Man Without a Face

MAN
WITHOUT
A FACE

The Autobiography
of Communism's
Greatest Spymaster

MARKUS WOLF

with Anne McElvoy

PublicAffairs

NEW YORK

PUBLISHED IN THE UNITED STATES BY PUBLICAFFAIRS™,
A MEMBER OF THE PERSEUS BOOKS GROUP.
PRINTED IN THE UNITED STATES OF AMERICA.

Book design by Jenny Dossin.

REPRINTED BY ARRANGEMENT WITH TIMES BOOKS, A DIVISION OF RANDOM HOUSE, INC.

ALL PHOTOS, UNLESS OTHERWISE NOTED, ARE FROM THE AUTHOR'S COLLECTION.

Library of Congress Cataloging-in-Publication Data
WOLF, MARKUS, 1923–
MAN WITHOUT A FACE : THE AUTOBIOGRAPHY OF COMMUNISM'S GREATEST SPYMASTER /
MARKUS WOLF ; WITH ANNE MCELVOY. — 1ST PUBLIC AFFAIRS ED.
P.   CM.
INCLUDES INDEX.
ISBN 1-891620-12-6
1. WOLF, MARKUS, 1923–   .
2. GERMANY (EAST). MINISTERIUM FÜR STAATSSICHERHEIT—BIOGRAPHY.
3. SPIES—GERMANY (EAST)—BIOGRAPHY.
4. INTELLIGENCE SERVICE—GERMANY (EAST)—BIOGRAPHY.
5. GERMANY (EAST)—POLITICS AND GOVERNMENT.
I. MCELVOY, ANNE, 1965–   .
II. TITLE.
DD207.7.W65A3   1999
327.12'092—DC21   99-13467
[B]   CIP

3 5 7 9 10 8 6 4 2

For Andrea

Without a maximum of knowledge, you are unable

To put spies successfully in place.

Without humanity and justice you are unable

To send scouts ahead.

Without sure instincts and a penetrating mind you are unable

To judge the authenticity of a report.

Sensitivity! Sensitivity!

Sun-tzu, Chinese general, fourth century B.C.

The Art of War

Contents

Introduction

For thirty-four years I served as chief of the foreign intelligence service of the Ministry of State Security of the German Democratic Republic. As even my bitter foes would acknowledge, it was probably the most efficient and effective such service on the European continent. We gathered many of the strategic and technical secrets of the mighty armies arrayed against us and passed them via Soviet intelligence to the command centers of the Warsaw Pact in Moscow. It was widely believed that I knew more about the secrets of the Federal Republic of Germany than the chancellor in Bonn himself. Indeed, we placed agents in the private office of two chancellors, among the thousand or so we had infiltrated into all sectors of West German political life, business, and other areas of society. Many of these agents were West Germans who served us purely out of conviction.

I saw my personal and professional life as one long arc that began with what was a grand goal by any objective standard. We East German Socialists tried to create a new kind of society that would never repeat the German crimes of the past. Most of all, we were determined that war should never again originate on German soil.

Our sins and our mistakes were those of every other intelligence agency. If we had shortcomings, and we certainly did, they were those of too much professionalism untempered by the raw edge of ordinary life. Like most Germans, we were disciplined to a fault. Our methods worked so well that we unwittingly helped to destroy the career of the most farsighted of modern German statesmen, Willy Brandt. The integration of the foreign intelligence service into the Ministry of State Security meant that the service and I were charged with responsibility for both internal repression in the German Democratic Republic and cooperation with international terrorists.

It is not easy to tell the story of this intelligence war from what was our side of the vanished Iron Curtain so that it will be understood by those who have spent their lives on the other. In recounting my story of a unique battle in the Cold War, I seek no pardon as a representative of the losers. Our side fought against the revival of fascism. We fought for a combination of socialism and freedom, a noble objective that failed utterly but which I still believe is possible. I hold to my beliefs, although they have been tempered now by time and experience. But I am no defector, and this memoir is not a confessional bid for redemption.

From the time I took over East German foreign intelligence in the 1950s until my photograph was surreptitiously snapped in 1979 and identified by a defector, the West had no idea what I looked like. They called me "the man without a face," a nickname that almost makes our espionage activities and the intelligence war between the East and West sound romantic. It was not. People suffered. Life was hard. Often no quarter was asked or given in the war between the two ideologies that dominated the second half of our century and paradoxically gave Europe its longest era of peace since the fall of the Roman Empire. Crimes were committed by both sides in the global struggle. Like most people in this world, I feel remorse.

In this memoir I have attempted to recount from my side the facts in full as I know them. Readers, reviewers, and historical specialists may examine them, credit them, and challenge them. But I reject the accusations of some of my countrymen that I have no right to recount and examine in detail the successes and failures of my career. In Germany there has been an attempt, through the courts and elsewhere, at a settling of accounts to ensure that only one version of history prevails. I seek neither moral justification nor forgiveness, but after a great struggle it is time for both sides to take stock.

Any history worthy of the name cannot be written only by the winners.

Foreword

By Craig R. Whitney

When a country is its own worst enemy, having the world's best foreign spy service can't help, as the leaders of East Germany discovered when that Communist country collapsed like a house of cards in 1989.

The irony does not escape Markus Wolf, the man who built the East German espionage agency and led it for thirty-four remarkably successful years. East Germany needed spies, its insecure Communist leaders thought in the early days of the Cold War, because West German economic superiority, coupled with NATO military might, threatened to overwhelm it. But despite 4,000 espionage agents and 109,000 secret police informers in the huge State Security Service, which had one informant for every 150 East German citizens, the Communists did not recognize until too late that it was their own internal flaws, the fatal fault lines of any system built on repression and coercion, that would bring them down.

For personal reasons, Wolf retired at his own request in 1986 and moved to a sixth-floor apartment overlooking the Spree River in the center of what used to be East Berlin. It was a choice location in the Communist scheme of things, in a neighborhood restored by the regime to recall the atmosphere of prewar Berlin; cobbled pedestrian streets and craftsmen's shops tucked into buildings whose bright pastel colors were meant to evoke an eighteenth-century past. After the Berlin Wall collapsed in 1989, tabloid newspapers called Wolf's apartment a luxury penthouse, typical of what the masters of the State Security Service—the dreaded "Stasi," as Germans called it—allowed themselves but denied all ordinary East Germans. The descriptions were always overdrawn.

There are ninety-nine steps to the sixth floor and the building has no elevator. Even in his mid-seventies, Wolf is still fit enough to negotiate the stairs. In the dingy entryway, someone has scrawled "Stasi pig" on Wolf's aluminum mailbox, an act that would have meant immediate imprisonment in the Communist days. A few blocks away his son from a previous marriage now earns pocket money in a pizzeria under the railroad tracks of the Friedrichstrasse S-Bahn station, the primary border crossing for visitors between east and west used during the Cold War days. Wolf is a man who has fallen a long way.

Unlike some of his Stasi colleagues, Wolf never saw the intelligence business as a way to enrich himself. Wolf is a compelling presence, well over six feet tall, trim and gray-haired with an interesting, elongated face, penetrating brown eyes, and the long-fingered, delicate hands of an intellectual. His German is elegant and expressive. He chats about Goethe and Brecht or Tolstoy and Mayakovski with equal ease, and he has a sense of humor. To while away the time during a brief forced exile (his second) to Moscow after German unification in 1990, he put together a book called *Secrets of Russian Cooking* (*Geheimnisse der russischen Küche*), a charming mix of recipes for beef Stroganoff, blini, and piroshki with cartoons and clever anecdotes from the spy business.

But seeing him today, one can't help but wonder what Wolf would have been as a West German: a general, perhaps, or foreign minister, or the head of some great German enterprise. He would have been successful, no doubt, prosperous and proud, perhaps with a few more pounds around his middle and a Mercedes in his driveway. But instead he lives in the petit bourgeois way of East Germany's Communist leadership, a collection of aging mediocrities to whom he feels loyalty but also intellectual superiority. In one of the harshest and most repressive political environments in Europe, he succeeded and survived by his wits, using his education and his charm to persuade Westerners to betray their own country for the Communist cause. Given how pitiful that cause was in East Germany, the real question is how so brilliant and intelligent a man could squander such great gifts on so wretched a system.

•

Ironically, Markus Wolf did begin his life in West Germany. Born in 1923 in Hechingen, a small town in Württemberg in southwestern Germany, he was the first son of the well-known dramatist, author, and homeopathic physician Friedrich Wolf, a Jew and a Marxist. Like her husband, Wolf's mother, Else, was an active member of the German Communist Party. After the Nazis came to power in 1933 the Wolfs were marked for arrest, and Markus's father fled to France. Else, Markus, and his younger brother, Konrad, soon followed, and in 1934 the family found political asylum in Moscow.

There, for the next ten years, the boys underwent the educational, cultural, and political conditioning of Communist Russia. Konrad returned to Germany in 1944 as a soldier in the Red Army. Markus studied aeronautical engineering in Russia and, in 1945, at the age of twenty-two, was sent to Germany on German Communist Party orders to help build a propaganda radio station in the ruins of Berlin.

Wolf's fluent Russian and his exposure to Communist ideals from the cradle onward put him at ease with the Red Army authorities in the Russian occupation zone of eastern Germany and with the other German exiles and survivors who were placed at the head of the German Democratic Republic in 1949. Whatever else he might have done, Stalin had saved the Wolf family from the Holocaust, and that fact, plus the heady sense of power that came from suddenly being put in charge in the first Communist state on German soil, always outweighed whatever Markus Wolf would later discover about the dark, repressive side of communism.

It did not take long for Wolf's talents to become evident to his elders, who sent him to Moscow as an East German diplomat for a few years and then brought him into East Germany's budding foreign intelligence agency, making him its chief in 1952, when he was not quite thirty. A year later, the agency merged foreign intelligence into the State Security Service, making Wolf a quasi-autonomous deputy chief of the Stasi as head of its Hauptverwaltung Aufklärung, or "Main

Intelligence Directorate," where he eventually acquired the rank of general.

In the precarious first days of East Germany's existence, there were plenty of foreign threats to worry about. West Germany's Federal Republic, by far the larger of the two successor states to the defunct German Reich, asserted sole claim to historical legitimacy and would not have diplomatic relations with any country that recognized its eastern neighbor. To Western eyes, there was little that seemed democratic about the German Democratic Republic, and most of the countries that risked West German ire by establishing relations with the east were either Soviet satellites or fellow travelers.

During these early, volatile years, the East German minister for state security was Erich Mielke, a thuggish veteran of Communist intrigue from another generation sixteen years Wolf's senior. A more complete contrast between two individuals is hard to imagine. Mielke was born into a working-class family in Berlin at the end of 1907, grew up in a hardscrabble milieu, and joined the Communist Party in 1930. Imprisoned after murdering two Berlin policemen in 1931, he escaped and fled to Moscow. Sixty-two years later, he was convicted of the crime on evidence he had locked away in his Stasi safe. But as head of the GDR's secret police machine, Mielke, obsessed with the threat of internal subversion, turned East Germany into the most ruthlessly efficient police state in Eastern Europe.

When communism collapsed, Mielke became an object of universal loathing. Wolf, too, spares him little sympathy. He portrays Mielke as a tyrant, a boss against whom he fought a constant bureaucratic struggle to preserve the independence and autonomy of his espionage domain. But at the same time, Wolf also denies responsibility for many Stasi activities that seem closely related to foreign espionage, such as the "shoot to kill" orders given to the border guards who manned the Berlin Wall. He denies ordering the death of foreign moles. He denies any connection to the Stasi's Section XXII, which granted temporary asylum to terrorists and used them as agents of subversion against the West.

Section XXII kept track of such radicals as West Germany's violent Red Army Faction, whose members murdered a dozen industrialists and high government officials in the 1970s; Ilyich Ramirez Sanchez, the international terrorist who called himself "Carlos"; and various members of the Palestine Liberation Organization. The Stasi occasionally used these terrorists as agents of subversion in the West, granting them temporary asylum in East Germany. It was a Stasi colonel who released more than fifty pounds of high explosives to Carlos's German deputy in 1983 before the bombing of the French consulate in West Berlin. As Wolf relates here, other Stasi officers in Section XXII knew of the plan by Libyan diplomats to bomb a West Berlin nightclub frequented by GIs, an explosion that killed four people and wounded more than two hundred in 1986 a few months before Wolf's retirement. But the East Germans did nothing to stop them.

●

From the start in the 1950s, Wolf's main assignment was ferreting out what West Germany's leaders had in mind for the vastly smaller East Germany. Under his leadership, East Berlin practically pitched one long no-hitter in the spy game with West Germany. Wolf's service "turned" West German agents, sending them back across the Wall to spy for the Communists instead. It recruited businessmen and legislators of both the left and right wings and probed them for information about West German economic and political policies. It sent "Romeos," attractive single men, to woo the many frustrated single women unhappily wedded to their jobs as secretaries to Bonn politicians. Wolf's service lured defectors to the Communist cause so often that it became an embarrassment. These defectors included West German intelligence and counterintelligence officials who had problems with alcohol, financial worries, or doubts about devoting their lives to the cause of a U.S.-led alliance in their divided country: "Probst," "Günter," "Kohle," "Komtess," "Mauerer," and finally "Topaz"— Rainer Rupp, Wolf's top spy in NATO's Brussels headquarters, who was not detected until after the Cold War was over. (After his release from prison in December 1998, the neo-Communist Party of Democratic Socialism caucus in the German Parliament wanted to hire Rupp as a consultant, but backed down under heavy fire.)

●

Wolf endured setbacks, to be sure: defectors from communism like Werner Stiller, who brought West German intelligence 20,000 pages' worth of microfilmed documents that enabled West Germany to uncover a score of undercover agents and, incidentally, the first picture in three decades of Wolf, until then a "man without a face" in their files. But these setbacks were outnumbered by his triumphs.

Wolf's service sent "moles" by the dozens burrowing into West German society on a bet that, given enough time and luck, some would work their way up close to the top of West German political parties and provide valuable information about German planning for military contingencies and, even more important for East Germany's strategic relationship with the Soviet Union, U.S. military and strategic intentions in case the Cold War turned hot. Among the moles were Günter Guillaume and his wife Christel, who infiltrated into West Germany in the mid-1950s as "Hansen" and "Heinze" to try to work their way up the Social Democratic Party hierarchy in Frankfurt. They succeeded beyond Wolf's wildest dreams when Guillaume became an aide to Chancellor Willy Brandt in 1972.

When he was unveiled as a spy, Guillaume brought Brandt down in 1974. This was arguably the worst defeat East Germany ever inflicted on itself before its collapse fifteen years later. Brandt's "Ostpolitik" had improved relations between the estranged countries. Bonn had finally stopped fighting the Communists and begun making diplomatic approaches instead. But the Communist leader, Erich Honecker, mistrusted Brandt's Ostpolitik, seeing West Germany's relationship with Moscow as a threat to East Germany's legitimacy. So in East Berlin, Wolf escaped retribution for bringing about the chancellor's fall.

A list identifying all of Wolf's agents would fill many volumes. Wolf has identified only those who died or were caught and tried. Despite his vast network of moles and agents, Wolf often felt frustrated by the results of his spy game. What did these agents accomplish in the grand scheme of things? "Almost all the papers that NATO produces, stamped 'secret' and 'cosmic,' that we go to great lengths to obtain are on closer inspection not even good for use as toilet paper," he wrote in his private diary in late 1974. It was the same on the Communist side, he mused – vast, swollen bureaucracies producing mounds of useless paper. In Moscow, in Warsaw, in East Berlin, the machinery ground on, trying to protect, defend, and perpetuate an indefensible system whose fundamental flaw was the belief that human happiness and prosperity could be forced onto people by an all-powerful Communist bureaucracy.

On both sides of the ideological divide, the bureaucrats whom John Le Carré dubbed "espiocrats" tunneled deep into opposing territory, infiltrated their moles, plotted and schemed, but in the end, they accomplished little that fundamentally changed life for people on either side. In Afghanistan, the CIA made life miserable for the Red Army, armed the mujahideen with air-to-air Stinger missiles, and eventually drove the Russians out. But what replaced them was an Islamic fundamentalist tyranny even more repressive than Communist rule, and soon there were worries that the Stingers would find their way into fundamentalist terrorist hands. In Eastern Europe, it was not the CIA or its West German equivalent, the BND, that caused the collapse of communism and the Warsaw Pact, but the accumulated frustrations and inherent political, economic, and social contradictions of Communist society.

Wolf would not begin to ruminate publicly about the flaws in the Communist system until it was too late, in a memoir of youth and Communist idealism published in East Germany only months before the Berlin Wall came crumbling down in 1989. The memoir, *Die Troika*, a continuation of a project begun by Wolf's brother, Konrad, before his death in 1982, was one of the few attempts ever made in East Germany to explore, even timidly, the mistakes made by Communist leaders in Moscow and elsewhere in the name of Stalinism. Despite Nikita Khrushchev's earlier efforts, such criticism had become possible in the Soviet Union only after Mikhail Gorbachev became leader in 1985 and introduced perestroika, an effort to reform communism that undid it instead, just as Khrushchev had feared loosening all the restraints would do. Honecker was having none of it in East Germany, and there Wolf's book caused a sensation.

But where Wolf actually stood in the eyes of his compatriots did not become clear until after the people of East Germany finally took to the streets that autumn to demand freedom. In a speech in Berlin in October 1989, Gorbachev made it clear that the half million Red Army troops in East Germany would not use guns or tanks to beat them down. That speech numbered communism's days in East Germany. The demonstrations soon swelled beyond control in Leipzig, Dresden, and Berlin, and when Wolf appeared and offered his services in the cause of reform, he was booed off the stage. East Germans wanted freedom to travel, deutschmarks, Mercedeses and BMWs, and all the rest of the material wealth West Germans had, not warmed-over reform communism. Plans for reunification were moving forward like a juggernaut.

On October 3, 1990, East Germany would cease to exist, absorbed lock, stock, and barrel into the Federal Republic of Germany. The reunified Germany had scores to settle with Markus Wolf. When the clock struck midnight on the long-awaited day, Wolf knew he would go to jail. Quietly, he began sounding out friends in the KGB about the prospects for asylum in Moscow.

●

It was not only the West German authorities who had scores to set-tle with Wolf. The CIA had plenty of them, too. By 1990, the U.S. agency was in deep trouble. Its main enemy and raison d'être over the years, the Soviet Union, was in the process of collapse. But a dozen or so of the Soviet agents the CIA had recruited and nurtured with immense difficulty had been discovered and executed, betrayed by a U.S. citizen whose treason would not be unmasked until his arrest four years later, in 1994—Aldrich Ames. In 1990, all the CIA knew was that somebody was selling its innermost secrets, with lethal results. The CIA may well have thought that Wolf could help lead it to the traitor.

On May 22, Gardner A. Hathaway, recently retired as the CIA's assistant director for counterintelligence, appeared at Wolf's dacha, a log cabin under the pines on the northeast outskirts of Berlin, with a bouquet and a box of chocolates for Wolf's wife, Andrea, in hand. He had an extraordinary proposition. Help us, Hathaway urged, and we'll get you out of Germany to the United States before they come to arrest you in October.

Take me to the United States first and we'll talk there, Wolf says he counter-offered, but Hathaway insisted: no agreement to cooperate, no ticket. Wolf admits that he was tempted by the offer, though he could only speculate about what kind of help the CIA wanted from him. It already had a microfilmed list of all of his agents, he was sure, a list covertly acquired from disaffected or greedy HVA officers (the CIA eventually confirmed that it had such information but in early 1999 refused official demands by the German government for its return), but perhaps the CIA wanted additional information that went beyond the list. It may also have wanted to tap Wolf's knowledge of Soviet operating methods to enable the counterspies in Langley, Vir-ginia, to track down Moscow's agents, too.

By deciding not to tell what he knew, Wolf angered Washington, and with Bonn breathing down his neck, he saw no choice but to flee Germany yet again, like his father before him. He still had help in high places in Moscow, friends like Vladimir A. Kryuchkov, his Russian counterpart, who had become the head of the KGB. Six days before October 3, Wolf and Andrea, thirty years his junior, slipped out of East Berlin, escaped across the border to Austria, and a few weeks later exfiltrated themselves—Wolf knew the technique well enough, after all—through Hungary and Ukraine to Russia.

But the world Wolf had known in Russia was fast disappearing. For Gorbachev, the key to Russia's future was not the KGB but good relations with Germany and its chancellor, Helmut Kohl. Wolf was a symbol of the discredited past, and when Wolf's friend Kryuchkov joined an unsavory attempted coup against Gorbachev in August 1991, Wolf knew Russia would not shelter him much longer. A month later, he headed back to Germany.

Wolf turned himself in at the Austrian border and was immediately arrested, then freed on bail provided by friends and former associates in East Berlin. To his astonishment, he learned that the Federal Republic of Germany intended to charge him with treason. Since he had been leading a spy service against the Federal Republic from Berlin and Berlin was now once again the capital of Germany, the prosecutors charged, Wolf was to be tried not as a foreign spy, but as a German traitor. His case looked grim. Klaus Kinkel, a former chief of the Federal Republic's intelligence service, was serving as the German justice minister and by bizarre coincidence had also been born in Hechingen.

Wolf's trial in Düsseldorf, in the same fortified basement courtroom where Günter Guillaume had been convicted almost two decades earlier, began in the spring of 1993 and concluded that December with a guilty verdict and a six-year sentence. It took the German equivalent of the Supreme Court until mid-1995 to set aside his conviction and point out the absurdity of the logic behind it. Wolf could not possibly have committed treason when he was running East Germany's spy service, the high court ruled, because East Germany had been a sovereign state recognized by Bonn for nearly two decades of that time. Besides, Wolf had never set foot on West German soil to do any spying himself. He was no more guilty of treason than was Yevgeny Primakov, then head of the successor to the KGB in Moscow.

So prosecutors tried another tack, indicting Wolf again in 1997 on more ordinary criminal grounds—charges that he had ordered kidnappings and coercions of people from across the East German border in the 1950s and 1960s, crimes that had also been illegal under East German law at the time they were committed. In May 1997, again in Düsseldorf, Wolf was convicted on three of those counts and given a two-year suspended sentence instead of a jail term. Running short of money to pay his mounting legal bills, Wolf decided to claim moral victory and forgo an appeal.

But the authorities were not finished with him yet. In January 1998, they tried again, calling Wolf as a witness in the trial of Gerhard Flämig, a West German legislator charged with spying for East Germany during the Cold War. Wolf refused to answer key questions and, with his seventy-fifth birthday approaching, was jailed three days for contempt of court. His seven-year-old grandchild sent him a drawing of a birthday cake with a file glued onto it, as if he could somehow saw his way out of jail, but Wolf's lawyers eventually got a higher court to dismiss the contempt citation. Wolf was once again free, but his freedom grated on his many former enemies in Germany who were determined to make him squeal.

•

The United States, either for its own reasons or at the request of the Germans (Klaus Kinkel had become the German foreign minister in 1992), was playing the same game. Though Israel, long known for its fear of potential terrorists, welcomed Wolf on a 1996 visit, the United States refused to grant him entry. When Wolf's publishers asked him to come to the United States to help with the final editing of the first edition of this book, U.S. authorities used his alleged terrorist connections as a pretext for denying him permission to set foot on U.S. shores.

The letter Wolf received on March 12, 1996, from the U.S. consulate-general in Berlin accused him of a crime even the West German authorities had not laid to his charge:

Dear Mr. Wolf,

With reference to our telephone conversation of yesterday we confirm that the State Department of the USA denied you the entry into the United States of America under section 212(a), paragraph 3(B) of the U.S. Immigration and Nationality Act.

In accordance with paragraph 3(B) foreigners who participated in terrorist acts are excluded from entry into the United States of America. Paragraph 3(B) includes different kinds of terrorist acts, among them the preparation and planning of terrorist activities as well as the provision of material support to persons that committed or planned acts of terrorism.

The Ministry of State Security of the GDR actively encouraged and promoted international and state-supported terrorism. As deputy Minister of State Security of the GDR and former head of the foreign intelligence service of the Ministry of State Security of the GDR you held a decision-making position and participated in determining the policy and the objects of that Ministry. You are thus responsible for acts resulting from that policy.

On that basis the decision was made that you participated in terrorist acts.

At the time being, the State Department of the United States does not think that it will be able to apply to the Immigration and Naturalization Service to obtain an exceptional permission for your entry into the United States.

Best,
Glen C. Keiser
U.S. Consul

In his own flawed English, Wolf appealed to President Clinton a week later.

Mister President,

Confidence in your person as well as misgivings about the wheels of administrative bureaucracy have induced me to apply to you personally with the request to endorse my application for entry into the United States of America.

The visit to your country is of an importance to me that exceeds the reasons given in my visa application that has been refused by the State Department. It is my intention to meet in New York my publisher to attend the final editing of my book manuscript. The reasons stated in the refusal of my application for entry include an allegation I cannot tolerate uncontradicted. Doubtlessly there are reasons for a critical review as to my course of life, the cross roads of which are related in the book to be published by Random House. I will have to answer questions related to history, and painful questions as well.

Those countries of Europe that named themselves as socialist, and among them East Germany, have failed, and so have their claims to serve a utopia of mankind. On the evening of my life, I question myself in the forthcoming book since when and where we have erred, where we have seen the errors too late, and where we have made ourselves guilty. There are many questions. Therefore I am not willing to carry the burden of criminalizing allegations as well. The claim made in the State Department's decision that I had been involved in terrorist activities is as unfounded as it is untrue. You might see that from my enclosed appeal.

Many a trait in your life and your policy, of an unconventionality that struck me as remarkable with President John F. Kennedy already, have encouraged me to take this unusual step. To you, the burden of unjustified and unwarranted allegation is not unknown either. So I remain, confiding in your sense of justice and with the best wishes for you.

yours respectfully.

Whether Wolf's letter was flattery or outrageous provocation—and the president might have reacted to it either way if he ever saw it—the letter got Wolf nowhere. A year later, as the book was being published, State Department spokesperson Nicholas Burns said Wolf would still be denied entry. "We think it [a visa] is inadvisable for someone who spent his entire career as an opponent of free Germany, West Germany, as an opponent of the German people, and someone who is anti-American and trying to bring down our government and sponsor terrorist attacks against us; why would we give him a visa? So, he is not coming to the United States. He can write his best-selling books, but he won't be able to enjoy the United States throughout the rest of his life if we have anything to do with it," Burns said at a State Department press briefing.

Asked why Wolf would be turned back at any port of entry when people like the Russian foreign minister Primakov and the Palestinian leader Yasser Arafat were now welcome, Burns said, "We have a very good relationship with Yevgeny Primakov. He is the Foreign Minister of one of our friends, a friendly country to the United States. . . . Markus Wolf is an unreconstructed communist who believes in state terrorism against the United States. There's a big difference."

There was also a big difference between the terrorism charge and the truth about why U.S. authorities didn't want to let Markus Wolf inside the United States. High-ranking U.S. officials later admitted that the CIA suspected that Wolf still hadn't told all he knew. Years after the demise of the USSR, the agency was reeling from the damage that U.S. traitors working for the KGB had done to it. The CIA suspected that Wolf or his former colleagues knew of others who were still in place. It wanted those names. In early 1998, the head of German counterintelligence, Volker Foertsch, came under investigation as a possible Russian mole. The investigation ended for lack of evidence.

If the U.S. authorities were waiting for Wolf to help them out, he would soon disappoint them. Cold War intelligence was a complex, colossally expensive game, one that ran by its own logic and its own rules. The cardinal rule was not to be outdone. But when you were outdone and fell into the enemy's hands, you never told them anything they didn't already know. Both sides had played by these rules during the Cold War and quietly maintained a system of trading captured agents that rewarded those who held their tongues. Even amid the ruins of his greater political failure, Wolf remained stubbornly proud of his professional achievements. He was not going to sell out his honor for a trip to the United States. So Yevgeny Primakov, now Russia's prime minister, is welcome any time, but Wolf remains persona non grata.

●

So for many reasons, this is not a "tell-all" book. Wolf continues to be a controversial figure, partly because he insists on not seeing his life as the abject failure his erstwhile enemies keep insisting it is. The book's omissions will disappoint readers who expected a confessional, but then confessions in the spy business are usually fatal, and Wolf is a man who obviously enjoys life. Read Wolf, instead, for a fascinating glimpse, if only a glimpse, into the seductive mind of one of the great spymasters of our times, a man marked by the Holocaust, and then by the Cold War ideological divide, who stood on the opposite side of that divide from most readers. Perhaps he has the right to take some secrets to the grave.

The Party, the State, and the Ministry of State Security

The state

Erich Honecker, general secretary of the Central Committee of the Party, chairman of the State Council, head of the Party and the state

Politburo of the Socialist Unity Party

Regional party secretaries

Hermann Axen, politburo member for international affairs

Günther Mittag, politburo member for economic affairs

Erich Mielke, politburo member, minister of state security

Egon Krenz, politburo member for security

Heinz Kessler, politburo member, minister of defense

Erich Mückenberger, politburo member, chairman of the Party Control Commission

International Relations Department of the Central Committee

Ministry of Foreign Affairs

Alexander Schalck-Golodkowski, KoKo (Commercial Coordination)

Various companies

Department of the Central Committee for Security Questions

Party Control Commission

Ministry of State Security (central administration)

Regional branches of the Ministry of State Security

Organization of the Ministry of State Security

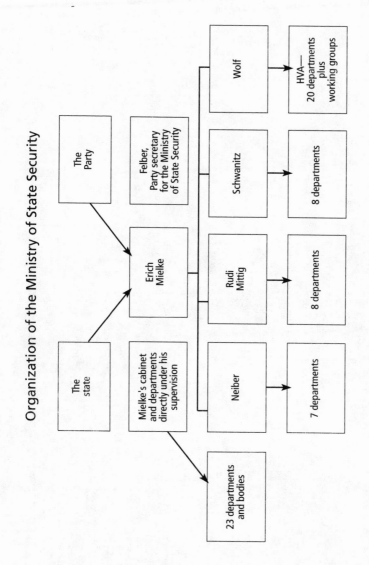

Man Without a Face

I

The Auction

In the summer of 1990, the two Germanys were preparing for their reunification after four decades of separation and hostility that began in the postwar order drawn up by the victorious Allies in 1945 and was solidified by the superpower conflict that followed. My life's work, committed to the ideal of socialism, was crumbling before my eyes. My own country, East Germany, which had failed to live up to the demanding title German Democratic Republic, was facing a shotgun marriage with Europe's economic powerhouse, West Germany. The process of winding up an independent East Germany was already under way, and though I did not know what a unified Germany would mean for Europe, I knew one thing very well: I was about to become a wanted man.

The date for unification had already been set for October 3, 1990. Everywhere I looked, I saw my homeland and the system that had created it being consigned to the scrap heap. Souvenir hunters were gleefully buying up the medals and uniforms that had until then been so proudly worn in the East. But my own mood was far from festive, or even nostalgic.

Although we were all Germans, with a common language and culture that went far deeper than the barbed-wire divisions of postwar

Europe, ours was a special kind of hostility. But this was not only an internecine affair, Germans against Germans. The scores to settle between the capitalist and the Communist Germany were part of the global reckoning with the legacy of Marx and Lenin and the injustices perpetrated in the name of their vision of socialism. My country was the most eloquent expression of the global division between two hostile ideological camps after the end of World War II. That division was coming to an end with a speed no one had expected, East or West.

I had always seen the task of running our intelligence service as carrying a particular responsibility in the Cold War. In a song I helped write from a Soviet model to inspire young recruits, I placed their job on "The Invisible Front." This was no overstatement: For four decades after the Second World War ended, we considered ourselves at war with the forces of capitalism arrayed against us.

The cynosure of our work was in Berlin, where for most of the time the separation between the two systems was fixed in permafrost. Strategists and politicians on both sides assumed that if there was to be a third world war, Berlin was the most likely place it would begin. But following the destruction of the Berlin Wall in November 1989 and the opening of East Germany's gates to the wider world, the German Democratic Republic quickly ceased to exist as a nation. The denouement of my life's work in the total collapse of the state I had served had been literally unimaginable. Four years before the Wall came down, feeling trapped within the ossified bureaucratic structures around me, I retired from the service to try my hand at writing; under the stagnant leadership of the ailing Erich Honecker, I could see no realistic possibility of change from within. But even I was taken totally by surprise with the rapidity of the state's decline. For many, the end, when it came, was not pleasant; people have talked to me about their humiliation.

The members of the East German security services, which had been one of the GDR's principal supports, were declared Public Enemy Number One by the media, the politicians, and the courts. This was an inevitable development, justified to some extent as part of the painful process by which the citizens of a collapsed regime face up to the reality of their past.

On January 15, 1990, irate crowds stormed the headquarters of the Ministry of State Security on the Normannenstrasse and discovered the vast records that the ministry had maintained from spying on its own citizens. It was like living inside an inexorably closing trap. My mood was one of withdrawal and resignation. I knew that all hopes of reforming the socialist state were now shattered (there were some who had seen me during my years of retirement as a potential reformer in the mode of Mikhail Gorbachev). I needed to find a temporary way out of this overheated country.

I headed to Moscow, the city of my childhood, which had offered my family a refuge from Hitler and where a large part of my heart has always remained. Contrary to popular belief, there was no carefully conceived contingency plan for my escape. I was writing my own memoir of the events of 1989 and needed time and space to finish it quietly. But I knew that unification was likely to mean my arrest; there had been a formal warrant out for me in West Germany shortly before the collapse accusing me of espionage and treason. The sharks were circling.

My half sister, Lena Simonova, put me up in her dacha and her apartment in the famous House on the Embankment, home to the favored within Moscow elites since the thirties. I can never enter the ornate doors of this apartment house without remembering how grand our dreams were as young Communists in Moscow, where we had fled from the Third Reich with our parents. Now, looking out over the frozen Moscow River in February, I felt safe again. The sharp winter air stimulated thinking. I would take long walks around the narrow streets of the old Arbat, reflecting on my life and the vicissitudes that had brought me, a native of southern Germany, to Moscow as a young boy, to divided Germany as a man, and now back to Moscow as a pensioner.

The other purpose behind the trip to Moscow was to find out how far our old allies in the KGB and the Kremlin would support me and my colleagues in the intelligence community now that our state had literally collapsed. There had been no great rush of comradely support from our Moscow friends during the stressful past months. Like us, they had been completely unprepared for what happened. The supposedly eternal brotherhood to which we had raised our glasses down the years was now a ragged band. Where once the hot lines between Moscow and East Berlin had hummed all day on the various levels of communication between two allies, there was now no exchange. Letters went unanswered. Awkward silences reigned.

I was inundated with letters from former officers in my service, the HVA (Hauptverwaltung Aufklärung, or "Main Intelligence Directorate"—the foreign intelligence department), complaining that they had been left alone to face the wrath of their countrymen now that the excesses of the Ministry of State Security had been revealed. People were furious when they discovered the extent to which the internal surveillance network reached throughout the country. Although my own work in the HVA had never focused on the 17 million people of East Germany but only on other countries' intentions toward the East bloc, I knew there would be little appetite for discriminating appraisal of the subtle distinctions between departments of the Stasi (as the Ministerium für Staatssicherheit, of which my service was a part, popularly—and derogatorily—was known; the term would not have been used by an employee of the ministry, and I avoid it).* And I needed to know what help we could expect now as members of what had once been the Soviet bloc's best intelligence service.

On my arrival I was welcomed as usual in the southwestern suburbs of Moscow at the vast building in Yasenovo that houses the KGB's First Main Directorate, the heart of its foreign intelligence operations. The head of foreign intelligence, Leonid Shebarshin, and his senior staff greeted me warmly. We had known each other for decades. They brought out the vodka and solicitously inquired about my living conditions in Moscow. But it soon became clear that the KGB, hostage to the power struggles that had erupted in the last and uncertain phases of Mikhail Gorbachev's rule, was no longer able to offer substantial help.

My case and the fate of East Germany's espionage officers, agents, and moles were considered so politically sensitive that they were being handled directly by President Gorbachev himself. I understood that my contacts with the Kremlin were to run through Valentin Falin, a prominent Central Committee member and Gorbachev's foreign affairs adviser, whom I knew well for his important work on Soviet-German relations. The involvement of Falin, who enjoyed high

---

*Indeed, to my knowledge the term Stasi became popular after the events of 1989. Even Western media and propaganda had mostly used SSD to encourage identification with the Nazi past. East Germans used names like The Firm or KONSUM (Coop), etc. I shall use the term Stasi in this book for the benefit of my readers. Even most of my former employees have stopped having difficulties with the term.

renown in West Germany, implied that I was considered a potential political embarrassment: He had been given the awkward job of attending to my needs without unduly annoying the West.

It was not the first time in my life I had found myself in the position of having to rely on Mother Russia to save me. But contrary to widespread belief, I had had no formal contacts in the upper echelons in Moscow since I left the foreign intelligence service in 1986. The head of the KGB in Berlin, first Wassily T. Shumilov, then Gennadi W. Titov, focused all their attention on Erich Mielke, the minister of state security, and avoided contact with me. Some people have claimed that, together with the reform Communist Hans Modrow, I was preparing a coup against Honecker. But although I had warned Falin and several other colleagues in Moscow that the regime in East Berlin was near the breaking point, I had never asked for nor received support for any attempt to influence the leadership after Honecker's fall, which was the result of a putsch against him inside the politburo.

In fact, I would go as far as to say that the Russians avoided contact with me after I retired beyond those occasions demanded by loyalty and courtesy. During my visits to Moscow, Falin and Shebarshin spoke freely of my concerns about East Germany, but they were wrapped up in the problems of perestroika. After the Wall fell, events moved with such speed that it was virtually impossible to keep up with them. It was probably already too late when, on October 22, 1990, I addressed a letter to Gorbachev that said:

> We were your friends. We wear a lot of your country's decorations on our breasts. We were said to have made a great contribution to your security. Now, in our hour of need, I assume that you will not deny us your help.

The letter went on to ask the Soviet leader whether he would request an amnesty for East German spies as a condition of his agreement to unification. A message came back from the KGB chief, Vladimir Kryuchkov, saying that Gorbachev had sent his ambassador in Bonn to discuss my request with Chancellor Helmut Kohl. In fact the ambassador was directed instead to Kohl's chief of staff, Horst Teltschick. They had discussed an amnesty during the summer of 1990 before the

Allied talks on unification but reached no agreement. Kryuchkov thought that Gorbachev would bring up the matter again in the summit at Arys, in the Caucasus, to finalize the details of unification. It was not a very promising reply. For the first time, I began to have serious doubts about Gorbachev's loyalties. Surely he would not just deliver us defenseless into the hands of the West Germans, our old enemies?

But when he agreed to unification at his meeting with Chancellor Kohl in the Caucasus on July 14 to 16, 1990, Gorbachev absolutely failed us. At the final talks, he refused to put forward our request for immunity from prosecution. His overriding concern now was to keep his image bright in the West, having conveniently forgotten that he too had once been a Communist. The West Germans were prepared to discuss immunity for those who had worked for East Germany, but when the matter arose briefly at the meeting, Gorbachev waved his hand and told Kohl that the Germans would manage this problem sensibly themselves. It was the Soviets' ultimate betrayal of their East German friends, whose work for over four decades had strengthened Soviet influence in Europe.

●

As the mergers and sell-offs of East Germany's industrial assets and institutions got under way, another top secret auction began. It was an auction for me, or, more precisely, for my intelligence knowledge and services. And the price was the highest of all: my freedom.

The first bid came out of the blue and from an entirely unexpected quarter, my old enemies in West German counterintelligence, the BfV (Bundesamt für Verfassungsschutz, the Federal Office for the Protection of the Constitution), the very organization to which I had assigned moles and double agents who had dug away in its dark and secret tunnels for decades.

In March 1990, the first free elections since 1945 took place in the East, bringing to power a Christian Democratic government, strongly supported by Chancellor Kohl's ruling coalition in Bonn. This was a caretaker administration whose job was to steer East Germany toward unification while minimizing upheavals. Its interior minister was a sharp-dressing, rather brash young man called Peter-Michael Diestel,

who had emerged from one of the conservative parties founded in the
East in the heady aftermath of East Germany's collapse.

By this time, Erich Mielke, for many years the GDR's minister for
state security and my immediate superior until my retirement, was
already under arrest, and the pressure on former agents and officers of
our service to divulge their secrets was growing daily. Betrayal was rife,
and deals were being struck between our old employees and the West
Germans. The bargain usually was freedom from prosecution in
return for East German secrets. Intelligence officers feared that they
would spend the first years in a unified Germany behind bars. I
received calls every day from desperate men begging me to do something. Already, I knew of two suicides among senior officials in the
ministry. My own son-in-law, Bernd, who headed a section in the HVA
department responsible for espionage against West German counterintelligence, had recently been offered freedom from prosecution and
half a million deutschmarks in exchange for his knowledge about his
spies' activities and their former targets.

He rejected the offer but, shattered by the abrupt end of his career
and the demise of the system in which he had wholeheartedly believed,
plunged into a deep depression and attempted suicide. Like dozens of
others whose lives rightly or wrongly had been tied to the failed system, he felt spent and useless. Their psychological supports had been
pulled out from under them, and their sense of worth and ideological
certainty collapsed overnight along with the Berlin Wall itself.

At this moment, Diestel called me at my dacha in Prenden, near
Berlin, and invited me to meet him at his house. It was clear from our
first meeting that he was acting on the orders of the West German interior minister, Wolfgang Schäuble. But unlike others among our new
politicians, he did not seem to take any particular pleasure in my misfortune. On the contrary, he endeavored to create a convivial atmosphere
between us. Despite the wide differences that had opened up politically
in the East (and I could not be further apart from the ultra-Conservative
Mr. Diestel), our shared past meant that a residual empathy remained.

"How about a spot of supper and a chat about developments?" he
asked breezily. He said his assistant would make the arrangements.

A few days later, up rolled a blue BMW, the new chariot of the
politically powerful, which had replaced the Citroëns and Volvos

favored by the Communist leadership. I could not help wondering which members of the old leadership the driver had chauffeured until a few months ago but thought it tactful not to ask.

To my amusement, we were served supper by men I recognized from the old security ministry. "What I am going to make you now is an offer in absolute confidence," said Diestel. He explained that the West Germans were unhappy with the progress of their attempts to dissect the extensive and industrious East German intelligence service by analyzing the data left behind when the Communist system it served had unceremoniously collapsed. My successor since I had left the service in 1986, Werner Grossmann, and another senior officer, Bernd Fisher, who had been ordered to guide the West Germans through the maze of material, were not coming up with the names of remaining agents and moles and a sufficiently precise summary of what they knew. Interior Minister Schäuble was impatient, convinced that his own investigators had failed to master the scale of our work.

"Who better to explain it to them than the man who set it all up and made it run like clockwork?" Diestel urged as he refilled my glass. He was not simply asking a favor. There was of course to be a reward: freedom from prosecution for treason against the West German state. "Jump into my car," he said, "and ride to Boeden's office with me [Gerhard Boeden was then the chief of West German counterintelligence, the BfV]. Give us between ten and twelve names of really big agents in the West and some help in figuring out what damage your side has done, and we'll see that there will be no charges against you."

Boeden, he added, was ready to guarantee my free passage without risk of arrest if I would agree to talk to him. The offer had clearly been carefully arranged, with the welcoming Boeden patiently waiting a few miles away to add his hospitality to Diestel's. There was even talk of my offering my knowledge to assist West Germany's antiterrorist services.

Now it was my turn to negotiate. I said that I appreciated the offer of freedom from prosecution but that I also had a responsibility to my former employees and agents.

After a while Diestel grew bored by this tug of war. "Mr. Wolf," he said, "I think you know that we are all going to prison one way or the other. The only question is how the food and conditions will be when we get there."

He was highly flattering about my reputation as one of the world's top intelligence chiefs.

I sensed that he knew a lot about me and was trying to sort through his preconceptions and see which ones proved out when we actually met. Indeed, in the time-honored manner among intelligence operatives, he offered a minor piece of information about himself in the hope of receiving a major one in reply. He told me that he had been stationed in West Berlin in the 1950s and followed the early years of my career closely. I surmised from his conversation, although he did not confirm it, that he had also been the CIA station chief in Moscow.

"You are a man who is hardworking and intelligent," Hathaway said.

First the carrot, I thought to myself—where is the stick? We drank what seemed like oceans of coffee. I smoked, to the evident distress of my guest. Finally, my patience snapped.

"Well, gentlemen," I said, "I don't suppose you've come all the way here to compliment me on my pretty eyes. I guess you must want something from me, too."

Both men laughed, relieved to cut through the waffle at last. Hathaway's voice dropped.

"You are a convinced Communist, we know that. But if you would like to advise or help us, you could work with me. No one else need know. We could arrange that, you know. We can do that sort of thing."

My brain picked up the signals of this coded language and moved into top gear. Here was an emissary of the United States, our chief Cold War enemy, preparing to offer me sanctuary against the revenge of its NATO ally, a united Germany.

"California," he continued in his easy German, "is very agreeable. Great weather all year round."

"Siberia is agreeable, too," I joked, painfully aware of the bizarre way real conversations in espionage can sometimes imitate the style of spy novels.

We laughed, which gave me a moment to think.

"The thing is, I don't know America. It would be difficult for me to imagine a life there."

Hathaway said Webster wanted to invite me to CIA headquarters in Langley, Virginia, to discuss a deal. He continued: "You could have a disguise or face-lift if you would feel safer that way."

It was all I could do not to laugh out loud at the thought of returning in my advanced years to the ruses of the youthful spy.

"I am happy with my looks as they are," I retorted.

Again, a brief, dry laugh came from my interlocutor. He added that a considerable sum of money would be on offer. We did not discuss the details, but I knew that my officer in charge of our espionage against America, Jürgen Rogalla, had been offered a million dollars by the CIA station chief in Berlin to tell what he knew and had declined it. We talked politely about the effects of the collapse of communism and the good reputation of the service I had run.

"Of course," he said, "you must do something for us."

Fearing a repeat of the German offer of names for freedom, I said that I was not prepared to give away the identity of any of my agents.

"There would be something in it for you, of course," said Hathaway.

This phrase had an unfortunate effect on me, probably because it recalled that mixture of wheedling and high-handedness with which I had dealt with agents in my own time. Who the hell did these people think they were talking to?

"Gentlemen," I responded, "I have had an awful lot of experience at what you are attempting now. I know exactly what you are thinking. You want a lot from the partner but the partner isn't so forthcoming. One has to be patient. One can discuss things and get a lot out of a conversation before anything becomes formal."

That was the politest version of my thoughts. My inner voice was dying to tell Hathaway that he had it all wrong, that he was talking to me as if I were some two-bit agent he could buy and sell. I wanted to tell him directly that it was not like that, that we should talk properly on the level that should be expected from two people who knew this game inside out.

"But you have to help us," said Hathaway again.

"That would be true if I were offering myself to you," I said, hardly bothering this time to hide my irritation. "Then you could ask me what I was going to bring to the party, so to speak. But I'm not offering. It is you who are talking to me."

"Yes, yes," said Hathaway hastily, "it's true I have come to Berlin specially to talk to you."

"There are always limits to this kind of discussion," I said. "My limit is that I will not betray anyone who worked for me. No names. If you still want to talk to me, invite me to America formally and then we can talk properly, like grown-ups. I need to see your country before I can decide anything."

"But your security here is not very good," interjected Hathaway, reminding me that if I stayed in Germany, only a few weeks remained until my certain arrest, as I knew all too well.

"There's always Russia," I replied.

At this, my interlocutor suddenly came to life, sensing that he might be bidding against at least one other powerful rival.

"Don't go to Moscow," he said. "Life there is hard. Think of Andrea. Come to a country where things would be pleasant for you, where you can work and write quietly. In my opinion, that is only possible for you in America now."

The prospect of sunning myself in prosperous retirement in California or Florida rather than sampling the dubious delights of a German prison may seem enticing. But I still felt uneasy at the prospect of delivering myself to the CIA as its hostage. What if they decided to turn the screws on me? Presumably they were also taping the conversation, and they could always claim that I had invented the meeting if the whole business turned sour. I wanted a greater commitment from them before we talked further, so I requested some form of invitation to America, perhaps from an organization fronting for the agency.

My visitors were unhappy with this idea, explaining that they operated under a quota system for the agency's foreign guests that was difficult to exceed. More likely they were nervous about the West Germans finding out about the deal. After all, even an attempt to recruit such a senior and long-serving figure in the enemy camp as I was amounted to massive treachery by the Americans toward their allies in Europe and especially Germany. I suggested finding a tame publishing house or film company through which they could invite me as an author—the time-honored method of making a covert approach. That was certainly the way such a deal would have been set up in the Eastern bloc, and I would have thought it was well within the CIA's capabilities to find some organization to issue an invitation that could then be transformed into a permanent stay in America if we struck a deal.

There was a long silence, followed by Hathaway shaking his head. But they plugged away regardless, insisting that I could make a valuable contribution to the agency without directly betraying my men. Gradually it became clear to me that, unlike the West Germans, they were primarily interested not in my work for East German intelligence but in my knowledge of the KGB and the structure of Soviet intelligence.

"Gentlemen," I said, hoping to speed up a conversation that was beginning to weary me, "I don't know which part of the service you are from, but I can guess. There is something very specific you want from me, isn't there?"

Finally Hathaway got down to brass tacks.

"Herr Wolf," he said softly, "we have come because we know that you have operational information that might be useful to us in a particularly serious case. We are looking for a mole inside our operation. He has done a lot of damage. Bad things happened to us around 1985. Not only in Bonn but elsewhere, in places with which you are familiar. We lost some men—maybe thirty to thirty-five, and five or six in the apparatus."

He seemed to know his way around Soviet intelligence and knew who ran its foreign arm and its operations, which had led me to conclude early in the conversation that he was a highly placed American counterintelligence man. We spoke guardedly about great Soviet traitors—Penkovsky, Gordievsky, Popov—men whose change of loyalties had helped the Americans keep pace with Soviet espionage. He admired a Russian colleague of mine, General Kireyev, head of foreign counterintelligence in Moscow, with whom I had planned some joint operations against the CIA. He seemed to know something about those enterprises and tried to open a discussion about Felix Bloch, an American diplomat suspected by the CIA of having been recruited by Moscow but never prosecuted owing to lack of evidence. I guessed that there had already been some painstaking research at Langley into my cooperation with the KGB and that this had raised hopes that I might know the identity of the mole they sought.

I did not. This sort of information was protected very tightly by the Soviets. Neither would I, despite our formal fraternal alignment, have told the Soviets the identity of my top moles or agents. At the most, we might indicate shyly to one another that we had "someone sitting" in the enemy camp, but no more.

It was clear from Hathaway's earnest approach and tenacious attempts to lure me into the American camp that the CIA was in a state of panic about its penetration. They must have had to swallow hard to bring their problem to me. Moreover, they were risking a substantial breach with their West German partners in approaching me. In such desperate straits, even the firmest ideological loyalties are stretched to the breaking point.

On May 29 they came back again, but we came no closer to reaching an agreement to invite me formally to America. Hathaway said that he would report back to Webster and that if I wished to pursue the matter, I should contact him. They were clearly hoping that, under the more imminent threat of arrest, I would agree to come under their wing, and on their terms. Charles stepped in at that point and spoke to Andrea, describing the pleasures of life in America to her. Before leaving, they handed me a toll-free telephone number in Langley, and we exchanged code words for future contact. I had not delivered or promised them anything. They were, I knew, playing a waiting game, and my situation could only get worse.

By mid-August the German bid brokered by Peter-Michael Diestel had fallen through completely. I felt that my options were running out fast. The CIA evidently guessed as much too, because they made contact with me again through the same channel. We arranged another meeting in my dacha and Hathaway referred, once again, to what he delicately described as my "disagreeable situation." Webster, he added, was still refusing to offer me a personal invitation, but the offer still stood of asylum in the States in return for my helping in the mole hunt. This time Charles was more talkative. He explained that if I decided to seek their help, I should send my wife, Andrea, to the Bahnhof Zoo station in the western part of Berlin and call a certain toll-free number. She was to introduce herself as Gertrud and say, "I want to talk to Gustav." My escape would be planned thereafter from Berlin, where the man who called himself Charles would be in charge of my case.

From this, I assume that the mention of the code-name Gertrud would automatically switch the call through to both Langley and the

Berlin CIA station simultaneously. It would not be too difficult to snatch me then, probably by air, as the Soviets had done when they spirited the disgraced leader Erich Honecker out of East Germany aboard a military plane to Moscow. Having arrived in 1945 on one of the first flights of returning German Communists from Moscow after Hitler's demise, I mused that it would be an ironic ending to fly out of Berlin forty-five years later under the cover of the Americans.

There was one more meeting, this time in my city apartment, at the end of September, but it brought no improvement in the American offer.

At that, the West German public prosecutor obligingly announced that police officers would be dispatched to my door at midnight on October 2 to arrest me. The tabloid *Bild-Zeitung* had sent a representative with an offer to pay the legal costs of my defense for exclusive coverage of my arrest. I told them I would think about it. It was all a well-planned circus, which I had no wish to be part of. I told the *Bild* reporter that I had no plans to leave Germany. This was almost true, because I certainly had a strong desire to leave Germany for a while, but no idea where to go. By refusing to turn traitor at Bonn's behest, I had, in effect, closed off the option of staying in Germany without having to face trial and very probably prison.

Only much later did I discover the identity of the mole who was causing the CIA such heartache. His name was Aldrich Ames, the most damaging traitor in the history of American espionage. Ames used his position in charge of detecting Soviet counterintelligence operations worldwide to sell the Soviets the names of America's agents, effectively destroying the American intelligence network in the Soviet Union from the inside. For nine years he served Moscow, under both the Communist regime and the rule of Boris Yeltsin, in this job and later in the anti-narcotics department. In the process he earned $2.7 million, making him without doubt the highest paid mole in history. My visitor from Langley was no mere emissary of William Webster, but Gardner A. Hathaway, who, I later read, had retired as chief of U.S. counterintelligence only a few months before he first visited me.

A veteran officer of the CIA's Operations Directorate, Gus Hathaway had been in his job for just over a year when the signs began to multiply that a traitor was at work high in the agency. He was one of the few who knew how heavy the losses of American agents inside the Soviet Union were—ten executions and dozens of harsh prison sentences—and had complete understanding of how this traitor within the ranks was bleeding U.S. intelligence.

I had done some casual research and something about Hathaway fascinated me. When I learned he had just retired I felt a certain empathy for him as an intelligence pensioner. Like me, he had been unable to draw a line across his life and simply devote his remaining years to gardening, holidays, and the family pleasures we all imagine we will enjoy in retirement. He was captive to the deathly puzzle he had spent his last working years trying to solve: Who was his own agency's serial traitor? I remembered the way his eyes had held mine as he in effect confessed the CIA's failures in short, spare sentences. It must have cost him dearly in pride to travel to Berlin and ask for help from a former enemy. But he was professionally and privately obsessed with tracking down Ames. His mole-hunting unit was secret even within the CIA. It was staffed mostly by retired officers to further ensure secrecy and was called the Special Task Force. It included a female senior counterintelligence analyst—rare in the CIA or any other intelligence service—who had studied a Chinese CIA mole who had gone undiscovered for thirty years and a respected colleague from the Soviet division. I was impressed by the range of skills Hathaway had sought out. He did as I would have in his position and kept his team as small as possible. Using retired officers was an especially clever move, since any attempt to draw in the CIA's own Soviet department risked warning or even recruiting the mole himself. The motto of all such operations should be: Tread softly.

Ames was eventually discovered by the CIA's rival, the Federal Bureau of Investigation. I doubt Hathaway's difficulties arose from lack of experience or knowledge. More likely, he was not a very creative person and was, as some of his colleagues said, a rather bureaucratic man. But I do not fault him for failing to identify the traitor who had been attacking American intelligence like a malevolent bacillus from within. The thankless and exhausting task of tracking down a traitor always seems much easier in retrospect than in prospect. The clues always seem so obvious—but only after the hunt has caught its prey.

Looking for quirks in behavior is the right way to locate a mole. But many people in any profession—to say nothing of the high-stress pro-

fession of espionage—have alcoholic, behavioral, or marriage problems, feel underappreciated, or need more money than they can honestly earn. Intelligence workers are encouraged by the secretive milieu
in which they live or work to feel that the rules governing others do not
apply to them. Members of a department that worked as intensely as
the CIA's Soviet team must have come to know the enemy's mind-set so
well that it became easier and easier to slip into his way of thinking,
especially if, as in Ames's case, the bonds to one's country and agency
have been whittled away by feelings of inferiority and frustration.

When he was formally recruited by the Soviets in 1985, Ames was
run by the KGB resident (the officially assigned KGB officer) in the
Soviet embassy in Washington, Stanislav Androsov. A year later
Androsov was replaced by Ivan Semyonovich Gromakov, whom I had
known since the 1960s as the head of the KGB's German section
(Department 4 of the First Main Directorate). Though I knew he spoke
German, I had no idea his English was also fluent, and thus I was surprised when I heard of his Washington appointment. Squat and jovial
with thick glasses, he had an unnerving habit of roaring bloodcurdling
toasts to the success of the KGB. I never spoke to him about his prize
catch, but I can easily imagine how delighted he was when, stationed as
he was in the heart of enemy territory, Ames landed in his lap.

When the story of Ames's treachery emerged, I was stunned that he
could have carried on undiscovered for so long and that American
counterintelligence proved so incompetent and desperate as to be
forced to resort to the help of an enemy spy chief to find him.

It may seem odd that I was even prepared to talk to the CIA. After
all, I had no real desire to leave Germany and had formally declared
that I had no intention to emigrate. I rejected outright the claim of the
West, as victor in the Cold War, to administer its version of justice to
me and my colleagues; to me this claim was tainted by the motive of
revenge. The principal attraction of the CIA offer was that it would
remove me temporarily from my country in the first days after unification. I knew that in those first weeks and months, the appetite for
revenge would run high. If possible, I wanted to avoid the Russian
option, since disappearing to Moscow would send the wrong public
signals about my relationship with the new Germany, encouraging
those at home who wanted to pursue me. There would be accusations

that I had gone to Moscow to hand over the names of agents, a story that had already circulated during my two-month stay at the beginning of 1990. This was not the case. I was far too concerned about securing freedom from prosecution for myself and for my ex-employees, agents, and moles to play go-between with the Soviets.

Had the CIA been prepared to receive me in America, I would have seriously considered its offer as a dramatic if temporary solution. But my fear was that, if the deal foundered once I had flown to the States without a formal invitation, the CIA could present me as having offered myself and effectively blackmail me into cooperating with them on their terms. With the arrogance of a great intelligence service, the CIA assumed that I was so desperate to work with them that I was prepared to place myself in the vulnerable position every good defector tries to avoid—being trapped into negotiations on enemy territory. Although Hathaway had specifically come to Berlin on September 26 and we had already packed our bags, our last conversation drudgingly moved in circles.

●

What neither the Americans, the Russians, nor the West Germans realized was that one other significant secret bidder had entered this curious auction. And that was Israel. I am a Jew, unusual for a man in the upper reaches of Soviet bloc intelligence. Or to be precise, I am half Jewish, since my mother was a Gentile. But I am Jewish enough to have been categorized and persecuted under the Nuremberg racial laws promulgated in 1936 if the Nazis had caught up with my family as it fled, first to France, then to Russia. My ideology and the ruptures of the Cold War should have made me an adversary of Israel. But I have always retained an interest in Jewish affairs, and the traditions of my family were such that I regarded myself as having a Jewish heritage, if not the faith.

My first contacts with Tel Aviv came very late and were an unexpected, if welcome, consequence of my appearance at a rally on November 4, 1989, calling for a change in the regime in East Germany. There I met a woman called Irene Runge, an academic who ran the Jewish Cultural Association, founded in East Berlin during the eighties after the decades of repression of the Jewish tradition in the East, which was a consequence of the GDR's alignment with the Arab world. I gave Irene an interview for use in an Israeli newspaper, and I attended a meeting of her association as a guest, but thought no more of it.

In the summer of 1990, she called me out of the blue with the news that a Rabbi Tsvi Weinman, a senior Orthodox figure in Jerusalem, wanted to make my acquaintance. It was a Friday, which meant the Jewish Sabbath would begin at sundown and that he could not meet me in person. But I telephoned him and we exchanged pleasantries and agreed to meet during his next visit to Berlin. Soon after, he turned up again, claiming that the main reason for his presence was a visit to the Jewish Cultural Association. I invited him to my apartment, where he arrived punctually, a man of around fifty with a broad-brimmed black hat but no other external sign of a typical orthodox Jew. He inquired solicitously about my position as someone with a Jewish background and experience of persecution who was facing a political trial in Germany. He carefully avoided any mention of my former work, but asked whether I would like to visit Israel. I began to wonder whether Weinman's interest in me was entirely attributable to cultural matters. Shortly afterward I received an invitation from the Israeli newspaper *Yediot Ahranoth* to visit the country.

Inquiries about Weinman produced the whisper that he had worked for the Mossad in his youth. He himself was quick to deny this, saying that he had been in the army but had never worked in intelligence. We telephoned frequently and I looked forward to my trip, imagining the crestfallen faces in Bonn, Moscow, and Washington when they saw the headlines reporting my sudden presence in Israel. I guessed that the Mossad might be interested in gleaning from me what I knew of the Palestinian groups and their operations, which was very little, but I decided to cross that bridge when I arrived in the Holy Land. At any rate, the visit offered the possibility of a new escape route from Germany. I was not going to look that gift horse in the mouth.

Two weeks before unification, I received a sudden call from Weinman. He sounded depressed and a trifle embarrassed. The visit was off. The newspaper had lost interest, he said, owing to the appearance of a critical book about the Mossad and its methods that was causing a furor. It was not the right time to entertain me. I understood immediately that the Israelis had gotten cold feet at the last moment, doubtless fearing that any service I might render could never be offset by the damage that their excellent relationship with West Germany would suffer through my presence in Israel. The door of hope that had opened so temptingly slammed shut. But Tel Aviv did not sever its links with me entirely. After the call from Weinman I received another from the newspaper, offering me a visa and flight ticket at a later date. I arranged for it to be left for me in Vienna. But when I checked on it a few weeks later, there was nothing. If there had ever been such a ticket available, it was no longer there.

By now the pressure was intense, and I knew that the German authorities were eager to see me behind bars. Where could I escape to, and what would be the cost of refuge? There were no compelling options, and I was running out of time.

2

Out from Under Hitler's Shadow

My father, Friedrich Wolf, born in the Rhineland in 1888, came from a devoutly Jewish family. In his youth, his parents wanted him to become a rabbi, but he rebelled and insisted on studying medicine instead. His path to Marxism culminated in 1928, by which time he was already forty years old, and he arrived at this secular faith via a convoluted route. He was not one of the German intellectuals primarily fired by the 1917 October Revolution in Russia. Of petit bourgeois Jewish origins—his father was a businessman—my father floated through a pacifist and utopian period with ideas gained from Tolstoy, Strindberg, Upton Sinclair, Nietzsche, and Kropotkin, before the horrors of the First World War. He served in the Kaiser's army and was severely wounded—but he suffered equally from the uncaring insolence of the German officer corps, which helped inspire his radicalism and antinationalism. His disappointment in the defeat of the German revolutionaries who sought to establish a just and egalitarian state in 1918 and then in the first years of the Weimar Republic moved him to embrace the promises of social and economic harmony made by Marx and Lenin.

But our family had always had a radical streak. Father used to tell me that his political education had begun at the age of five, when he was taken by his grandmother to see the Kaiser unveil a monument to the nineteenth-century German ruler Friedrich Wilhelm. As the crowd cheered the ruler and craned their necks for a better look at the monument, she lifted up the boy and said sternly, "Fritzsche, that is no hero you see, that is the cannon-happy prince who shot at the workers." She was referring to Friedrich Wilhelm's bloody suppression of the liberal 1848 revolt in Germany. My mother, Else, also had a contrary streak. Ten years younger than my father and a beautiful blonde from the Rhineland, she had broken with her family when she married a Jew.

Even in death my father remained a figure of great controversy. On the neat main square of the small town of Neuwied, on the banks of the Rhine south of Bonn, hangs a commemorative plaque recording his birth on December 23, 1888. Nearby, a street was also named after him to mark the hundredth anniversary of his birth. The erection of the plaque brought Neuwied as close to civic uproar as it ever got, since my father, besides his fame hereabouts as an experimental doctor and playwright, was also a fervent Communist, a type of local hero not often celebrated in cozy West German towns.

After the fall of East Germany I finally had a chance to revisit Neuwied. It was a disconcerting feeling to stroll the streets in the other half of my own country, of which I knew so much but had seen so little. Throughout the Cold War years I had never ventured into West Germany. The few trips I did take outside the Eastern bloc in my decades as East German chief of espionage were essential operational ones, usually to meet agents whose security forbade their traveling to us.

I was born in Hechingen, a small town in rural, Catholic southwest Germany. It was January 19, 1923, during the years of rampant inflation so uncontrollable that my parents were often relieved when my father could collect his medical fees from rural patients in the form of butter and eggs. We were a lively household, eccentric by the staid standards of the locality. Life was little changed when we moved to Höllsteig, on Germany's southern border with Switzerland.

My father was a fitness fanatic who took great pleasure in honing his athletic body to near perfection. He was also an early proponent of naturism. As a result many of our family photographs show my father, me, and my brother, Konrad, almost three years younger, stark naked and doubled up in gymnastic contortions. Koni and I thought this was quite normal, despite the giggles of our classmates when we showed them the photos. Many such pictures appeared as anatomical illustrations in my father's best-selling book *Nature as Healer and Helper* (*Die Natur ols Arzt und Helfer*), a homeopathic tract written while we were in Höllsteig, in which my father dealt with, among other things, the effect of living and working conditions on the health of individuals. Such ideas would later become commonplace as what we now call preventive medicine. Back then, however, they were regarded as unorthodox, and my father was frowned upon by the medical establishment, which saw that his analysis of the causes of illness led into an altogether wider debate about society and the conditions of the poor that they wished to avoid.

But the book was a huge hit with the public, selling thousands of copies, and it became a kind of compulsory layman's bible on health care. In fact, it became such a standard text that, years later, it even escaped the Nazi ban on books by Jews. The book's financial success made it possible for our family to move to a pleasant house in Stuttgart, a city with a long tradition of the arts dating back to the liberal princelings of its free-thinking court.

My mother was quiet and gentle but a person of great courage, whether undergoing the Nazis' rough house searches or those of the secret police in Stalin's Russia. During Stalin's reign of terror, she once offered shelter to the family of an arrested man, an act that could well have led to her own imprisonment or worse. Also during our Moscow exile, upon hearing that my half sister Lena's mother had been arrested in the Volga region, she made her way from the capital to rescue and bring Lena back home to us.

It was our mother who raised us during our father's long romantic or political absences, but he played an important role in absentia by sending letters full of advice on how to be correct and honorable socialists and human beings. Without doubt, he was the strongest political influence on my young life. Our mother suffered greatly from his affairs with other women. These produced a small brood of children, half brothers and sisters to Koni and me, whose own children have straddled the barriers of the Cold War. To this day, I have relatives in Germany, Russia, and America as a result of his amours.

These adventures were frowned upon by outsiders but caused Koni and me little concern. It was simply part of our childhood for Father to announce from time to time that we would soon meet a new half brother or sister. These children of different mothers were treated by my own mother with great tolerance as part of the family. The marriage survived these other relationships and my parents remained together until his death in East Germany in 1953.

Friedrich's activism was impressive: He renounced the Independent Social Democrats in 1928, joined the Communist Party of Germany, and ran for the Stuttgart municipal council as a Communist, receiving 20 percent of the vote. His pro-abortion play of 1929, *Cyanide*, landed him in jail briefly and made him a national voice of radical politics. In 1931 he was jailed again, this time accused of performing abortions for personal gain. After he and his codefendant were cleared of all charges, they left Germany for the Soviet Union, then returned in the same year.

Koni and I went to a school run on the lines of the great liberal German educational reformers of the time and were encouraged to explore the countryside and express ourselves freely. Both my parents being Communists by now, my younger brother, Koni, and I joined the Communist youth organization, the Young Pioneers, while we still were in Germany. We tied on our red neckerchiefs with great pride and listened to tales of the Revolution in the "great Soviet Union." The family atmosphere decisively influenced the rest of our lives, with the exception of the vegetarianism my parents practiced. Our mouths watered at the cold cuts and German sausage in our school friends' box lunches, and my brother announced, "When I grow up, I'm going to eat a whole ox." But the more lasting impression was left by their love of nature and bodily fitness, and their radical politics embodied in my father's plays about the struggles of the peasants and workers staged in the touring Workers Acting Group Southwest. I began to feel like a political warrior, taking collections for striking metal workers, going on campaign events, and listening to the grown-ups' vigorous arguments during the last days before Hitler came to power.

As a child of Communist parents in Germany, I came to perceive Stalin as a wise and distant figure, like the benevolent magician in the fairy tales. I often imagined what life must be like in the "great Soviet Union"—for years I thought that was the country's official name—and concluded that it must be very white, covered in snow, and full of good people, guided by the wizard. My brother, Koni, better blessed than I with the ability to put his thoughts in imaginative form, spent hours drawing pictures of the great leader in the guise of a fairy-tale hero. But at that time I had no expectation of ever experiencing Soviet reality for myself.

After the National Socialists came to power in 1933, our life in Germany became intolerable. The burning of the German Reichstag in Berlin and the Nazis' false accusations that Communists had been responsible for it produced a witch-hunt against the Left. My father, at risk as both a Jew and a Communist, fled into hiding in Austria. During one of the many house searches that followed, I answered one of the brown-shirted SA men cheekily. He pressed me up against a wall and threatened that I would end up "in the Heuberg" if I did not betray my father's whereabouts. The Heuberg was the first concentration camp in our region, to which political opponents were sent. The adults spoke of it in whispers, and I was puzzled about what went on there, but at that age I still interpreted the conflict between the Nazis and the Left as a sort of gang fight. I knew that those men in the brown shirts were profoundly, even tribally, different from our family and I already saw myself as a young fighter.

It was about this time that I first became aware of my Jewish heritage. After one exceptionally brutal search in which I remember that my brother and I were particularly furious because the thugs crashed through our nursery, trampling our precious toys and books, my mother, marshaling all the serenity she could to hide her inner terror, took us on a bicycle ride through the lush Swabian countryside to visit my father's uncle, Moritz Meyer, whom we knew familiarly as "Öhmchen."

Öhmchen was considered a little weird in the small town of Hechingen. After a legal career, he had retired to live with his goats in the forest and enjoyed a modest reputation as a miracle healer. It was almost certainly his influence that converted my father from conventional medicine to homeopathic cures and natural therapy, and my father dedicated his book on natural healing to him. Our bicycle visit was during Passover, so he could give us only unleavened bread, which did not delight our childish appetites, but he compensated for this disappointment by telling us grave and exciting stories from the Torah and explaining the meaning of Jewish festivals.

A few months later, my mother, brother, and I were smuggled into Switzerland with the help of Communists there; the Party was by then illegal. From there we proceeded to France, where we were officially deemed "unwanted foreigners" and had to be hidden by friends on the little island of Bréhat in Brittany, where we were joined by my father. There he worked finishing his play *Professor Mamlock*, the first literary witness to the persecution of the Jews in Germany. Even before its German-language premiere in Zurich, it was performed at Jewish theaters in Warsaw and Tel Aviv and enjoyed huge successes around the world. A film based on the play was made in the Soviet Union and again much later by my brother, Koni. When the film ran in New York, in 1939, it helped make my father's name known in America.

The Nazis' response to the success of this play—never, of course, performed in Germany under their rule—was not long in coming. Our possessions were seized and my father's name was placed on the official list of authors of "harmful and undesirable writings." Soon afterward the entire family was stripped of its German citizenship and by 1937 not only his name, but my mother's, mine, and my brother's, would appear on the state's wanted list. That made us boys feel very grown up. If there is such a thing as a single event that forms a man's politics, for me this was it: to be listed as a criminal by one's own country.

Had we not been hidden in Switzerland, we all too easily could have shared the fate of our Jewish relatives whose names were later inscribed forever in the Yad Vashem Memorial in Jerusalem. Öhmchen, for example, did not survive the Holocaust. A German prisoner of war in Moscow told me that he had been taken away and had perished in the Mauthausen concentration camp in Austria. He was over eighty years of age when he died.

Sixty years later, wandering through Hechingen's manicured streets, I remembered my great-uncle and felt a shudder run down my spine, a sensation that only a German can feel when he looks into the faces of men his own age and wonders how they behaved during the period of Nazi rule: How much did they know, and how many guilty memories had they suppressed? Perhaps cities are better at swallowing the traces of the past. It is in the small towns of Germany that my mind turns to uncomfortable thoughts about my compatriots.

By now the Nazis had frozen our bank accounts and confiscated our property. The asylum we were offered in the Soviet Union came as a lifesaver for my parents, Koni, and me. With the help of a friend, the dramatist Vsevolod Vishnevsky, my father had found a small two-room apartment on Nizhny Kizlovsky Lane, one of the winding nineteenth-century streets in the old center of Moscow behind its main street, the Arbat, beloved of writers and intellectuals. In March 1934, my mother, brother Koni, and I followed him there.

We adjusted slowly to a strange language and culture, fearful of the harsh manners of the children who shared our courtyard. "Nemets—perets, kolbassa, kislaya kapusta," they would shout after us: "Germans—pepper, sausage, sauerkraut." They laughed at our short trousers, too, and we begged our mother for long ones. Finally she gave in with a sigh, saying, "You're proper little men now."

But we were soon fascinated by our new environment. After our provincial German childhood, the bustling city, with its rough and ready ways, thrilled us. In those days people still spat the husks of their sunflower seeds onto the pavement, and horse-drawn traps clattered through the street. Moscow was still a "big village," a city with peasant ways. At first we attended the German Karl Liebknecht School (a school for children of German-speaking parents, named after the Socialist leader of the January 1919 Spartacist uprising who was murdered in Berlin shortly thereafter), then later, a Russian high school. By the time we became teenagers we were barely distinguishable from our native schoolmates, for we spoke their colloquial Russian with Moscow accents. We had two special friends in George and Victor Fischer, sons of the American journalist Louis Fischer. It was they who gave me the nickname "Mischa," which has stuck ever since. My brother, Koni, anxious not to be left out, took the Russian diminutive "Kolya."

The Moscow of the thirties remains in my memory as an era of light and shadow. The city changed before our eyes. By now I was a rather serious teenage boy and no longer thought of Stalin as a magician. But as the new multistory apartment blocks soon appeared around the Kremlin, and the amount of traffic suddenly increased as black sedans replaced the pony traps, it was as if someone had waved a powerful wand and turned the Moscow of the past into a futuristic landscape. The elegant metro, with its Art Deco lamps and giddyingly steep escalators, hummed into life, and we would spend the afternoons after school exploring its vaults, which echoed like a vast underground church. The disastrous food shortage of the twenties abated, but despite the new buildings, my family's friends, mainly Russian intellectuals, lived cheek by jowl in tiny apartments. There were spectacular May Day parades. The exciting news of the day carried highlights of the age, like the daring recovery of the Chelyushkin expedition from the pack ice of the Arctic Ocean after its conquest of the North Pole. We followed these events with the enthusiasm that Western children devoted to their favorite football or baseball teams.

With similar passion Koni and I both joined the Soviet Young Pioneers—the Communist equivalent of the Boy Scouts—and learned battle songs about the class struggle and the Motherland. As Young Pioneers we marched in the great November display on Red Square commemorating the Soviet revolution, shouting slogans of praise for the tiny figure in an overcoat on the balustrade above Lenin's tomb. We spent our weekends in the countryside around Moscow, gathering berries and mushrooms because even as a city dweller our father was determined to preserve his nature worship as a way of life. I still missed German delicacies, though, and found the sparse Soviet diet, with its mainstays of buckwheat porridge and sour yogurt, desperately boring. Since then I have learned to love Russian food in all its variety, and if must say so, I make the best Pelmeni dumplings (stuffed with forcemeat) this side of Siberia. But I have never developed a great fondness for buckwheat porridge, probably as a result of having consumed tons of the stuff in my teens.

In summer I was dispatched to Pioneer camp and elevated to the role of leader. I wrote to my father complaining about the miserable gruel and military discipline that prevailed there. Back came a typically optimistic letter, bidding me to resist the regime by forming a commission with my fellow children. "Tell them that Comrade Stalin and the Party do not condone such waste. Quality is what counts. . . . Under no circumstances must you, as a good Pioneer and especially as a Pioneer leader, quarrel! You and the other group leaders should speak collectively with the administration. . . . Don't be despondent, my boy."

The Soviet Union was now our only home, and on my sixteenth birthday, in 1939, I received my first Soviet papers. Father wrote to me from Paris, "Now you are a real citizen of the Soviet people," which made me glow with pride. But as I grew older I realized that my father's infectious utopianism was not my natural leaning. I was of a more pragmatic temperament. Of course, it was an exhilarating time, but it was also the era of the purges, in which men who had been feted as heroes of the Revolution were wildly accused of crimes and often condemned to death or to imprisonment in the Arctic camps. The net cast by the NKVD—the secret police and precursor of the KGB—closed in on our émigré friends and acquaintances. It was confusing, obscure, and inexplicable to us youngsters, schooled in the tradition of belief in the Soviet Union as the beacon of progress and humanitarianism.

But children are sensitive to silences and evasions, and we were subliminally aware that we were not party to the whole truth about our surroundings. Many of our teachers disappeared during the purges of 1936–38. Our special German school was closed. We children noticed that adults never spoke of people who had "disappeared" in front of their families, and we automatically began to respect this bizarre courtesy ourselves. Not until years later would we face up to the extent and horror of the crimes and Stalin's personal responsibility for them. Back then, he was a leader, a father figure, his square-jawed, mustached face staring out like that of a visionary from the portrait on our schoolroom wall. The man and his works were beyond reproach, beyond question, for us. In 1937, when the murder machine was running at its most terrifyingly efficient, one of our family's acquaintances, Wilhelm Wloch, who had risked his life working for the Comintern in the underground in Germany and abroad, was arrested. His last words to his wife were "Comrade Stalin knows nothing of this."

Of course, our parents tried to keep from us their fears about the bloodletting. In their hearts and minds, the Soviet Union remained, through all their doubts and disappointments, "the first socialist country" they had so proudly told us about after their first visit in 1931.

My father, I now know, was fearful for his own life. Although his wife and children had been granted Soviet citizenship because we lived there, he spent much of his time abroad and so was not a citizen. He was, however, still able to travel on his German passport, even though his citizenship had been revoked. He had already applied for permission from the Soviet authorities to leave Moscow for Spain, where he wanted to serve as a doctor in the International Brigades fighting against General Franco's Fascists in the bitter Civil War there. Spain was the arena where the Nazi military tried out its deadly potential, practicing for its later aggression against other vulnerable powers. Throughout Europe, left-wing volunteers were flooding to the aid of the Republicans against the Spanish military insurgents. For many in the Soviet Union, fighting there also meant a ticket out of the Soviet Union and away from the oppressive atmosphere of the purges. Decades later, a reliable friend of the family told me that my father had said of his attempts to reach Spain: "I'm not going to wait around here until they arrest me." That revelation wounded me, even as a grown man, for it made me realize how many worries and reservations had been hidden from us children by our parents in the thirties, and how much sorrow must have been quietly harvested around us among many of our friends in Moscow.

My father never did reach Spain. For a year, his application for an exit visa lay unanswered. More and more of our friends and acquaintances in the German community had disappeared and my parents could no longer hide their anguish. When the doorbell rang unexpectedly one night, my usually calm father leapt to his feet and let out a violent curse. When it emerged that the visitor was only a neighbor intent on borrowing something, he regained his savoir-faire, but his hands trembled for a good half hour.

Perhaps he had some protector in the leadership of the German Communist Party in exile. I know that he corresponded with one of the main figures, Wilhelm Pieck, at this time and that Pieck had great respect for him. Perhaps he was just lucky. At any rate, he had been given permission to leave Moscow in 1938 and had gone to France, where at the outbreak of the Second World War he was interned—ironically, as an enemy alien because of his German passport. Even worse, after the Nazi invasion of France in the summer of 1940, he and the other inmates of the Le Vernet camp were due to be turned over to the German authorities, which would have meant certain death for him. He might actually have had a chance to emigrate to the United States, but because it meant putting down on the application that he had never been a Communist, he refused, ever loyal. My mother had for the previous three years pestered the authorities in Moscow, from where he had tried to flee, in an attempt to obtain Soviet citizenship for him so he could be repatriated. He was finally made a citizen in August 1940.

But by then the Hitler-Stalin Pact of August 1939 made the lives of German émigrés in Moscow more difficult than ever. The authorities, who honored our status as the hounded victims of the evil Reich, were now under orders not to exacerbate ill feeling toward Hitler. It was particularly difficult for families like ours, which had been driven out of Germany by the Nazis, to comprehend the Soviet leader's deal with them. As budding agitators in the Komsomol (Young Communist League) youth movement, we were told that it was Stalin's only way of saving the great Soviet Union from attack, and that the Western powers were hoping that our Communist nation would "bleed to death" on the Nazi sword. It seemed a convincing enough explanation at the time, although we sensed that for our parents it was anathema that the Communists had made a deal with the very dictator they had fled.

Anxious to fit into our new milieu, Koni and I had Russianized ourselves as quickly as possible. We spoke the language all day at school and with our playmates, hearing German only in our apartment in the evenings. I was delighted to be called Mischa by the other boys, which meant that I could be taken for a Russian. We went to bed listening to broadcasts of Hitler's manic screech proclaiming the glory of the Reich.

After I finished secondary school I began studying aeronautical engineering, my dream subject. That changed abruptly on June 22, 1941, when Hitler's Wehrmacht attacked the Soviet Union with ferocious might in Operation Barbarossa. With the German army nearing Moscow in 1941, the families of Writers Union members, including our own, were evacuated to Alma-Ata, the capital of Kazakhstan, four thousand miles from Moscow. The horror of the three-week train journey across the Urals remains vivid for me. Our train crawled along the track, shunted to the sidings every hour or so to allow the trains heading to the front to pass from the other direction. My father tended Anna Akhmatova, the great Russian poet, who was sick and frail. Two of her husbands had disappeared in the purges and a son was in an internment camp. I was allowed to take her the allotted food ration of four hundred grams of black bread and some tepid water. She lay, sunken and weary, the soul of Russian literature, now officially deemed an "unperson" by the authorities, but still idolized among intellectuals as they traveled together on the Writers Union train.

Alma-Ata was a bleak place where we were isolated from news of Moscow, let alone the world beyond. Physically beautiful and normally inhabited by only four hundred thousand people, Alma-Ata suddenly was jammed with a million refugees, and living conditions became crowded and harsh. In 1942, Koni joined the Red Army, from which I was at that time exempt because aeronautical engineering was an essential occupation. I was still at that optimistic age where it did not occur to me that any harm could befall him, despite the rumors of heavy Russian losses. While exempt, I did receive military training, and as the tallest in our group, I regularly had to carry the heavy tripod of the Maxim machine gun on my shoulders in temperatures above one hundred degrees Fahrenheit. Our bread ration remained only five hundred grams, and I can truly say that was the only time in my life I knew what hunger was. But some help and variety came from the exiled Moscow intelligentsia, especially the Moscow film studios. In the evenings we called on the great director Sergei Eisenstein, who read us passages from his script for the film *Ivan the Terrible*. When filming began, we were enlisted as extras, serving as the invading German knights who were repulsed. Because of my parachute training, I got stuntman's roles, which gave me triple pay, and that helped relieve the wartime boredom and privation.

Halfway through my studies, a mysterious telegram arrived, signed "EKKI Vilkov." The four letters EKKI stood for the Executive Committee of the Communist International, the Comintern, and it was signed by the man who headed its department of personnel and cadres. I was ordered to travel first to Ufa, the capital of the remote autonomous republic of Bashkiria, where the Comintern and the leadership-in-exile of the Communist Party of Germany had been transferred away from the siege of Moscow.

The Party had decided to send me to the Comintern school, at the small village of Kushnarenkovo, forty miles from Ufa, where Communists from occupied European countries and Korea prepared for the liberation of their homelands and were trained for future political assignments. I was schooled enough in the discipline of a Communist youth not to question the decision, despite regretting that my dreams of designing Soviet planes were now unlikely to be fulfilled. But despite any such regrets, I was also utterly convinced that the fight against Hitler was more important and honorable than my studies.

Life in the Comintern, an organization whose task was to promote the international proletarian revolution, was conducted in an atmosphere of great secrecy, which made me feel very grown up. It was ingrained in my character that if the Party asked something of us, we responded obediently. They said, "Jump," we said, "How high?" Conditions of utmost secrecy prevailed at the school. We were given false names—mine was Kurt Förster, which I thought sounded very dashing. Although all of the young Germans there knew each other from Moscow, we used only these new names to address each other—an early training in covert methods. We were taught how to use submachine guns, rifles, and pistols, how to handle explosives and hand grenades, and how to use the "conspiratorial techniques" of meeting and message passing that are the basis of espionage. Our political education was oriented toward the time after the expected victory over Hitler. The firm assumption was that we would organize a common front of all antifascist and democratic forces.

But we also received a thorough grounding in propaganda skills. In one of the lessons, someone from the group would be picked to present the arguments of our Nazi enemies as convincingly as possible, while the others would have to counter him with antifascist precepts. I enjoyed this challenge of getting as deep into the enemy mind as possible and made my pro-Nazi arguments clearly and with great passion, while the duller students, fearful perhaps of endangering their record as convinced young Communists, would parrot the textbook explanations unenthusiastically. Once, my classmates were scolded for failing to respond sharply enough to the fascist rhetoric I assumed. "What on earth would you all do if you ever had to argue with a real Nazi?" the teacher thundered. My only real competition in these bizarre contests of ideological wit came from Wolfgang Leonhard, who years later, in 1949, would flee East Germany for Yugoslavia and become a leading

Sovietologist in Germany and later at Harvard and Yale. One of the many ironies of my life is that Professor Leonhard eventually used the argumentative skills he honed in the Comintern against the Soviet system, while I continued to deploy mine in its defense.

At the Comintern school I also met my future wife, Emmi Stenzer. I had never met a woman so utterly absorbed in her political task, which she saw as a dedication to her father, Franz Stenzer, a Reichstag deputy who had been killed by the Nazis in Dachau in 1933. She had a Spanish boyfriend when we first met, and it was only after we left the Comintern school and met again in Moscow that we fell in love. I was fascinated by her independence and strength of will after the harshness of her young life, which had been spent in an orphanage in the grim industrial town of Ivanovo after the arrest of her mother in Moscow during the thirties in one of the wholesale roundups of foreign residents on suspicion of anti-Soviet activity (her mother was later released).

Bertolt Brecht wrote to his wife, Helene Weigel, about the importance of "the third thing" that was always there between them—their shared attachment to the Cause—as a living part of their relationship. Nowadays that seems easy to mock, but in times when political beliefs can lead to death or imprisonment, they become very much part of the emotional as well as the intellectual fabric of a life. Despite the fact that I divorced Emmi after nearly three decades of marriage and have remarried twice since, she continues to be a soulmate and maintains her early tie with my whole family by running the Friedrich Wolf Archive in Berlin.

On May 16, 1943, my life took yet another abrupt turn. We arrived in our classroom to find a notice on the blackboard informing us that, owing to "the differences in conditions between the countries that had become the bearers of Nazi tyranny and the freedom-loving peoples," the Communist International and its school was to be dissolved. Of course there were hidden political reasons for this. Dissolving the International was Stalin's compromise with the Western Allies, who saw the Comintern as an agency fomenting revolution in their own countries.

I had been extremely lucky in the timing of my recruitment. The previous set of graduates had been parachuted into Germany to make contact with resistance groups but fell into a trap set up by Third Reich counterintelligence, which had been sending false radio transmissions that the Soviet authorities interpreted as valid. They were caught by the Gestapo and Hitler's military counterintelligence and executed. Their sacrifice spared our intake group a similar fate. Instead, we worked on a machine-maintenance crew on a nearby farm and unloaded barges on the Belaya River.

We were nevertheless surprised at the decision. Hadn't our teachers told us that the International was eternal, the highest element in the Party? But the whole education had been directed toward training us to follow orders without question. We had learned to accept whatever the Party ordered as the right thing, and waited patiently for new instructions.

Probably because I was the son of a noted author, the Party leadership saw fit to make me an announcer and commentator on the German People's Radio (Deutsche Volkssender), the voice of the German Communist Party on Radio Moscow, so I returned to Moscow. I became a full Party member at the age of twenty and attended meetings in the old Hotel Lux in the room of Wilhelm Pieck, later the first president of the German Democratic Republic. It was there, in a hotel that had been at the center of the purges of foreign Communists, that I first met the men, like Walter Ulbricht and others, who were to rule my country after the war.

Emmi meanwhile was sent to the front to deliver negative propaganda in German through a microphone as part of the psychological warfare campaign. She would walk up and down within sight of the enemy lines, shouting into her amplifier that the war was all but over and calling on German soldiers to capitulate. She was seriously wounded at Gomel, and on September 24, 1944, fearful that we might never see each other again, we were married. We remained separated, however, during the final months of the war.

Victory over Nazi Germany was finally celebrated the following May, and I will never forget the joy with which my parents and I joined the jubilant crowd of Muscovites. Koni was already on German soil and participated in the final assault on Berlin, during which he earned six awards for bravery. He sent us a letter saying that he was waiting for us, and I started to pack up the possessions of my teenage Russian life. In the Comintern school, we knew that we were being prepared for a return to Germany after an eventual Allied victory. That time now had arrived.

3

Stalin's Pupils

I was eleven years old when I left Germany and went to Moscow, and it would be another eleven years before I returned to Germany. I have often been called "half Russian" in jest, patronizingly, and sometimes critically, but I have never taken it as an insult, and the patronage of the Russians was an essential element in my career. My fellow German Communists knew that my early life had been shaped in the Soviet Union and by the profound spirit of the Russians. My very closeness to the Soviet Union gave me an authority that in later years I could use with firmness in disputes.

When I visited Moscow later on official business, I would slip out of my formal German identity as soon as I could and into the familiar guise of a Muscovite, wandering through streets and chatting with people more familiar to me than Berlin and Berliners. I would head to our old apartment building on Nizhny Kizlovsky Lane, now marked with a memorial plaque for my father and brother, and visit many of my old friends in the Arbat. With my old friend Alik, who had lost a leg during the war and had become a professor of German, I would walk through our old neighborhood to Gorky Street, now called Tverskaya again as it was before the Revolution. As students we had spent many hours queuing for seats at the famous Moscow Art Theater to see the great Tarasova play *Anna Karenina*, or watching Michoels, a star of the Jewish theater, located near our school. We loved the Russian classics and also the nineteenth-century European masters—Heine, Balzac—as well as Galsworthy, Roger Martin du Gard, and the tight and powerful style of Hemingway. When we had a reunion in the summer of 1941, we rowed into a secluded curve of the Moscow River and recited poetry by Aleksandr Blok and Sergei Yesenin.

For years, my leaving Moscow produced a pang of homesickness, but unlike some of my German friends who settled there, I never was tempted to remain in Moscow for the rest of my life. Germany was still my *Heimat*, and here was the calling for which my Comintern training and radio experience had prepared me. I was twenty-three years old, a sophisticated and ambitious young man who remained naïve about what I would face back in Germany. Our training had been heavily ideological and concentrated on the mopping-up operation we would perform in the defeated territory. We could not imagine the shock of facing our own countrymen after the collapse of their world, a vast national defeat, and the ignominious end of the dictator who had entranced them.

We young Communists returning from Moscow saw ourselves as bearers of political enlightenment, who would show by our example how much better the Left was than the Right. Our initial orders were not to impose Communist structures in the Soviet occupation zone of Germany, but to create a broad antifascist alliance, albeit one engineered by us. This was not a mere tactic but in our eyes and those of all Communists a necessity: We had learned from Hitler how the Left could be eradicated. Stalin was, in fact, initially skeptical about the chances of creating a Soviet-style government in part of Germany and wanted to keep his options open with the Western Allies.

Our return was much more cruel and unpleasant in fact than we could have imagined. My brother, Koni, reflected on it years later in his film about young people coming face to face with unimaginable barbarity, *I Was Nineteen*. There he contrasted the boyishness of the young hero with a society in chaos, where town hall mayors were hastily hauling in the Nazi flag—or sometimes just cutting out the white circle and the black Swastika in the middle—as the Red Army approached.

While Koni, as an officer of the Soviet military directorate, was helping to establish the foundations of a post-Nazi administration in the Soviet zone, I was ordered to Berlin as part of the Party apparat. The shrill, bearded Walter Ulbricht, who had emerged as the leader of the German Communists in exile, set off from Moscow to Berlin with the gentler figure of Wilhelm Pieck and a small advance party in April. The rest of us flew a month later, on May 27, in a military version of the Douglas DC-3, all wearing brand-new civilian suits. From the air, all that we could see below were the ruins of war.

We were a mixed bag—old Communists and German prisoners of war who were children of old Communists. No one had any idea what to expect, and we talked and wondered what we might encounter. We did not even know whether the Communist Party would be permitted in Germany. Of idealistic talk about building a new Germany there was none. We realized that our first task would be the fundamental one of organizing daily life simply so that Germans could survive.

Emmi came with me, the first time we would be staying together as husband and wife. For the two of us the return to our homeland was an exhilarating and painful affair as we took in the devastated landscape of vast ruins that had been Germany's towns and cities. We had caught a fleeting glimpse of the wreck of Warsaw on the way in. It was utterly destroyed, smoke rising from the rubble as if from a funeral pyre. Our aircraft was the first to land at the freshly reopened Tempelhof airport in Berlin, which three years later was to serve as the hub of the Allied airlift during the Berlin Blockade. The destruction of Berlin seemed so complete as to exclude any thought of reconstruction.

As children of the Comintern, we were possessed by a powerful sense of purpose. We wanted to purge our own people of their Nazi past and believed wholeheartedly that the socialist ideas in which we had been reared could cleanse and renew Germany. But it was harder than I had expected for me to get used to living among people who had cheered on Hitler and Goebbels. The majority seemed unable or unwilling to comprehend what the Nazis had done with their help or in their name. Hardly anyone felt a sense of guilt or responsibility for what had happened. Emmi recalled overhearing a group of women discussing the report on German war crimes that was carried by the radio station where I worked. "German men," they said, echoing the ultranationalist Hitlerian language to which they had listened for the last twelve years, "would never do anything like that."

In the view of many Germans and much of the world we returned from the East bearing with us another dictatorship. But we did not see ourselves, as the West would later taunt, as swapping a Brown for a Red tyranny. We German Communists had perhaps the most complete blind spot of all the foreigners in Moscow about Stalin's crimes, since we had been rescued from death or imprisonment in Germany by the Soviet Union. Any other doubts about what was going on were overshadowed by events under Hitler's brutal regime, and I was incapable of seeing our socialist system as a tyranny. For me and my generation of Communists, it had been a liberating force. There was perhaps a rough streak in its methods, but we always felt that it was essentially a force for good and it would have been futile to try convincing me otherwise.

This approach was to determine our thinking throughout the Cold War. It meant that whenever we heard an unflattering portrayal of our own side our first question to ourselves was not "Is this true?" but "What are they trying to hide about themselves by accusing us of this?" Once this mental defense system had been perfected, few criticisms could hit home.

We were also naïve. I had hoped that after the shock of the defeat, more Germans would be grateful for their deliverance from Hitler and embrace the Soviets as liberators. The reality was rather different. In the tenement block in which I lived, I would overhear our neighbors arguing over who would move into the more spacious and airy apartments at the front of the building, from which a Nazi family had been evicted. The collapse of Germany as a world power had not destroyed its people's petty ambitions for their own "Lebensraum," I thought bitterly. My temper worsened when I heard from others that the family laying claim to the apartment on the basis that they had never been Nazi Party members were noted local *Denunzianten*, who had betrayed five Communists to the authorities.

How could I have been so blind to the irony of our claims to be installing a humane and peace-loving order? I can only answer that the part of me that had in my years in the Soviet Union become half Russian sympathized at some emotional level with the desire for revenge for the horrors inflicted by Germany. I supposed that after a good rout, the desire for revenge would subside and we could build a new German-Russian relationship, devoid of the desire to dominate each other.

A few days after our arrival, we were summoned before Ulbricht one by one. Curtly, he told us our roles in the administration of the Soviet zone. I was directed to Berlin Radio to work as an editor; it was a huge complex in Charlottenburg, in the British sector, that had been Josef Goebbels's Reichsradio and was now in Soviet hands. At first I resisted Ulbricht's orders, since I had been trained as an engineer and knew too little about the techniques of agitprop—although I had been exposed to it as a child, when it was a formative experience in the resistance to Nazism. When I asked him when I would be allowed to finished my aeronautical studies in Moscow, he snapped, "Just do your job. We have other things to worry about than building airplanes." Despite my initial misgivings, when I went out to do reporting and foreign policy commentary (under the alias "Michael Storm") I found the work interesting. Located far from the Soviet sector, in the British sector, our station was literally an outpost in the Cold War that was just beginning. Our distance from Party headquarters in East Berlin meant that we could operate with some independence. I did have a small brochure that Ulbricht had written back in Moscow giving the Party line and stressing the common fight against fascism, but, initially, that was the only political directive I had.

Now and then I ran across Ulbricht. In a program I ran called "Tribune of Democracy," he spoke for the Socialist Unity Party (SED) (actually, the Communist Party, created from the merger of the Communists and Social Democrats in the Soviet zone in 1946). His piping high voice and unmistakably provincial Saxon accent made anything but a pleasant impression on the listeners. With the dangerous honesty of youth, I suggested that he should let an announcer read his texts while he took some voice training. His face colored with annoyance. It is a wonder my career ever prospered in East Berlin after that clumsy start.

We tried to make the station accessible and lively by answering listeners' questions about supposedly taboo subjects such as the fate of hundreds of thousands of German prisoners of war held in the Soviet Union, the way minor Nazi functionaries were being dealt with, and the new, foreshortened border of Germany along the Oder and Neisse rivers; surprisingly, these were not taboo for the Soviet control officers at the station. Our biggest struggle was against the orders of the Soviet control officers to broadcast hours and hours of boring speeches. One was a seemingly interminable speech at the United Nations by Soviet foreign minister Andrei Vishinsky, which heralded a roughening in relations between Moscow and the Western Allies. This kind of thing drove many of our listeners into the arms of the newly founded RIAS, the Radio in the American Sector.

There were other problems, too. We were not able to report freely about the relationship between the German population and the Soviet occupation forces, nor about the rape and pillage that had accompanied the Red Army's march to Berlin. The brutal campaign against the defeated population, particularly in East Prussia, was an open secret. Like all Germans, we were horrified at the news, and we felt that the only way to bring Germans and Russians together was to speak openly about war crimes of any kind. The German Communist leadership was furious, since the behavior of the guilty troops in the Red Army made it even more difficult to win people over to our side. We had our opinions but could not express them openly, and the more civilized Soviet officers also quietly admitted that such atrocities never should have been allowed to happen. But the very word "Russian," which had been assiduously used by the Nazis to awaken primeval antagonisms, was once again associated by many civilians with fear.

As German Communists, we did not protest against these atrocities as much as we should have, and for two main reasons. The first was that it ill-behooved a German to criticize the Russians for their brutality, after all the havoc wrought by the Wehrmacht during its invasion of the Soviet Union. In those of us who had left Hitler's Germany, there was probably a grain of hatred for those of our own people who had allowed themselves to become the instruments of the Third Reich. The second reason was simply that we suppressed our doubts about the Russians' behavior for ideological reasons.

People have asked me how it could be that I, a reasonably sophisticated young man from a cultured family, could block out of my mind so many of these uncomfortable events. I was curious enough to listen to these accounts, but the words skimmed past me, filtered by the ideological net in my mind. In the postwar chaos of revenge and suspicion, there was no shortage of injustice, but we focused on ensuring that Nazism would never infect Germans again. Indeed, the great majority of the listeners who wrote us were far more concerned with stamping out the vestiges of Nazism than with the fate of some who might be injured in the process.

When Soviet occupation officials carried out mass arrests of ex-Nazis and assorted opponents of Stalin, thousands of Social Democratic opponents of Nazism were swept up, and some ended up in labor camps that, ironically, had only recently been Nazi concentration camps. We knew very little about that, and what we did know we viewed as cruel Western propaganda. For example, the West Berlin Social Democratic paper, *Telegraf,* published a story that in the cellar of the residential house where I lived people were being interrogated and tortured by a police section known as K-5. I publicly denied this completely and accused the paper of inventing not only torture but the very existence of a section K-5. Only later, when I was appointed to the Ministry of State Security, did I discover that K-5 did indeed exist and it had been torturing suspects in that very basement.

Throughout my career I overlooked, minimized, or rationalized similar episodes, and I can only remind the reader again how my character was formed in the struggle against fascism; we came to feel that against such tyrannical opponents, almost anything goes. In due course, under the influence of Nikita Khrushchev's secret 1953 speech before the Twentieth Party Congress, in which he revealed Stalin's crimes to his Communist supporters and then to the world, I slowly began to feel somewhat differently. But at the time and for much of my life I had no doubt that we Communists stood on the side of social renewal and justice. This had helped excuse the Moscow show trials during the purges, and now the exigencies of the nascent Cold War would help us overlook such acts as attacks on German Social Democrats who had survived the Nazis. In individual cases I did what I could, but I found few such cases. Perhaps I already felt exempt from some moral norms, a sense bolstered by a confidence that the Communist machine could never turn against me, one of its children. I never thought of myself as a victim. Nor did my father, and perhaps that is one reason we survived. He even wrote to Stalin in 1945, complaining that he had been barred from returning to Germany as a Jew, and when the notorious "doctors plot" of Stalin's last years provided an excuse for a revival of anti-Semitism in the Soviet Union, neither he nor I was touched. Just as in the time of total insecurity and threat before the war, in the chaos after the war I felt it was not my task to undermine those on my side who were fighting evil.

I did of course know of many of the terrible crimes of the Stalin era even while they were under way; anyone who says he knew nothing is a liar. These are not things I look back on with pride. I even spoke about them to our German Communist leaders. But then and now, I never put the crimes of the Communist regime in the same class as those of the Nazis, and if there was anything that persuaded me it was impossible ever to equate the two, it was the awful facts that emerged at the Nuremberg war crimes trials of the Nazi leaders.

●

In September 1945 I was dispatched by the radio station to report on the Nuremberg war crimes tribunal. Until then I had learned of events in Nazi Germany through Soviet propaganda, which concentrated on the fate of German Communists. But we also knew something of what had happened from the tales of our own family that reached us in Moscow and from my father's writings about the beginnings of what came to be known as the Holocaust. We were very slow, however, to see that the unique dimension of the slaughter of the Jews was at the heart of National Socialism. But here, as if on a dissection table, the anatomy of National Socialism was laid bare and the full extent of the Holocaust first became apparent to me.

As the son of a Jewish Communist family, I shuddered to find myself sitting opposite the surviving principal figures of the Nazi era. Wandering in the ruins of Nuremberg, formerly known as "Germany's jewel box" but now forever associated with the racial laws to which millions of Jews fell victim, I was suddenly, coldly, aware of how completely we Communists and the other opponents of Hitler had failed to prevent this slaughter, and vowed that nothing like it should ever be allowed to happen again on German soil.

For that reason I found the defeated Germans' resentment of the Soviet occupiers exasperating. To my parents I wrote rather naïvely that the Red Army's "generosity is taken for granted and people complain constantly. They simply do not seem to have grasped the extent of the catastrophe Hitler has visited on Germany. They do not understand that the chance of a new beginning is being offered them."

●

Germany formally split into two political entities after the 1948 currency reform in the three Western occupation zones led to their consolidation as the new German *Bundesrepublik*, or Federal Republic. In response, the German Democratic Republic was officially founded in October 1949, with torchlight processions, mass marches, and patriotic songs. To some more sensitive Socialists, it all looked uncomfortably like the old displays of Nazi power. But I saw it as a great historical moment in German-Russian relations. Shortly afterward I was summoned by the Central Committee and told that I had been chosen to help cement this link. On November 1, I was to move back to Moscow as counselor to the new East German embassy there. To take the job I had to give up my Soviet citizenship and once again become officially German. We arrived in Moscow on November 3, 1949.

The elegance and ease of diplomatic existence was a relief after life among the ruins in Berlin, and we greatly enjoyed our family life in Moscow. And it was family life: While I had been reporting the Nuremberg trials in 1946, my first child, a blond, gray-eyed son we named Michael, was born, followed by his sister, Tatjana, in 1949. Emmi, who disliked the artifice of the embassy world, also had the chance to throw herself into her Russian studies and begin a doctoral thesis on Dostoyevsky.

It was as first counselor in the embassy of the German Democratic Republic that I finally met Stalin, a significant experience to me even after so many years. Talking to friends of my generation, I find that Stalin still figures occasionally in all our dreams, perhaps as a flashback to the mass parades we witnessed on Red Square, during which the intensity of the crowd's adulation overwhelmed all other sensations, or to the portraits and statues of Stalin—long disappeared from Moscow—that made us think that we were living in the presence of a demigod.

In fact, however much I may direct my adult mind toward an objective appraisal of his evils, this semimystical aspect of my experience of

Stalin refuses to go away. It may even be good that it has not receded entirely, for it always reminds me of how important and powerful a dictator's charisma remains, persisting even beyond the revelations of his iniquity.

The most vivid memory of my short career at the embassy is of a reception given for the Chinese leader Mao Tse-tung in the great ballroom of the Hotel Metropol, in February 1950. I was standing with my back to the entrance doors when a sudden hush fell on the room. Turning around, I saw Josef Vissarionovich Stalin standing a few feet away from me. He was wearing his famous Litevka tunic with its stand-up collar. He wore no insignia or medals. Surprisingly small and tubby, he had a shining bald pate. These features were in stark contrast to the images of *Vozhd*, or "Great Leader," cultivated in films and portraits. I did a double take, first in disappointment but then with a sort of pride. "At least he looks like a normal man," I thought. "All these stories about a personality cult must have been invented without his knowledge."

As chargé d'affaires, I stood in for the ambassador on this occasion, sitting up front where the heads of both delegations exchanged their toasts. While Zhou En-lai, China's foreign minister, and his Soviet counterpart, Andrei Vishinsky, were speaking, Stalin lit one powerful Herzegovina Flor cigarette after another (these were the special long Russian paper-tipped *papyrosi* he favored). Later he pronounced several toasts of his own. In one he praised the modesty and solidarity of the Chinese leaders. Then, portentously, he lifted his glass to the peoples of Yugoslavia, who he said would one day resume their place in the socialist family of nations. Only two years earlier Yugoslavia had been cast into outer darkness on Stalin's orders, after the charismatic Yugoslav leader Josip Broz Tito had refused to bow to the Kremlin leader's personality cult and demanded more autonomy in the running of the multiethnic Balkan state than Moscow would allow. We in the faithful countries looked on Yugoslavia with a mixture of fear and wonder that Tito had the audacity to challenge Stalin's wishes.

We doted religiously on the Soviet leader's every word. For me, as for most of the guests at the reception, Stalin and Mao were far more than human beings. They were monuments of history. I still had no inkling of the coming Sino-Soviet split, but I do remember thinking that it was remarkable that Mao did not say a single word all night. I wondered whether this was a sign of the famed Chinese inscrutability.

Not every experience in my two-year diplomatic career was so impressive. For a reception marking the second anniversary of East Germany's founding the controversy was not about a split in alliance or a rogue Communist state, but about what to wear. As always, the younger diplomats argued with the chief of mission, who wanted us to wear morning coats with tails to mark the solemnity of the occasion. Not possessing tails, we favored business suits. In the end, we reached a compromise, which was dinner jackets with black ties. At the time, however, only socialist countries recognized the GDR, and for most of them, black ties were rejected as bourgeois attire. For all our later notoriety as an obedient Communist satrapy, the German Democratic Republic still clearly carried the traits of its ordered Prussian past during its early years. To our immense embarrassment, the only attendees in such formal dress besides us were the waiters. When Nikolai Krutitsky, the Orthodox metropolitan archbishop of all the Russians, got up to take his leave and I accompanied him politely to the cloakroom, he fumbled about for some time under his heavy robes before finally producing three rubles and handing them to me solemnly as a tip.

●

In August 1951 I received an urgent message to return to East Berlin for consultations with Anton Ackermann—whose real name was Eugen Hanisch—the East German foreign secretary and a leading strategist in the politburo. He greeted me at the Foreign Ministry in the morning, inquired after my health, and told me to appear, after lunch the same day, in such-and-such a room in the grandiose Central Committee building. I was mystified—until I turned up for the afternoon appointment to find the same Comrade Ackermann behind a different desk, this time in his capacity as a member of the politburo. This absurdity was a result of Ackermann's insistence on secrecy and the separation of powers between the Party and the state apparatus, which in practice were congruent.

Ackermann had been entrusted with building up a political intelligence service, and I was to be assigned to it, sharing responsibility for the "enlightenment of the young state." Put more bluntly, I was to become a spy. It was again an order, and as usual at that time, I did not question it or even reflect on the impact it would have on my life. The Party had sent me to the Comintern school. The Party had assigned me to the Moscow and Berlin radio stations. The Party had dispatched me to Moscow as a diplomat. If the Party thought that I was useful for intelligence work, so be it. I was proud that the leadership trusted me enough to involve me in confidential work. This sense of unquestioning discipline is the hardest thing for Western observers of our system to understand, but without comprehending the sway the Party held over us and the way it defined choices for Communists of my generation, it is impossible to understand, let alone judge, our lives.

On August 16, 1951, I started work at the brand-new Institute for Economic Scientific Research, a cover name for the building that concealed East Germany's embryonic intelligence network. My new career began with a ride with Richard Stahlmann in a huge eight-cylinder Tatra limousine, very grand for the time. Stahlmann, who had been entrusted with the task of starting up our operations, was a professional revolutionary and an imposing figure whom I admired. His real name was Artur Illner, but he had worked for so long in the covert Communist world that everyone, even his wife, used his code name as if it were his real name. A member of the German Communist Party since 1918, he had been made a member of its "military council" in 1923. Like everyone else from the old guard, he rarely talked about a past that contained too many secrets. He did, however, regale me with anecdotes about his missions to the Soviet Union, Britain, China, Spain, France, Sweden, and the United States. He had near legendary status as "Richard the Partisan" in the Spanish Civil War and was a close confidant of Georgy Dimitrov, the Bulgarian Communist accused by the Nazis of plotting the Reichstag fire. Stahlmann had been with Dimitrov when the Gestapo came for him, but the two of them had kept their nerve, even after the rough arrest and questioning. Dimitrov later referred to Stahlmann as "the best horse in the stable," a background that gave him a lot of pull with the new East German leadership. He was on a first-name basis with them all, and whenever obstacles arose in setting up the intelligence service, he would visit Prime Minister Otto Grotewohl at home and the problems would promptly disappear.

These problems usually concerned money and resources. We were very starved for cash in the early years, and hard currency took months to work its way through the official channels. Occasionally Stahlmann would visit the finance minister and come back with his battered briefcase full of crisp notes. When Czechoslovakia thoughtfully delivered twenty-four Tatra cars for the GDR government, Stahlmann somehow managed to siphon off half of the shipment for the use of our still tiny service, so that even when we were still operating out of cardboard boxes, we could travel in style. Stahlmann understood that such accoutrements helped boost the service's status in the eyes of the government, and that departments that try to operate on the cheap normally attract the attention of budget cutters.

Our first meeting was in Bohnsdorf, a suburb southeast of Berlin. No one could quite remember the day of the meeting and there was no written record, so we later declared September 1, 1951, as the date of the founding of the intelligence service. Soon after, we moved to an office in a former school in the Pankow district of East Berlin, near the restricted area where the Party and government leaders lived—a sign that we were accepted as indispensable.

In the beginning there were only eight of us and four Soviet advisers, including a senior NKVD man who was introduced as "Comrade Grauer." Andrei Grauer had served as a Soviet intelligence officer in the USSR's Stockholm embassy. He was a highly experienced operative, and we sat at his feet, wide-eyed at his accounts of moles unearthed, services penetrated, and heroic agents. From him we learned how to form the basic structure of an intelligence service, which divides its duties and targets the enemy at its vulnerable points. Alas, his own career ended badly some years later. He became compulsively distrustful, a combination of professional deformation with the atmosphere of Stalin's Soviet Union, I suppose. He and Ackermann, the formal head of the intelligence service, became bitter enemies, and Grauer became obsessed with the notion that Ackermann was suspect. After a while Grauer had to be recalled to Moscow. I later heard from embarrassed Soviet intelligence friends that he was in fact a schizophrenic suffering from acute paranoia. The watchfulness that had once made him a top intelligence officer had taken him over.

Within government and party circles the cover name for our service was the Main Directorate for Economic and Scientific Research (Hauptverwaltung für Wirtschafts-Wissenschaftliche Forschung). This was not in the slightest concealing, since the very words "main directorate" reminded anyone in the know about such matters as the Pervoye Glavnoye Upravleniye, or "First Main Directorate," of the KGB, which was responsible for its espionage operations. In 1956, the foreign intelligence service was renamed Die Hauptverwaltung Aufklärung—HVA for short—which translates as "Main Intelligence Directorate."

Our Soviet advisers played a strong, even domineering, role. At first our section chiefs drew up all their work plans under the watchful eyes of these advisers, who followed extremely bureaucratic Soviet methods, which drove us crazy. Besides copying regulations and other papers by hand, we had to spend hours binding them neatly into file folders, a procedure introduced by the czar's secret police before the Revolution. No one knew the rationale for this procedure, but no one questioned it either.

The structure of our apparat was an exact mirror of the Soviet model. The diction of our guidelines betrayed their translation from the Russian and laid down the main goals of our future work. These were the gathering of political intelligence about West Germany and West Berlin; scientific and technical intelligence in the areas of nuclear weapons and delivery systems, atomic energy, chemistry, electrical engineering and electronics, aviation, and conventional weapons; and, last but certainly not least, intelligence about the Western Allies and their intentions regarding Germany and Berlin.

A small, independent department of the HVA called "counterintelligence" (*Abwehr*) was directed at monitoring and penetrating the Western secret services, but it immediately came into conflict with the Ministry of State Security, which had its own more elaborate surveillance department. Even when we were taken into the ministry, in 1953, this conflict persisted and counterintelligence remained under the direct control of the ministry. The bureaucratic wars cut us off from crucial information about operations inside our own ministry, especially in later years when counterintelligence operatives began operating with foreign terrorists.

People often ask why Moscow created our service as a German competitor to itself. But Stalin correctly assumed that Germany in the postwar period would be a difficult area for Russian services to penetrate, and that a solid domestic service in what began as the Soviet sector of Germany would give us pride in our work, thus advancing Soviet interests. Initially our Soviet advisers received all the information we had, right down to the cover names of our sources and our individual cases, although we gradually began protecting our sources and providing our Soviet liaison officers with selected information.

My first assignment was as deputy chief of analysis under Robert Korb, a former colleague of mine at Radio Moscow. Korb had profound political knowledge and an enormous command of facts and breadth of learning. I learned a great deal from him about things that had nothing to do with our work, such as Islam, the complicated background of Israel, and the religious conflicts of the Indian subcontinent. He was a brilliant analyst who taught me to regard field reports with skepticism, and we soon came to the conclusion that a careful reading of the press could often produce results far superior to secret reports of agents, and that our own analysts should draw independent conclusions from diverse sources in order to evaluate raw intelligence material. This insight has remained with me ever since.

An original in behavior as well as thought, Korb could hold the attention of an audience with a wit and sarcasm that often did not include much respect for the dignitaries he had to brief. Since I shared his irreverence, we found we had much in common. Although loyal servants of the state, we tried to keep our distance from the missionary zeal of some of our political leaders.

Our outfit grew rapidly and we moved again from Berlin-Pankow to a bigger building on the Rolandufer in the center of East Berlin. I was soon promoted as deputy in the newly founded foreign intelligence service to Gustav Szinda, a man with many decades of experience in covert operations in Spain and elsewhere for Soviet intelligence.

Unfortunately, neither Szinda nor I had much idea of where to start against a West German service that had emerged, practically unscathed, from the collapse of the Nazi Reich. Leading intelligence figures who had served Hitler were now working for their new masters in a small, mystery-shrouded Bavarian village called Pullach. We had to look it up on the map when its name first started appearing in the press. This was an unknown world to us and seemed quite beyond our reach, although with time, we would become very familiar indeed with its workings.

I initially came across the name of General Reinhard Gehlen, the first leader of West German intelligence, in a headline in the London *Daily Express* that read HITLER'S GENERAL SPIES AGAIN — FOR DOLLARS. The byline was that of Sefton Delmer, a journalist known for his connections with British intelligence; during the war he had been in charge of the British counterintelligence radio station Soldatensender Calais. Delmer's report caused a furor. It revealed not only that the Nazi intelligence old boy network remained intact, but that the new espionage services in the Federal Republic contained numerous former SS men and military intelligence experts who had operated under Hitler in France and elsewhere. Gehlen himself had been head of the Nazis' military espionage unit against the Red Army. Through the Gehlen Service, as it came to be known, the Americans, who were giving the orders in West Germany's intelligence sphere pretty much as the Russians were in the Eastern bloc, had access to the old Nazi connections.

There were also rumors about the role of General George S. Patton, Jr., who was said to be extending his protection to certain high-ranking German officers. Worriedly, I realized that the postwar goal of a Europe at unified peace was no longer tenable. The muzzles had been loaded on both sides. The peace won at such sacrifice now appeared very fragile. Europe was divided, and the fault line ran right through Germany.

West Germany's chancellor, Konrad Adenauer, threw in his lot with the American "policy of strength" and the strategy of rolling back communism professed by John Foster Dulles, whose brother, Allen, was the chief of the U.S. intelligence service, the Central Intelligence Agency. Soviet power had pushed west at the end of the war; now Washington was prepared to summon up all the political, intelligence, economic, and, if necessary, even military strength of the United States and its allies to counterattack. Gehlen recognized the opportunity the new clash provided for him to exert a direct influence on policy. He met with Adenauer before the West Germans took over his intelligence service from the CIA and was given extraordinary powers and support. That included the control of files against domestic political enemies, including Social Democrats who were in parliamentary opposition to the Christian Democratic government. In the West German armed forces and its state bureaucracy, loyal servants of the

Third Reich once again held top positions, and former Nazi officers ran Gehlen's organization.

The name of Hans Globke, one of Adenauer's closest advisers and ultimately a secretary of state in the chancellor's office, became a synonym for this kind of infiltration. A former high-ranking official in Hitler's Interior Ministry, Globke had been the author of an authoritative commentary on the Nuremberg racial laws that legitimized violent discrimination and eventually led to the Nazis' Final Solution. Globke would serve as Adenauer's secretary of state for ten years.

In this frantic atmosphere, Berlin in the 1950s succeeded Vienna as the heart of espionage operations in Europe. As many as eighty secret service agencies with their various branches and front organizations were operating in the city. In the Americans' and Russians' covert offices, masquerading as everything from plumbing companies and jam exporters to academic and research bureaus, sat whole groups of case officers recruiting and running their respective agents who could easily travel between the sectors of Berlin and the two halves of Germany in the days before the Wall dividing the city and the nation was erected in 1961.

It was also before the West German economic miracle began and therefore was a time of shortages and economic desperation. Offers of food or advancement lured people into spying. But while the West Germans could resort more easily to financial offers, we were still operating on a shoestring and had to pursue a more ideological approach. Many of our moles in West Germany, particularly in politics and industry, were not Communists but worked with us because they wanted to overcome the division of Germany and believed the policies of the Western Allies were only reinforcing it. We lost some of these moles later when the Wall went up and presented them with the symbol of a divided Germany literally set in concrete.

The minutiae of setting up the brand-new espionage service took up most of my time. My attention was focused on the West, and I worked hard to familiarize myself with the political shifts in the United States and Western Europe and to keep up with the development of their postwar intelligence services.

We had to acquire new sources in the political, military, economic, and scientific and technical centers on the other side. This was easier said than done, since the security requirements in our own apparatus imposed by the Soviets were extremely strict. Thousands of recommended candidates had to be screened in order to come up with a handful who were acceptable. Those with Western relatives were ruled out, as were most who had spent the war years as refugees or prisoners of war in the West. Contrary to rumors that still persist, we did not knowingly employ former Nazis inside our apparat and regarded ourselves as morally superior in this regard to the West Germans.

We had access to some of the Nazi files on party membership in the Third Reich, which we would use to persuade those in the West who had suppressed their past collaboration with the Nazis to cooperate with us. Many others volunteered to work with us, claiming that they regarded it as a kind of moral reparation for the harm they had done in the past. That was looking at it kindly. The real reason was more likely that they wanted to insure themselves and their new careers in the West against unwelcome revelations from our side at a later date. In German, we called this *Rückversicherung*, literally a kind of "backward insurance" for the past. Through the West German Communist Party we inherited the services of a politician in the Free Democratic Party named Lothar Weihrauch (who later served in West Germany's Ministry for Common German Affairs), who supplied a great deal of political information until we discovered that he had committed war crimes when he held a high position during the German occupation of Poland. We then cut him off. We also recruited another former Nazi, an ex–storm trooper code-named Moritz, who was helpful during our political battle against the European Defense Community (which was finally blocked by the nationalism of the French rather than anything our intelligence service did to discredit the project).

The past was a powerful weapon among the spy services, and both sides were unashamed to use blackmail. Just as we sought to bring down politicians or senior figures hostile to us by revealing their Nazi complicity, the West Berlin Committee of Free Jurists, an anti-Communist organization made up of lawyers who had fled the East, produced their own booklet of Eastern functionaries who had managed to conceal Nazi Party membership. But since almost all of our senior intelligence officers and the political elite had been in exile or in the underground during the Third Reich, we in the East won that particular propaganda battle hands down.

Some Nazis tried to make the switch to our side by hiding their past. Soon after I started work, a junior member of the staff came to me in a state of great embarrassment to say that he had noticed a man working in the interrogation department who bore the telltale SS tattoo on his arm. Interrogation was the roughest department within the ministry, and I would not have liked to be exposed to some of the thugs who worked there. I could well imagine how someone who had a taste for such work from the previous regime might have felt at home there. We removed him quietly from the post.

The blackmail that went on was a dirty and compromising game and was played by both sides. Some former Nazis in the West offered their services to us out of a kind of contrition, others for money, or to prevent their unmasking as former collaborators with the Nazi regime. The Soviets had more blackmail opportunities because they held the captured Nazi files, and they took in such people as former SS-man Heinz Felfe, who had held the rank of *Obersturmführer* in the Nazi intelligence organization, the Reich Security Office (Reichssicherheitshauptamt), and had found postwar employment with the Gehlen Service. Felfe became a Soviet double agent, betraying all the main achievements of the West German service to Moscow and doing damage on a scale accomplished only by such double agents as Kim Philby, George Blake, and Aldrich Ames.

•

One of our first opportunities to penetrate the Allied services came from Communist Party intelligence in Germany. In the nineteenth century the German Social Democratic movement had developed clandestine services to deal with the Kaiser's repression. The Communist Party of Germany (Kommunistische Partei Deutschlands, or KPD), steeled by even harsher treatment by the authorities (its early history was dominated by the early murders of the Spartacists Rosa Luxemburg and Karl Liebknecht), copied the Social Democrats by developing its own intelligence network. This structure soon built up close connections to the leadership of the Comintern in Moscow and the secret services there.

The brains behind the Party intelligence network in the twentieth century were Ernst Schneller, murdered in 1944 on Hitler's orders, and Hans Kippenberger, for whose death in 1937 Stalin was later responsible. This network, devoted to acquiring scientific-technical and military information to be passed to the Soviet Union was, during the Hitler years, the source for the famous intelligence network Rote Kapelle—in English, the "Red Orchestra."

The Red Orchestra was one of the biggest resistance organizations. A few of its members were Communists, and a small portion were agents of the Soviet intelligence services (NKVD and GRU, military intelligence). The first challenge I faced was trying to check the worth of establishing a new Communist network. I soon came to believe that the new network built along the lines of the old could not be trusted. The British, in particular, had done sterling work in turning a number of the Communists they had held as prisoners of war. They also were highly successful in turning some of the Communist wartime emigrants as well as several new, young agents of the newly established network.

A good example of just how compromised the network was is the case of Merkur, whose real name was Hans Joachim Schlomm. I came across him while going through mountains of paper, most of it uncollated, looking for leads into the Western secret services. I studied the files, which indicated he had contacts with the West German counterintelligence service, known as the Federal Office for the Protection of the Constitution (Bundesamt für Verfassungsschutz, BfV), based in Cologne. He also had numerous connections to the political world nearby in Bonn. His recent reports to the Party were impressive in their detail, variety, and depth, including inside information on political parties in the West German parliament, eyes-only material from the foreign and other ministries, and organizational data about the counterintelligence service. On the surface, he seemed to be a dream source, so I sent a man to find him in Schleswig-Holstein, where his file said he would be. Merkur claimed he had been waiting patiently for our call and without hesitation accepted an invitation to Berlin. He was to be my first agent.

He appeared punctually at a safe house, a villa on the outskirts of Berlin. A tall, slim man of thirty, he seemed to fit his profession, that of an electrical engineer. He explained that he had been associated with the Communist Party as a university student in Hamburg, worked for

Party intelligence, and on its orders joined a right-wing youth organization, ultimately working his way to Bonn as private secretary to Dr. Fritz Dorls, chairman of the Socialist Reich Party. I then questioned him at length, but something seemed strange; his answers about people he claimed to know did not correspond with the files. We sent him back to West Berlin and invited him to come the next day. I went over his files again.

When he returned, I played the intellectual, and Szinda, the tough guy. "Enough, you shit," Szinda would say to signal he was losing patience with our potential operative. As the contradictions of his tale mounted, Merkur finally acknowledged that as early as 1948 he had been infiltrated by the British into Communist intelligence, that he was still working for them, and that the material he had been providing us had been planted.

The investigation then fell to Erich Mielke, number two at the Ministry of State Security (founded on February 8, 1950) and eventually its chief, who was already suspicious of our service, which he viewed as competition. This tough old Stalinist had not gotten along with Szinda since their days as comrades in the Spanish Civil War, and he had little but distaste for me. Mielke arrested Merkur as a double agent and put him on trial, which resulted in a prison sentence of nine years.

The Merkur case set off alarms not only in the West but in our service, where we concluded from his interrogation and testimony that he knew far more about Communist Party intelligence and its relations to other organizations than an undercover agent was supposed to know. At that point we realized we would have to check out everyone in the underground Communist intelligence groups, which had a total of forty to fifty agents. As if putting together a puzzle, I started questioning liaison officers and couriers who had been sent into West Germany from the GDR, so that our suspicions would not be telegraphed to the agents themselves. What they told me about violations of the rules of covert operations made me suspect danger of penetration.

So I sat down and started drawing a diagram of the connections and cross-connections among the existing intelligence networks, which began to look like a huge web. Like the trained aircraft engineer I was, I drafted what I called my "spider's web" on a sheet of graph paper. On the diagram I connected all of the couriers, safe houses, and the like. I colored suspected double agents red, sources blue, and residents green. The lines and boxes also identified personal and professional relationships. Special symbols marked suspicious circumstances or suspected contacts to opposing services. To the uninitiated, the diagram would have meant nothing, but to my eyes, it began to take on a clear outline indicating possibilities for expanding and deepening our work. It was also essential to obtain a clear picture of how deeply this service had been penetrated from outside.

I finally concluded that if the Western secret services wanted to, they could easily liquidate the whole network. In actuality, they were probably not that clever or efficient, but the risk remained, especially to the Communist Party, if the old espionage network were to be turned or unmasked. So I decided instead it would be better for us to liquidate the network and abandon all our Communist contacts in West Germany.

With my spider's web rolled under my arm, I made an appointment to see Walter Ulbricht, to whom at that time all intelligence services were directly responsible. I stressed the absolute confidentiality of what I was about to tell him. Instead of calling me to his office, he invited me to his home in the Pankow enclave, which was known not very fondly to East Berliners as the "little town." The leader's rooms betrayed the taste of a trained carpenter for solid, middle-class furnishings, embellished with carved ornaments.

I unrolled my chart on Ulbricht's dinner table and laid out my findings in detail. Together with Ackermann, whom I had spoken to before the meeting, I had decided to break off all contacts with Communist Party intelligence in West Germany and drop all agents with any kind of connection to it. The fact that the West German authorities were already preparing to outlaw the Party—it was finally declared unconstitutional in 1956—played an important role in our thinking. Ulbricht agreed with my proposal, and from then on West Germany's Communist Party of Germany was forbidden territory for our service, as was its eventual successor, the German Communist Party, which was reestablished during more liberal times in 1968.

In 1952 we recalled our agents, and even the most loyal Communists were placed in isolation under a sort of "villa arrest" and subjected to tough questioning. People often ask what method we used in such cases. It was based on psychological pressure against men and women accustomed to drawing their sense of identity and self-esteem from membership in a group of like-minded people. When that trust is suddenly withdrawn, the psychological pressure on them becomes acute. There was no need to threaten them or issue formal warrants of arrest. Addressing them as suspects and monitoring their replies was enough to convince us that they were innocent and that we had found no more double agents. Of course, there was no question of redeployment in the West. They were warned not to talk about what had happened. All of them kept their word about this, as good comrades do.

Some had done courageous work fighting the Nazis. One had even been in a camp in France with my father; we kept him isolated in an apartment for weeks before clearing him. To some we gave pensions and to others lowly positions in the provinces, where they labored under suspicion.

In 1956, after Khrushchev's secret speech to the Twentieth Party Congress, we rehabilitated most of these withdrawn comrades with medals and decorations. Bruno Haid, who had fought with the French Resistance during the war and had been withdrawn and sent to a factory in Karl-Marx-Stadt as a minor functionary, eventually rose to be the GDR's deputy chief prosecutor. He accused me of using brutal methods reminiscent of Stalin's secret police chief Lavrenti Beria in shutting down the Party network—I did not—but he did eventually, if grudgingly, see my point when he learned about double agents like Merkur.

A few of our "preserved" sources were not withdrawn and were eventually reactivated, though kept strictly isolated from newer contacts. Why did we do this? Quite simply, we discovered that the penetration had not gone as far as we feared. The West didn't know any more security miracles than we did.

4

The GDR Comes of Age, and So Do I

In December 1952 I received a message from Walter Ulbricht, the East German leader, summoning me to the Central Committee building at the busy intersection of Lothringer Strasse (later Wilhelm-Pieck-Strasse) and Prenzlauer Allee in the center of East Berlin, not far from Alexanderplatz. At the entrance I was given a pass, which the guard carefully inspected along with my identity card, although security was not as tight and the building itself not as imposing as it became when the headquarters moved to Werderscher Markt. Even then, however, one could discern a hint of the growth of an elite that eventually would isolate itself from the people.

I presented myself in Ulbricht's outer office. He was in a meeting, but after a short time he appeared, neatly dressed and with his famous pointed beard. He invited me into the adjoining office of his wife, Lotte, his closest colleague. I knew her well from our work together at the German People's Radio in Moscow. She greeted me warmly. Ulbricht offered me a chair and sent his wife out. He and I had met several times, and he dispensed with pleasantries, coming quickly to the point. That was his way: curt, businesslike, concentrating on the essentials, and never looking his interlocutor directly in the eye.

Drily, Ulbricht informed me that Anton Ackermann, who had led the foreign intelligence service since its founding, had asked to be relieved of his responsibilities for reasons of health. I knew that Ackermann's physical health was not at issue, but that Ulbricht distrusted Ackermann's talk of a peculiarly "German road to socialism," as distinct from the Soviet model. Ulbricht was able to move against Ackermann because he had been caught having an adulterous affair, forbidden in the puritan milieu of East Germany in the 1950s.

"We are of the opinion that you should take over the service," said Ulbricht. That was a royal "we"—or, more precisely, "we" meant the Party leadership. He did not ask me whether I thought I was up to the job, nor did he invite further discussion.

I was caught quite unprepared. Not yet thirty years old, I did not have a prominent place in the Party hierarchy. I asked Ulbricht how the foreign intelligence service would report to the Party leadership, and he replied that I would be answerable directly to him.

Not a quarter of an hour later, I was out on the street again, my head swimming. When I returned to my office, Richard Stahlmann, acting head of the service since Ackermann's demise, was waiting for me. I was uneasy about his reaction; a man of his reputation and experience does not ordinarily relish yielding power to a young upstart. But he was beaming with relief as he unlocked the safe and gave me the few files inside; he had never been strong on paperwork, and that would be an important part of my job. He slid the keys across the table to me and said, "It's all yours. Good luck. I'll be there if you need me." I was more than a little proud as I hurried out to get a new suit for my first day behind the big desk.

The reasons for my selection after only sixteen months of intelligence work are unclear to me even now. But the German Democratic Republic had been founded only in October 1949, and its officials had to learn on the job. Ackermann apparently had recommended me as his successor, and I am sure that my upbringing and connections with Moscow weighed heavily. Sometimes I am asked why I accepted this appointment in a service that was part of a structure of repression. First of all, I did not see the intelligence service as part of a repressive structure. And refusal would have been impossible, given my understanding of duty, Party discipline, and the demands of the Cold War.

One very frequently voiced Western criticism of our behavior during the 1950s was that we could not have been blind to what was happening because we knew the signs from our experiences during the Moscow purges. This was wrong. Our experience of life in Moscow had precisely the opposite effect. There was always an excuse in our minds: Stalin had to be vengeful because he was fighting a barbaric enemy. We never came to terms with the scale of the lies perpetrated in the Soviet Union of the twenties and the thirties; consequently, we could not recognize the lies, half truths, and vendettas that accompanied our attempt to secure the Soviet Union's strategic gains in Eastern Europe.

We in turn had to compromise our grand ideals with murky practices because the United States and its European allies were trying to destroy our attempts to bring socialism to German soil. And on it went, the roll call of excuses, until we were awakened from the dream in 1989. I still refuse to accept the judgmental stance of those who say our system was built only on the Lie, but I have to admit that it was, in great part, built on excuses.

After I took over as head of the foreign intelligence service, Ulbricht kept direct control of it for only about half a year. By the spring of 1953 it had been brought under the wing of Wilhelm Zaisser, a member of the politburo and, simultaneously, head of the Ministry of State Security. He had a past that commanded respect in the East. Before the war he carried out secret missions in China and directed the Eleventh International Brigade in Spain. Zaisser and I worked well together, which is to say that he left me to my own devices. I was given only an hour with him each week and my time always ran out before I could tell him what was worrying me. A passionate student of Marxist theory, he was much keener on discussing the translation problems of the new German edition of Lenin's collected works, which he was editing, than in listening to my report. Those vast manuscripts were usually sitting on his desk instead of intelligence reports.

Shortly after Easter 1953, the first bombshell of my career fell. In an incident that later became known as the Vulkan affair (*Vulkan* is German for "volcano"), Gotthold Kraus, who served on the staff of our economic intelligence unit, became our first defector. I took it as a heavy personal blow, and it made me realize that our young service was still far from secure. Moreover, he went during the holiday weekend and his absence had not been noticed for several days. His head start gave West German counterintelligence ample time to extract from Kraus everything he knew about East German agents on their territory and arrest them before we even realized they were in danger, let alone could attempt to call them back. Franz Blücher, the vice chancellor of West Germany, announced at a press conference that thirty-five agents had been arrested as a result of Vulkan's information. This was an exaggeration; no officer would ever have been allowed to know the identity of so many agents operating in a hostile country. It turned out that West German counterintelligence, overexcited by their first big coup, caught in its net a number of innocent businessmen who did deals in the East but were certainly not spies.

But Gotthold Kraus's betrayal cost us dearly: at least half a dozen fully operational agents, including Andrew Thorndike, the gifted documentary filmmaker whose professional work we had used as a cover for his espionage activity. He came from a famous Hanseatic family, and through his connections we tried to penetrate the powerful political and economic circles of Hamburg. Though he was not in West Germany at the time but in the GDR, he was arrested by means of a simple trick: West German counterintelligence sent him a telegram notifying him that his aunt had fallen ill. He went to West Germany and was arrested. Fortunately there was no proof of his activities and he was released. He came to East Germany and lived a blameless life making films on our side of the border. Zaisser gently reproved me: "Mischa, you have to learn more and more about many things."

The following months were spent reorganizing our whole operations along more efficient lines. The search for suitable, reliable candidates was difficult and costly. Checking their political reliability, their personal ties, and their character took time. We sought young, politically motivated citizens, convinced socialists who believed in serving our country and cause. We were not concerned if candidates to be agents had relatives in the West, in contrast to our policy for potential officers at headquarters, who were barred from employment if they had any. In fact, Western relatives could be quite useful in helping an aspiring agent bypass refugee camps and enter the Federal Republic.

Each agent's training was personally supervised by the man who would be running his operation, and special training was added if there was a scientific or technical objective. Once accepted in West Germany, agents usually began their assignments with an inconspicuous period of manual labor to help overcome the bureaucratic barriers of getting established in the West. We therefore preferred candidates with crafts-man's skills or practical experience in a profession. Almost every one of the students and budding scientists who emigrated in the early years found employment in research facilities or companies of interest to us— the federal government's nuclear research facilities in Jülich, Karlsruhe, and Hamburg; the Batelle Institute in Frankfurt, which had been set up by the United States; Siemens, Germany's largest electronics company; and IBM Germany or the giant German chemical companies BASF, Hoechst, and Bayer. Because we assumed that Germany's traditional arms manufacturers would—after the storm over German militarization died down—eventually resume military production, we also placed peo-ple in companies such as Messerschmidt and Bölkow.

Some of our people were able to work their way into areas covered by strict secrecy regulations, others into highly paid management posi-tions. We also exploited official and private connections between sci-entists in the two Germanys, a relatively simple matter because the tenor of the times left them with a great feeling of uneasiness about the threat of atomic, biological, and chemical weapons. Those who were badly shaken by the results of their participation in wartime atomic weapons research were especially good targets for our agents.

•

Stalin's death in March 1953 had come as a great shock to the Com-munist body politic, unleashing a furious power battle in the Kremlin and insecurity within the leadership of the countries of Eastern Europe. My own response, like that of many believers, was one of great grief coupled with a sense of confusion. We had lived so long under the guidance of Stalin that life after him was difficult to imagine.

Ulbricht had bet on the triumph of the hardest of the hard-line forces around Stalin. In order to curry favor with the new regime, he doggedly pursued his policy of "accelerating socialism," meaning heavy taxes and tight credit, which stifled small-scale enterprises and drove the self-employed into bankruptcy. Large farms and agricultural companies suffered under the sudden drive to perfect the socialist economy. The activities of the church were further curtailed.

These policies ran up against fierce resistance. The farmers and small producers responded by working inefficiently or, where they could get away with it, not at all. In December 1952, the East German prime minister, Otto Grotewohl, warned of impending shortages of food and other essentials. But Ulbricht paid no heed. He saw resistance to his plans through the prism of pure Stalinist ideology, according to which the class struggle would intensify and accelerate as the radical change to socialism progressed.

In the spring of 1953 a 10 percent rise in production quotas for factories, plants, and building sites was decreed, accompanied by stiff increases in the price of basic foodstuffs. Emboldened by the injustice of having these burdens imposed from above, people began complaining openly in shops and factories. During the first four months of 1953, over 120,000 people fled the country. The same thing was to happen thirty-six years later, in 1989; on both occasions, the leaders were too sclerotic to react to the hemorrhage with anything more than phrasemaking and mock heroics. "We will be purer when the class enemy has gone," Ulbricht is said to have remarked as the factory workers, teachers, engineers, doctors, and nurses joined the exodus.

Fearing that the instability could lead to a full collapse of the East German state and frustrated by Ulbricht's pig-headedness, Moscow intervened. Lavrenti Beria, then fighting for power against others in the leadership installed after Stalin's death, oversaw the preparation of a paper entitled "On Measures for the Amelioration of the Situation in the German Democratic Republic." The very fact that the Kremlin would even concede that such a thing could exist in the Eastern bloc was a stunning admission in those days long before glasnost.

Like naughty schoolboys, the leading members of our politburo were called to Moscow and ordered to put Beria's ideas into effect as soon as possible. This would have meant promoting small enterprises, abandoning Ulbricht's command economy, and relaxing his drastic limitations on such ideological "enemies within" as the liberal intelligentsia and the church. As little as the leadership in East Berlin liked it, Beria's goal was to fatten up East Germany to sell it off to West Germany in return for its neutral or even demilitarized status.

I spent the runup to the 1953 uprising in East Berlin at the beach on the Baltic, reading Hemingway and playing with my children. It is not very edifying for an intelligence chief to admit this. This rare holiday came about at the instigation of Wilhelm Zaisser, my superior. He had snapped at me when I had pressed him once too often about the state of our financially strapped foreign espionage service.

"Mischa, there are more important things going on just now," he said, and then, by way of amends, "When did you last have a holiday? You drive on up to the Blue House and then we'll see."

It was a great honor to be invited to the Blue House in Prerow, the security minister's official resort on the Baltic coast. There, in a well-appointed government dacha, I read about the first admission of panic by our politburo on June 16. It was a communiqué in which both the party politburo and the government admitted to serious mistakes and announced the reversal of the measures raising production and raising food prices. Investment in heavy industry was to be cut, production of consumer goods increased, and private businesses that had been forced to close by Ulbricht's heavy-handed tactics were to be reopened. It was a complete U-turn by Ulbricht, but it was too late.

On the morning of June 17, Radio in the American Sector (RIAS) reported that construction workers had marched from the Stalinallee to the House of Ministries (the same building that had housed Hermann Goering's aviation ministry during the Third Reich). The workers were demanding cancellation of the new industrial quotas and improvement of their wages and conditions. The building had been cordoned off by riot police and the mood was volatile. The strikers were calling for Ulbricht and Grotewohl to come out. Fritz Selbmann, the industry minister, emerged to try calming the crowd, but to no avail.

Versions differ as to the extent to which the Western intelligence services, more precisely West Germany's front organizations backed by the Americans, were involved in promoting the spread of the uprising. There was substantial infiltration in industrial areas, and to all those who wanted to effect the downfall of the East and bring about the unification of Germany it was clear in the course of those days in June that this was their big chance. But it was the Party's internal mismanagement of the economy and Ulbricht's repressive leadership that had brought things to this pass. Ulbricht eventually managed to reappear, but he did not dare to venture before the demonstrators, who were by now shouting "Down with the *Spitzbart!*" in reference to his pointed goatee, proudly sculpted after Lenin's. Instead he chose the comparatively safe surroundings of a party activists' meeting to make a response; there, his raw, authoritarian style disappeared, and he seemed uncertain and unfocused.

By evening RIAS had taken on the role of coordinator of events, broadcasting calls for demonstrations with precise information about times and places. One factory after another joined the strike. Processions of demonstrators converged on Berlin's Potsdamer Platz, where the four Allied sectors converged. From the West, groups raucously demanding the overthrow of the Communist regime were also streaming to the Brandenburg Gate. At 1 P.M., the Soviet commander of the city declared martial law and tanks moved in.

I decided to return to Berlin. As we approached the city of Neustrelitz, about halfway along the route from the Baltic coast to Berlin, our car was stopped by Soviet troops at a roadblock. My special identity card proved useless. Despite our protests, we were locked up with other "suspicious persons" in the cellar of the command post. There I had a few hours to ruminate on who really ran things in our part of Germany! It was only thanks to my knowledge of Russian, including some of its coarsest slang, that I was finally allowed to talk to the commander, introduce myself properly, and thus continue the trip.

I eventually arrived at my house in the Pankow district of East Berlin, the part of the city where the leadership lived. The workers from Bergmann-Borsig, a big machine-tool, heavy-engineering, and household-appliances conglomerate, had marched directly past the house and my father narrowly escaped being beaten by a mob in the center of town. He was sure that many of the young demonstrators came from West Berlin and said that they reminded him of the brown-shirted thugs who filled the streets during Hitler's early days. Nowadays that sounds like typical Communist propaganda, but it is important to remember that these events took place just eight years after the collapse of National Socialism in Germany and it was not uncommon to feel that, to borrow a line from Bertolt Brecht, "the bitch that gave this birth is still in heat."

We were stunned by the violence and hatred that had welled up in our midst. For people like me who were insiders in the new society, it was a rude awakening as to just how unpopular our beloved system had become. The dead never really were counted, but the total was between one and two hundred, and it became clear to me that the notions of "fascist adventurism" and "counterrevolutionary putsch" conjured by our leadership were pure propaganda. But this did not shake my own commitment. I fondly imagined that we could learn from this revolt and put the lessons to good use in our future management of the state.

As head of foreign intelligence, my job was to search for evidence of any involvement by external forces in the uprising. I was aware, even then, that this was a bit of a game intended to provide excuses for the leadership when the Soviets slammed its incompetence. It was not difficult to gather newspaper and magazine articles, books, and other documents demonstrating American and West German plans to liquidate our republic; they were the mood music of international relations at that time. The American ideologue James Burnham, in a book entitled *Defeating Soviet Imperialism*, called for subversive methods inside the territory of the Eastern bloc, including the use of "underworld circles" to instigate, "combined actions for the removal of Communist power" spearheaded by our old CIA-backed foes in West Berlin, the Brigade Against Inhumanity (Kampfgruppe gegen Unmenschlichkeit—KGU) and the Investigative Committee of Free Lawyers (Untersuchungousschuss Freiheitlicher Juristen—UFJ).

We discovered from one of our agents in the U.S. military mission that the CIA chief, Allen Dulles, and his sister, Eleanor Lansing Dulles, a State Department official, had been in West Berlin the week before the uprising. (The agent, named Bielke, was the translator for the local representative of the AFL-CIO, a man named Baker, whose job it was to penetrate the GDR trade unions.) We also picked up a cable sent by Walter Sullivan, the *New York Times* correspondent in Berlin, to his office in Manhattan, which read: "There would never have been any unrest if it had not been for the RIAS broadcasts. From 5 A.M. Wednesday morning, the propaganda station of the U.S. in Berlin was sending detailed instructions to all parts of Germany."

It was our job to collect intelligence on the background of the uprising, but we had no control over what conclusions the leadership drew from it. Ulbricht put unexpectedly heavy emphasis on a piece of information we had barely noticed. On the evening of June 16, the West Berlin trade union organization had planned a steamboat excursion and invited their colleagues in what was left of the independent East German unions. Our source reported that invitations had not been sent by mail but delivered on the telephone and that the words "steamer trip" had been used in every call. Ulbricht immediately seized on them as the code words that had triggered the events of June 17, which was an obvious exaggeration.

The great irony of the uprising was that it actually consolidated Ulbricht's power. After an upheaval of that magnitude, there was no question that the Soviets would risk further instability by unseating him, and in any case Beria had just been eliminated in the first post-Stalin purge. Zaisser and Rudolf Herrnstadt, editor of the Party newspaper, *Neues Deutschland*, both favored a reform course, and Ulbricht thus had the perfect excuse to force out his rivals. All were replaced by his uncritical supporters, and Ulbricht himself moved with Stalinlike ruthlessness to destroy his opponents.

A climate of uncertainty and mistrust was created that would sour the rest of East Germany's existence, and I sensed this at the time. But my worldview and convictions remained unaffected, something that Western readers will find mystifying. Why, after the bloodshed on our streets and Ulbricht's purge of people we knew to be honest, did we not consider distancing ourselves from him or criticizing him? According to the ideology and the practice introduced in all Communist parties after Lenin's death, anyone who publicly attacks an incumbent secretary general renders service to the class enemy. For a Communist, this was the equivalent of blasphemy for a devout Roman Catholic.

The accused purged by Ulbricht received the charges against them in silence. Their failure to speak out on their own account can perhaps only be understood by those who have experienced Stalin's purges and understand that Party discipline was a binding force. These men had devoted their whole lives to the revolutionary movement and a confrontation with the Party would have meant a complete break. They kept silent for another reason as well: They knew things were hopeless; saying anything would only make things worse.

Among the victims of Ulbricht's consolidation of power were Rudolf Herrnstadt and Wilhelm Zaisser. Before the war, Herrnstadt had worked for the GRU (Glavnoye Razvedyvatelnoye Upravleniye), the Soviet military intelligence, and had built up an excellent network in Warsaw. Two agents he had recruited, his first wife, Ilse Stöbe, and Gerhard Kegel from the German embassy in Moscow, had provided advance information about a German attack in 1941. It must have been dreadful for him to learn how his former services now counted for nothing. Herrnstadt's case moved me most deeply. Even though he was an official unperson, in the 1980s I eventually managed to commission a documentary film for my young agents recording his espionage successes. At least he would have honor among spies, if not officially.

Much later, I read the notes that Herrnstadt wrote as he worked in the State Central Archives in Merseburg. Even here, one senses again and again the agonizing question: "Am I smarter than the Party?" The question tormented him even though he was the victim of Party-sponsored injustice and could see the ossifying effects of official doctrine. Like Zaisser and Ackermann, he kept his doubts to himself and buried his reflections in notes for future generations, bound by the conspiracy of silence that affected so many disgraced Communists. They all stood by the basic rule of a Communist: Never harm the Party.

None of them could have lived with even the suspicion that they were providing ammunition to those attacking our hard-won power. Intellectuals had an extra burden to bear, struggling to gain the trust of a party devoted to the triumph of the working classes. My father and other writers and thinkers routinely suffered the indignity of humbling themselves before aggressive questioners in Party meetings. In East Germany, the word "intellectual" had a disparaging ring in both the Party and the Ministry of State Security. Many tried to defend themselves from accusations of "elitist thinking" or "immodesty" by stressing their acceptance of the leading role of the working class and biting their tongues about the idiocies perpetrated in its name. Without acknowledging the power of such thinking, it is difficult to explain how I could have kept the faith during the years still to come.

The removal of Wilhelm Zaisser as minister of state security had both personal and organizational consequences for my service. I remained in my job and was nominated as deputy to the new chief of the service, Ernst Wollweber, who cared little about operational details but was intensely interested in the political information we gathered. When discussing it he would pace back and forth across the carpet in his office, a small, round man with a permanently dying cigar clenched between his teeth. Nothing could keep him tied to his desk once he began speculating about the various persons, connections, and contradictions in the West and what possibilities they might create for us.

Wollweber could not have been more different from Erich Mielke, who was responsible for counterintelligence, which dealt with rooting out domestic spies. Mielke was opposed to my control of espionage abroad; he considered himself my rival and actually schemed against me not only when we were equals, but later when he became my superior as head of the Ministry of State Security. Part of the Communist Party's hit squads against Nazi gangs in the 1930s, he was merciless in rooting out enemies. In 1953, however, he was still smarting from a Party decision to examine his competence as a result of the 1953 uprising. I was thus elevated to the status of one of Wollweber's deputies before he was, which he held against me for the rest of his days. Years later I learned that when Wollweber was finally thrown out, the KGB resident in Berlin, Yevgeni P. Pitovranov, and the Soviet ambassador to the GDR, Georgi M. Pushkin, were discussing a successor for Wollweber with Ulbricht. Pitovranov said, "Why are you looking? You have a successor—Wolf." But Mielke got the job; he was Ulbricht's watchdog.

Mielke was a warped personality even by the peculiar standards of morality that apply in the espionage world. He was a fitness fanatic. He was afflicted with an obsession for collecting data, not only on suspected dissidents, whom he ordered to be placed under round-the-clock surveillance, but on his own colleagues. Desperate to unearth traitors in the leadership, he promised me high honors if I could obtain from the U.S. Document Center in West Berlin, where Nazi files were stored after 1945, some sort of proof that any East German politician had been a collaborator under the Third Reich. Nothing escaped his notice, no detail was too mean to land in the red files he hoarded in his office safe.

Once I received a report from a puzzled employee of my service, who had seen Erich Honecker, later the East German leader and at that time the head of the Free German Youth, surreptitiously slipping through the backstreets of East Berlin after dismissing his driver at dusk. It was clear to me that Honecker must have been visiting a secret girlfriend, although he was married to a fellow functionary at the time. I joked to this effect with Mielke, saying, "Well, we hardly need to keep that in the files," and made to throw away the report. "No, no," came the head of counterintelligence's hasty reply. "Let me have it. You never know." It joined other unflattering details of Honecker's life in his red boxes, to be discovered decades later in 1989, when the public prosecutor searched Mielke's office.

Purges, once started, are difficult to stop. Four years later, Wollweber was ousted in another Ulbricht machination and Mielke was installed as minister for state security. Mielke would remain in the top security job until his farcical exit in 1989, when he quit office with a forced valediction before the East German parliament and the words "I love you all."

5

Learning by Doing

Germany in the early 1950s was a huge web of declared and undeclared connections, secret shame, and covert loyalties on both the Right and the Left. Nothing was certain, no one could be trusted completely, appearances deceived. The result was a nervous intensity and suspicion, captured by Billy Wilder in his films about life in the American zone—particularly *A Foreign Affair*—and by my own brother in his films about the early years in the Russian zone. The official accounts people gave of themselves were like masks. "Every second person in the country was in the underground resistance," my father used to joke bitterly after hearing fanciful accounts from Berliners of how they had covertly fought Hitler. "Unfortunately, they never met."

Both German states claimed their goal was the reunification of the country. I myself did not believe it was even conceivable in the foreseeable future because of the conflicting interests of the victorious powers that had divided Germany after the war. In Washington and in London, too, the June 1953 unrest in East Germany confirmed their conviction that the strategy of rolling back Soviet power would work. Hopes for unification were further eroded through political, economic, and, not least, military pressure—the rearmament of West Germany and its integration into the Western military alliance were high on the West's agenda. Nevertheless, the leadership of the GDR clung to the slogan of German unity—even though so many of its citizens had left the country.

The main preoccupation of our rulers was the struggle to establish a distinct identity in the East. The inherent fragility of the "second German state" was never far from their minds. This gave rise to a cult of patriotism that verged on the absurd. We adopted dress uniforms; I had no less than five, no small achievement for someone who had never served in the army. One of the odder ideas that Ulbricht espoused during this period was a return to military symbolism—a distinct about-face, given that we had criticized the West Germans for continuing the militantly nationalist traditions of Hitler's Wehrmacht. Traditional military music was also revived and was played publicly for the first time in East Berlin at the Soviet bloc World Youth Games in 1951. Like many Communists who had been brought up to view this blend of militarism and music as having prepared the ground for Nazism, I found this disturbing. When the marches were played I turned to the Russian Jewish writer Ilya Ehrenburg, who was on the reviewing stand beside me, and asked him what he thought of the spectacle. He gave a classic Russian shrug of resignation and replied, "The Germans were always fond of marching."

●

Our fledgling service meanwhile was trying to learn its trade in less flamboyant ways, although it did not always work out that way. The early years of a new espionage undertaking are always prone to the workings of Murphy's Law, and the scientific-technical sphere offered abundant potential for errors and misjudgments.

During the 1950s, thousands of the GDR's citizens streamed across the then practically open borders into West Berlin and West Germany. Their numbers increased considerably after the uprising in June 1953, and nearly 500,000 of the nation's 18 million people fled in the following three years.

It was not very difficult for our agents to swim along in the stream. They were usually young, convinced Communists, and they laid the cornerstone for many of our later successes. Although they were usually picked up and questioned in the refugee camps once they got to the West, they still had a good chance of blending in with the mass of newcomers if equipped with a believable cover story, such as a wish to join relatives in the West. We used different pretexts: An agent might say that he had been caught trying to hide his past membership in the Nazi Party or the Waffen SS, or that he had made negative comments about our government's policies. We even put such "stains" into personnel files kept on these agents that were maintained by other ministries in order to enhance the credibility of the charges should West German counterintelligence somehow get their hands on an agent's file. I shied away from staffing my department with people who had relatives in the West, since I believed that the Western services could more easily penetrate us—as we did them—through family links and pressures.

For each person we sent across we had a predetermined mission, and each agent was trained by a staff handler responsible for the mission. We limited training to the elementary rules of espionage and tips on acquiring the information we wanted. It made no sense to train these agents in subjects and skills that did not concern them; in some ways, it would make their operations more risky by unnecessarily complicating their mission. In some cases we retrieved agents from the West and brought them back to the GDR for additional training when the appropriate time came.

The fact that we were sending our agents into West Germany, a country with the same language and culture, was clearly an advantage. Obviously, it was much more difficult for the Soviet Union to infiltrate agents in the United States or vice versa. As the two German states grew apart, such infiltration became more difficult, and the building of the Berlin Wall cut to a trickle the heavy flow of émigrés in which we hid our agents. This meant cover stories had to become even more foolproof. But even then the West was at a disadvantage, since migration from West to East was extremely rare and carefully observed. On the other hand, the West had less need to send people across: They could instead simply buy people from our large pool of dissatisfied citizens.

To overcome the bureaucratic barriers to becoming established in West Germany, most of our agents there usually began their assignments with a period of simple, manual labor. For that reason, we often preferred candidates with craftsmen's skills and practical experience in a profession.

Not everyone went this route, however; as mentioned before, almost every one of the scientists and science students who emigrated at that time found a spot in companies or research facilities that were of interest to us. We also obtained information through informal contacts with West German scientists. Many felt great uneasiness about the threat of atomic, biological, and chemical weapons. Badly shaken after the atomic bombs dropped on Hiroshima and Nagasaki, they offered our agents ample opportunity and subject matter for informative discussions.

Some of our people were able to work their way into areas that were covered by strict secrecy regulations. Others gained highly paid positions of corporate leadership. But penetrating the secrecy of the military and political centers of Bonn, where the big decisions were actually made, was far more difficult.

●

After the upheavals of 1953, the summit of the foreign ministers of the Allied powers in Berlin the following year became our most pressing concern. It was the first time such an event had occurred on our doorstep and I was unsure what intelligence activities were expected of me. As usual, the Soviets demanded from us a precise plan of action. More in hope than expectation, I struggled to prepare one that would yield a sudden surge of high-quality information from my officers.

Moscow sent a special adviser who perused the large diagram on my desk and, like a mechanic spotting an engine leak, said, "Of course, you'll be needing a '*malina*' for the duration." I was mystified. *Malina* is the Russian word for "raspberry," but surely our KGB friend was not thinking of fruit desserts. It emerged that he was using the word as slang for brothel, to which our agents would lure stray officials from the conference to unburden themselves with a little high living.

This was years before I had developed any clear strategy for using sex in espionage, but I was unwilling to let my Russian colleague know I was so naïve. At breakneck speed, we turned a little house we sometimes used in the southern reaches of East Berlin into a combination brothel and entrapment center with bugging devices in the living room and a camera with an infrared flash hidden in the bedroom light fitting. In those days such devices were very primitive, so the photographer had to squeeze into the bedroom's tiny linen cupboard and stay there until the people he was observing had left.

The next problem was finding the ladies. We approached a senior police official who had been head of the vice squad in Berlin. (Curiously enough, control of prostitution and pornography was shared by East and West between 1945 and 1949.) He was a down-at-the-heels gumshoe who knew all the haunts of prostitutes and where they could be found now that the oldest profession had gone underground in our puritan new state. Unfortunately, he directed us to the Mulackstrasse area, which has always represented the bottom end of the Berlin flesh market. My then boss, who after a lifetime in espionage was unshockable in such matters, phoned me up with the glum message, "You wouldn't consider getting your leg over any of these even a mark."

Against ideology, we had to rely on the instincts of free enterprise. At a milk bar on Karl-Marx-Allee we found some more attractive girls who, despite making an honorable living by day, declared themselves ready to make a less honorable one by night on behalf of their socialist Fatherland. The plan was to send scores of our agents to the West Berlin press center and restaurants and bars in the vicinity of the foreign ministers' meeting place. They were to invite officials and advisers for a few drinks and, if the evening looked promising, bring them back to a "small party" in the *malina*, where female company was guaranteed.

So far so good. But in the middle of the night, my phone rang with news of an "unexpected development." The madam had demanded a thorough hygiene check and discovered that one of the girls was less fastidious than she had claimed: She had crabs. I ordered her withdrawn from the operation.

The conference began, our team waited impatiently for action, but no guest materialized. The ministerial coteries must have been unusually moral that year, because the only taker, and on the very last night, was a West German journalist. Drinks and snacks were duly produced, the ladies took up position. But in all the bonhomie, our man in charge of the evening accidentally drank the glass of spirits containing the aphrodisiac intended for the guest. To round things off, there was to be a showing of pornographic films. Of course they were banned in the East, but somehow they were produced by the former head of the vice squad whenever the need arose. While our man could barely take his eyes off the film, his quarry showed not the slightest interest in either it or the women and withdrew to the kitchen, where he sat chatting with the maid.

The next day the journalist was the only one with a clear head. He had understood the game and declared himself ready to work for us. It was a conquest of sorts, but hardly worth the effort. The disappointed waitresses had to be paid off and sent home with strict instructions not to gossip about the fiasco.

There was a strange postscript to the affair. When we sent an agent to meet the journalist, in his place appeared a colleague named Heinz Losecaat van Nouhuys, who claimed to work for the popular West German newsmagazine *Der Spiegel*. Whether they had arranged the swap or it had been organized by West German counterintelligence, I never knew. But Herr van Nouhuys proved an extremely willing agent, and although I had my suspicions about his claims to have information from ministerial circles, the information he supplied us over the years matched other reports. His journalistic career took him to the editorship of *Quick*. This right-wing mass-circulation magazine staunchly opposed the East, but he continued to work for us there.

We started using the Leipzig trade fair to make contacts with the business community, and through them conservative politicians and public figures who believed that by cooperating with the East they were somehow ensuring there would be no full rupture between the two halves of Germany. East-West business deals negotiated there were subject to the strict Western embargo on strategic goods, which could be something as basic as steel pipe. The restrictions made it natural for businessmen to set up confidential contacts and arrange illegal transactions, and one department of the Central Committee was responsible for under-the-table deals, although we later took over much of its work. I would often go to Leipzig posing in the well-worn cover of a senior trade official or a representative of the Council of Ministers.

That is how I met Christian Steinrücke, who was involved in wholesale steel trading in West Germany. Steinrücke was on good terms with such leading industrialists as Otto Wolff von Amerongen, whose family's steel company had pioneered trade with the Soviet Union in the early 1920s and helped build the Manchurian railway. When I dined with Steinrücke one evening, I told him I was a general in the East German Interior Ministry, and we got on famously. The next morning, at a closed meeting of the West German Iron and Steel Federation, he introduced me as his colleague to its director, Ernst Wolf Mommsen. With Steinrücke shepherding me about, not one of the gentlemen in this secretive elite seemed to notice my presence, let alone mind it. Steinrücke was married to a Wehrhahn, the daughter of one of the mightiest families of German capitalism. Her brother was Adenauer's son-in-law—my ears tingled with excitement when I heard that—and even better, her sister-in-law was the niece of Cardinal Frings, the most senior figure in the West German Catholic church.

Our contact lasted many years. To help keep it alive, I invited Steinrücke to dine with me from time to time and invented a whole alternative family life for myself. I took a small villa in Rauchfangwerder with a pretty announcer from East German television playing my wife. Pictures of her children were hung on the walls whenever Steinrücke was due for a visit. As the arms business grew more sophisticated, my conversations with him became increasingly valuable, and by the mid-1970s he was an adviser to the Lockheed Corporation with good links to the head of the West German air force and a knowledge of the activities of Franz-Josef Strauss, the Bavarian political leader and West German defense minister. I never made a formal approach to him, nor spoke to him about spying for us, although he should have guessed my role if not my real identity. The end of the connection was unwittingly provoked by me because of Steinrücke's friend, Dr. Walter Bauer.

Bauer appeared to be a modest businessman who traded West German tallow for East German felt in the Lausitz region of East Germany. This hardly seemed to be the basis of a decent fortune, which Bauer clearly possessed. Our suspicions were justified. Some time before 1945, he had taken up a senior position in the Flick industrial conglomerate, prewar owners of the profitable Lausitz brown-coal region. His image as a small-time, rather shabby trader was contradicted by a photograph we found of him standing beside Konrad Adenauer at a church conference. We suspected his real mission was to help his employer keep a foot in the East on behalf of the big industrialists hoping for unification. Under our criminal code, that would have been both espionage and revisionist activity, which gave me something on which to hook Bauer, or so I believed.

I knew that he was also a close associate of a man called Hans Bernd Gisevius, who had been the contact during the Second World War between the middle-class German resistance and the OSS (Office of Strategic Services), the forerunner of the CIA. Armed with this material, I decided on a full frontal assault on Bauer. We met at the Johannishof, the hotel for government guests in East Berlin. Bauer, the furthest thing imaginable from a smooth, debonair agent, was a small, round man wearing an old suit.

Steinrücke, who clearly enjoyed his new game as go-between, had told him I was a high official in the Interior Ministry working on economic matters. We talked for several hours, and I played one card after another without success. Bauer had an answer or an explanation for everything he did and showed no fear or doubt under pressure, even when I told him that I knew of his contacts with the Americans. That was to be my trump card and it failed miserably.

This down-at-the-heels businessman turned out to be a highly skilled operator, too tough to be cracked by an eager young intelligence officer. He was too well-connected for us to blackmail him, which gave me a valuable lesson in what happens to agents who overplay their hand.

My supposition about Bauer was quickly confirmed when Steinrücke did not appear for his next meeting with me. He had been subjected to extremely embarrassing questioning by the American intelligence service, which told him who I really was and urgently warned him against continuing our relationship, a warning Steinrücke took to heart. He went on to deepen his ties with the German and American arms lobbies, which was what had intrigued me about him in the first place.

Through my brashness with Bauer I had lost a valuable contact who would have continued his work with us on the basis of a careful understanding. Over the years we refined our techniques of persuading people to work for us and came to recognize that it was unwise to try to persuade potential agents to sign on the dotted line. Many of those prepared for whatever reasons to deal with a hostile intelligence service will shy away from a formal commitment and actually prefer an ambiguous relationship. I advised my officers: If you think that the answer is going to be no, don't ask the question. Don't try to make the human material fit some preestablished pattern outlined by bureaucratic rules. Over the years we tried to shed the bureaucratic obsessions of our Soviet godfathers, and this worked well for us.

We were also very keen to penetrate the Krupp industrial empire and attempted to attract Carl Hundhausen, a board member with an artistic bent who seemed to understand the East better than his colleagues. He criticized the Bonn government's stance against intra-German trade, but it soon became clear that he saw his contact with me as little more than a means to advance Krupp's interests.

At a congress on German unity, we happened upon Heinrich Wiedemann, a campaigner for German unification and an old friend of Joseph Wirth, the former chancellor of the Weimar Republic. To my delight, Wiedemann said that speeches against the strengthening Washington-Bonn alliance were not enough and hinted that he wanted capital from us to set up a business in Bonn. A contract was drawn up that guaranteed us a share of his company's earnings, a rare excursion for my intelligence service into venture capitalism, and with our support Wiedemann opened the Office of Economic Aid for Fixed-Salary Earners, a lobbying group with access to ministries and their employees. Through this channel, we were able to forge a contact with Rudolf Kriele, a department head in the Federal Chancellery responsible for defense policy and military alliances. A powerful official who frequented our lobbying office, Kriele downed Rhine wine and gossiped about the inner workings of German politics.

This excited our ambitions. We planned to expand the office into an illegal residency (the intelligence trade term for a deep undercover operation), which would become a contact point in times of tension between East and West. We installed an agent with equipment to record conversations with visiting officials and receive, process, and transmit information back to us. We also recruited Wiedemann's girlfriend, whose boss worked in the Chancellery, and gave her the code name Iris. But there was one awkward problem. Wiedemann, for all his gifts of persuasion, was not a particularly good businessman, and the cost of operating the office considerably surpassed its earnings, a fact that could not be concealed from the outside world for long. We operated under the assumption that West German counterintelligence had access to tax records and would soon start wondering where the money was coming from. The end came more quickly than I expected when a defector fled to the

West from our headquarters, and we were forced to withdraw our agent because of the risk that the defector might expose him to Bonn.

The consolation prize was Iris, though our joy in her was diminished when her boss was moved from the Chancellery to the Ministry of Science and Education. There for a decade, she passed us details of sensitive research projects supported by the government and helped us plan our own scientific and technical espionage.

Along with Wiedemann's office, a fascinating hostess in Bonn also seemed to offer great promise during the early 1950s. We had seen her potential when we came across the name Susanne Sievers in going through the list of Western prisoners held in East Germany and awaiting release through an amnesty. She had been arrested by our counterintelligence during a trip to the Leipzig trade fair in 1951 and sentenced to eight years in prison for spying. Her file listed her profession as freelance journalist, which intrigued my staff. A colonel arranged a meeting before she knew that she was to be released. In the visitors' room, our man found before him a tall, slender woman in her mid-thirties. Her strong and self-confident personality radiated through her drab prison garb, and she still discussed her arrest as an injustice, making no attempt to curry favor with her captors. But she also talked about Germany's problems and Adenauer's pro-American policies. Our man inquired whether she might be willing to continue the conversation in other circumstances. Her release followed and they met on the Warsaw Bridge in East Berlin, where it was agreed that on her return to the West, she would pass information to us. We gave her the code name Lydia.

To our delight, Susanne set herself up in a hospitable apartment in Bonn, in which she ran a salon where prominent people met to discuss politics and culture. We received valuable information about an organization on the extreme right of German politics called Rescue Freedom (Rettet die Freiheit), headed by the Christian Democratic politician Rainer Barzel. It had ties in Eastern European countries through émigrés and had an alliance with Otto von Hapsburg, a descendant of the Austro-Hungarian imperial family who was active in politics. Barzel would later come to haunt us when he rose to become chairman of the Christian Democratic Union and was its candidate against Willy Brandt, staunchly opposing Brandt's efforts to accord East Germany diplomatic recognition by the West.

Before her arrest by the East Germans, Susanne had had a passionate affair with Willy Brandt when he was mayor of Berlin. He had written her a series of intimate letters, which were made public in the 1961 parliamentary election campaign by Brandt's enemies, including Franz-Josef Strauss. It was her reports that first forced us to rethink our stereotype of Strauss as the fanatical enemy of socialism he portrayed himself to be in public. She saw him as a dispassionate pragmatist. When Lydia disclosed that Strauss and Brandt had made an appointment for a private meeting at her apartment, rumors arose of a grand coalition that would bring Social Democrats into government for the first time since the war. Brandt confirms these talks in his memoirs without mentioning the scene and his links to Susanne.

I often wondered what had motivated this woman to turn up for conspiratorial meetings in Berlin and report about organizations and persons who were much closer to her own political views than ours, especially after having suffered imprisonment on what I surmised were trumped-up charges. She certainly knew with whom she was dealing. Had she been a double agent she would have asked certain questions about our operations, but she never did. She accepted only compensation for her expenses, nothing more. As an alibi for her visits to Berlin, she invented a girlfriend in the Western part of the city.

Our contact with this extremely valuable source was abruptly severed by the erection of the Berlin Wall in 1961. She was one of several Western sources who stopped working for us then. But I believe that there was more to Susanne than met the eye, and there were hints that she had started to work for West German intelligence. She disappeared with Fred Sagner, a West German army major who had first told her about Rescue Freedom, to the Far East, where he was assigned to various embassies of the Federal Republic as a military attaché. By 1968 she was working for a spy network controlled by a West German agent called Hans Langemann, a contact of the CIA who controlled agents in Europe and the Far East.

It emerged that Susanne Sievers—once our helpful Lydia—later became a station chief for West German intelligence (Bundesnachrichtendienst—BND) in Hong Kong under the code number 150, running substations in Tokyo, Manila, Jakarta, and Singapore. West German intelligence files to which we gained access during the 1970s showed that she had received one payment of 96,000 deutschmarks, so her role must have been an important one. When Klaus Kinkel eventually became West Germany's chief spymaster in 1968, his first task was to clean out phony agents and put an end to harebrained schemes inspired by Gehlen, which were still the norm, despite the fact that two other men had led the BND since Gehlen. Susanne Sievers left the service and was said to have received 300,000 deutschmarks for her silence about the BND's involvement in domestic politics. I lost sight of her, and to this day she remains a figure whose real loyalties and significance remain an enigma to me.

•

Chastened by my mistake with Steinrücke, I realized that the secret to the political penetration of the Federal Republic lay in a wide variety of sources and solicitous handling of them once they had been contacted. On the right we had built up a contact with Günter Gereke, a German patriot and prewar parliamentarian who had been imprisoned for his opposition to Hitler and later joined the plotters who tried to assassinate him in 1944. In many ways Gereke was a paradigm of the staunch conservatives who ended up working with us. Many could not stand Adenauer, rejecting his notion of securing the rebirth of Germany with the help of an American midwife. Gereke protested by meeting with Ulbricht publicly and was expelled from Adenauer's party. We hung on to him as a valuable source in Christian Democrat circles, whence he reported generously.

When the news broke that Gereke's assistant had been an agent of British intelligence, it became clear to Gereke that the Bonn authorities were almost certainly working up a case against him, too, in the hope of discrediting all opponents of pro-American policies as Communist agents. We decided to move fast and told Gereke to move to East Berlin. This was the last thing that his social class had prepared him for, but in those days we were pretty straightforward, and he had little choice. He was finished anyway as a public figure in the West if Adenauer decided to make an example of him.

We produced him at a press conference in East Berlin, where he explained the reasons for maintaining contacts as a German patriot, a propaganda victory for us that delighted our leadership. Too delighted, in fact, since it awakened an unhealthy appetite for classy defections, regardless of the fact that a good agent in place is usually worth a dozen defectors. I once had a source, code-named Timm, a CDU deputy whose real name was Karlfranz Schmidt-Wittmack. A member of the committee for European Security Questions and the head of the defense committee of the CDU's youth branch, he was the protégé of powerful industrial figures and was on the ladder to the top of his party. I returned from a summer holiday in 1954 to find a note from Wollweber saying that Schmidt-Wittmack would have to be withdrawn to the GDR. I was furious at the thought that a man who was passing us documents detailing the terms for Bonn's entry into NATO should be sacrificed just for a press conference, and I knew how reluctant he would be to give up his prospering career to wither away in East Germany. But the matter was out of my hands. However sharp may be the instincts of an intelligence service, it is always the toy of the government it serves.

I felt that I had to break the news to Schmidt-Wittmack in person. The few political arguments I managed to devise did not satisfy him at all: He wanted to be more than a cog in the eternally turning propaganda wheel. I had no choice but to lie and say that West German counterintelligence was on his case and that his only chance of avoiding jail was to flee to the East immediately. He made his decision contingent on his wife's agreement. We assumed that, although she was familiar with his work for East Germany, she would hardly be thrilled at the thought of moving there. We persuaded him to write to her before he returned to Hamburg to wind up his affairs, and our courier sped back to Hamburg ahead of him, giving her time to come to terms with the shock. Forced to choose between having a disgraced husband in prison or taking up a new life in a pretty lakeside house in the East, she took the latter.

On August 26, 1954, Schmidt-Wittmack appeared before the press in East Berlin. He revealed that Adenauer had withheld important information about his intentions in foreign and security policy. As was usual in such cases, we added to the impact of the show by giving him extra information to disclose from other sources—in this case Soviet military intelligence—to wit, that Bonn, contrary to its public declarations, was planning an army of twenty-four divisions.

Schmidt-Wittmack was given a job as vice president of the foreign trade organization, but I always regretted the decision to bring him over and often wondered whether we hadn't sacrificed a future defense minister for the sake of a headline. Gereke became a functionary in the National Democratic Party, the East German party that represented old soldiers, craftsmen, and small businesses. It was not a particularly useful way for poor old Gereke to spend his days.

The most spectacular defector of those years arrived without any work on our part, and he was not even one of our sources. On the contrary, his job was to unearth and expose our agents and his name was Otto John, chief of West German counterintelligence (Office for the Protection of the Constitution). It is hard now to realize what a sensation this created at a time when the personal histories and current loyalties of all Germans were still suspected by their former enemies, and the left still had credibility.

An opponent of the Nazis, John disappeared from West Berlin after a service marking the tenth anniversary of the miscarried officers' putsch against Hitler on July 20, 1944. He was last seen in the West in the company of an old acquaintance, Dr. Wolfgang Wohlgemuth, a society gynecologist, and turned up on July 21, 1954, in the Soviet military base at Karlshorst on the outskirts of Berlin. There was evidence that the two had traveled into East Berlin in Wohlgemuth's car.

Panic ensued in the West, where the case was explained as a provocative snatch by Communist intelligence. But with splendidly comic timing, just as the government spokesman in Bonn announced that John had not left the Federal Republic of his own free will, the intelligence chief avowed on East German radio that he had come over voluntarily because, he said, Adenauer had become a tool of the Americans, who, in their "need for war against the East German soldiers . . . welcome those who have not learned anything from the catastrophe and are waiting for the moment when they can effect revenge for 1945." When he also said that Nazis dominated West Germany's intelligence networks, his words carried a great deal of weight.

But like many events at the height of the Cold War, this one was not entirely what it seemed. Here, for the first time, is the truth as I know it about the bizarre affair.

The key lay in John's wartime experiences, when he became a confidant of a small resistance group within Nazi counterintelligence that was plotting to kill Hitler. He was introduced to Claus Schenk Graf von Stauffenberg, the officer who eventually botched the assassination, and was given the task of determining whether the Allies would accept the plotters' suit for peace if they could get rid of Hitler. John, then working in neutral Madrid for Germany's commercial airline, Lufthansa, forged links with the American embassy and, in particular, with the military attaché, Colonel William Hohenthal, who had connections at the highest levels of Eisenhower's headquarters. John also sent a message seeking support from London through the British embassy in Lisbon.

Years later, John told me that he believed his message had been blocked by Kim Philby, who was at that time at the height of his powers as a KGB mole in British intelligence. The Russians were adamantly opposed to any deal between Hitler's German opponents and the Western Allies, lest a conservative putsch end with all of them banding together to fight Russia. "The documents I passed to Philby must have disappeared somewhere in his files," John told me long after Philby's death. "I don't think they ever reached London."

When the plot failed and the plotters were mercilessly hunted down and murdered, John managed to flee via Madrid and Lisbon to England. The journalist Sefton Delmer took him under his wing and gave him a job in the evaluation department of his news network. After the war, John gave to the British evidence that was used in the trials of Field Marshals von Brauchitsch, von Rundstedt, and von Manstein. With this background, it was hardly surprising that he was appointed head of West German counterintelligence, located in Cologne in the British occupation zone.

John was no natural ally of the former Nazi Reinhard Gehlen, who had been placed in charge of foreign intelligence by the Americans, nor of the Nazis around Adenauer, nor of Adenauer himself, who like many West German conservatives felt that the Stauffenberg plot had smacked of adventurism. John would have preferred an appointment in the fledgling diplomatic service, but, he later told me, a career there was out of the question because it remained staffed by a circle of diplomats that had surrounded the Nazi foreign minister, Joachim von Ribbentrop. To add insult to injury, the deputy president of the

Gehlen agency, Olaf Radtke, had been moved over to the counterintelligence service, clearly to keep an eye on John. It is scarcely any wonder that by 1954 he was feeling desperate and that his appearance in the East one sunny morning in July was seen as a defection.

The truth is entirely different and far more bizarre. John had never intended to defect. Dr. Wohlgemuth was a Soviet agent who decided that he would use his friend's demoralization to lure him to the East. My Soviet colleagues swore that they gave him no encouragement, but I can well imagine Wohlgemuth saying to his control officer, "I can get you Otto John." Whereupon the skeptical Soviet intelligence man would have replied, "Fine, we'll believe it when we see him here."

What is certain, however, is that the last independently verified sighting of John was in Wohlgemuth's car as the two crossed into East Berlin in the middle of the night. I surmise that John either must have been very drunk or had been drugged by his friend. The two had been spotted weaving their way through a string of nightclubs, drinking to the memory of their dead comrades in the resistance. When the unwilling traveler woke up, it was in the Soviet barracks in Karlshorst, a nightmare for the man who was head of West German counterintelligence. I believe they were as surprised by John's appearance in their hands as he was because they called in General Yevgeni P. Pitovranov, head of the KGB station in Berlin, and a certain Mr. Turgarinov, the representative of the Information Committee of the Foreign Ministry under W. M. Molotov, to decide how to best put him to use. John knew that he had been fatally compromised and that, as a virtual prisoner in Karlshorst, the Soviets held the key to his fate. He faced prison back home, and his career was over.

After he had made his public appearance and the shock had begun to sink in back in Cologne, the Soviets as usual dumped the damaged goods on us. John was in a state of utter disorientation, so our first concern was to provide a circle of friends for support. We put him in touch with Hermann Henselmann, the chief architect for the city of East Berlin, and Wilhelm Girnus, whom I knew from my Berlin Radio days and who shared some of John's old anti-Nazi acquaintances. The Ministry of State Security provided bodyguards to protect against a snatch by the Western services, but they did not do a very good job. Seventeen months after his appearance in the East, John disappeared with just as little ceremony, leaving a meeting at Humboldt University in East Berlin to speak with a Danish journalist named Bonde-Henrickson. The two men climbed into Henrickson's car and sped back to the West through the Brandenburg Gate.

That was in 1955. Thirty-seven years later, in April 1992, I sat with the eighty-three-year-old John in a restaurant overlooking the spot beside Humboldt University whence he had fled back to the West. He was still furious that, on his return to the West, he was sentenced to four years' imprisonment for betraying his country. He served only eighteen months, which suggests that the West Germans were unsure of the extent of his guilt. Of the "defection" to the East he told me, "I lost consciousness and woke up in Karlshorst. I never had the slightest intention of going East." He said that he had never felt at home in East Berlin and had simply decided after a year that he had had enough and sought contact with someone who could help him leave.

When all was said and done, our famous defectors had little strategic value. Yes, Adenauer was forced by a defector's disclosures to admit that he was discussing the rearmament of Germany. And the resilient influence of old Nazis in Bonn had been disclosed in such a dramatic way that the subject emerged on the political agenda and stayed there. But West Germany soon joined NATO anyway. We did not succeed in our aim of preventing its accession to the Western alliance, or even slowing it down.

6

Khrushchev Opens Our Eyes

Like most people in the Communist world, I was unable to root out my own admiration for Stalin and Stalinism for many years. The catalyst for my awakening was to be the world's most public secret speech, delivered by Nikita Khrushchev at the Twentieth Congress of the Communist Party in Moscow in February 1956. The exact origin of my long and painful process of breaking with Stalinism is hard to ascertain; the slivers of doubt that penetrated my ideological defenses in the foreboding atmosphere of East Germany in the early fifties were probably the beginning. But the event that shook my carefully nurtured worldview and that of many Communists of my generation was Khrushchev's speech in which he disclosed Stalin's crimes. After that, though we could still claim to be faithful Communists, we could no longer claim to be innocent.

Until February 1956, Stalin's portrait still hung over my desk, showing him lighting his pipe, a benevolent father to the nation. One day that month, the Western newspapers arrived in a thick bundle as usual. I always read *The New York Times* and the Paris edition of the *International Herald Tribune* to ascertain the drift of the American mind. I also read a variety of West German newspapers and magazines, including the tabloid *Bild-Zeitung*, which, while lurid, often had better inside information on intelligence than its worthier rivals. I looked at *The Times* of London and *Le Monde*, too. This global reading matter was one perk of my job. Western newspapers were forbidden in the East, on the spurious grounds that they contained seditious statements against the Communist world, but in truth because the politburo knew in its heart of hearts that their rendition of life behind the Iron Curtain was in many particulars too close to the truth for their comfort.

At the Party Congress, Khrushchev, having finally triumphed in the complex and bloody power struggle that followed Stalin's death, denounced the dictator, revealing that, of the 139 members and candidates of the Central Committee elected in 1934 at the Seventh Party Congress of the Communist Party of the Soviet Union, 98 had been arrested and shot. Of the 1936 delegates at the Congress, whose proceedings our parents had solemnly recounted to us as teenagers, well over half had been condemned as counterrevolutionaries and very few survived. Khrushchev concluded that Stalin's cruel repression violated all norms of revolutionary legality.

This was a language that we Communists, accustomed to the whitewashing of the slightest defect in our enterprise, had never encountered. Now that the corpse of that system has been laid open to a thorough autopsy, we would find the language of Khrushchev's accusations against Stalin rather vague and partial. But at the time, it was as if we had been hit on the head with a hammer. When I finished reading the text of the speech in a Western paper, my first reaction was to take down Stalin's portrait from the wall and kick it into a corner. I could not claim that what I read came as a complete shock—I knew too much from my own experiences of Soviet life for that—but it was a source of great pain to peer into the real abyss of his crimes. It was as if, at one stroke, our worst fears about the system to which we had pledged our lives had come true.

Filtered through Eastern Europe via the Western media and word of mouth, Khrushchev's volcanic speech helped escalate the dissatisfaction in Poland and Hungary. The Hungarian uprising of October–November was a direct result of Khrushchev's denunciation. The reform leader in Hungary was Imre Nagy, whom I had known in Moscow from 1943 to 1945, when he was chief of the exile Hungarian radio station while I was a correspondent for German People's Radio. We often took the same bus home after the late shift. Nagy, with his characteristic Hungarian mustache and round face, was always calm and good-humored and easily made friends among Moscow's overheated exile groups. Now I was confident that he, along with the Moscow leadership, would work out a course in Budapest that would restore calm. The tanks withdrew from Budapest following the first few days of the uprising and Nagy promised liberalization.

But it was too little, too late. The protests and bloodshed continued and the Soviet tanks returned on November 4. The Soviets were constantly on my emergency telephone line with the same question: What will NATO do? I was far from confident. On the one hand, there was ample evidence of covert NATO preparation against the Soviets. On the other, there were hints from our sources that the West was holding back because it feared escalation. I crossed my fingers and radioed Moscow: "NATO will not intervene."

If I had been wrong—and I was far from sure—my career would probably have ended, though that would have been the least of it. But I was right, and Nagy became the Soviets' scapegoat. They promised Nagy and other Hungarians at the Yugoslav embassy freedom from prosecution, but they broke their word. They kidnapped him from the Yugoslav embassy, took him to Romania, and executed him after a farcical secret trial; it was all a relapse into the worst ways of Stalinism. Later, the head of Hungarian foreign intelligence, Sandor Rajnai, confided to me that he was plagued by guilt over his personal role in interrogating Nagy. "Mischa," he said, "that sort of thing must never happen again."

Hungary, with its images of mob slaughter and mutilation, was a bitter lesson for all of us. While it may have temporarily enabled Moscow's dogmatists to label reformists as counterrevolutionaries, for many thinking Communists the uprising's complexities were perplexing, its messages mixed. The old Leninist questions would flood back into my mind: Should we risk such hard-won power? Freedom for whom and against whom?

In the Ministry of State Security we held a meeting in March 1956 to discuss the significance of the Moscow Congress. Ernst Wollweber was still in charge, so we were spared meetings of the type conducted by his successor, Mielke, whose idea of a debate was for him to speak for an hour and then dismiss us. I spoke out and welcomed the way our Soviet colleagues had confronted their past and expressed my relief at losing the burden of suspicions that had troubled me for years. Mielke was horrified. "I have never suffered under any burden," he said. "I have no idea what Comrade Wolf means." He went on to say that he had known nothing of any repression in the Soviet Union and added, for good measure, that there was none in East Germany, either.

Of course our country could not avoid some consequences of the thaw. Eighty-eight German prisoners convicted by Soviet military tribunals were freed, and a further seven hundred convicts were released from jail early. Inside the Party, the disciplinary proceedings against Anton Ackermann, Franz Dahlem, Hans Jendretzky, and several other disgraced (since 1953) Central Committee members were canceled. Reform plans were suddenly hauled out of functionaries' file drawers. Within our own Central Committee, searching discussions began on the establishment of a market system under socialism, which could only work with some form of democracy. I served on a mixed study commission that included specialists on economics, banking, politics, the military, and the security services. Economics has never been my strong suit, but I listened with great interest. I even began to feel my way intellectually toward an acceptance of a greater share of private property and to question more closely the relationship between freedom of expression and the state doctrine of adherence to the teachings of the Party.

But Ulbricht kept the lid on. Just two months after the Moscow Party Congress, the East German politburo voted against any further discussion of errors, lest it give ammunition to the enemy. Discipline was restored under such absurd phrases as "conquering the imperfections on our forward march." I was one of many in the Party who, having hoped for fresh impulses, bowed to its almighty discipline once again. Nevertheless, the Twentieth Party Congress was the first step on a long journey toward what we would later come to know as perestroika and glasnost, the beginning of an arc whose end would be described in 1989. I too would have to undergo a bumpy journey until I would be able to embrace new ideas and leave behind the intelligence service and its strictures on my thinking.

●

The geopolitical explosions in 1956 further undermined any hopes of change. The events in Poznan—where in the wake of Khrushchev's revelations there was a strike by Polish workers, bloodily suppressed by Polish forces—the uprising in Hungary, and the Suez crisis all forced us to think again in terms of the Cold War. From our vantage point, all we could see was that the two superpowers' respective allies were disciplined when they attempted independent policies—Hungary by Moscow, and Britain and France by Washington. The world was divided into spheres, and we knew which one was ours.

I ask myself whether I would have acted any differently if I had been in power. I hope so, but I am not so sure. When I spoke to Yuri Andropov in the early 1980s about problems of reform—the topic happened to be Poland, not Germany, but the questions were the same—I asked this liberal Communist why he had so little influence in these matters. "Comrade Wolf," he replied, "whenever anyone becomes general secretary you have about a year to influence him. As he becomes surrounded by his own people they tell him he is the greatest thing and applaud his every move, and it is too late." Andropov cited Nicolae Ceauşescu of Romania, who during his early years seemed to strike an independent course from Moscow before quickly becoming a tyrant.

I can already hear my critics jeering that it took me twenty years to put my thoughts into practice. But so it was. The foundation of all my thinking about the Cold War was that the West and its system did not present an acceptable alternative. At that point and for many years to follow, I could not have undertaken any step, even a mental one, that would have helped move my country or the others in the Warsaw Pact closer to a capitalist system. It remained my unshakable belief that the socialist system, for all its terrible failings, represented a better potential model for mankind than the West. When it came to the crunch, for all the growing doubts I had about Communist practice, I believed that we must never cede influence in Europe. A long, anguished entry in my diary in 1968 reads:

Power structures have developed in this transitional period on the way to true Socialism which have their own rules and an independent existence. They are governed by strongly subjective factors and interests.

These structures, apparats and functionaries can sometimes abuse power against people in ways that seem to have little to do with the Revolution.

This mixture of fervent belief and uncomfortable doubt plagued most intelligent Communists. But the temptation always remained to bury these uncomfortable questions and concentrate instead on the technological and scientific gains made by our system and on its modernizing influence on backward societies like Russia and China. Anything else was put on ice until socialism became more stable. The fact that changes were not possible at that time lay in the nature of both the system itself and the tensions of the international situation. They made any acceptance of reform seem like admission of failure, which was automatically counted as victory for the West. Such were the circles of the devil in which we revolved, year in, year out.

•

After the upheavals of 1956, Khrushchev's principal concern was diffusing the conflicts and tensions of the Eastern bloc in order to concentrate on his ambitious economic plans at home. His strings of statistics and optimistic speeches were greeted by many of his own colleagues with mild amusement, but he really believed that under his guidance, the country could not only catch up with but overtake America's prosperity. This was religiously but maladroitly translated by Ulbricht's advisers as "overtake without catching up" (*überholen ohne einzuholen*), a proposition our general secretary spouted for a long time before anyone dared bring to his attention that it was a logical impossibility.

There was also some discreet laughter at Khrushchev's fascination with corn, which he believed was the secret weapon to solve his vast nation's food shortages. During his first visit to East Germany in 1957 Mielke and I took him to the republic's most impressive cereal-producing plains in the Magdeburg region, where he met agronomists who could enlighten him to his heart's content. He carefully wrote down all the figures, and I later heard that he had made the lives of his own functionaries a misery on his return, chiding them for lagging behind the production levels of even the GDR.

Khrushchev's primitive manner and lengthy speeches caused a certain amount of irritation back home, but in East Germany, where we were sentenced to listen to Ulbricht's wooden delivery, Khrushchev's spontaneity was most impressive. He enjoyed the best reputation of any Soviet leader until Gorbachev came along, but unlike Gorbachev he was a simple man with an innate understanding of how ordinary people feel and think. He could talk for hours about his native Kalinovka with sentimental pride, all the while displaying a hearty disregard for diplomatic niceties.

I remember one incident after the farewell reception in East Berlin, at the conclusion of Khrushchev's visit to the GDR. The inner circle had retired to the Soviet ambassador's rooms in the embassy for a last drink. Anastas Mikoyan, the elderly chairman of the Supreme Soviet, suddenly became sleepy after a few glasses and did not want to make the trip out to Castle Niederschönhausen in the Pankow suburbs, the official residence for state guests, preferring instead to stay overnight in the embassy. Ulbricht was dismayed because he had arranged for the route from Niederschönhausen to the airport to be lined the next day with loyal East Germans waving farewell to the visitors.

A charged exchange followed, until Khrushchev interjected, "Anastas, there is no point arguing with Ulbricht. The Germans are hopelessly fastidious." Ulbricht turned a choleric shade but said nothing.

The next day, en route to the airport after his obligatory night at the castle, Mikoyan was in a bad mood. Making his protest against his hosts' determination to confront him one last time with obedient rows of East Germans lining his route, he fell asleep in his car. From his seat, Khrushchev turned to me and said quietly, "Back in our factory in Kalinovka, we once had a German craftsman called Müller. One summer, he brought his fiancée with him from Germany. He was very proud of the fact that he would not lay a finger on her until they were lawfully married. This story got about the factory, and a friend of mine called Vaska saw his chance. He serviced the lady all summer long. So you see, Comrade Wolf, German fastidiousness is not always a good thing."

No doubt Khrushchev could be a primitive man and his limited intellectual capacity and lack of experience of other parts of the world permitted him to ignore the grim shortcomings of his own country. He was also incapable of coming to terms with the wider consequences of his secret speech, proving in the end that he was still firmly tied to the old system and its ways of thinking. But he was a politician of conviction, not a bureaucrat, and he believed passionately in his ideology, to the extent that he would often sacrifice diplomatic advantage for the sake of argument.

●

By 1956, the conflict between the superpowers had become rather like Bertolt Brecht's depiction of the Thirty Years' War in his play *Mother Courage*: It had taken on its own momentum. On both sides, the arms industry, the politicians, and the intelligence services lived well from this flourishing business.

Early one morning toward the end of April 1956, I was awakened by my housekeeper with an unusual greeting: "The minister is waiting for you at the garden gate." I was immediately on the alert. Peering through a gap in the curtains, I saw an aging, tiny Volkswagen beetle parked below. My suspicions deepened still further, since this was not the way East German ministers of state were apt to travel. Mystified and edgy, I seized the loaded pistol I kept by my bedside table, pushed it into my dressing-gown pocket, and made my way downstairs to the front door.

In front of me stood the plump figure of Wollweber, with a cigar butt between his lips. Gesturing toward the car, I asked if everything was all right. He explained that he had been roused from his sleep by an emergency call from the Soviets and decided to save time by borrowing a neighbor's car instead of waiting for his guards and limousine driver. "Get a move on, Mischa," he chided, "you won't believe what they've found."

We rattled through the empty streets toward Schönefeld airport. Behind Alt-Glienecke, about five hundred yards from the American sector border and just outside a cemetery wall, we saw a group of figures in the gray dawn light. Half were Soviet soldiers, digging energetically. They were watched by others I knew to be the top brass of Moscow's military intelligence in Berlin. A spy tunnel had been unearthed.

The soldiers had already dug a deep trench, and we looked on, fascinated, as they climbed into it and cut through a tubular metal structure in the rough soil. Inside was a metal door. Its locks melted under the white heat of their blowtorches and it was yanked open before our eyes. Silently, the mine sweepers and bomb disposal men descended, checking the cavity for booby traps. They found none. The inventors of the tunnel had not expected to share their secret. The advance guard beckoned us to climb inside.

I found myself in a room the size of a large study. There were two chairs and a small table in the middle. Along the walls ran bundles of cables, carefully divided. Each bundle had an amplifier attached before it ran back into the main cable on the other side. Signals were picked up, magnified, and diverted to a specially built hut five hundred meters away, in West Berlin. It was a perfectly designed underground listening post.

How sophisticated the tunnel really was I was only to learn in detail from my Soviet colleagues later. The Americans had discovered that under this stretch of earth ran the main prewar telephone cable link to the south of what was now East Germany. Three of these cables had become dedicated lines for the military. They included the so-called Ve-Che line (from the Russian abbreviation for "high frequency," *Vysokaya chastota*), which linked Moscow with the Soviet military headquarters in Wünsdorf, south of Berlin.

It takes no imagination to realize this was an intelligence man's dream. The Americans could pick up conversations about weapons acquisitions, shortages, technical deficiencies, and code names for newly developed weapons technology between the defense ministry in Moscow and the East Berlin base in Karlshorst, the biggest in Eastern Europe. They could also listen in on operational planning and the arguments over the constant budget difficulties plaguing the Soviet military.

The Russians had great faith in the security of their Ve-Che lines. They had developed a new technique of filling the tiny wires inside the cable with pressurized air. This registered any sag in the current going through the wire—which occurs whenever a bug, however sophisticated, is affixed.

As a child of the Stalin years in Russia, I never believed there was such a thing as a line that could not be tapped, and I still don't. (The extent to which the Russians trusted their special lines even after the discovery of the tunnel was demonstrated to me several years later when, during a visit to my KGB counterpart in Berlin, he blithely handed me the telephone for a chat with Yuri Andropov, who was then sitting in his Moscow office as chief of the KGB.)

The British and U.S. secret services had first constructed a little hut just over the border in the West to pick up the messages in safety. They designed it with a cupola so that it looked like a meteorological installation, diverting attention to the top from its real business underground as the source of any possible radio signals.

To get around the difficulty of the minute sag in current when the lines were tapped, British engineers had built a tiny amplifier for each of the several hundred telephone wires inside the three big cables. It was a technical marvel and I would guess that without the tip-off received via the KGB, the tunnel would not likely have been found independently by our side.

We groped our way along the tunnel in the darkness and silence, with only a weak flashlight beam to help us. I caught a glimpse of white cardboard and shone my beam at it. There, underground on the subterranean line dividing two systems and ideologies, some intelligence man with a well-developed sense of humor had placed a tiny roll of barbed wire and a piece of cardboard bearing the message in black pen, "You are entering the American sector." Here I was, one of the prime enemies of the CIA, sharing this private joke of American intelligence workers! For the first time during an extraordinary morning, I pinched myself to make sure I was not dreaming.

Of course, there was one flaw in the conception of this intelligence marvel that not even the most brilliant technicians could have repaired: The Soviets knew about the tunnel from the start, thanks to their brilliant double agent in British intelligence, George Blake. But while by this means they protected their own conversations, they never told us anything, leaving us unguarded and exposed. This was lamentably not out of character for the Soviets: For them, intelligence generally flowed in one direction only.

I already had an inkling that there was a highly placed British agent working for the Soviets in West Berlin. The Soviets naturally kept details a tight secret, but one of the generals had been unable to resist boasting to me that he was running a big operation inside the British camp. But the Soviets wanted to let the Americans finish their masterwork so as to be able to evaluate their technological expertise. The

Americans fell into the trap. Soviet intelligence watched the monitoring operation for about a year and then blew open the secret.

Blake was eventually arrested and imprisoned in 1961, only to make a sensational escape to the Soviet Union five years later from London's Wormword Scrubs prison. Even after he had settled in Moscow and established a new family, the Soviets were nervous about allowing him to travel. Finally they gave in to his pleas for a holiday and sent him, with a minder, to one of our ministry's retreats on the island of Usedom in the Baltic Sea. Blake came to visit in East Berlin four times in all, always with his KGB guardian in tow. I invited him to address our trainee agents about his adventures with the hope of fostering a sense of belonging and tradition within the Communist espionage community.

By the third visit, Blake's minders seemed more relaxed and permitted his Russian wife to accompany him. He also requested a private meeting with me. We are about the same age and we immediately warmed to each other. I was particularly struck by his British habit of understatement. While his wife went shopping, enjoying the relative bounty of East Germany's state stores after the shortages in Russia, we sat in a guest house exchanging stories. He was a brilliant linguist, being fluent in Arabic, French, and Dutch, and by now also spoke fluent German and Russian, albeit with the accent of an English gentleman that he apparently had picked up at Cambridge University.

Blake told me that the original idea for the tunnel had come from the British side. After his return from Korea, where he had been deputy station chief for Britain's Secret Intelligence Service in the region, Blake had been involved in a similar venture in Vienna. The plan to tunnel through to the Soviet military mission from the British Military Police headquarters in Vienna's Simmeringstrasse ran into technical difficulties but seemed a promising approach. Because he had been involved in the project, he was asked to consult with the Americans on the Berlin tunnel.

After his imprisonment and escape to Moscow, Blake and I met once again, in the company of my brother, Koni, for the premiere of his film *Mama, I'm Alive!*, which told the story of German prisoners of war in Russia. It was a cozy evening, during which we talked about Russian films and books. Even for a former spy, he was more than usually reserved when it came to discussing the more grimy details of the business. He did tell me that his friendship in Moscow with Kim Philby had proved a tremendous support. It struck me then that Blake suffered terribly under his reputation as a callous agent and wanted to be regarded as an idealist. Despite his commitment to the Soviet cause, I also had the feeling that he refused to accept that he really was the traitor his country considered him to be. He was perhaps less intelligent than Philby, whom I also knew and admired immensely. Both seemed relieved to have someone to talk to who understood their commitment to the socialist system and shared a critical view of its course in Moscow. Long before Gorbachev, they were also confident that change could come from within.

Although both Philby and Blake were given posts in which they could use their knowledge, no one can pretend that life is easy for agents withdrawn after an active life in the West, particularly to a country struggling under as many contradictions as the Soviet Union. Philby was a more outgoing character than Blake, confident, suave, and relaxed in company. He too came several times to East Germany for holidays and enjoyed a long evening talking with old friends and comrades over a few drinks. But after a few years in Moscow, his view of the Soviet Union became more sober. He would complain to me bitterly about the miserable economy and the gap between the rulers and the people. It always amused me that the British think they are the first to have discovered such obvious truths as poor consumer goods and bureaucratic mix-ups. Philby did not have much opportunity in Moscow for conversation with cultured people, but I do not agree with Western accounts that he was miserable in Moscow. The truth is that he had no other option, but Philby was able to manage better than other spies.

I got the impression that the KGB arranged holidays to countries like East Germany and Hungary, where the standard of living was much higher than at home, as a way for people like Philby and Blake to let off steam. The KGB lived in fear that their prize Westerners would go back home and deal a propaganda blow to the Kremlin, and such escapes were not particularly difficult. Philby told me that the British secret service in Moscow found ways of making several offers for him to return.

Philby loved the East German countryside and when he visited we talked about many things—books, ideas, even cooking; we made Pelmeni dumplings together so we could compare our versions of this dish, with its highly individualistic combination of ingredients. After one visit he presented me a copy of his memoirs with the dedication: "To Comrade Col.-General Wolf, With high esteem and great gratitude for a wonderful reception in the DDR, Kim Philby." It was a West German edition of the book and he added as a postscript: "The FRG [Federal Republic of Germany] translation leaves much to be desired. K.P." Perhaps he thought it only polite to knock West Germany when making a present to the head of East German foreign intelligence. At any rate, this codicil amused me in its indication of Philby's pedantic concern for accuracy.

Philby and Blake rank among the tragic figures in the history of intelligence services. Their professional achievements were great, whatever one might think of their politics. The peculiar sadness of Blake's fate is that he lost his homeland not just once, when he fled England, but twice, when the Soviet Union collapsed and he was left to live out a withdrawn life in an adopted homeland that had abandoned his cause. Philby, who had participated in many of the century's great events, starting with the Spanish Civil War, was perhaps the more fortunate to have died in time. It never bothered me that Philby was a traitor to his country, because what he did, he did out of conviction. He was convinced from the start that the Soviet Union was the country that best represented his antifascist ideals. If you have conviction in life, you follow the road you have set for yourself and do not deviate from it—no matter what terrible things you may see along the way. Of course, each person's path and priorities vary. There were people like Arthur Koestler, who set out espousing the Communist ideals of justice and equity and then turned away from them because of Soviet excesses. That also happened to my old friend Wolfgang Leonhard. I once found it difficult to understand them, but I speak to Leonhard and I think we understand each other now.

●

With the regularization of the rules of the Cold War, spies also appeared less like agents of the devil on the other side and more like pieces—often pawns—in the game between East and West. They were more likely to be held by the rival intelligence services after capture than to be shot, although at times executions did take place, very often when a politician wanted to send a message either to his own people or to the other side. This change made me realize that exchanges could become an important part of our intelligence arsenal. I started to look more systematically among those held by our side for possible exchanges with our agents held in the West.

In Germany, this practice became formalized through the services of Wolfgang Vogel, the East Berlin lawyer who represented the GDR's interests internationally, and Jürgen Stange, his West German counterpart. As the years passed, it became easier to arrange exchanges across the Iron Curtain, even when a long sentence was involved. Vogel made a small fortune providing the links between enemy powers.

The first important international East-West swap involved Francis Gary Powers, the U.S. spy-plane pilot who was shot down in 1960 over the Soviet Union. It caused great political embarrassment to President Eisenhower, and the mishandling of the affair ruined his summit with Khrushchev in Paris. I had the eerie experience of watching Powers's trial in the ornate Hall of the Trade Unions in Moscow, where Stalin's show trials had taken place in the thirties. I was in town on unrelated business and decided to go along. I sat on a hard bench underneath the deceptively tranquil pastel ceiling, decked with glittering chandeliers more suited to a ballroom than a courtroom.

This was the first time since Stalin's death that a spy trial had been held so openly, and talk of the Powers trial dominated that summer in Moscow. Ordinary Muscovites hovered around the courthouse, curious for a glimpse of the American who had fallen out of the Soviet skies. My KGB colleagues whispered that the general secretary himself intended to confirm the verdict and sentence.

Powers appeared in the dock, a little confused by the judicial instructions he was receiving in Russian. He had a soft, boyish face and the habit of wrinkling his brow deeply when he did not understand a question. His pleasant and somewhat naïve manner awakened in me a twinge of sympathy, even though he was working for the other side. Through a stone-faced interpreter, he responded readily and at length to the prosecution's questions, confirming the nature of his mission and who he was working for. "You fool," I whispered under my breath.

As it turned out, Powers's naïveté and cooperation with the Soviets were the very thing the superpowers needed to facilitate their first major spy exchange. Powers was sentenced to only ten years in jail, and my KGB friends explained that this relatively lenient sentence was a signal to Washington that Moscow was ready to go ahead with a spy swap.

On the other side of the Atlantic, KGB colonel Rudolf Ivanovich Abel was in a federal penitentiary in Atlanta. The son of a St. Petersburg worker of German ancestry who had embraced bolshevism enthusiastically and met Lenin on several occasions, Abel (whose real name was William Fischer) had been surreptitiously settled in America by the KGB in 1947, where he assumed the guise of a photographer and painter named Emil Goldfus. From his studio in Brooklyn he ran a string of agents dealing in government, trade, and military secrets before being arrested in 1956 and sentenced the following year to thirty years in prison. Vogel was instrumental in arranging the swap of Powers for Abel on February 10, 1962.

Several years later, Abel came to East Berlin to brief my service about his experience. The KGB had given him the title of general and placed him in charge of their Anglo-American network. He also addressed my recruits, and I arranged several gatherings with my senior officers in his honor. He could be a convivial man, given the right company, and after toasting each other's espionage successes, we turned to discussing the theater of the twenties and thirties, and even my father's plays. Abel was a modern-day Renaissance man with a lively interest in chemistry and physics and a particular enthusiasm for Albert Einstein. His paintings—which he had used in Brooklyn as a front for his espionage work—were rather good. I still possess a few small drawings he left me as souvenirs. After his death in 1971, his widow had to lobby the Soviets hard to allow his real name to be placed on his gravestone underneath his KGB name. They could not lose the habit of keeping secrets, even when one of their prize agents was dead and buried.

Another sign of the virulent routine of the Cold War emerged after the angry summit meeting between Khrushchev and President John Kennedy in Vienna in 1961. The full seriousness of their quarrel became evident to me when Khrushchev returned home to address his military and highlighted the importance of West Berlin. From two of our sources—one in the British military command in Berlin and another at NATO headquarters—we learned about hectic American preparations for countermeasures in case Moscow ordered a second Berlin blockade. As I leafed through the classified documents that had been reassembled like an elaborate jigsaw puzzle from bundles of microfilm, I realized that just one unwise step on either side could lead to war. And it would start here, in Berlin.

A top secret American organization called Live Oak had been set up in 1958 by the then secretary of state, John Foster Dulles, and placed initially under General Lauris Norstad, the NATO commander, for the express purpose of countering a new Berlin blockade. One day I was brought a transcription, signed by Norstad, of the key parts of the "Initial Probe of Soviet Intentions." This document, which I obtained through a source in the British military headquarters in Germany, remains classified in the United States as of this writing almost forty years later. If the low-level harassment of military vehicles traveling along the hundred-mile corridor between Berlin and West Germany were to escalate, the Live Oak plan proposed dispatching a military convoy to insist on Western access to Berlin and test the Soviet reaction. The document went on to propose more extensive military options. First a battalion of U.S., British, and French troops would probe the corridor. This would culminate in the ultimate level of force, a division made up of three countries' troops moving down the corridor to assert the West's rights to access to the city. Only U.S., British, and French troops would be involved, since they were the only ones with the right to send troops through East Germany to their occupation zones in the Western sector of Berlin.

I am not prone to panic, but Live Oak chilled me to the core. Sources in Moscow told me Khrushchev was talking endlessly about Berlin. He had even told the U.S. ambassador Llewellyn Thompson that resolving the Berlin question was a matter of his "own prestige" and that he had "waited long enough" to make a move. Knowing Khrushchev's stubborn pride intensified my fears. Great powers have gone to war often enough to protect the fragile prestige of their leaders.

What I did not know at the time was that there was strong opposition to Live Oak within NATO itself. Many years later the CIA declassified documents reporting that Britain's chief of defense staff, Admiral Lord Mountbatten, had hectored Kennedy about the plan:

What would happen to a battalion on the Autobahn? The Russians would blow up a bridge in front, a bridge behind, and then sell seats for people to come and laugh. If that's a farce, a division would be a tragedy. It would need a front of thirty miles to keep moving and it would be seen as an invasion of East Germany and lead to all-out war.

I was relieved to hear that Britain's old warhorse showed a shred of common sense about the adventurism of Live Oak. The Live Oak staff was not acknowledged by NATO until 1987, when they were allowed to wear a SHAPE (Supreme Headquarters, Allied Powers Europe) badge on their uniforms, like other NATO staff. The organization was not actually dissolved until after German unification. Thankfully, its importance in U.S. strategic thinking decreased after Khrushchev decided that he did not want to risk war over what was essentially a German problem. Instead, he looked for a different solution, and it turned out to be one cast in concrete.

7

A Concrete Solution

When the Cold War is recalled as just one of the clashes of great empires, and the German Democratic Republic has become a footnote in the history books, my country will perhaps be remembered as the one that built a wall to keep its own people from running away. The image of the Berlin Wall dividing not only a great city but the two ideologies and military blocs that competed for the future of mankind remains the most powerful symbol of the postwar division of Europe and indeed of the brutality and absurdity of the Cold War itself.

For me, one who lived and worked behind the Wall after it was erected in August 13, 1961, and devoted my efforts to the security and advancement of the system that built it, the Wall was always an expression of both strength and weakness. Only a system with our confidence in its founding ideology could have managed to divide a metropolis and draw a closed border between two parts of one country. And only a system as vulnerable and fundamentally flawed as ours was would have needed to do so in the first place.

Thus I knew in my heart of hearts that the GDR was doomed when, on the night of November 9, 1989, I switched on my television to learn that the GDR's citizens had been declared free to travel beyond the country's borders and saw the first crowds streaming through the suddenly opened border. A country as dependent as ours was for its very existence on internal stability could not survive the impact of this. It was as if reality had been suspended. Dazed, I sat with my wife watching pictures of East and West Germans embracing each other in the no-man's-land of the Berlin border. Some were still in their carpet slippers, as if sleepwalking into a night that would determine the fate of Germany and Europe for years to come.

Of course the border had never been entirely closed. It was open to East German travelers on official business, who first had to be vetted and found fit as "travel cadres." This meant that they were politically reliable, had no close relatives in West Germany, and were not privy to any sensitive information about East Germany. Since the relaxation of restrictions in the 1970s, when relations between the Germanys had improved, pensioners were allowed to travel on the logical—indeed cynical—ground that if they stayed in the West, it would not damage the Eastern economy and would even save the state the payment of their pensions. And naturally, my agents in the field and the couriers who took messages to our sources were allowed to travel to the West, armed with false identities.

People who could leave the country were greatly envied by the population at large; travel fever was acute in this country of nontravelers. I had traveled less widely for pleasure than most middle-class American college students, which is something that Western commentators tend to forget when they talk about the lives of the members of the nomenklatura. For all my privileges, I had never visited the Prado, the British Museum, or the Louvre. All of us led lives that were narrow, though mine was less so because the espionage business took me to Eastern Africa, the wilds of Siberia, the shores of the Black Sea, the forests of Sweden, and the softness of the subtropics in Cuba. I was privileged to have a fine apartment, a car and driver, and pleasant holidays at the invitation of other secret services in the Eastern bloc. But these were always connected to my job and status; in the end, the wider world was sealed off to me, too.

Even though we did not enjoy the ease and independence of even the modestly wealthy citizen in the West, I was well insulated from the hardships afflicting ordinary people in my country. From the Soviets we had inherited the system of nomenklatura privileges. It started in

1945, when functionaries, scientists, and others useful to the Communist cause received extra amounts of goods in short supply, which we called *payoks*, from the Russian word for rations. After that it took hold as a habit, as such things do, and became institutionalized in a department called "personal security," which of course grew to have a staff of five thousand. Our privileges eventually became formalized in a system of connections through the Foreign Trade Ministry, ensuring that the top servants of the state were not confined to the often second-rate products of their own country. It was all strictly hierarchical. Special shops stocking Western goods were available to the politburo. After they had taken their pick the rest was passed on to us in the intelligence services, whereupon the other ministries and trade departments then got their share. It was very simple and made for a comfortable life. I was too weak to say no to these privileges, and years later I admitted this to students who asked. They were satisfied with the answer, because they understood the human predicament presented by such privilege. Of course, if I had fallen from grace, the perks would have disappeared overnight.

But aside from these perks and my rather unusual ports of call, I lived the life of a bureaucrat, the servant of my political masters. At first we worked at night—Stalin's hours—just like the upper levels of the Soviet bureaucracy. After Stalin's death Mielke worked long days starting at 7 A.M. and often lasting until 10 P.M., although later I think he tried to look like he was in his office when he was not. I often envied the autonomy of those working in my service. They could roam on special missions and make their own hours, but my working day was tied to my superiors' schedules.

I woke up about 6:30 or 7 A.M., jogged, and did exercises for my back—it has given me trouble since my youth—and got to the office at about 8:15 A.M. I had a driver and a secretary at first, and later two secretaries and a personal assistant, known as *referent* in German. The members of my private office were very close and the personnel rarely changed; my principal secretary began with me in 1954, my third year as chief of the HVA, and remained thirty-three years, until my retirement.

I began my day looking over important papers, reports from section chiefs, and sometimes reports from agents. In the last ten years the paper flow became too heavy and I depended on a summary prepared by the analysis department, composed of secret material, a digest of current events, and material from news agencies.

The HVA was divided into about twenty departments, including separate groups to oversee agents and information in West German ministries, political parties, unions, churches, and other institutions; military espionage; the United States, Mexico, and the rest of the world; NATO and European Community headquarters in Brussels; counterintelligence; disinformation; scientific and economic information from West Germany; technological espionage departments specializing in basic industries, electronics and scientific instruments, and aeronautics and aerospace; embassies; frontiers; training and translation; and a department to analyze and evaluate the raw information flowing in from all the others.

Four or five days a week I would confer with my deputies and with each of those department heads under my personal control on the progress of their work and important projects. I had to read every report that was sent up to the leadership. Mielke did not edit my reports but kept some from Honecker, saying, "They won't be too happy to read this." I usually lunched with my deputies and the secretary of the Party together in the courtyard of the ministry's office in the Normannenstrasse in the Lichtenberg district. We exchanged information and swapped stories, but even within the closest confines of the ministry we always referred to our agents and even the "legal" residents in our embassies by their code names, lest their real identities leak, thus putting them at even greater risk.

Vast stretches of this work were very boring. Intelligence is essentially a banal trade of sifting through huge amounts of random information in a search for a single enlightening gem or illuminating link, so I varied my routine by insisting on running ten or twelve agents personally. As far as I know I was the only chief of any of the world's principal intelligence agencies to do so. This gave me the opportunity to get out and meet them from time to time in safe houses in the Berlin suburbs or—what I preferred—in Dresden and other places where there were fewer Westerners for visiting agents to encounter.

This routine was of course broken by unexpected events, especially arrests of our agents abroad. Usually our first news came from the media, which did not always get a spy's name right, so we would have to figure out whether it was our spy or someone else's. Sometimes I would find the head of a department waiting with the bad news, especially if it was a defection. We trained ourselves to go over each loss step by step and tried never to panic among ourselves; there would be panic enough when the minister asked for an explanation.

Rather than placing blame, it was far more important to find or figure out who else might be endangered by an arrest or defection. We would radio quick warnings to agents in code, but since agents could not always tune in every day, we might find it necessary to phone their homes directly with a coded warning. If, for example, our agent was a businessman, the flash warning might be something like "Our next meeting must be postponed." We avoided obvious tip-offs like "Your aunt in Dresden is very ill." We did have certain signals, such as a nail in a tree or a cross on a mailbox an agent passed every day that he could check, but this was not the case for every agent.

During my last ten years on the job I usually worked until about 9 P.M., six days a week, with only Sunday as a full day off. I had very little social life, although I tried to attend a play or a concert at least twice a month. Exchange visits to intelligence services in friendly countries, or visits to Berlin by their delegations, provided rare and welcome opportunities for visits to museums and the theater. On weekends I tried to get to my dacha in the small village of Prenden, twenty miles northeast of Berlin, and there I did all I could to protect my civilian life from official intrusion. When my boyhood friends from Moscow, George and Louis Fischer, visited Berlin in 1985, they were surprised to find that I had no bodyguards shadowing me in the country and moved with ease and freedom. Mielke did have a bodyguard and once ordered me to get one, but I managed to get rid of him. My driver took special training to protect me but never bothered to carry his pistol. I left mine in my safe.

Whatever my doubts about the system I served, such a life of privilege, responsibility, and occasional fascination would be hard for anyone to give up to campaign for change, especially someone who, like me, believed change could only come from the top down. This may sound strange from a man in my position of supposed influence, but my influence was limited to my own service, where I had my own space.

Günter Gaus, the first West German ambassador to East Germany, a highly intelligent man with a great understanding of our problems,

used to call the GDR a community of niches. A large part of our population turned away from the problems of public life, ignored questions of official policy, assiduously followed private pursuits, and
defended their private space. I also had my niche, and, as paradoxical
as it may sound, that niche was my service. I could not change.

This description of our lives might give rise to the impression that I
led the deplorable life of an apparatchik, doing my work only so that I
could enjoy special and rare privileges. Not so. My work at the top of
the intelligence service satisfied me. I was convinced of its necessity,
and I was deeply committed to it. I deliberately and successfully
dodged opportunities to move into higher positions closer to the centers of political power. I also refused an offer of promotion to media
chief, a job that would have put me in charge of propaganda. Even my
children urged me to refuse this promotion, since it would have put
me too close to the political leadership and would inevitably have
caused conflicts.

●

In the days before the Berlin Wall was raised on August 13, 1961, it
was clear to me that some sort of drastic action was imminent. The
mood in the eastern part of the city was grim. Labor and goods shortages mounted weekly. Passing a line outside a shop one day, I heard an
old woman cursing in the broad Berlin dialect, "They can launch the
Sputnik, but you can't get a green vegetable in the middle of summer.
That's socialism for you."

Who could blame young people if they chose to put their talents to
work across the border, where they could earn money and buy goods
those back home could only dream of? In their minds, they were not
betraying a state, they were simply moving to another part of Germany where most of them had friends or relatives prepared to help
them make a start.

Since the founding of East Germany in 1949, 2.7 million people
had fled to the West, half of them under twenty-five. I could not help
wondering whether the youngsters in my own family would have also
gone if they had not been part of a committed socialist clan. On
August 9, 1961, the number of refugees recorded in the reception

camps of West Berlin was 1,926, the highest ever in a single day. The state was hemorrhaging its workforce, losing people who had cost money to train and without whose contribution living standards would sink further. I felt that we were swimming through mud.

The official accusation on our side was that the West was bleeding the East dry. Stripped of its rhetorical pathos, I knew this meant that West Germany's attraction was rising with its new prosperity and that people were prepared to sacrifice their family links and the cosseted security under state socialism for the uncertain promises of capitalism. Of course the official explanation for the Wall was never in the least credible for me—that our borders had been closed as a protective measure against imminent aggression or penetration by foreign agents. But with the building of what in the East was officially called "the antifascist protective barrier" and in the West was labeled "the wall of shame," all of our lives were changed overnight.

I not only understood the real reasons for the Wall but formally supported them. I believed there was no other way to save our country at that time. We had inherited the historically economically weak part of Germany and thus started from a lower base, even without the mismanagement that compounded our difficulties. In addition, East Germany had been stripped by Soviet forces of industrial machinery and even infrastructure items such as railroad track, which they viewed as reparations. West Germany, by contrast, was able to build up its part of the country with Marshall Plan money. I held to the illusion—as I now realize it was—that with changes in the international situation and sensible domestic reforms, our standard of living would step by step catch up with the West's. I believed that the validity of socialism, of a planned economy, would assert itself and, as we said among ourselves at the time, the day would come when the West would take over the Wall to keep people out! Indeed, in the late 1970s and the 1980s, some of our agents and sympathizers in the West asked whether we really needed to restrict travel because living standards had improved to the point where most people who traveled from the GDR would return. But in 1961, it was a choice between the Wall or surrender.

At the risk of damaging my reputation as the man who really knew what was going on in East Germany, I have to confess that the building of the Berlin Wall was as much a surprise to me as everyone else in

August 1961. I can only conclude that Erich Mielke, who handled some of the covert planning of the operation, kept this information from me out of malice. Like millions of others, I heard the news that a wall was being built across Berlin on the radio on the morning of August 13. My first reaction was one of pure professional fury. I should of course have been told of this in advance, since I had to continue running agents across the border, the nature of which had radically changed overnight. So secret had the building plans been that we could not coordinate with the head of the border troops in advance to ensure that our couriers could continue traveling West to collect secret material from our agents across what became without warning an impenetrable frontier.

I spent most of my time during the following days ensuring that our men were given hastily drawn papers passing them through the control points to the West to make their assignations on time. This was more than a matter of convenience. Espionage relationships are based on absolute reliability. Once the links break down, vulnerable agents are frightened and the machinery of intelligence gathering grinds to a halt.

We now had to devise cover stories for our couriers to give a plausible explanation to the guards on the other side as to why they had the right to cross to the West when the rest of their countrymen did not. To the Western services, the sealed border was an unexpected boon because it filtered out large numbers of ordinary people and allowed allied counterintelligence to concentrate its resources on the much smaller number of citizens now allowed to cross, usually on some form of state business, such as trade officials, approved academics, and ordinary citizens occasionally given permission to cross on urgent family business.

As I traveled around East Berlin in my official car, I would find myself diverting the driver so I could look at the building work with a mixture of fascination and horror. My own close family were all in the East, so I did not experience the personal trauma of separation. But the Wall produced countless bizarre incidents, one of which touched me as my father's son.

On one stretch of the River Spree a fleet of pleasure boats operated from Treptow Park, sailing only as far as the border with the Neukölln section of West Berlin before returning obediently to their moorings in the East. The boats were named after German socialist writers, among them my father. One day, just after the Wall was built, the good ship *Friedrich Wolf* merrily sailed west in one of the more unusual escape stories of that era. During an evening outing, the ship's cook and his family got the captain drunk and persuaded him to sail full steam ahead past the amazed guards into West Berlin. There they jumped ship and waded to the bank and freedom. The captain collapsed into a drunken stupor on deck. When he sobered up, he shamefacedly sailed home, to the even greater surprise of the border guards, where he faced stern disciplinary proceedings. My mother, who ran the Friedrich Wolf Archive, was then telephoned by the distraught spouse of the ship's captain, begging for help.

"Can't you do something?" my mother asked me over dinner that night. I knew that my father would have viewed the adventures of his boat with his eye for comedy, so I pleaded for clemency for the poor captain. He was spared a prison sentence, but I could not rescue him from the humiliation of a transfer outside Berlin. He ended up working on a grimy steamer in an industrial area that was a safe distance away from any border.

The altered situation also increased tension between my own foreign intelligence (*Aufklärung*) service and the counterintelligence (*Abwehr*) department, which was in charge of border security. Relations between these two branches of an espionage service are never warm, as anyone who has followed the history of infighting between the CIA and the FBI will know. In our case, by now they were very frosty indeed. I refused to hand over a list identifying our agents and other informants who needed to cross the border, since this would have made us vulnerable to betrayal from officers in departments over which I had no control.

It took weeks—months in some particularly difficult cases—until we could reach a new modus vivendi. We found ourselves in the paradoxical situation in which the controls imposed by our own side were far more draconian and difficult to negotiate than those of the West Germans. One case that presented me with a headache was that of Freddy (not his real name), our most important informant inside the Social Democratic leadership in West Berlin. I do not name him here only to spare his family, but Social Democrats of that era will certainly recognize him. A figure larger than life and a bon vivant, he was a loud and persuasive voice in the Social Democratic Party's (SPD's) executive and had good connections to Bonn—a king maker rather than a king, but not less useful to us for that. He had returned long after the end of the war from American captivity, which held bad memories for him. A Party member in his youth, he had been drawn into its intelligence network. In fact, he had been infiltrated into the SPD in 1950 on the orders of one of our veteran handlers, Paul Laufer, who would later run Günter Guillaume, the spy in Chancellor Willy Brandt's office.

Freddy took to the Social Democratic cause with gusto and, disillusioned by events in the East, stopped regarding the Communist cause as his own. For a while it seemed that we had lost him. But we were persistent with people we wanted to keep. I took on his case myself in an attempt to obtain the high-quality information I knew he possessed about the SPD's internal wrangling over its policy toward East Germany. Nevertheless, he categorically refused to speak into a tape recorder or tell us anything about his colleagues in the Eastern Bureau of the SPD, the organization in West Berlin that worked to restore social democracy to the East—in our eyes one of the most treacherous institutions operating on the other side of the Wall. Attempts to inveigle him into political discussions almost always ended in terrific rows, with Freddy damning Ulbricht as a Stalinist idiot.

At first Freddy and I would meet in a small apartment that served as a safe house for our service in the Bohnsdorf district in the southern part of East Berlin. But the atmosphere was strained and in 1955 I hit on the idea of changing the meeting place to a small, informal country house belonging to acquaintances from my Moscow days. I used the optimism engendered by the Twentieth Party Congress to adjust our relationship. Freddy was impressed by Khrushchev's rejection of Stalin and his crimes. "You see," he would say triumphantly, "I was right. I told you things had to change." I would share my own enthusiasm for Moscow's "New Course" with him—we now were free to speak about the past and to discuss problems in the party, cultural freedom, the economy, etc.— and we would sit for hours in a tiny smoke-filled room debating the future of the Soviet Union and its allies. At last I was getting somewhere. It was clear to me that Freddy would only tolerate his role as informant if our relationship was based on friendship. He was also not averse to an occasional drinking spree, so just before his fiftieth birthday, I invited him to meet me in a small villa at Rauchfangswerder by a lake, the one we had used in the disastrous *malina* escapade. Here, hidden from prying eyes, we sat on a summer afternoon quaffing ice-cold sparkling wine and, as the evening wore on, a case of beer. I had to drink hard to keep up with my new friend and had warned my assistant, who was responsible for getting us there and back and making sure we were undisturbed, to stay as sober as a judge so that when we brought Freddy back to the West at least one of us would have his wits about him.

By now Freddy was unstoppable, pouring out grievances about the Americanization of the Federal Republic and heaping scorn on the politics and personal life of the rising political star of West Berlin, Willy Brandt. Just before midnight we headed back to the city. I had the driver park the car some distance away and the two of us swayed unsteadily through the silent Treptow Park toward the border crossing. We had just got within earshot of the border guards when Freddy burst into revolutionary songs, roaring out "When We Were Striding Side by Side" and "The Internationale." I sobered up at once, told Freddy in rather uncomradely terms to shut up, and diverted the driver to the next crossing point, where we dropped him off. Warning him to keep his head down and say the very minimum demanded at the border, I stood back in the shadows to watch him cross.

My heart was in my mouth, since he had reached that uninhibited stage of drunkenness marked by a complete disregard for the consequences of what one says or does. My greatest fear was that one of the policemen on the Western side would recognize him as a local celebrity and note that he was crossing blind drunk in the middle of the night—enough of a scandal to end his career even if espionage was never suspected. The tottering figure made its way to the control post. At the last moment, he turned around, waved his arms triumphantly, and shouted in my direction, "We'll drink a thousand more glasses together, you and I!"

I swore under my breath, but there was nothing more I could do. In the days that followed, I scanned the newspapers anxiously in search of any repercussions. But the drunk have the devil's luck, and Freddy's reputation remained intact.

It was always more risky for public figures to attend meetings in the East via the official crossing points. Eventually Freddy gradually revised his opinion of Brandt and became a close associate of the young mayor. He no longer could risk coming to us openly, drunk or sober. We were forced to think of a new solution and resorted to a minutely planned and operationally complex setting for our exchanges of views: the allied transit route that led through East German territory to Berlin.

We assumed that the road was extremely well monitored by West German counterintelligence, just as it was by our side. Both sets of law enforcement officers registered the time each car entered the route and the time it emerged, either in West Berlin or at the West German border. There was also a strict speed limit of 100 kilometers an hour, so the appropriate time for covering the route could be calculated almost exactly, and there was no possibility of stopping for anything but the briefest transfer of material.

Moreover, our own traffic police monitored the rest stops and the route's winding sections on surveillance cameras. I was very unenthusiastic about letting counterintelligence in on the details of my work, so I decided to avoid the formality of asking them to suspend observation while I met my agent. Instead, with Freddy's agreement, we designed a much more exciting and comfortable way to keep in touch. I approached this with some trepidation, but no matter how senior, a spy is always an adventurer, and I still relished rolling up my sleeves and taking an occasional risk myself. We agreed that Freddy would leave West Berlin in the late afternoon so that the light would be fading by the time our meeting took place. He scheduled the trip to coincide with party business in Bonn, which was a plausible cover.

Just before he set off from West Berlin, I left the East in a dark blue Mercedes with a Cologne license plate and a driver with false Western papers. Since no one in the West knew what I looked like, I did not bother with a disguise and simply wore the typical clothes of a businessman. At the first service station outside the city boundaries on the Berlin-Munich transit route, I had my driver stop to fill the tank and have a cup of thin East German coffee in the service station. I sat there waiting until I saw Freddy's car pass.

This proved highly entertaining. The East German truck drivers—taking me for a Westerner after I offered them Western cigarettes—would start bellyaching about the situation in East Germany. It was a rare opportunity to hear what ordinary people were really thinking from my perch high on the ladder of East German seniority. If they had known they were complaining directly to a top Stasi officer, they would have been horrified. I remember one trucker cursing the privileges of the East German elite after I had spun a story about being a successful traveling salesman from the Ruhr. "Those apparatchiks of ours probably live as well as you do," he said "The difference is, you achieve something and they don't." The real Markus Wolf was a bit nettled by this judgment, but I simply nodded in agreement.

As soon as Freddy passed the rest stop at his statutory 100 kilometers an hour, we whipped out a special sign allowing me as one of the high officials my trucker friends had just been berating to drive faster than the speed limit. We roared off at around 150 kilometers an hour, the time and distance calculated so that as we pulled even with Freddy's car, we were approaching one of the exits from the Autobahn reserved for forestry trucks and the police. Then we shot off into the woods, out of sight of the surveillance cameras and other drivers. Silently and as fast as his bulky frame could carry him, Freddy slipped into my car and my driver into his. Both cars then set off, leaving the hidden exit with headlights off so as not to show up on the cameras or to any patrols flying overhead. There was a moment of exhilaration when we both realized we had completed this delicate maneuver successfully. "This is far more interesting than politics," said Freddy wistfully.

My permission to speed gained us enough time for a conversation. As we sped along the Autobahn, we chatted comfortably, and Freddy handed me some material. It also gave me a chance to give him instructions in absolute privacy. Just before the exit, we would stop at another parking place under cover of darkness and wait for Freddy's car (with my driver) to catch up. Freddy would get into his own vehicle again. The trouble with this ruse was that we were not the only ones to have discovered it. As time went by, the Western services also started to use it, and so did the dozens of organizations that began helping East Germans escape in the trunks of cars. The illegal exits and service stations became the focus of renewed interest by our own counterintelligence. They started to draw the net tighter and tighter, and I feared that one day my own watchful counterespionage colleagues would discover one of my meetings. I had to revise my earlier decision and request that the observation monitors be switched off for assignations with foreign agents by myself or my officers.

This worked for a while, but I then feared that West German intelligence had discovered a way of checking on us, so that if the monitors were switched off for ten minutes or more, it became obvious that some suspicious operation was under way and border controls could be tightened at the other end. In time I reverted to the old ways and chanced the operation without taking the risk of tipping off counterintelligence. I was so nimble and exact that I was never caught by either side. The method worked not only for Freddy but also for a good political informant from Bonn, a liberal politician named William Borm, who provided information on the Bonn parliament.

Freddy died a few years later, his heart failing a couple of days after one of our Autobahn assignations. I suppose his constitution could not keep up with his intensively busy political life, his lordly drinking and eating, and the extra strain of covert work with us. But after the sticky early period, he never showed any regrets. He had become hooked on the excitement and the feeling that he was exerting special influence. As honorable employers, we always put aside a pension for the wives of agents, even if, as in Freddy's case, she had not been told about his work. Now we were in the embarrassing position of having to send an officer to tell her that she was entitled to money because her husband had worked for the East. I don't know if she ever suspected him, but she took the news very calmly. One thing my job taught me is that women know far more about their husbands than the men think they know.

Even after the Wall was built, some stretches of the border in the countryside remained permeable for a while. I took the opportunity to push scientific and technical agents, even some who were not fully trained, into the Federal Republic, but we had to become increasingly clever in faking identities. The Western authorities began to demand more proof of identity and biographical details. The use of computers also made it easier for them to check information against other files held abroad or by different authorities.

But as fast as the West Germans worked out ways of checking against infiltrators, we developed new ways to bamboozle them. It was a marvelous and exhilarating race. We had the advantage of being able, for example, to use the identities of people killed in the Dresden bombings as covers for the agents we settled in the West, but there was always the chance that an unexpected survivor might turn up and blow an agent's cover. This happened increasingly often as the West German counterintelligence's computer net was widened and deepened, so that we eventually halted this macabre maneuver.

But I also had a lot of trouble with our own people seeking to centralize records. Erich Mielke, my superior as minister of state security, was desperate to have me provide a central index of agents. I refused point-blank. The tug of war over this persisted to the day I left office. I was proud to say that under my tenure nowhere in my directorate did there exist a single record of all our spies. I was determined that no card index or computer disc should ever hold all our operational details. Instead I developed a process through which the identity of a source could be determined only if three to five key details were already available. Before a search could continue, each detail had to be checked blind against the other. We did have information cards on perhaps hundreds of thousands of individuals, including many names in the West, ranging from Bundestag members to industrial leaders to members of the Allied Control Commission. Separate card registers for our own people were kept in each department; a department would handle at most sixty to a hundred sources, agents, couriers, etc. Each card carried a code name, address, territory, and file number. The number referred to a dossier containing real information on the individual spy. The small stack of cards in each department was usually kept in the custody of a trusted senior officer. Anyone seeking a dossier would have to justify his request to this officer, and if the dossier did cover a spy, the handler had a cover story ready. In war or times of high tension, the officer's job would have been to remove a spy's file from the ministry to our temporary headquarters.

Any unauthorized person going through the cards and files would have had to physically trawl through a massive quantity of paper in search of a match. Such a conspicuous operation to match the code name of an agent with his real one would inevitably attract attention, quite the opposite of what would have happened if even these separate files had been on computer discs. The ungainliness of the operation troubled me little because I and my senior officers kept the names of most important agents in our heads. Ever since I first used the model of the spider's web to identify connections between existing spy networks in Germany after the war, I had found it perfectly easy simply to slot new names into my head. I rarely had to remind myself of the real identity of an agent or his field of operation. In its own way, this decentralization increased our security. When we did have treachery in our own ranks, the absconding officer only knew about the cases he handled himself or the rumors he had picked up from loose talk—which, however fiercely discouraged, always goes on in a large organization.

In the 1950s we were able to draw quite heavily on the aristocratic families of West Germany. Some felt that they had to assuage the guilt of their class for failing to stop Hitler's rise to power. Others found themselves without a role and were even barred from using their titles in the new Federal Republic. Many were alienated by Chancellor Adenauer's antinational, pro-American stance. They still had a strong desire to be involved in affairs of state, and many seemed to look on their cooperation with us as a sort of secret diplomatic endeavor. I never met one who thought of himself as a traitor.

Nevertheless, some were betrayed by Max Heim, the head of our section responsible for work against West Germany's ruling Christian Democrats, a subdepartment of Department 2. He defected about two years before the Wall went up, revealed the state of our knowledge about the governing parties in Bonn, and then led West German counterintelligence to several of our agents.

Among them was Wolfram von Hanstein, who had used his prominent public position in the West to build up a variety of useful contacts. His father and grandfather were renowned academics and writers, and Hanstein wanted to follow in the family tradition of gentlemen scholars. Before the war he earned his living and a certain modest reputation writing historical novels. He refused to be drafted and spent the war underground, ending up in Soviet captivity, where he turned to communism. He settled in Dresden, devoting himself to the Communist cause. Before von Hanstein and his wife went West at our request, they deeded their Dresden villa and its grounds to the state, and it was passed to the Ministry of State Security. In Bonn, his humanistic outlook and family name helped propel him swiftly to the top of West Germany's main human rights lobby. He was friendly with

Heinrich Krone, Adenauer's special minister for security questions, and with Ernst Lemmer, the Christian Democratic minister who oversaw relations between the two German states. He also informed us prodigiously about the activities of the SPD's Eastern Bureau and infiltrated many other anti-Communist organizations. Even during his six-year jail sentence, he continued working diligently and made contact with three fellow prisoners who later worked for us. After his release, von Hanstein asked to come to East Germany, where he died in 1965.

Another agent betrayed by Heim was Baron von Epp. The descendent of a nobleman who had supported Hitler from the earliest days of the Nazi movement, von Epp sought to atone for his family's shame by working for us. When he was uncovered and imprisoned, I was sorry to see him go, although not altogether surprised. A wild card, the baron had approached our service declaring himself ready to undertake terrorist activities and was disappointed when we told him that we needed far more discreet and diligent help rooting out useful confidential material.

Before the 1969 elections, which gave the Social Democrats their best postwar result and paved their way to power, it was particularly important for us to follow the shifts in the Bonn landscape. At just the right time, there appeared one of the more eccentric agents I ever had the pleasure to meet, the tycoon Hannsheinz Porst. I have dealt with all sizes of intellects who were committed to the Communist cause for all sorts of reasons, noble and venal, but never have I come across such a compelling and even honest figure, in his own peculiar way. He was small and sporty, with the energetic manner of a young businessman. The first thing I had to get used to was the fact that during our conversations only one of his eyes looked at me; the other had been damaged on the very last day of the war, when a grenade exploded in his face.

Our connection to Porst came about through his cousin, a man called Karl Böhm. Both had grown up in Nuremberg, and during Porst's childhood Böhm had taken the role of older brother, confidant, and inspiration. Soon after the Nazis came to power, Böhm was arrested as a Communist and sentenced to six years in the Dachau concentration camp. The young Porst was unable to understand why his revered relative had been taken from him and waited eagerly for his return, despite the discreet warnings from his parents that people sometimes did not return from the camps.

When the sentence was over, Hannsheinz's father found work for Karl in his small photographer's studio. It was a brave step for an apolitical man, but he had a reputation as a hard worker who kept his nose clean. The photo business grew throughout the thirties, and by the time war broke out, Porst senior had built a business that thrived on taking pictures of handsome young men in uniform, often the last photo their wives and families would ever have.

Because of his Communist record, Böhm ended up in one of the fearsome Strafbataillons. To these the Nazis consigned soldiers deemed ideologically unreliable, treating them accordingly by assigning them suicidal missions. But Böhm survived the war. Porst spent his time as a frontline anti-aircraft officer. When they were reunited, they decided to build a publishing house together. Porst later told me, "Karl would tell me of his radical ideas for a new, peaceful society, and in the midst of the hypocrisy that followed 1945, I was so glad to listen to a man saying such things who had been prepared to face persecution for them, a man in whom theory and practice did not contradict each other."

After the war, Böhm continued to speak of communism openly and favorably, and as a result the U.S. authorities refused the cousins a business license. Incensed, Böhm fled East, leaving cousin Porst behind. He in turn went to work for his father and proved himself a talented young entrepreneur, presiding over the tenfold expansion of the company within a decade. With his share of the company profits he bought a printing press on the outskirts of Nuremberg, which ended up as one of the largest and most profitable in the new West Germany.

Böhm too made his way, albeit in a different world with different values, and became a success in East German publishing, which was controlled by the state through the Ministry of Culture. Böhm's job was director of the Office for Literature (Amt für Literatur). This office harbored what was called a legal residency of my foreign intelligence department, a small team of one or two officers operating out of the ministry's publishing division. Whether Böhm put them onto Porst or whether, as I heard at the time, the first contact was accidental, I do not know. At any rate, in the mid-1950s the two undercover agents got talking to the young entrepreneur at the Leipzig trade fair and found him sympathetic to the East's concerns about West German rearmament. An approach was made to Porst; he was asked to join Adenauer's Christian Democratic Union and inform on it for us.

This was a push too far for the independent-minded businessman. He arranged a meeting with his cousin and said he would be happy to help the East discover more about West German politics but would not be its puppet. As luck would have it, I dropped in on Böhm that summer in Karlsbad, the Czech spa where he was being treated for high blood pressure. "My cousin is very much his own man," Böhm told me. "He won't be taken for a ride or ordered about. But he wants to hold talks about the big political picture between the two Germanys. Why don't you take him on yourself?"

My first meeting with Porst was at Böhm's weekend house outside East Berlin. Porst did not bother to mute his criticisms of the GDR. When I tried to protest that many of our excesses were responses to threats from the West, he shook his head like a management consultant examining a badly run factory and told me our problems were mainly homemade, starting with the discourteous treatment of travelers at the border and ending with the bureaucracy and inefficiency that bedeviled our economy. "Look at those dreadful state shops," he spluttered. "If I ran them they could be as attractive and profitable as my own photo shops back home."

In those days I was still rather sensitive to such criticism, trapped in the mentality that dictated that one look on the bright side of all things socialist. I was nettled at having this catalogue of failure read out in such a businesslike fashion. But there were some points I had to concede, like the abysmal dullness and one-sidedness of our media.

Despite his warts-and-all understanding of the East, Porst believed that the socialist system there, particularly its welfare system and antifascist tradition, represented a worthy alternative to West German capitalism. A subtle indication of this political leaning was a formula he had developed for sharing ownership with his employees. Like many of our businessmen-agents, Porst was constantly in search of a way to indulge the more imaginative side of his nature. He could instantly switch from a tough analysis of his decision to introduce Japanese cameras and electronic goods to the German market—the strategy that had made him a millionaire—to indulging in romantic visions of a better, more just, and socialist Europe.

I was fascinated by the details of his work and keen to know more about the world of big capitalism, which we condemned but did not really understand. He on the other hand wanted to discuss Marxist theory. Perhaps there was a capitalist crying to get out of the socialist in me, and vice versa in him. At any rate, we formed a close association that went beyond the details of espionage.

He told me he that he could not face joining the Christian Democrats, disliking its militarist strain and Prussian values. They reminded him of the conservative Catholic prewar Center Party, which had proved ineffectual when faced with the threat of Hitler. Instead, he joined the Free Democrats, the natural political home of entrepreneurs. Using his close links via this postwar center party, he was able to sound out leading figures like Walter Scheel, who later became president of West Germany, and the Free Democratic Party leader, Erich Mende. Mende did not suspect Porst of being an agent but knew of his connections with the GDR. With some public figures, there was a fine line between ordinary discourse and cooperation with a foreign power.

When old man Adenauer was finally forced to resign in 1963, his successor, Ludwig Erhard, offered Mende a place in the cabinet. Mende, a die-hard liberal, was against bringing his small party into a coalition with a conservative government, but I realized that Mende was sympathetic to the idea of détente and persuaded Porst to convince his friend to join the government. Mende finally did so as minister for German affairs, in which post I regarded him as susceptible to our influence.

We would never have approached a minister with the clumsy request to become a formal source. But as long as he was chatting away with old friends and colleagues who reported to us, we did not need to. We even gave Mende a code name, Elk. Cases like this, where a public figure was code-named in a file containing his views, caused great confusion after the collapse of East Germany. It was assumed that a marked card in our filing system meant the subject had knowingly signed on with us. But there were many people we were content to run in the gray middle ground as sources without pushing them too hard, lest they be reminded of their loyalty to their own country and turn away from us.

When we decided to hunt around in Foreign Minister Hans-Dietrich Genscher's background for compromising material, we gave him the code name Tulip. He was terribly annoyed after 1989 to discover this. He had always been particularly circumspect in his contacts because he hailed from Halle, in the East, and knew enough of our methods to guess that we paid him close attention. Of course, we plumbed his past, read all mail between him and old friends and family in his native Halle, and kept an eye on him when he visited. Questions had been raised about Genscher's relationship with the Soviet authorities during his student days in Halle, and we investigated them thoroughly. I can state with confidence that Genscher had nothing to hide in his youthful past.

Soon after he had joined the Free Democrats on our behalf, Porst approached us with an unusual request. He wanted to become a member of our own Socialist Unity Party. This was a new one on me. I consulted comrades who knew their party statutes inside out. They said that strictly speaking, it was impossible for someone who was not an East German citizen to become a full member of the Party. Even the West Berlin branch of our Party was registered as a separate organization, the Socialist Unity Party of West Berlin.

But I objected that we could hardly deny Party membership to a man working for our cause in the West, and an exception was made. After two years as a candidate member, the time period young Communists had in which to prove themselves mature and responsible enough to be confirmed, our entrepreneur was received into the Party, the first and last millionaire in its ranks. We showed him his little red membership book, but it was kept in East Berlin, locked in a safe. He seemed a touch disappointed by this, but we never let any such documents out of our hands when the bearer was operating abroad. "You can't exactly carry it with you," I comforted him. "Imagine what would happen if you dropped your wallet and the police found out that the tycoon Hannsheinz Porst just happens to be an East German Communist!"

Porst's contacts in both the business and the political spheres were so important to us that we decided to send over a liaison officer to make it as easy as possible for him to pass his reports on to us. He certainly did not think of himself as a spy, and there was never a question of training him in conspiratorial methods. An officer code-named Optic was assigned to him under a false identity and a cover story that he had fled the East. Optic became the private tutor to Porst's children, which gave him an excuse to be in the household. But Optic was far more than a courier. He supplemented Porst's reports with his own contacts in Bonn as well as in the German Industrial Institute and the various entrepreneurs' associations. This grew until we had to appoint yet another resident agent, code-named Eisert, to back up Porst and Optic.

Our first fears for Porst came in the early sixties, when I discovered that he had shared the secret of his activities with his private secretary, Peter Neumann. I suspect that this mistake sprang from Porst's peculiar mixture of naïveté and arrogance. As a wealthy entrepreneur with thousands of employees, several villas, and a private plane at his disposal, he simply expected life to be made as comfortable as possible and his staff to be unfailingly loyal. But he was wrong.

For the time being, however, all was well. Porst and I would pass hours discussing ways to steer industry and inter-German trade to overcome the Bonn government's Hallstein doctrine, which denied recognition to any third country that recognized East Germany, forcing it to choose and thus dissuading all but the pro-Soviet countries from doing so. In a sense, our contacts with people like Porst allowed us a semblance of diplomatic contact with the West, albeit on a covert level.

Porst talked of founding a newsmagazine to promote détente between the two Germanys at a time when the West German media heavily opposed it. I was skeptical that an outsider could pull it off, but to my surprise, he managed to launch a TV and radio newspaper supplement called *RTV* as the foundation of a larger and more politically influential magazine.

Then, in 1967, disaster struck. Porst was betrayed by Neumann, and to our great shock the incriminating evidence was supported by none other than our man Optic, who presumably saved his own skin by informing on Porst.

In a statement after his arrest, Porst continued to maintain that his cooperation with my service had not amounted to treachery. His dramatic announcement said:

> It is true that I am a millionaire and a Marxist. I was at once a member of the Free Democratic [Liberal] Party of Germany and the Socialist Unity Party [Communist] of Germany. I gave the Free Democrats money for their campaigns at the same time that I paid my dues to the Socialist Unity Party.

I live here and held political discussions over there. Is that really such a contradiction?

I say: No.

Alas, the state prosecutor did not follow this logic, and the court sentenced him to two years and nine months in jail. Porst's composure never faltered throughout his trial. Asked to describe his contacts with me, he told the court:

> General Markus Johannes Wolf . . . could be friendly, while keeping his distance. He had no reservations about discussing ideas, even when these did not belong to the official repertoire. He is of the same vintage as myself, wears well-cut suits and is not without humor. I have to say that they weren't all like that.

For years, this kind description of me would appear in newspapers, accompanied by a picture of a suave-looking man who certainly was not me. I never did find out who he was, but I suppose since the West had no photo of me to use, they had to make do.

Today, of course, in the former East Germany the red neon signs of the Porst photo shop chain twinkle in the city centers just as they do in the rest of the country. So in the end my friend did get his wish to see the market work profitably and efficiently in the East. The sad and thankless thing about both of our lives is that to make that happen it took the collapse of a system that half of him and all of me believed in.

●

The closing of the border meant that the methods of my service became inevitably more complicated and, unfortunately, more expensive. Communication with sources, the transport of agents, preparation of new contacts—all required hard currency that was now more difficult to acquire. I also needed hard currency for technical assistance to agents, listening devices, high-frequency radio boosters, deciphering machines, and other equipment in which we were rapidly falling behind America and West Germany. Our best hope was to buy one piece of the latest equipment and try to copy it cheaply. Almost all such equipment was on the U.S.-managed list of goods forbidden for export to the Eastern bloc, so we had to find people to secure the equipment without its being traced. I also needed hard currency to pay agents in the West and entertain potential informants. I made a practice of not stinting on this. Westerners liked being courted by an espionage service, and the more lavish the welcome, the greater the chance they would feel flattered and respond positively. If one of my agents in West Germany had maneuvered himself close to a political, diplomatic, or business figure in Bonn and invited him for a drink or a meal, he wanted a restaurant with class—not too flashy or fashionable but the sort of good, solid place that suggests sound money and refined taste. The wine would have to be serious, too. Any well-placed Westerner thinking about offering secrets to us had to feel that he was dealing with a reliable, well-funded enterprise. I would never have dreamed of doing things on a shoestring like some of my Soviet counterparts, whose meanness with money was legendary and whose manners often revealed their limited horizons.

In the early days, obtaining hard currency to pay for these needs was done unsystematically. But as the service grew, so did our operations, and by the time the Wall was built, we needed more cash than our old methods of financing provided. It was because of this need for funds that I first got to know East Germany's financial wizard, Alexander Schalck-Golodkowski. Schalck, or Alex, as he was known, was a massive man with copious chins, a barrel chest, and a booming voice. I was introduced to him in the mid-1960s by my deputy, General Hans Fruck, who had been the chief of the vast East Berlin department of the Ministry of State Security. There he had dealt with two East German businessmen, Simon Goldenberg and Michael Wischnewski. Contrary to popular belief in the West, private entrepreneurs did exist in the East, but they occupied a shadowy position in society and their activities were carefully monitored by the state, so that in the end, most of them were under the control of the Ministry of State Security.

The GDR's need for hard currency was always far greater than the earnings of its modest exports. Goldenberg and Wischnewski made a deal in which the state shared their profits in return for allowing them the freedom to trade goods and stocks. Schalck cut this deal with them as an ambitious official in the Ministry for Inter-German and Foreign

Trade. The funds were transferred via Schalck to the Central Committee of the Socialist Unity Party and were used in part to finance some political groups in West Germany and other countries. But Schalck was too sharp an operator to stop there. From the late 1960s onward, when rapprochement between West and East Germany was just beginning, the leadership hived off this part of the foreign trade organization and created a new, covert organization, run by Schalck. Its goal was simple: to acquire, through almost any means necessary, hard currency for the GDR.

We needed a go-between who knew the Western stock market, its banking procedures and hidden rules, and Schalck was the perfect candidate. He had autonomy, but he was not in the end independent. The Western businessmen and leaders who dealt with him were unaware that Schalck was secretly a colonel in the Ministry of State Security, and that his real boss was Mielke. Schalck also reported directly to Erich Honecker, the party leader who succeeded Ulbricht, and Günter Mittag, who was the politburo member in charge of the economy. Schalck's status was that of an "officer for special tasks," and through his close links with the Science and Technology Department of the HVA, he was able to obtain embargoed Western computer equipment and high-technology goods. My department helped Schalck determine which Western suppliers might be prepared to sell to the East. Our industry and military were prepared to pay double the going rate.

Schalck named his fiefdom Kommerziale Koordination, KoKo for short, a canny move that made it sound respectable in its full form but also zippy and thoroughly modern to Westerners in its shorter version. The organization grew rapidly under Schalck's management—in fact, Schalck was soon known as the *Devisenbeschaffer*—literally "currency acquirer."

The most lucrative source of hard currency came through secret negotiations between the GDR and West Germany's government and several of its leading churches. The calculus was cold and simple: We traded people for goods, which we could then use ourselves or resell for hard currency. Between 1964 and 1990 the GDR released over 33,000 political prisoners and over 215,000 citizens to reunify families and received payments from the West of more than 3.4 billion deutschmarks. Schalck administered much of this money.

Until 1989, Schalck's background and the very existence of KoKo was a secret to those outside the tightly knit world of West German high finance, and of course to people in the East. My personal dealings with Schalck were conducted mainly at the Leipzig trade fair, which I viewed as a golden opportunity to size up potential recruits among West German businessmen. My deputy, General Hans Fruck, was in charge of all State Security operations during the fair. The whole thing took on such an air of gamesmanship that Fruck, against all the rules of espionage, was a prominent guest in the grand old Astoria Hotel and could be found every evening at a table in the back of the restaurant surrounded by his circle of East German businessmen and foreign trade representatives, including Schalck.

Every department in the Ministry of State Security wanted some of Schalck's time, knowledge, and, ultimately, equipment and money. In all of this there was ample room for siphoning off funds with the help of careless accounting. In 1982 Mielke and Schalck agreed to tighten control of the dealings between the Ministry of State Security and KoKo. Instead of the ministry's departments' dealing with Western firms directly on Schalck's recommendation, all business ran through Schalck's office. Once a year a meeting would take place with Schalck, his deputy, Manfred Seidel, Werner Grossmann, and me to plan for the year ahead. I had a budget of about one million deutschmarks for special acquisitions via KoKo—less than 10 percent of our annual hard currency expenditure. The rest came from the state budget.

The Ministry of State Security also made use of the dozens of shell companies Schalck had founded as covers for every kind of business, from importing cars to clandestine shipments of art sold to Western dealers from state collections, to replenish our empty treasury. Our ministry's central budget financed our technical work—falsifying passports, running specialized photo laboratories, and the like—while these companies helped us obtain embargoed products like chemicals and microelectronic equipment. For members of the leadership Schalck could provide cars, videos, furniture, and other luxuries.

I was not close to Schalck, but we did meet socially once on the Black Sea coast, where we had both booked a vacation. I was impressed by his ready wit and the way he seemed to have evolved from an East German trade functionary (usually an uninspiring species) into a grandiloquent figure, towering above petty ideological quarrels. He treated the East-West conflict as little more than a minor hindrance to conducting business, which was his first love. But he used other people, no matter what their convictions. He was a shrewd and fundamentally rather cold man.

By 1983 Schalck's importance had reached such proportions that he was entrusted by Honecker and Mielke with one of the most sensitive financial tasks possible on behalf of a state: saving it from bankruptcy. He negotiated a loan of one billion deutschmarks, which allowed East Germany to service other outstanding loans to Western banks. Honecker, determined to buy popularity, had imported increasing amounts of consumer goods and had spent huge amounts on his pet housing program, and the books simply did not balance. Through the good offices of the März brothers, Bavarian wholesalers who bought quality meats from the East (making fillet steaks extremely difficult to find in our country, despite high beef production), Franz-Josef Strauss was persuaded to back the loan in return for improvements in travel arrangements for Germans who wanted to visit their families in the East. Schalck and Strauss became political confidants and would indulge in high-level gossip, which Schalck would then report to the Ministry of State Security. Out of this bizarre, multisided deal encompassing deutschmark loans, meat exports, conditions at border crossings, and political reconnaissance came, I suspect, more good than evil. But I also suspect that a lot of individuals were enriched in ways not strictly in accordance with the regulations.

After unification, German courts spent years trying in vain to establish how much of this activity was illegal. Some criticized Strauss for backing the loan because it only helped perpetuate the East German state. But in the end, it was the sum of the political, economic, and human bankruptcy of the regime that killed the state, not its immediate financial woes.

Looking back, I often ask myself whether things could have been different. My judgment is that East Germany could not have survived as a state socialist system long after 1961 without a closed border. The economic pressures, coupled with the inherent instability of being half a country (and traditionally the poorer half, at that), were simply too strong. But the seeds of the divided Germany's demise began to sprout as soon as the border was fortified and the first concrete slabs put in place along the demarcation line. Cutting off the access of our people to the more attractive part of Germany was a brutal and effective solution, but it was only a short-term one. In the long run it was a disaster. I now see in the moral campaign against the East, which gained strength and conviction by the brooding symbolism of the Wall, one of the decisive reasons for the eventual outcome of the Cold War. No amount of expertise on our part in planning, diplomacy, or the darker arts of espionage could have prevented that.

8

Spying for Love

The link between romance and espionage is no invention of mine. Since time immemorial, security services have used the mating game to gain proximity to interesting figures. But if I go down in espionage history, it may well be for perfecting the use of sex in spying. My Romeo spies gained notoriety across the world by winning women's hearts in order to obtain the state and political secrets to which their targets had access. When it began, I had no idea of the harvest it would bring for us. As far as I was concerned, it was the one instrument among many available to a cash-strapped and inexperienced intelligence service. The historical precedents were, however, promising.

In the fourth book of Moses we are told how God ordered Moses to send forth men into the land of Canaan and bring back intelligence. Twelve were chosen, one from each of the tribes, and one was even given a false name—Joshua, who was Hosea, son of Noon—entirely according to the practice of intelligence agencies. After gathering reports about the giants in Canaan and the agricultural policies of this land of milk and honey, they cut off a vine so heavy with grapes that two of the agents had to carry it home on a pole between them. When Joshua became Moses' successor, two of his emissaries to Jericho spent the night in the house of Rahab, a woman of easy virtue. Thus the two oldest professions in the world first encountered each other. The King of Jericho's counterintelligence people informed him that two strangers had spent the night at Rahab's. When Rahab saw the guardians of morality approaching, she hid the spies on the roof and told the investigators that she had indeed entertained two gentlemen, but that they had left. I like to imagine that she thus saved the necks of two very spooked agents. One of Rahab's heirs in the love-and-espionage business was Mata Hari, a Dutchwoman who performed useful services for Germany in the First World War but was an awful spy and was tried and shot by the French in 1917. I would not have kept her on my payroll.

In the twentieth century, women began to be useful to intelligence agencies in roles other than as kindhearted prostitutes and seductresses. They took over the formerly male jobs as secretaries to important figures and, with the rise of feminism, became secretaries of state, advisers to politicians, senior academics, and bearers of state secrets themselves. So it was not surprising that the male counterpart to Mata Hari should come along, the Romeo spy.

My own first Romeo began work in the early fifties. His code name was Felix and his real identity remains a secret to this day. As a student he had impressed our senior officers on their regular recruitment trips through the provinces scouting for potential agents. These trips mirrored those of East Germany's sporting scouts—who were actually employed by another division of the Ministry of State Security and who went talent hunting for pint-sized gymnasts and other athletes in the school playgrounds. I flatter myself, I believe, that my service achieved a similar record of success in the world rankings of Romeo spies.

Our screening process was extremely rigorous. For every hundred candidates our staff found through the Party, the universities, or the youth organizations, only ten would be interviewed, after we had studied their backgrounds and records. Of that number, only one might end up working for us.

In the spring of 1952 I traveled with a senior colleague to the small town in southeast Germany where Felix was an engineering student. He was a clever, earnest fellow, but when we disclosed who we were and what we wanted, he was surprised and unenthusiastic because he worried about breaking off his studies. But we urgently needed men to work undercover in the West and persuaded him that life as a spy was not so bad. Certainly it paid better than an anonymous job somewhere in the state apparatus.

As with all novices, we started Felix off with a practice mission. His was in Hamburg. We told him that it was a genuine emergency to enable us to evaluate his judgments and actions under pressure. After a preliminary meeting with a contact near the main train station, he was supposed to pick up material from a man on the jetty. We had taught Felix the various methods of determining whether he was being followed. He intently studied our diagrams showing the visual angles from which surveillance is possible and how to avoid certain positions in a crowd. Of course, no matter how many diagrams someone studies, one can never be certain. I have known of agents with decades of experience who came to grief because they were sure they were unobserved when they were in enemy sights. The basic rule, even for the most advanced spy, is never to assume that you are not under surveillance.

Our student got off the train and was immediately convinced someone was following him. He broke out in a cold sweat but could not break away from his tail, a figure in a gray overcoat who seemed to turn up wherever he walked. By the time he got to the bridge, he was convinced that a whole legion of men in gray coats was behind him. The fact that these unappealing garments were the fashion in those days did not stop him from thinking that every gray coat he saw must be worn by an undercover man from the other side. So he gave the contact waiting on the bridge the agreed warning signal, shifting the newspaper under his arm to a particular angle to indicate that the mission should be aborted. The transfer of materials did not take place.

Later, when Felix had proved to be an excellent operator in Bonn, we would laugh at this false start. But it also contained a vital lesson for me when it came to evaluating trial sessions. Not every agent is born a James Bond. When it comes to a crucial situation, it is the experienced, cautious, methodical spy who has the necessary strength to stay cool and calculate risks wisely.

Felix established himself in the West with false papers and started work as a sales representative for a company based in Cologne selling hairdressing and beauty supplies. We wanted him to penetrate West German counterintelligence (the Federal Office for the Protection of the Constitution), which was based in Cologne. But his sales trips to

Bonn soon focused our interest on the Chancellery then headed by former Nazi Hans Globke, who, as one of the many born-again democrats, was a close confidant of Chancellor Adenauer and a voluble opponent of communism.

We were not happy with the quality of information we were getting from Adenauer's circle. We had no genuine leads, not even the basic tool for understanding any institution, the internal office telephone directory—to say nothing of any information about the people listed in it. So we decided to divert Felix to the chancellor's office. Not that we had any idea how a traveling shampoo salesman could penetrate such a carefully guarded place, but our curiosity about Adenauer and our shortage of inside information and contacts meant that we had no choice but to give Felix a try.

Felix himself came up with a starting point. He said he would mingle with the crowd at the bus stop closest to the building at the end of the working day and see if he could make some acquaintances. After a few false starts, he did indeed meet a dark-haired secretary from the chancellor's office, whom we code-named Norma. They began a friendship that soon blossomed into romance and enabled him to learn something of the operations of the chancellor's office.

Once he became established as Norma's young man, Felix was invited to meet her colleagues for bowling or office excursions on the Rhine pleasure boats. Turning on his southern charm, he could be the life and soul of the party, telling jokes, dancing with the women, and drinking heartily with the men. Norma was glad to have a boyfriend. She was no beauty and, as far as we were concerned, was a means to an end. But human nature is unpredictable. Felix developed genuine feelings for her.

They moved in together, but marriage was normally out of the question for any of our agents who had been given a false identity, usually borrowed from another citizen who was dead or had emigrated. The West German authorities checked birth and christening records of those who wanted to marry, and in Norma's case her status in the Chancellery would entail a thorough security check on her prospective spouse. So the majority of our agents had to insist that they were not the marrying kind, were still married to an old spouse, or spin some similar fable.

This first Romeo espionage affair continued nicely for several years. Felix never told Norma his real job, which would have ended the relationship, or worse. One day we heard from a mole we had planted inside the Office for the Protection of the Constitution that security had shown an interest in Norma's partner and was running a check on him. We had to pull Felix back to the East with great speed. She returned from work one day simply to find him gone without explanation. The unfortunate woman must have been devastated to discover that her lover had disappeared, but in a choice between saving an agent and saving a romance, I had to be ruthless.

Not for the last time, I had to develop my qualities as an agony uncle. Poor Felix was in a terrible state when he returned to East Berlin. I emptied two bottles of vodka with him one night at one of our country safe houses as he poured out his heart to me. But while his heart was aching, his head, thankfully, continued to work. He passed on a tip about another woman who he thought might be open to establishing contact with us, a middle-aged person full of joie de vivre who was a secretary in Globke's Chancellery.

There was no obvious reason to assume that this woman would work with us. But from his personal contacts Felix had formed the impression that she might be influenced by a good-looking man with a self-confident manner and a good cover story. It was the 1950s, and the postwar shortage of men was keenly felt among lonely, middle-aged secretaries yearning for a partner, a gap in the market we helped fill with eligible bachelors of our own.

After exhaustive examination of a number of candidates, we chose Herbert Söhler, code-named Astor. He was an amateur pilot who had been on the staff of Field Marshal Kesselring during the war. After being taken prisoner by the Soviets, he had been converted to communism in the prison camp. His Nazi Party membership and his contacts with other officers who had worked for Kesselring blocked his career path in the GDR, so he accepted infiltration into the West on our behalf with enthusiasm and military precision.

A few of his friends had settled in Bonn as West Germany began to move toward rearmament. The time was ripe for former military men to decide for good which side they were on in the battle for their divided homeland. It was not difficult for us to send him in this direction, particularly in the wake of the failed 1953 uprising, which had demonstrated the full extent of Soviet control in East Germany and prompted a good numbers of waverers to go West.

Söhler moved to the Bonn area and found a job as a real estate agent. He joined the nearby flying club at Hangelar, whose members included many government employees seeking weekend adventure. It did not take him long to make contact with Gudrun, as we had now code-named the secretary Felix had mentioned. Our hopes were soon fulfilled. She saw Söhler as a good catch, while he soon discovered that memos about Adenauer's contacts with Reinhard Gehlen, the spy chief, passed across Gudrun's desk. She became his girlfriend. After a while, he suggested he should try to recruit her by posing as a Soviet intelligence officer. This seemed strange, but we soon discovered that he had the right instinct. Gudrun recognized the Soviet Union as a global power while she rejected the GDR's claim to be a legitimate nation-state. Söhler related his wartime experiences: the destruction caused by Hitler's armies and the inspiring Russian cultural officer who lectured him in prison camp about the ties between the Russian and German peoples.

We decided to conduct her formal recruitment in an isolated vacation spot in the Swiss Alps so that we could beat a hasty retreat with Söhler if she reacted badly to our proposal. We always tried to avoid directly propositioning a West German on the territory of the Federal Republic, since it is an old counterintelligence trick to shadow a suspected recruiter, prime his intended target, and then film the recruitment to gain evidence of espionage activity and grounds for immediate arrest. Inviting a potential recruit to a meeting with senior intelligence officers in East Germany or elsewhere is also a useful final test of readiness to enter into a binding espionage relationship. At this point even the dimmest soul understands the nature of the offer without anything actually having to be said.

In this case, our careful planning and wooing of Gudrun in expensive Swiss restaurants turned out to be superfluous. Söhler must have been a master at the art of persuasion, because the recruiting turned out to be a formality. This taught me that many women who are recruited by the men they love often sense that their partners are working for the other side, even if they may be unwilling to admit it to themselves for a long time. After that, we never underestimated the fact that the secretaries might suspect that our men were agents, even if this knowledge was suppressed. That also meant that the Romeo must have a quick and safe path back to East Berlin if his prospective Juliet balks.

Unfortunately, Söhler developed a serious lung disease, which ended his work for us. We called him back to the East, where he later died of his illness. All attempts to interest Gudrun in another romantic intelligence partner failed. Some women became hooked on the espionage itself—the excitement and intimacy of a shared secret—and they could be directed toward another partner if the first had to vanish for security reasons. Others were one-man women, and there was nothing we could do about it. Gudrun was one of these. Contrary to popular rumor, we never tried blackmail to retain them. The risk of their running back to the West Germans full of repentance and bearing a colorful and propagandistically effective tale was too great, and so, regretfully, we said good-bye to Gudrun.

With the information she had provided we were, however, finally able to launch our campaign against Globke. This led to his resignation in 1963, a net gain for us in the removal of an obsessive opponent of East Germany while simultaneously bringing to the West's attention the extent to which ex-Nazis served the West German government.

●

My conviction grew that women recruited by our Romeos could provide top-quality information, but the more we used the tactic, the higher the risk of its discovery. Sooner or later, the bubble had to burst, but amazingly, this did not happen until 1979. Ingrid Garbe, a secretary in the West German mission to NATO in Brussels, was arrested by West Germany for spying for the East. The media there presented this as the biggest case of treason in the history of the Federal Republic. The truth was, from an intelligence point of view, Garbe was important but not indispensable. We had others. But the fact that she was a woman seemed to awaken dim memories of Mata Hari. The stereotype of the "spy for love" was born and the press could not get enough of it.

In March, the news agencies announced the defection of Ursel Lorenzen, a member of NATO's general secretariat, to East Berlin. To the consternation of her NATO colleagues, she appeared without warning on East German television, explaining that she had chosen to reveal her inside knowledge of the organization.

Ursel had been with NATO for twelve years, most recently in the Operations Directorate, where she had access to planning papers and details of crisis management at headquarters. Of special interest to us was her information about procedures in the situation room, where all political, military, and intelligence reports were assembled and evaluated and where NATO prepared its most important assessments, the East-West Studies.

After Ursel's defection, Imelda Verrept, a Belgian secretary at NATO, also asked for asylum in East Germany. While the leadership in East Berlin boasted of these defections, they put me in a thoroughly bad mood. The sudden public appearances in the East of these women, while useful propaganda for the Communist leadership, were in fact an informational loss for our service. The triumph of having NATO employees seek asylum in East Germany, however pleasant a change it might have been from Easterners demanding shelter in West Germany, paled beside the usefulness of having them in place in the enemy camp and delivering their valuable secret intelligence.

In the spring of 1979, while I was on a skiing trip, another report came in, of the arrest of an Ursula Höfs, a secretary in the West German Christian Democratic Party headquarters, along with her husband. Her name meant nothing to me at first, since at headquarters we only used our agents' cover names and held the real ones on a need-to-know basis. Not wanting to risk a telephone call to East Berlin to find out which of our spies she was, I hurried back, listening to the reports on West German radio and trying to figure out just whose cover had been blown.

One week after the disappearance of Ursula Höfs, the defection of two more Bonn secretaries hit the headlines. Inge Goliath had worked for Werner Marx, a head of the CDU's major think tank for foreign, defense, European, and inter-German policies. She had been delivering strategy papers on defense and Cold War policies for ten years, and in this nervous climate, we felt that it would be safer to withdraw her. The very next day, the tabloid *Bild-Zeitung*'s headlines screamed NOW BIEDENKOPF'S SECRETARY IS GONE TOO. A photograph showed Kurt

Biedenkopf, the popular chairman of the Christian Democrats and deputy leader of the party. Smiling beside him was his assistant, Christel Broszey. Christel had behaved impeccably as an agent under orders to leave. Betraying no fear, she left her boss with a cheery wave and the words, "I'm off to the hairdresser's. See you tomorrow"—never to return.

The newspapers reported she was a "supersecretary," who had regularly been placed among the top five in the professional championships in both typing and stenography. These qualities had impressed both Biedenkopf and his two predecessors and had also proved extremely useful to us. Because Christel had worked for three different Christian Democratic Party chairmen over a long period, it was impossible for the West Germans to figure out the extent of her knowledge and exactly what damage she had done. One week later Helga Rödiger, secretary to Manfred Lahnstein, senior civil servant in the Finance Ministry, also said a casual good-bye to her boss and headed for East Berlin. Rödiger was a valuable source, since Lahnstein was an expert on the monetary structure of the European Community and a close adviser to Helmut Schmidt as he rose from finance minister to chancellor.

Escape routes for our agents were always agreed to in advance. The agent was usually told to fly via countries considered to be low risk, such as Belgium, Holland, or Switzerland, and to arrive at an East German border control with a West German passport cover containing no document inside. The border officials knew this agreed-upon signal. The guard would call a superior, who would, under guise of waving the person through, take the fleeing agents into a small side room and make contact with us on a special telephone.

I was distraught and puzzled. The only thing most of the secretaries had in common was that their husbands or the men they lived with were our agents living under aliases in West Germany. Probably these men had registered as doppelgängers in the name of West Germans who had emigrated. Presumably each fleeing Juliet suspected that her cover was about to be blown. But how had the authorities discovered their real identities as our agents?

It was clear to me that the West Germans had succeeded in cracking some of our infiltration methods. Until then we had arrogantly assumed that these methods were safe, but I quickly decided that we had to start over. We made a painful but necessary decision to call home some more of our female agents together with their Romeos. For Ursula Höfs and her husband, this order had come too late. They were tried and sentenced to two years in prison.

The 1979 arrests turned out to be the result of the replacement of Günther Nollau as head of the Office for the Protection of the Constitution (West German counterintelligence) by Dr. Richard Meier. He introduced a high degree of professionalism—far too high for my liking—and made it clear that loyalty to the service was more important than party or political connections. He devised something called Operation Registration, a meticulous examination of the background of all those who might be suspect.

At first we could not see what these setbacks had in common. I noted in my diary:

> A comprehensive reexamination of all resettlements and visits from abroad has been commenced by West German intelligence, something that we had not hitherto considered possible or practicable. This is causing severe headaches. For better or for worse, we are going to have to accept a degree of defeat and refrain from trying to infiltrate people or, in some cases, consciously accept the fact that we are taking a big risk. This is a real life-or-death struggle and the opposition is breathing down our necks. On the outside it does not seem dramatic at all, but it causes inner tension and insecurity. One must have strong nerves to survive, but still not allow one's skin to grow too thick.

I never forgot that behind every case was a human being who had put his trust in us and his life on the line. A spy chief who callously sacrifices his agents in pursuit of his own goals soon loses the respect and trust of those working on the invisible front.

My puzzled suspicions about West German investigative procedures continued as our losses mounted. Often in the wake of an agent's arrest in the West, we would start investigations at headquarters on the suspicion that a mole might have worked his way into our department that prepared false passports. Suspicions like this are the worst kind of poison for an intelligence service, undermining the trust on which the entire operation is based and sometimes crippling it. Especially damaging were West German arrests of valuable sources that turned out to have resulted from the unmasking and interrogation of controllers whom we had infiltrated into the West. We had to pull numerous agents back to the East, but still could not divine how the West Germans were discovering our secrets.

At first all we had to go on were hints from one of our sources about a comprehensive reexamination by counterintelligence in Cologne of all cross-border travel into West Germany. We were informed that a small army of bureaucrats, mainly pensioners, had apparently been installed in the offices where foreign visitors or people moving from one region to another are required to register their new residence. This team of granddaddies was carefully combing the files for certain characteristics. We had no idea what they were looking for, although the term "screening profile" kept popping up in all our incoming reports from the West. I set up a working party, reporting directly to me, to figure out what criteria the West Germans were using to weed out suspicious figures.

We already knew that solitary male travelers between the ages of twenty-five and forty-five years were supposed to be questioned if they were carrying a small amount of hand luggage or if their clothing or haircut did not match perfectly with their identity papers. What we did not know until much later was that West German intelligence had spotted certain characteristics typical of East Germans. As hippie fashions spread in the West but were discouraged in the East, young Western males, particularly if traveling casually, tended to have long hair. Our recruits, often teachers, wore their hair short, but even the short haircuts differed subtly between the two Germanys. As for the East German teachers, good training could do a lot for them, but turning one into a convincing hippie was nearly impossible.

Once alerted by the train guards, undercover men based at the main railway stations would watch the suspect's behavior after he left the train. For instance, very few native Easterners could resist making a detour to shops near the station to look at the unfamiliar goods in the windows, in which Westerners had little interest. Such tiny differences were being carefully monitored.

These tactics of Operation Registration became evident to us only after years of confusion. Ironically, it was Meier himself who gave the game away. He chose to introduce himself as the new head of the service with a grand drumroll, announcing the arrest of sixteen East German agents who had been smuggled in through third countries. Newspapers spoke of a total of forty additional investigations. This news ended our speculation about whether it was possible for the West Germans to filter out the minute number of our people who were mixing in with hundreds of thousands of travelers. Meier thus effectively confirmed the methods he was using to detect our agents. Painful as this setback was, we were able to recall a lot of our endangered agents and suspend the infiltration. Had he kept quiet about his successes, he might well have been able to keep our side guessing for a very long time about his methods. By targeting the arrests more carefully or waiting until the suspect had made contact with the whole range of sources before moving in, he could have done a lot more damage. Showmanship in a service chief tends to build up a glamorous reputation at the severe risk of sacrificing his achievements.

As usual in one of these big psychological operations, the West German Interior Ministry moved quickly to demand that our agents give themselves up before they were caught—a common bluff in the great game of inter-German espionage. However, this attempt made little impact. Cooperation with us had become part of the lives of most informants and undercover agents, and they were generally immune to such invitations. For most of my agents, such immunity was due to a mixture of political conviction, a resistance—nurtured by us—against psychological warfare, and a natural aversion to giving themselves up. Every human being lives in hope that he or she will be spared the bitter cup. So it was, at least in most cases, and, if not, it was too late anyway.

Hansjoachim Tiedge, a leading official in the Office for the Protection of the Constitution who defected to us in 1985, told us that Cologne had discovered no fewer than two hundred suspected false identities over a decade. Between 1972 and 1982, the final score, according to my reckoning, was some thirty of our agents exploded, i.e., arrested in West Germany, and three times that number withdrawn by us to the East in time. Since agents once pulled back can never be used in the same territory again, Operation Registration cost us about a hundred good operatives—a big blow.

Despite his hunger for publicity I must give Meier credit for a carefully orchestrated campaign intended to unsettle our network and its control centers in West Germany. He next began to target me personally and spread rumors about my "imminent demise." The *International Herald Tribune* ran a story headed, IS MISCHA WOLF LOSING HIS TOUCH? Another Western paper landed on my desk bearing the headline WOLF WORKS OVERTIME.

But the truth of the matter was somewhat less sensational; work went on, and while we adapted our methods to Operation Registration, we did not moderate our efforts. Consider Helga Rödiger, codenamed Hannelore. The man who had recruited her had to be recalled because of a scare about his security. Keen not to lose her, we looked through our files and found another Romeo candidate, a young agent code-named Gert who had been infiltrated into the Federal Republic. He had taken the identity of a West German citizen named Robert Kresse, who had emigrated to New Zealand.

I decided to oversee the match myself, partly because I was curious to meet Helga, whose work for us had been outstanding, and partly because she had told us that she had a choice between moving with her boss to the Finance Ministry or staying in the chancellor's office. She sent a coded message through her courier to East Berlin asking what she should do: an unusual embarrassment of riches. On the one hand, a source in the Chancellery was of great importance to us. On the other, she had a close working relationship with her boss; he trusted her with confidential information about budgets and internal politics. We had no idea whether she could achieve similar results in the Chancellery.

The Winter Olympics in Innsbruck, Austria, in 1976 provided good cover for a meeting. Helga rented a holiday bungalow near the village. On our first meeting, she declared herself ready to accept one of our agents in the West as her go-between. We promptly produced Gert. I watched them hopefully at dinner, but there was no sign of early attraction between them. In any event, we concluded that the Finance Ministry was the safer option for her, and so she moved and continued sending us secrets.

In time, a relationship did indeed blossom between Helga and Gert. It proved to be a genuine and lasting one. After we had to withdraw her, in 1979, he too was called back to the East, where they were finally free to marry. The service took place in the picturesque town of Wernigerode in the mountains and I was a guest of honor, as befits the matchmaker.

●

As might have been expected, my Romeo agents had become the subject of frenzied analysis in the Western intelligence world. They also caught the popular imagination. The *Bild-Zeitung* put together a photo montage with twelve women in our pay under the headline THE SECRETARIES WHO SPIED FOR LOVE. A weekly-magazine cover story showed a naked bosom decorated with East German medals. I sensed that Western services were concerned about our success rate and were obviously devoting time and money to cultivating their own image of the victims in the media. The secretaries were relentlessly portrayed as pitiful, misused victims, all of a certain age, single and hungry for love, delivered helpless into the arms of misfortune.

In order to increase the deterrence value, West German state security maintained that the Romeo spies used the affections of their conquests cold-bloodedly, only to disappear at the first scent of danger. But an internal report by Herbert Hellenbroich, then deputy head of West German counterintelligence, admitted more prosaically, "The relationships arose for the main part without pressure or blackmail. Neither did money play a major role. Usually it was ideological motivation or simply attraction that lured the women."

The truth is that we rarely spotted vulnerable Little Red Riding Hoods and targeted them specifically, unless—as in Söhler's case—we had a tip from one of our men. The way that it usually worked was like this: When we sent a young male agent to the West with a specific espionage task, we would say to him, "OK, you are likely to have a private life like anybody else, but if you do happen on a secretary, and a well-placed one at that, so much the better." The rest was up to him. Of course, not every man is automatically attracted to a secretary, but one has to remember that our agents were extremely loyal people of conviction who were used to making sacrifices and accepting personal restrictions for the sake of something they believed in.

Contrary to the wilder rumors, they were not schooled in the *ars amatoria* back in East Berlin. Some were better than others at this sort of thing. They were sharp operators who realized that a lot can be done with sex. This is true in business and espionage because it opens up channels of communication more quickly than other approaches.

●

I would be failing to give a truthful picture, however, if I did not reveal in detail some of the more exotic and tragic operations in which my men took part. There were two super-Romeos, each with a different style and area of operation. The first was Roland G., a king of melodrama.

Roland G. was the director of a small but well-regarded East German theater in Annaberg in the Erzgebirge mountains, the sort of place gifted actors and directors would wind up when they were considered too politically risky for the main city theaters. He was known for his wonderful performance of Faust in Goethe's play about a man hungry for all human experience who seduces and disgraces a simple girl called Margarete. Highly intelligent, fine-featured, and with an actor's talent for disguise, he was a perfect Romeo candidate. I had a regional branch office in Karl-Marx-Stadt (rechristened Chemnitz after unification) with a reputation for conceiving wild schemes and baroque projects, and officers there spotted Roland G.'s abilities and also his love of good living. In 1961 he was sent to Bonn with instructions to approach a woman named Margarete, an interpreter at Supreme Headquarters, Allied Powers Europe (SHAPE), NATO's command center, then located at Fontainebleau near Paris.

Because of the international aspect, Roland G. was given a foreign identity. He soon perfected his role as Kai Petersen, a Danish journalist who spoke good German with a Scandinavian lilt—no problem for a good actor. Margarete, lovely, unmarried, and very Catholic, worked diligently inside NATO and lived a quiet life. Three of our agents had already tried and failed to win her stout heart. Roland G. was made of sterner stuff. He managed to arrange a trip to Vienna with her, showing himself an attentive suitor by introducing this shy woman to the voluptuous Italian nudes displayed in the Kunsthistorisches Museum, escorting her to the Spanish Riding School, and finally to the extravagant Dehmel café for rich cakes and Viennese coffee—all, of course, at the expense of our intelligence service. Sometimes, his outlays would strike the case officer as rather high, even for such a recruit, but he was a wise man and knew that espionage offered Roland G. a long leash and large budget to enjoy luxuries denied him in puritan East Germany.

One night, after a successful evening at the Burgtheater, she repaid his attentions with a single kiss and the words, "I have never had such a lovely time with anyone before." They spent their first night together and the next morning he emptied his heart to her—some of it anyway. He told his new love that he was an officer with Danish military intelligence, explaining that small nations like Denmark often felt left out in NATO and needed their own confidential information.

Margarete accepted this and was delighted when he said that, in the course of his work, he would often be in Paris and would love to see her there. She agreed to help him by supplying NATO secrets. From time to time, he would meet her in a small hotel and she would disclose details of her work, in particular the preparations and evaluations of the alliance's military maneuvers. This gave us an excellent idea of how the organization perceived its own strengths and weaknesses, knowledge vital to the Warsaw Pact's own planning. She also delivered useful logistical information from the naval and ground forces departments where she worked as an interpreter from time to time.

The Soviets—with whom we naturally shared this information—were not so easily satisfied. They were extremely keen for the ultimate prize: NATO's deployment plans and the exact targeting and timing of its nuclear weapons for a first strike against the East. Occasionally Marshal Koshevoi, the supreme Soviet commander in East Germany, would appeal to my pride when trying to wheedle NATO's nuclear war plans out of me.

"You [East] Germans are so good. Can't you get us some more of the coordinates?" he would say, alluding to the exact map locations of the NATO bases, which the Soviets wanted to knock out first in any nuclear conflict. With terrifying bonhomie he would continue, "We don't need your papers. All we need are those coordinates, and we can drop a bomb on them and slice right through the West."

I was rather sore about this, since I prided myself that my service was able to deliver more in-depth analytical information than a load of map grid references. Nevertheless, while we helped Moscow in its search for most of the coordinates in Europe, we never succeeded in filling in the whole picture, probably because the Pentagon had the good sense to keep such essential data well away from its West German allies, whom they regarded as far from leak-proof—and not without good reason.

Meanwhile, Margarete was suffering pangs of conscience like her agonized namesake in Goethe's story. Her peace was gone, her heart was torn, as the great German dramatist put it. It had taken a long time to persuade her to pass on the documents we needed, even to a man whom she loved and who was, allegedly, from the harmless Danish intelligence service. And her strict Roman Catholicism made her uneasy about continuing an affair outside of marriage.

The main thing our man had in common with the heroes of popular spy fiction was a taste for pretty women and luxurious destinations, so the couple spent Christmas and New Year's of 1962–63 in the pretty resort of Arosa, Switzerland. There she told him she was unwilling to continue both the espionage and romantic partnership without undergoing a full confession in the presence of a priest and receiving a firm offer of marriage. Thinking on his feet, Roland G. said that marriage was out of the question because his work for Copenhagen meant that he could be called away at any time for long periods.

As for Margarete's desire to confess her sins, although Roland G. knew that the Roman Catholic church's rules on the confidentiality of the confessional were absolute, he also knew that a good agent takes no risk. So he asked Margarete to wait until a reliable Danish priest could be found. For this of course he did not look in Denmark but in the branch headquarters of our intelligence office in Karl-Marx-Stadt, where his request caused quite a stir. We had tricks up our sleeves, but producing Danish-speaking Catholic priests to order was not one of them. But Roland G. had promised, and an intelligence service, like a gentleman, always endeavors to keep the word of one of its men.

We managed to create a "Potemkin marriage"—a facade—using an agent dressed up as a military chaplain. He was taught how to conduct a confession, but his Danish was nonexistent, so we had to send him off on a crash course to learn a few words of greeting and farewell for the sake of verisimilitude and, more important, to replace the broad native twang of Saxony in his German with a suitably Nordic accent. We found a small and infrequently used church in a Jutland village, and when the coast was clear our man slipped into the priest's side of the confessional and Margarete was ushered in to bare her soul to him. It should come as no surprise that this priest proved understanding in the extreme and told her to carry on spying with the blessing of the Lord.

I had worried that the whole business was likely to end up in a messy farce, but to my surprise it worked. Sometimes in the game of spying, the most bizarre ruses succeed and the simple ones fail. As for the moral side of things, I am often asked today whether I felt guilt or shame about such machinations. On the whole, the honest answer would be no. In retrospect, some things did get out of hand, but at the time we believed that the end justified the means.

Margarete's links with us ended when we withdrew Roland G. from West Germany because we feared he had come under scrutiny there. For a while she continued to work with a successor Romeo, but that combination proved unproductive. Her involvement in espionage had always been for Roland G.'s sake. When he was gone, there was no real motivation for her to continue.

Our other top Romeo, unlike Roland G., was a man whom no one would suspect of having that kind of allure. His name was Herbert Schröter, an inelegant name in German, and he was built to match: bullish, with a square head, broad shoulders, and a loud voice. It remains a mystery to me what it was about him that was so attractive to women, but there must have been something, because in the course of his career he managed to persuade two highly placed and resourceful secretaries to spy for us. He was, alas, a source of ill fortune for the women involved. Through no fault of his own, both ended up under arrest, while each time he was able to slip free. His story demonstrates what a random game of chance Romeo espionage can be. Sometimes the tactic can lead to true and lasting romantic relationships, sometimes to tragedy.

We had sent Herbert to the Alliance Française in Paris in the early 1960s. This establishment was a favorite recruiting ground for us, known as the secretaries' sandpit because government employees were sent there to learn French. There he met the nineteen-year-old Gerda Osterrieder, a bright and slender girl. An affair began, and in time he revealed his real identity to her. She agreed to obtain a transfer to the

Foreign Office and become an informant for us, a task she carried out with astonishing enthusiasm and efficiency. Beginning in 1966 she was employed at Telco, the decoding center of the Bonn Foreign Office, where all telegrams from embassies abroad were deciphered. Herbert's cover in Bonn was as a commercial agent.

Telco's working methods were, to say the least, casual. In those days reports arrived on tickertape. Gerda was able to slip whole bundles of the stuff into her capacious handbag and ferry it out of the building without a single security check. In 1968 she was sent to Washington for three months as holiday relief and was employed as a decoder in the West German embassy, where she outdid herself on our behalf, passing on reports on the state of relations between Bonn and Washington as well as the West German ambassador's judgments on American domestic and foreign policy. Later in the same year, Gerda and Herbert continued their joint efforts for us in Bonn. Five years later, she was moved to Warsaw. Her relationship with Herbert suffered under the strain of separation, and she began drinking heavily, but we left Herbert in West Germany, lest a move to Poland arouse suspicion.

Unfortunately for us, she found comfort with a West German journalist who, it transpired, was an undercover agent for Bonn. To this man she revealed that she was passing information to us, and he persuaded her to confess. At least her personal loyalty to Herbert was sufficiently intact for her to telephone him just in time. Her message—"Go to our friends. It is very important"—was a previously agreed-upon warning signal that allowed him to flee to East Berlin before the net closed in.

What happened then was the sort of drama that occurs often in spy fiction but seldom in real intelligence work. Herbert was back with us, having escaped arrest by a whisper. Gerda was holed up in the West German ambassador's Warsaw villa to keep her away from any undesirable contacts with her former masters. We received news that two West German intelligence officers had arrived to question her.

That night my emergency telephone lines were burning up because I was still clinging to the hope that Gerda might change her mind and return to us. I contacted my colleagues in Polish foreign intelligence, who agreed with me that every possible attempt should be made to hinder her departure. This was not a simple operation. I was always uneasy when another socialist country was dragged into an inter-German espionage affair, in particular Poland, whose national pride did not easily accept the fact that we monitored its relations with West Germany. Even before the rise of Solidarity, relations between East Berlin and Warsaw were touchy, and I rightly guessed that if our mission failed, I would receive a stern lecture from my counterpart, Miroslav Milevski, a strong nationalist and the chief of Warsaw's foreign intelligence who later became Poland's interior minister.

We set up a last "rescue line." As the deputy head of the West German mission shepherded our quarry to the airport and passed the final customs control, an undercover Polish agent stepped forward and offered her asylum in Warsaw. For a moment Gerda hesitated, and the West German diplomat froze, terrified that he was going to go down in diplomatic history as the man who lost a confessed spy to the Communists right there, on the airport tarmac. Finally, however, Gerda shook her head and boarded the Lufthansa plane.

Back home in Düsseldorf, she was tried for espionage "in a particularly serious instance" and received a three-year sentence, shorter than usual because she had obliged the West Germans with details of her past work for us. We had tried a daring rescue and failed. I was in a sour mood about the whole affair and thought we had slipped up in our handling of the romance between Gerda and Herbert by being too cavalier. Moreover, we now were stuck with Herbert, a bluff and awkward man. He would never fit in at headquarters and had been unmasked as an undercover agent through Gerda's return to the West. To gain time to think, I sent him off to the Black Sea in Bulgaria for a holiday.

A few weeks later back he came, extremely pleased with himself: "I think I've got you another useful girlfriend." My jaw dropped.

On the beach he had met a stunningly attractive brunette named Dagmar Kahlig-Scheffler. He introduced himself under yet another false name (he had been through so many identities down the years, I wonder whether even he could remember them). Now he was Herr Herbert Richter. Dagmar told him that she was on holiday recovering from a painful divorce. Herr Richter declared that he too was a divorcé and understood how tough this could be. Then he began a holiday romance with her. One afternoon in her room, he leafed through that week's newsmagazine and to his consternation caught sight of a lengthy report of Gerda's trial. And there was his photograph, too, right next to Gerda's and clearly recognizable. Her favorite was presented in lurid detail as the devil incarnate, wrecker of women's lives. He had little choice but to confide his identity as Schröter the Eastern agent to his new girlfriend.

Fortunately, she was impressed by his honesty, and the two continued the romance. Since Herbert was persona non grata in the Federal Republic, we had to invite Dagmar to East Berlin for weekends. She was working as an assistant to a Munich journalist, which was not a very interesting prospect for us. As time went on, she made it clear that she was so grateful for the cozy weekends in the East that she would not decline work on our behalf. We proposed that she learn French and stenography, paid her tuition, and even paid for her small daughter to attend a Swiss boarding school.

Dagmar moved to Bonn at our request, but her training was still insufficient for her to obtain a government job. But we did not give up—I think our patience far exceeded that of any other espionage service. She took a job as assistant to a university professor. Aided by his excellent references, she managed after a year's employment with him to land a post in Chancellor Helmut Schmidt's office in the autumn of 1975.

The early weeks of such a deployment were always tense for us in East Berlin. Security had been tightened, and there was now a ten-week probation period during which a new employee's background and acquaintances were checked out. Dagmar passed with flying colors. Of course, we had to stop her trips to East Berlin but arranged for her instead to meet Herbert in Vienna, Geneva, and Innsbruck.

We gave her the code name Inge and she worked for us for several years, passing to us information on the internal workings of the Schmidt team and the mood in the Bonn leadership. We were particularly interested in her reports on the strained atmosphere at Schmidt's first meetings with President Jimmy Carter to discuss European security. She was a hardworking secretary, popular with her colleagues for her readiness to stay late if work demanded and to fill in on the late or holiday shift for colleagues with family responsibilities. In these quiet hours, she would busy herself doing the office photocopying, preparing an extra copy for us or microfilming important documents when no one was looking.

Her bond with Herbert was very strong, despite their geographical separation. Dagmar wanted desperately to marry. In accordance with our usual rules, we warned against it, but fearing that she might quit our service, we set up another of our Potemkin weddings. We made out an East German identity card for her in her maiden name and flew her from Bonn via Vienna to East Berlin, where she was taken to a registry office in the Lichtenberg district not far from our ministry's headquarters in the Normannenstrasse.

All the formalities were observed. The official asked Dagmar and Herbert if they were free to marry and delivered the standard speech about lifelong commitment and the seriousness of matrimony. Rings were exchanged and the wedding march was played. Although the couple signed the marital register, unbeknownst to them the page was removed from the book and destroyed after they left the building. Years later, when Dagmar discovered after her arrest that her marriage, not having been properly registered, was null and void, she was furious.

Her career came to an end in 1977 through no mistake of her own. Suspicion fell on her control officer in the West, Peter Goslar, who had been settled by us in Düsseldorf with his wife, Gudrun, under false identities. The Goslars had been channeled into the Federal Republic via London, where we had given them a British identity as Mr. and Mrs. Antony Roge. But in the course of a computer-aided swoop on unusual resettlements from abroad, the couple caught the eye of West German counterintelligence. They were observed for some time, and when their apartment was searched, the officials found documents hidden in the vegetable basket and the bathroom. These included Schmidt's notes on a confidential conversation with the British prime minister, James Callaghan, who complained about the White House's inadequate grasp of European realities and used words like "arrogance" and "stupidity" to describe the Americans.

The investigation team did not take long to figure out where the notes came from. They filmed the Goslars' meetings with Dagmar. The next time they were away, their flat was searched again, yielding the briefing papers from Schmidt's office for the West German position at the London economic summit in 1978. Dagmar was arrested, tried, and sentenced to four years and three months in prison. During my own trial, I met an elderly guard in the Düsseldorf court who had seen a number of our secretary-spies. Dagmar stood out in his mind among all the others, and he told me, "She was the most fantastic-looking woman I have ever seen." As for Schröter, his glory days were also finished. He was forced to live a quiet life back in the East with no more exotic holiday romances.

•

Gabriele Gast was a rarity in a male-dominated field and became the most highly placed woman in the Federal Intelligence Service (BND), rising to the position of senior analyst for the Soviet Union and Eastern Europe. Her famously perceptive reports on East bloc developments landed on Chancellor Helmut Kohl's desk. What neither he nor her superiors at the BND knew was that they also landed on mine.

Gaby's case started out as a Romeo affair, although I would be reluctant to describe her as a Juliet because she was a brilliant woman who acted according to her own convictions and ideas. The daughter of a conservative middle-class family, she was a student member of the Christian Democratic Youth Movement, a robustly right-wing organization, and in 1968 visited East Germany to work on a doctoral thesis on the political role of women in the GDR.

In Karl-Marx-Stadt she met a mechanic called Karl-Heinz Schmidt; it would take two decades for her to discover that his real name was Schneider. The encounter was no accident. Schmidt/ Schneider was in the pay of State Security in Saxony and would later rise to the rank of major. Rough and ready, he had a sort of proletarian charm that can be fatally attractive to sheltered middle-class women. She found his old-fashioned Christian name too stuffy and affectionately called him Karlizcek. He courted her assiduously with trips into the countryside, and they spent a romantic summer together. Then he revealed his true status and introduced her to his superior, an experienced intelligence officer called Gotthold Schramm.

Gaby was fascinated by this unheralded insight into the internal workings of the East. When her new acquaintances asked her to cooperate with them, she hesitated until they told her she would be prevented from seeing Karlizcek again if she declined. She then agreed, returning to West Germany to continue her studies in Aachen but coming east every three months to receive espionage training and meet her boyfriend.

Her East German handlers began without firm plans for Gaby but thought of steering her toward a career in Bonn, perhaps in a ministry. At this point, however, fate took over. We were not the only ones interested in Gaby. Her doctoral supervisor was an eminent professor of Eastern European studies, Klaus Mehnert, who had contacts with the BND and was widely believed to be one of its academic recruiters. Gaby was his star student, and when she completed her doctorate in 1973 she was offered a coveted job as a political analyst in the BND's highly regarded Pullach Institute near Munich.

We were of course delighted at this turn of events. We kept our promise and allowed her to go on visiting Karlizcek. Soon afterward they celebrated their engagement in a safe house in the East. Schramm was on hand to open the Russian champagne and brought along a cassette with the recorded good wishes of the head of the regional secret service. We always paid great attention to the romantic side of such liaisons.

Gaby's work for us was flawless. She gave us an accurate picture of the West's knowledge of and its judgments regarding the entire East bloc. This proved vitally important to us in handling the rise of Solidarity in Poland in the early eighties. Blessed with an unerring eye for the sort of material that would interest us, she was a brilliant analyst in her own right and would plough through mountains of classified West German material on political and economic developments in the East bloc and Soviet Union, summarizing the points she knew would interest us in East Berlin.

If we required the original documents, she would microfilm them and conceal them in fake deodorant bottles. We initially instructed her to deposit them in the lavatory tanks of the trains traveling from Munich across the border to the East. Later this was deemed too risky as well as insufficient to accommodate the flow of information she was providing. A female go-between would meet her at a Munich swimming pool and they would pass the information between their changing rooms, which had been specified in coded radio messages we sent her from East Berlin.

During her many years with us, Gaby developed a highly professional satisfaction in what she did. She also continued meeting her lover, Karlizcek, for holiday assignations. We treated our lovebirds well, offering them vacations in the Alps or on the Mediterranean coast. But in time the relationship that had first ensnared her faded in importance for her. I think that she hung on to the not particularly prepossessing Karlizcek because she liked the occasional comfort the relationship offered and she was a strong-minded, independent woman who was unwilling to fall into a conventional partnership at home.

She also carried an extra emotional burden. Her brother's wife had adopted a severely handicapped child, which proved too much for the couple. Unwilling to have the child sent to an institution, Gaby took over his care despite the heavy demands on her time and energy. She was also preoccupied by what might happen to him if she were discovered. She suffered anxiety attacks and sometimes talked of cutting her ties with us.

I was determined not to lose her and in 1975 took the unusual step of meeting her personally in Yugoslavia. At first the atmosphere was strained, because no picture of me had yet appeared in the West and to her I was the faceless head of East German intelligence. But she soon recovered her composure and flung herself into a passionate debate about *Ostpolitik* and the internal situation in East Germany, about which she had no illusions. I asked about her personal situation, her life at work—of course, Karlizcek was there with her—and we also discussed how she might best advance her career prospects in the BND. I assured her that I would guard her identity in my service with absolute secrecy and give her our full support. Later, we would meet in other places such as a pretty house in Split on the Yugoslav Dalmatian coast, an unsuspicious holiday destination for our agents in the West that carried no great risk for me either.

The virulent Western media campaigns against me and threats to expose our agents served only to make her more determined, and her ideological commitment became firmer as the years passed. Like many young West Germans who had lived through the protest movement in 1968, she was convinced that the Federal Republic was not facing up honestly to the Nazi past. She once sent me a book about Nuremberg, where the Nazis had held their mass rallies and the victorious Allies later prosecuted them for crimes. She inscribed the book: "The Old still lurks beneath the facade of the New. Thirty years after Nuremberg, the struggle for the New must go on."

I cannot presume to say whether after her initial excitement over Karlizcek, Gaby was really in love with him. But I do know that she developed a kind of love affair with my service. There was a romance to her relations with us that she, who had not enjoyed straightforward relationships with men, found emotionally as well as professionally satisfying. This parallel may sound odd, but the care that is lavished on a good spy, the attention to his or her well-being, can become a substitute for personal ties. In Gaby's case, the human factor was particularly important, and we took care to reward her good work with meetings in the East. They offered emotional sustenance and thus were great treats for her.

She was very fond of two senior officers who took a fatherly interest in her. When one of them died, she arranged for flowers to be laid on his grave in rural East Germany. Her feelings toward me were less easy to define. She needed to feel wanted by me and I gave her my personal attention. I truly liked her and found her intelligence and sensibilities appealing. This was certainly the closest bond I ever formed with an agent.

Sometimes her messages carried the wounded tone of a lover who feels taken for granted. But the visits to East Germany offered her a feeling of belonging that she seemed to miss in her own country. She would meet Karlizcek in the Vogtland, a beautiful area not far from the Bavarian border. It was a rural idyll with a touch of nineteenth-century romanticism that thrived in remote corners of East Germany. She was looked after by a landlady called Linda, whose fluffy Vogtland dumplings and impenetrable dialect Gaby adored. Here her own language was spoken as she had never heard it and she could sample a German cuisine she had never tasted before. Such experiences were often a source of fascination for the Westerners we brought to the East. It was a delicate balance to continue with these trips, which offered her emotional sustenance but became increasingly dangerous. Every trip to the East was dangerous for agents who were prohibited from traveling there because of their sensitive positions in the West—especially in such organizations as the BND. Gradually we had to cut the visits short because of the security risks, and this distressed her.

Once Gaby wrote to me to vent her worries about the risks she was running as her career progressed up the ladder of West German intelligence. I sensed a cry for deeper reassurance and invited her for another visit to the East. She answered, "A meeting and conversation with you in the shelter of a homelike environment are and will always be for me worth making a special effort to achieve, however difficult the circumstances may be." I had to face up to the fact that Gaby, for all her other virtues, was not an easy-care agent. We met seven times in the course of her work.

This feeling of belonging to a special community, an elite and secretive club fighting for a noble ideal, was, I often observed, of particular importance to Westerners from upper-middle-class backgrounds who had strong and complex personalities. Perhaps this goes some way toward answering the question I am incessantly asked about why such people flocked to work for us. What we offered them was the chance of mixing idealism with personal commitment, something that is missing in many modern societies.

In the eighties, Gaby threw herself into her work analyzing NATO's East-West studies and the effects of Ronald Reagan's aggressive anti-Communist policies. She shared my concern about the deepening stagnation in the Soviet bloc after the death of Andropov in 1984. By this time Afghanistan had become Moscow's ball and chain. We were both aware of serious mistakes in Soviet foreign policy and their effect on the entire socialist community.

To my surprise, from the end of the seventies she began to talk of the prospect of autonomous reform movements spreading outside Poland and through the other satellite countries. It was a view that shook me all the more because it reflected my own nascent insights, which I was not yet ready or able to articulate. Reality was moving further away from the official declarations and was boldly contradicting Marxist theory. I was plagued by a sense of unease but continued to suppress it.

Gaby's career was progressing by leaps and bounds. The trust she enjoyed can be gauged by the fact that in 1986 she was charged with writing a highly sensitive report for the chancellor on the alleged involvement of West German firms in the building of a chemical weapons factory in Libya. A year later she was made deputy chief of the BND's Soviet bloc political department, a giddily high position for a woman. We left it to her to decide what to deliver to us. Like her own colleagues in the West, we had absolute confidence in our expert.

The question then arises in this world of mirrors: Just whose analyst was she? I can say that she offered both us and the BND totally objective analysis. She knew our interests and could sum up the information we needed in crisp sentences in reports of four or five pages. Perhaps she compensated for her lack of emotional engagement by devoting all her formidable intelligence and energies to the intellectual task before her, whether for us or our enemies. What was most important for us was that we learned, through her, what the BND was thinking about Eastern Europe and about us, which enabled us to see the world through their eyes. Gaby worked for us out of deeply held conviction, but—as was the case with other valuable sources—excellent work for the other side was a prerequisite in order to get access to the information we wanted.

From her reports we also picked up leads on possible BND agents in the East, although that was secondary. More important, we got a wider view of the world through what the BND called its "yellow-stripe" information, about which very little is as yet known. This was the fruit of the BND's spying on the Federal Republic's own allies, much of it emanating from a German listening station code-named "Eismeer" (polar sea) near Conil and Cadiz on Spain's Atlantic coast. The presence of the listening station dated back to Nazi Germany's close relations with Franco's Spain in the thirties; the operation, code-named "Delikatesse" (delicacy), monitored communication lines from Europe to West Africa and North and South America used by the U.S. embassies and CIA stations. All of the BND transcripts that involved West Germany's partners were marked with a yellow stripe to ensure that they were not accidentally passed on, lest the other Allies learn what West Germany had overheard. West Germany, with technically trained secret service and police officers supplied with cipher technology, could theoretically decode the signals of fourteen friendly nations. It had a close partnership with the Turkish secret service, and during the 1982 Falklands war was the only service able to decode Argentina's radio traffic for the British. This West German technical proficiency, and our ability to tap into it via Gaby and other sources allowed us to piggyback our intelligence-gathering efforts: The West Germans did the dirty work of spying on their American allies, and we stole their information.

Much later, after the collapse of the GDR and Gaby's exposure, I often wished that I had let her go earlier so that we—and she—could cover her tracks better. Right up to the end she made no mistakes. Early in 1990, when we realized that unification was inevitable, my successor called her to a meeting in Salzburg to tell her that we were concluding our work and that all documents recording her cooperation had been destroyed.

But in the run-up to unification, a certain number of former employees of our apparat sought to secure immunity from prosecution by selling out others. The worst betrayal was performed by one of our senior officers, Colonel Karl-Christoph Grossmann (not to be confused with my successor as head of the service, Werner Grossmann). Although he had no direct knowledge of Gaby's identity or activities, he passed on the gist of a conversation he had overheard to the effect that our service had a very good woman placed high in West German intelligence and that she had a handicapped child.

This was enough to finger her, and she was arrested later in 1990 as she crossed the German-Austrian frontier for a final meeting with her handlers. I believe they were going to give her a long-service award. To the very end, such tokens of esteem meant a lot to her.

Much thought and more print has been devoted to why these women did what they did. All were West German citizens employed in the service of that state before they took on work for us. Some came to accept the socialist ideal out of conviction. But most just fell in love, and commitment to us followed commitment to a man. They knew that they might have to give up their family ties and a superior standard of living in the West for safety in East Germany, a country that few knew and whose public image was not the brightest. Many did indeed make new lives there after their espionage careers.

Ursel Höfs served her full sentence in the Federal Republic because she refused to rescind her application to leave for East Germany on her release. She was eventually allowed to join her husband in the East. Christel Broszey and her husband settled in the East German region of Thuringia and adopted a child. Later, to her great joy, the couple also had a baby of their own. Inge Goliath ended up living quietly with her husband in the countryside outside Berlin. Helga Rödiger moved with her husband to Berlin and stayed there after his death. I have met her only once, at a birthday party in the summer of 1996.

The transition to a different system was admittedly difficult for the women. Our policy was to help them live comfortably but as quietly as possible. After years of excitement serving a secret intelligence service, this came as an anticlimax in their lives. Christel Broszey was one who refused the quiet life. She badgered the local Party leadership until it found her a challenging job as a department head in a textile factory. There she railed against the inefficiencies of socialist management and introduced many improvements to her factory's labor practices based on her experience in the West.

I do not think that our service's recipe for success differed substantially from that of Western foreign intelligence services. We certainly had no patent on Romeo spies. West Germany's BND ran an agent in America under the name of Karl Heinrich Stohlze. In 1990 he approached a senior secretary in a Boston defense company, seduced her, and tried to recruit her in hopes of obtaining information for Bonn about U.S. research into gene-splicing technology. He taped calls during which she declared herself ready to engage in industrial espionage for Germany. When her nerve failed her he tried to blackmail her with the tapes. The affair ended messily with a suicide attempt by the woman.

Another BND Romeo was dispatched to Paris in 1984 with instructions to seduce the wife of an East German official at UNESCO and blackmail her into passing on information of East Berlin's policies and voting intentions at the U.N. This was picked up by our security officials at the embassy, and the man and wife were withdrawn before any harm could be done. A more unusual case arose in Oslo around the same time. The Norwegian counterintelligence service discovered through telephone taps that the wife of the East German ambassador was involved in a lesbian relationship with a Norwegian woman. Through other sources, we discovered that West German agents were planning to blackmail the ambassador's wife. The couple had to be hastily withdrawn.

The Romeos I have described in this chapter were not experienced Don Juans, much less Adonises. They were ordinary men who might pass by on the street without attracting a second look. When I reflect on their contribution to our work and some of the consequences for them, I have to admit that in several cases, the human cost was high in disrupted lives, broken hearts, and destroyed careers. I also regret that we allowed the liaison between Roland G. and his Margarete to become too deep and to go on for too long. The ends did not always justify the means we chose to employ. But it does irk me that Westerners adopt such a strident moral tone against me on the subject. As long as there is espionage, there will be Romeos seducing unsuspecting Juliets with access to secrets. After all, I was running an intelligence service, not a lonely-hearts club.

9

The Chancellor's
Shadow

Chancellor Willy Brandt was an engaging, intelligent, morally upright man and a compelling figure in postwar German history. He had an eye for the appropriate gesture—he fell to his knees in honor of the murdered Jews when he visited the Warsaw ghetto—and was honestly devoted to bridging the chasm between East and West Germany and the Communist and capitalist worlds. But we also knew him from his days in Berlin when he was one of the leading anti-Communists of the Cold War. When as leader of the government in Bonn he advanced his policy of reconciliation with the East—both East Germany and the rest of the Eastern bloc—known as *Ostpolitik*, we had every reason to want to be absolutely sure that he really meant to be our partner and was no longer our enemy.

The discovery that one of my agents had infiltrated Chancellor Brandt's private office abruptly ended Brandt's career at the helm of Germany. That is a responsibility that I bear and that troubles me even after his death. The question of why I did it, accompanied by the reproach "to Brandt, of all people," is one with which I will always be faced. The only justice I can now do to the late Willy Brandt is to explain in detail how the greatest spy scandal in postwar Germany happened and why.

On October 21, 1969, Willy Brandt, who as the young mayor of Berlin had watched in consternation as the Wall went up before his eyes eight years before, was elected West German chancellor. Three weeks later, a man called Günter Guillaume presented himself to the head of Brandt's office; he had been recommended by the labor leader Georg Leber for the post of junior aide to the chancellor with responsibility for links with the trade unions and other political organizations, and he was given the job. As simply as that, we secured a spy at the elbow of the leader of our prime target country.

We had never lost hope of penetrating the heart of Bonn, but no one expected to get so close to the top man. Nor would I have bet on Guillaume, whom we code-named Hansen, to be the one to accomplish this historic espionage coup. Like dozens of other young people, Günter, who had worked in an East Berlin publishing house with ties to the Ministry of State Security, and his wife, Christel, had been sent to the West on our orders in the mid-fifties, where they mingled with the tide of émigrés. Christel's mother, Erna Boom, a Dutch citizen, had settled in Frankfurt-am-Main and opened a tobacco shop. Christel always reminded me of an accomplished secretary—solid, self-reliant, unimaginative. Günter, on the other hand, was a shade larger than life, full of bonhomie and good at fitting in with any crowd.

Christel's family background and the presence of her mother in Frankfurt gave our couple the chance to evade the usual reception camps for East Germans and clear the bureaucratic hurdles erected by the authorities in order to aid secret service scrutiny of the new arrivals. We decided that our couple should try to make their career within the SPD itself as an operational cover. Both husband and wife progressed quickly in their roles as Social Democrats. Their rise to the top was not in our plan; they were intended eventually to act as handlers for our sources in the SPD. But they were simply far more energetic and industrious than we ever expected.

The Guillaumes lived in a comfortable apartment in Frankfurt, where they ran a copy shop and had a son, Pierre. Both were hard-working, Günter earning some extra money as a freelance photographer. In the predominantly left-wing milieu of the Frankfurt Social

Democratic Party, it was not long before the staunchly conservative Guillaumes caught the attention of right-wing members. The first leap forward was made by Christel, who was offered the job of head of Willy Birkelbach's office in the early 1960s. Birkelbach was one of those movers and shakers every party has who pulled a lot of strings in various quarters. He had a seat on the party executive committee, was president of the Socialist group in the European parliament, and was a state secretary in his native region of Hessen. He had access to NATO strategy documents like the study "A Portrait of War" and plans for nuclear emergencies.

Günter passed on this information on microfilm, handing it over in an empty cigar tube to a courier posing as a customer in his mother-in-law's shop. We maintained radio contact with him and Christel— rather too liberally in the early stages—at certain times and days of the month, using strings of encrypted numbers. Later we tightened up the process, reducing the volume of messages and changing the frequencies so that Günter would half grumble, half boast that he wore himself out finding our messages to him.

With the Social Democrats' historic adoption of a non-Marxist program at their conference in Bad Godesberg in 1959, the party became more interesting to us. The change in platform advanced the SPD's political fortunes and there appeared a distinct possibility it might enter the government. We encouraged Günter to concentrate on his own political career, and by 1964 he had become manager of the party's affairs for the Frankfurt district. We realized that his career was moving so fast that extra care was needed in handling him. The weak point in his story was that, as a supposed refugee and defector from the East, he should have had no contact with East Berlin at all. Once, while being driven to a meeting at one of the secret apartments we used for such business in East Berlin, he stopped at a road crossing to see a close acquaintance from his publishing days pass directly in front of the car. What would the man have thought if he had looked up and seen the same Günter Guillaume who was supposed to have fled this country? Pierre was also posing the kind of embarrassing problems children everywhere cause their parents by speaking plainly. In his case it was more than a mere embarrassment because he was in danger of innocently betraying his father. On one of Günter's visits to the East, the boy had been taken to the zoo by an officer with the thick accent of Saxony. On the way back to West Germany, Pierre imitated this most distinctive of Eastern dialects and asked Günter why the man spoke like that. His father felt the sudden strain that all spies must live with: the realization that their double lives have robbed them of the freedoms most citizens take for granted. He agreed that his secret visits to our headquarters should stop.

But his discipline and dedication never faltered. He rose to become a member of the Frankfurt city council and head of its SPD group. Guillaume's organizational abilities, along with his staunchly conservative position at a time of great ideological upheaval in the SPD, caught the eye of Georg Leber, the leader of the building workers union and later minister for transport in the grand coalition of 1966–69 between the SPD and the Christian Democrats. He needed a campaigner to help him secure the parliamentary nomination in his own constituency against the young left-winger Karsten Voigt. A solid and respected figure at the top of the party, Leber nevertheless faced a difficult fight for the nomination. The Left, encouraged by the radical mood of 1968, was determined to fight against the governing coalition of their own party with their ideological enemies, the Christian Democrats.

With Guillaume's tireless support and administrative help, Leber achieved a solid victory in the elections of September 1969. The Social Democrats emerged as the leading party for the first time since the war, and the situation could not have been better for Guillaume, who was associated with the result in one of the toughest constituencies in the country. Leber immediately promised to take him to Bonn. Observing this from East Berlin, we were pleasantly surprised but worried. His origins in East Berlin publishing were no secret, and in any case we knew that his placement in a government job in the capital would entail a far more thorough security check than he had undergone before as a mere worker bee in the Frankfurt party hive.

We ordered Günter and Christel to play a waiting game and not push for personal advancement in the new administration. They sat back and waited. As we had suspected, the security wheels ground exceedingly fine. Heribert Hellenbroich, later the head of West German foreign intelligence (Bundesnachrichtendienst), confirmed that Guillaume had been investigated like no one else before him—but without turning up anything. There had, however, been two vague tips from the evaluators in West Germany's counterintelligence (Office for the Protection of the Constitution, Bundesamt für Verfassungsschutz—BfV), and Horst Ehmke, the head of Brandt's office and thus responsible for personnel there, decided to confront Guillaume head-on with these suspicions.

Günter's reactions and his overall demeanor as he explained away his work at the Volk und Welt publishing house seemed so natural, as a stunned Ehmke would say later, that all doubts were put to rest. One man did continue to have an instinctive distrust of Guillaume and that was Egon Bahr, Brandt's most trusted adviser and the architect of *Ostpolitik*. Bahr told Ehmke that he was unhappy about moving Guillaume close to Brandt and said, "Maybe I'm doing the man a bad turn, but his past is too risky."

The reservations of the security services were swept aside with the explanation that denunciations of Easterners coming West were very common. Many émigrés felt that they had to dish out dirt on their fellows to prove their anti-Communist credentials with the West German authorities. In any case, several senior figures in the West German government had come from the East, including Hans-Dietrich Genscher, Brandt's interior minister and a member of the Free Democratic Party. Despite his origins, he was politically responsible for the BfV.

Other Social Democrats simply disliked Guillaume's ingratiating manner and habit of hanging around in the background during discussions that did not concern him; in hindsight it was not hard to see why he did this! But the new administration was above all determined to make a break with the past. Commitment, energy, and élan were far more important than a traditional, bureaucratic career path. This fresh approach benefited people like Guillaume who had no higher education or family connections behind them in politics. Patronage also counted, of course, and he had the congenial and influential Leber on his side. Thus, he was hired for the job, and with barely any effort on our part, as of January 28, 1970, we had our own man in the chancellor's office.

Guillaume seemed a sensible choice. Leber and other trade unionists wanted a trusted man in the Chancellery to help push the program of social and political reform, and, later, Brandt wanted a link with the unions. Within a year of his appointment, Guillaume had advanced to the newly created post of chief assistant responsible for liaison with parliament, government agencies, and the churches. One year later he was promoted to senior civil service rank and was directly responsible to the chief of the Chancellery, Horst Ehmke. But while Ehmke thought him competent, he never entirely forgot his unease about Guillaume's appointment.

•

I am often asked whether Guillaume helped put my service in a position to clearly judge the significance of Brandt's *Ostpolitik*. In other words, was the political risk of endangering Brandt's policy worth what we gained in intelligence? What we expected first and foremost from a source in the chancellor's office was timely warning regarding potential international crises. Watchfulness was Guillaume's priority. Before his move to Bonn, I had told him and other agents that we did not expect Brandt's new government to deviate from NATO policies or abandon the arms buildup. But I thought that it might well take steps toward easing tensions in Europe, a development that would merit close attention.

Guillaume's was essentially a political job and we used him to monitor the state of the Brandt administration, which was plagued from the start with internal strains and disagreements over its intentions in foreign policy, particularly toward the GDR and Moscow. In the run-up to the first meeting between Brandt and the GDR prime minister, Willi Stoph, in East Germany in March 1970, Guillaume gained access to some of the West German plans, which, combined with information from other sources, gave us a clearer idea of Brandt's intentions and fears.

Günter become steadily more valuable to us. For the SPD congress in Saarbrücken in mid-May 1970, a government office had to be set up to deal with the daily business of running the country. Guillaume was placed in charge of this office, which incidentally made him the liaison between it and the West German foreign intelligence service! He passed this test effortlessly—everyone commented on his efficiency and prodigious capacity for work—and subsequently received full security clearance.

Nevertheless, his real importance for us in East Berlin lay in his political instincts. Through Guillaume's judgments, we were able to conclude sooner rather than later that Brandt's new *Ostpolitik*, while still riven with contradictions, marked a genuine change of course in West German foreign policy. As such, his work actually aided détente by giving us the confidence to place our trust in the intentions of Brandt and his allies.

Guillaume's star continued to rise. Peter Reuschenbach, the SPD campaign director, was running for a seat in parliament and suggested that Günter take over from him in the run-up to the 1972 elections. Brandt had only been in office since 1969, so his term was far from up, but the Bundestag confidence vote on the Basic Treaty with the GDR had almost miscarried. We had helped Brandt scrape through by secretly paying Julius Steiner, a Christian Democrat, fifty thousand deutschmarks to buy his vote, but the narrow margin led the chancellor to call an early election for April 27, 1972. Our quick-witted, tireless worker was constantly by his side as the Social Democrats toured West Germany in their special election train.

During that period he grew close to Brandt and had an opportunity to observe his personal weaknesses. It was no secret that Willy Brandt was a compulsive womanizer and that his alleged romance with the journalist Wiebke Bruns continued throughout the election campaign. Unless Brandt's Norwegian wife, Rut, was on board (in which case she had the neighboring compartment), Guillaume's and Brandt's compartments were separated only by a thin wall. Guillaume soon realized that Brandt's adultery was frequent and varied. By now, our man was a trusted member of that set, and our only fear was that his opportunities to drink with his political cronies might blur his recollections. From what I know, the whole Social Democratic machine seems to have been lubricated by red wine. But a good agent knows how to hold his drink.

The coalition of Social Democrats and Free Democrats won an unexpectedly strong victory in the general election of 1972. For the first time in the history of West Germany, a non-Christian Democratic government commanded a clear parliamentary majority, which meant that *Ostpolitik* would go forward. During the television broadcast of the SPD's postelection party we glimpsed Günter cheerfully toasting the new chancellor along with all the rest of the Brandt team.

●

That autumn, another of our agents, Willy Gronau, code-named Felix, was arrested in West Berlin. He was director of the so-called Eastern Bureau of the West German Trade Union Association and one of our oldest sources. He was picked up while meeting his control officer from the East. It is unknown whether he or his control officer had come to the attention of the BND.

Guillaume and Gronau maintained professional contact with each other as part of their jobs, but neither of them knew that the other was an agent of East Germany. Our agents in the field were not even supposed to know about each other, let alone be in contact. But there must be some as yet scientifically unresearched law that says that people who are not supposed to find their way to each other always do. Gronau actually came to us with the tip that Guillaume would be a good catch for us and we might think about trying to recruit him! This caused a mixture of mirth and alarm back at headquarters. We were in the process of trying to pry these two from each other's company when fate intervened in the form of West German counterintelligence, and that was that for poor Gronau.

Given their acquaintance and similar political work, it did not seem odd to me that the authorities investigating Gronau questioned Guillaume as part of their inquiry. But his promotion as close adviser to the chancellor seemed a sure sign that the few suspicions arising when he was first hired had been swept aside.

By now Guillaume attended all the meetings of the party and parliamentary leadership of the SPD. He learned much as a scarcely noticeable, silent listener in the many conversations that Brandt liked to conduct in small groups. We tightened our security measures protecting Guillaume even further. Our contact with him was now kept to an absolute minimum. There were no more birthday greetings; only especially important information was transmitted, and that was done orally.

In July 1973 the first round of negotiations to set up the Council on Security and Cooperation in Europe (CSCE) were under way. Henry Kissinger, at that time security adviser to President Nixon, announced a strategic move called the Atlantic Declaration, according to which

Europe's NATO members would accept America's role as a global power in making defense strategy for the European continent. When Washington was seen pursuing separate negotiations with London and Bonn behind the backs of the other partners in order to push this forward, unrest grew within the alliance. The French in particular objected to what they viewed as an attempt to isolate them.

Small wonder that most of the communications the chancellor received on foreign policy issues during his holiday in Norway were devoted to the talks within NATO about the future of the Atlantic Declaration, then reaching a climactic phase. Guillaume was in charge of monitoring the telexes and preparing the official files Brandt received with his morning newspapers. A television team came to shoot a documentary at the chancellor's vacation retreat near Hamar. The cameraman shooting Guillaume as he stood by the code machine reading an incoming telex could hardly have known he was filming a master spy at work. All in all, Guillaume had time to copy three very important communications.

The first, on July 3, 1973, was the text of a letter in English sent by Richard Nixon in which he sought Brandt's help to pressure the French to sign the declaration. It was marked "private" and signed with a greeting in Nixon's own hand. The second was a detailed report from the West German ambassador in Washington about secret talks during which West German foreign minister Walter Scheel told Kissinger and Nixon that the declaration was a calculated push by Nixon to strengthen America's hand before the CSCE negotiations, and he saw no reason why the Europeans should automatically fall into line. Kissinger and Nixon also expressed their fears that the Soviet Union was making such advances in nuclear strategy that without technological reinforcement to NATO the Americans could no longer guarantee a nuclear first strike against a Soviet ground attack. The third document Guillaume tore from the chancellor's personal telex machine contained his adviser's skeptical response to the whole thing, urging Brandt to ignore American pressure and continue to pursue good relations with the French.

Further expressions of the European allies' opprobrium about the Americans chattered straight from the machine into the eager hands of Günter Guillaume. He perused British rejections of the American strategy. Paris went further in its rhetoric; Foreign Minister Michel Jobert accused the Americans of acting like firemen who set a fire so that they can rush in to put it out.

The time had come for Brandt to write a letter to his foreign minister laying out his position. But the chancellor was unhappy with his advisers' draft, which had been sent from Bonn, and worked on corrections for hours on end, suggesting different emphases and phrasing in green felt-tip pen. Brandt gave Guillaume the corrected version to send back to Bonn via his confidential telex. Guillaume, claiming that the original was too untidy to be given to the telex room as it was, typed out a clean copy. No one asked what had happened to Brandt's original.

Later, during Guillaume's trial, the public prosecutor stressed the fact that passing to the Soviet Union knowledge of the split within NATO

> could have reduced NATO's deterrent strength in the eyes of the Soviet Union, a deterrent strength predicated on the credible determination of the member states to a joint defense, genuine solidarity within the Alliance and a strategic balance of military forces. That could prompt the Soviet Union in its political and strategic considerations to take measures aimed at eroding the Western alliance and later to transform these into politically coercive measures.

In his memoirs, written in part to rub in the embarrassment of the affair to Bonn (after careful combing and adaptation by my service as disinformation—to protect other sources—and as positive P.R. for our work and its necessity), Guillaume strengthened the impression that passing Brandt's papers to us had been a major success for Soviet bloc intelligence. He concluded his reflections on the chancellor's Norwegian holiday:

> The holy of holies of Bonn sacraments was now in our holy of holies in Berlin.

By this he was suggesting that after copying the documents and placing them in a suitcase, he had passed them to East Berlin. This boast, which has since been accepted as fact, was to prove fateful for me many years later.

The regrettable truth, never before disclosed, is that we did not receive the enticing communications detailing the split between Washington and its European partners in such unguarded detail. Here is why: Our own worries about the Guillaumes began in the summer of 1973. Shortly after the stay in Norway, Christel began to worry that she was being watched. At first we had doubts about her concerns. It often happens that undercover agents, even very experienced ones, begin to see white mice. In perfectly normal situations they start to imagine that they are being followed or their movements recorded.

But the evidence hardened. Christel registered a clear case of surveillance in the garden of the Casselruhe restaurant in Bonn, where she would sometimes meet her courier. Two men had seated themselves close to her table. One of them opened a briefcase in her direction and she glimpsed a camera lens inside. In fact that was the very day Christel met her courier, Anita, and handed over the microfilmed documents from Norway, although fortunately the hand-over had been completed before the arrival of the men. The two women acted professionally, finished their drinks in a casual manner, and parted. As the courier walked through the city with the films in her handbag, she became convinced that one of the men was following her. She took a local train to Cologne, where she changed trams several times and ducked and weaved in the crowd as an agent is taught to do.

But she was unable to shake the tail. When she managed to move ahead of him and round a corner onto the riverbank, she decided to err on the safe side and dropped the package into the water below. Heinrich Böll dedicated his last novel, "Women in a River Landscape," to the Rhine and all the secrets it harbors. I could have helped him with an actual example.

When Guillaume was tried, the prosecution assumed that the Norway papers had reached us. We had instructed him to say nothing, but we decided not to disabuse the West Germans of the notion that we had done maximum damage. There was also a matter of Guillaume's pride. He was bitter about his lengthy sentence, but the one thing that comforted him—he was a rather vain man—was the knowledge that he was known worldwide as the German superspy. With our agreement, he spun the myth in his book that the handing over of the papers from Norway had been his crowning achievement.

One of the perils of being a spy chief is that you are not believed even when you do come clean. But I can say here that any search for Brandt's Norway papers in our files would be in vain, and not because they were destroyed in 1989: They would have been too old to be among the documents that had priority for shredding in the panic that followed the fall of the Wall. They are not there simply because neither I nor any of my officials ever set eyes on them. The only information we had came from the revelations inadvertently made by the West German side during Guillaume's trial. And they were relatively scant, given the original volume of the material involved.

West German counterintelligence had every reason to be suspicious about Guillaume's activities in the summer of 1973. The name Guillaume had caught the attention of a counterintelligence man while he was working on a different case. He was already familiar with Guillaume as a friend of Willy Gronau. No thread tied the two together, but that distinctive French name kept popping up. Particularly damaging was the fact that the case officer from our headquarters who had been arrested with Gronau in West Berlin had broken every elementary rule of secret service work: He had been carrying with him a slip of paper on which he had jotted down a few key words as an aide-mémoire. One of them was Guillaume, which he scribbled down because he had been told to urge Gronau to break contact with Günter, with whom we felt he was too close.

Guillaume's unusual name played a fateful role. If he had been called Meyer or Schultz, disaster might have been avoided. One more coincidence sealed his fate. The West German counterintelligence man who had noted the recurrence of Guillaume's name happened to sit down in the cafeteria one day with a colleague who was examining unidentified radio transmissions. They got to talking about their current projects, and this chance encounter proved to be Guillaume's undoing.

During the 1950s, my service had used the Soviet cipher system employed during the war to maintain contact with agents abroad. Each message began with a number, which was attached to a particular man or woman. It had long ago been cracked by Western services with the aid of computers. Once the fact had been established that each number represented a man or woman in the field, each call could be registered and collated. The telegrams were noted and eventually decoded. There was a file on every agent receiving the messages. The only remaining task for the other side was to put names to the numbers of the recipients.

As soon as we realized this, in 1959, we naturally changed the cipher and the calling method. We also made it a general rule never to make any concrete mention of people, places, or meetings in radio transmissions. After running a check on all our outgoing radio traffic, we were convinced that the messages we sent to the Guillaumes had given no indication of their identities. Alas, we overlooked the purely routine communications on birthdays, the New Year, or family events. Germans are very conscientious about such matters, and for our agents it emphasized the fact that they were part of our extended family. If we had been less conscientious, Guillaume might never have been discovered.

Several messages had gone out in 1957 to an agent identified as G. One sent birthday congratulations to G, the other to G's wife. The last said, "Congratulations on the Second Man." Sixteen years later, in that canteen in Cologne, plugging away at his unsolved cases of transmission intercepts and his mind jogged by his colleague, the investigator remembered the unsolved case of a supposed agent, G, who had become active toward the end of the fifties, had SPD contacts, and was important enough to receive congratulatory telegrams from his masters.

The message tracker got out the files and found the tantalizing messages. The one with its coy reference to the second man was the most puzzling. In fact we had sent it on the birth of Pierre, Günter and Christel's first and only son. The two intelligence men pondered this for some time until one of them declared that it alluded to the birth of a boy. They combed through the files of SPD people whose names had ever come up in other investigations. There, courtesy of the Gronau case, was Guillaume. Even then, our luck had not completely run out. I later heard from Klaus Kuron, our top mole inside West German counterintelligence, that the first suggestion that this man could be Guillaume was turned down by the analysis team, since he had only one son and the radiogram suggested that the newborn was the second in line. It took some bright spark, or perhaps a plain old-fashioned family man, to point out that the father is traditionally the first man in the family and the first-born son the second.

The next step was to decide how to proceed in acquiring decisive proof against Guillaume while avoiding further damage to Western interests. There were two options: start acquiring evidence immediately and push the inquiry on as quickly as possible, or leave Guillaume in place and monitor his connections. Cologne chose the second. In order not to raise Guillaume's suspicions, they first put his wife under observation, on the correct assumption that her husband's communications with the East ran through her. An obvious exchange of materials by her with a courier would have yielded the evidence they lacked.

So far, so good. But what happened next gives rise to the suspicion that not all politicians had Brandt's interest at heart. On May 29, 1973, Interior Minister Hans-Dietrich Genscher was informed of the Guillaume case by Günter Nollau, head of counterintelligence. In their testimony later before a parliamentary investigative committee, the two men gave different versions of what was said. Genscher and his chief of staff, Klaus Kinkel—later intelligence chief, justice minister, and finally foreign minister after Genscher's retirement—insisted that Nollau had spoken only of a suspicion and did not mention the evidence his agency had compiled in any detail. When Genscher informed Brandt of the conversation and of the recommendation from counterintelligence that Guillaume be left in place for observation, he apparently formulated it in such a casual way that Brandt acknowledged it only in passing and thought little more of it.

Nollau insisted until his death that he had given a strong warning, though eventually he shouldered the blame and resigned. The contradictions between the testimony of interior minister and the head of domestic intelligence led to rumors that Genscher had deliberately played down the importance of the information he had about Guillaume's case to let the full political force of the disaster fall on Brandt, as it did.

What are the possible explanations behind this? The first theory is that the ambitious Genscher, having seen that Brandt's government was in trouble, was already banking on his Free Democratic Party, which held the parliamentary balance of power, shifting its support to the Christian Democrats and that he was already having meetings with Helmut Kohl. Perhaps, but let us assume that Genscher and Nollau decided, for honorable reasons, to give orders not to change anything, to let matters take their course in order to harden the proof against Guillaume. In that case, Guillaume should never have been allowed to continue in his sensitive job as the chancellor's aide. If I had been Willy Brandt, my anger would have been directed first and foremost at Genscher.

The bald fact is that from the time counterintelligence informed Genscher that it was watching Guillaume until the day of his arrest, it gained not one extra crumb of evidence beyond what it already had. For one whole year, during which Guillaume continued to be entrusted with the top secret papers, those who were in on the secret tolerated having a spy close to the chancellor and handling the very state secrets they were supposed to guard. While we certainly laid down the kindling, others, including Genscher and Kinkel, lit the match to the fire that burned Brandt, and they allowed it to keep burning far longer than it should have.

Genscher must have been at pains to hide his dubious role when he told Parliament after Guillaume's arrest that a whole ring of agents had been flushed out. This was the only way to justify the delay in arresting our man. Having no ax left to grind, I can state that the story about a spy ring was a fabrication. The Guillaumes were a stand-alone spy couple.

●

After Christel's alert, we ordered both her and Günter to stop their intelligence work. Why did we not pull them out immediately? It was certainly a mistake not to do so, but it was not a matter of mere carelessness. I thought hard about whether to withdraw Günter. But the crude manner of Christel's surveillance misled us into thinking that there was no urgent suspicion about her husband. Georg Leber had by now become defense minister and offered Christel a job in his office as an assistant. We knew that that would entail a thorough security check and assumed her surveillance was the result of the job offer. Finally, we left the decision to the couple themselves, offering them the chance to return to the East if they believed themselves to be endangered. Neither saw any reason to do so.

Instead, we agreed to a cooling-off period. At this point I briefed Mielke. As I have already indicated, our relationship was not warm and I was keen to defend the independence of my department by running big agents myself. Only when our plans risked impinging on the political leadership did I clear matters with my superiors. In Guillaume's case, the political sensitivity of his position made it advisable to fill in the minister. Mielke agreed that it was best to play a waiting game. I consider it unlikely that he told Honecker or anyone else what was going on.

Nothing happened for several months, until February 1974. The Guillaumes themselves suggested resuming their intelligence work, but I recommended they remain in cold storage until the autumn of 1974.

It was during a vacation in the south of France in April that Günter saw that he was being blatantly followed by an entire swarm of French as well as German surveillance vehicles. But as he was driving home at night via Paris and Belgium the convoy vanished. It was a golden opportunity. His instinct and training should have told him that here was a chance to flee. The choice was still his.

The first reports that they had been arrested on April 24, 1974, caught me as much off guard as they did Willy Brandt, who learned the news at an airport as he returned from a visit to Egypt. Guillaume had gone out in style, but not the style we expected of one of our agents. When the police came to his house in the early hours of the morning with an arrest warrant, he cried out, "I am a citizen of the GDR and its officer. Respect that!"

This was disastrous, since it amounted to a confession of guilt without his even hearing the charges. With that statement, he spared West German counterintelligence and criminal justice authorities the major embarrassment that would have been caused by the lack of hard evidence against him. I had no explanation for this confession. After he came home to the East in 1981 and was allowed to write his memoirs for a limited audience, he tried to explain away his response by citing the early hour and the presence of his son. Certainly, Pierre played a huge role in Günter's life, and the father suffered from the burden of having to hide his real beliefs and his profession from his son. Pierre had grown up to be a Young Socialist on the party's left who saw his father as a traitor to the

Socialist cause. Something in Günter cried out to say to Pierre, "I am not what you think." Once I talked to Günter about the possibility of arrest and used the words, "Remain firm and confident." Perhaps in the mixture of early-morning bleariness and with Pierre looking at him in astonishment, his training and his instincts got muddled.

But there really was no excuse. A spy always has to be prepared for arrest. We trained our people very strictly on this. Confronted with an arresting officer, they were to give name, address, and date of birth as required by West German law and then say nothing other than to request that contact be taken up with the East German mission in Bonn, which would nominate an experienced lawyer. If that procedure was followed exactly, the burden of proof lay entirely on the West Germans.

But the truth—suppressed until now—was that Guillaume's marriage had been in trouble long before his arrest. He had a lover and wanted to protect her; he was returning from the south of France to move his things out of her flat. That was a serious mistake as well as a vain gesture toward the woman, a secretary, who committed suicide when she heard that he had been arrested for espionage.

In his remand prison in Cologne, Guillaume suffered as much from his sense of failure as from his harsh new environment. But our unmasked agent more than made up for his mistakes during his detention. He resisted all blandishments to exchange information about other agents for a reduction in his sentence.

Guillaume had admitted his mistakes. But what were ours? Had we not taken seriously enough the very early surveillance we spotted? Often enough during spy scares, there would be a flood of surveillance of innocent and guilty people alike. One sometimes had the impression that half of Bonn was employed watching the other. In the case of Guillaume, we were deceived by the amateurish nature of the tailing. But above all we were taken in by the fact that he was allowed to remain close to the chancellor. We thought it utterly inconceivable that a known agent would be left for a prolonged period of time in the inner circle of a leading statesman. Brandt and I were of one mind on this. In his memoirs, Brandt complained that the agent had been left in his immediate vicinity and added poignantly, "Instead of protecting the chancellor, he was made into an agent provocateur of his own country's secret service."

The professional mistakes that I and my colleagues made were of a different nature. In analyzing the dangers facing the Guillaumes, we completely overlooked the radio messages of fifteen years before, which we knew to have been decoded. We simply forgot about them. Only in the course of the subsequent investigation by the West German authorities were we reminded of their fateful significance.

After months of legal proceedings, the high court in Düsseldorf convicted Christel and Günter Guillaume. She was sentenced to eight years in prison, he to thirteen, which in other countries would be considered light, but in Germany the sentences were quite heavy. (German sentences for espionage were usually short in acknowledgment of the temptation and frequency of inter-German spying.) Throughout this testing time, the couple presented a unified face to the world and bravely gave no hint of any weakness in their marriage that could have been used to pry information from one or the other.

●

The Guillaumes' son, Pierre, was terribly shocked, and his father, almost deranged with worry, wrote pleading letters, making me promise to look after the teenager's welfare and turn him into a citizen the GDR could take pride in. This was not as easy as it sounded and demanded such commitments of time, personnel, and nervous energy that we seemed to need an entire department devoted to the lad. Of course it was hardly his fault. He had been brought up in an entirely different and anti-authoritarian milieu that encouraged individuality in dress, expression, and behavior. That wave thankfully had not washed over the Berlin Wall, and a kind of Prussian order still reigned in the schools of East Germany. But we found the most suitable school we could, where the headmistress was used to dealing with the rather spoiled children of East Germany's elite families. Several loyal activists in the Free German Youth and volunteers from families whom the secret services considered reliable were told to make friends with him. All to no avail. Pierre simply stopped turning up at school, and when he did he was disruptive and inattentive. Shortly afterward, he announced to our horror that he wanted to return to Bonn, where he had a girlfriend whose father was a

Conservative in the interior ministry. Every time Pierre took a trip to the West to see his father in prison, we thought that we might lose him.

We thus engaged in desperate measures to keep him. He had become interested in photography, so my department bought him the latest equipment and gave him a coveted apprenticeship at the best color magazine we could find. In the fullness of time, he got himself a new socialist girlfriend, an East German whose father was an officer in my service. Our relief was immense. But there was one more twist to the tale. A year or so later, I heard that they had both applied for permission to leave East Germany. Nothing could be done to dissuade them. We conceded defeat and sped their departure through the bureaucracy as quickly as we could, waving them good-bye with some relief. I had tried to keep my word to Günter as best I could, but there was no mistaking his disappointment. It was many years before the rift healed between father and son.

We advised Guillaume to remain silent in prison while we worked quietly to exchange him for Western agents. But the chances for a quick prisoner swap worsened with Brandt's inevitable resignation in 1974. His successor, Helmut Schmidt, insisted that Guillaume would have to serve his sentence "to the last day." The case became a political football, and not just in Germany. Washington and Moscow became players when Anatoly Sharansky, the imprisoned Soviet Jewish dissident, was proposed as a potential swap. One initiative followed another, but the years dragged on, to the detriment of morale among our younger agents. Fighting for the return of our captured spies was not just a moral duty but an important means of reassuring their colleagues on risky missions in the present and future.

In March 1981, Christel Guillaume was set free as part of a multiple exchange of agents. Günter's sentence still had eight years to run. One of the Westerners involved in the swap accused the government in Bonn of not doing enough to get its agents out of jail in the East. That increased the momentum behind the campaign, and Guillaume was finally exchanged in the autumn of that year.

On a gray October day he returned to the homeland he had set out to serve twenty-five years earlier. I arranged a reception for him at one of our secret country addresses. Anxious to make the homecoming as rewarding for Günter as possible, we sent his old handlers to meet him

at the border and bring him straight to the reception. Wearing his captors' good-bye gift of an ill-fitting chain-store suit, he arrived rather
dazed by his freedom. We filmed his return for a documentary entitled
Mission Accomplished, which we used in our training programs. I knew
that he was still sore about not having been exchanged earlier, so I
wanted to make it especially clear to him that he was viewed as a hero.

After the long imprisonment and worries about his family, he looked
pale and unsteady. Even so, he responded to my greeting, "Welcome
home, Günter, it's good that the long time has passed." He replied,
"Thank you for everything." I hastened to say that it was we who
should thank him, and there was a long exchange of mutual thanks.

Then he saw his wife, Christel, waiting at the side. Despite the difficulties the marriage had faced before and would soon face again, the
two threw themselves into each other's arms and embraced. It was
impossible not to be moved by this. They were given a pleasant residence and a few days alone together to sort things out. Christel had let
us know that she did not want to return to Günter, and this turned out
to be a terrible shock after the hopes for a reconciliation he had nurtured during the long years in prison.

His morale and his health were low, but his expectations were high.
I think he envisaged a job as my right-hand man, popping in from the
office across the corridor to give advice on running Western agents.
But he had been out of the game too long. I remember asking the doctor who treated his numerous health complaints what we should do
with Günter. The physician, who had treated several of the elderly
men in the political elite and had no illusions about their capabilities,
was blessed with a dry sense of humor, and when I sighed that the only
thing that would satisfy Günter was a place in the politburo, he
replied, "Well, one more or less won't make any difference."

Female companionship helps in such situations, and we assigned
Guillaume a pleasant middle-aged nurse, ostensibly to look after his
kidney and circulation problems, but also for a romantic trial. It
worked, and they married soon after and settled in a pleasant house in
the countryside outside East Berlin, Günter's reward for his services to
the republic.

Western assessments of Guillaume suggest that he had a split personality. It seems difficult for people to understand that a man like

Guillaume could serve two such diametrically opposed masters without suffering psychological damage. In order to reach the goals that have been set for him, an agent above all must preserve under the skin into which he has slipped the convictions that led him to the job in the first place. Guillaume succeeded in his task by getting close to Brandt, but this did not stop him from respecting the man for his many personal and professional qualities and for his achievements. During the formulation of *Ostpolitik*, Guillaume was convinced that he in his own way was contributing to this new understanding.

●

I have always maintained that the Guillaume affair was not the cause but only the pretext for Brandt's resignation on May 4, 1974, shortly after Guillaume's arrest. In his memoirs, Brandt argued that the discovery of a spy in his entourage should not have been a compelling reason for him to go. My own view is that he was the victim of difficulties within the SPD and a crisis of confidence in the leadership, caused not least by the uncomfortable triangle of power of which he made up one corner; Herbert Wehner, then whip of the parliamentary party, the second; and Helmut Schmidt, finance minister and Brandt's successor, the other. Guillaume's reports had made it clear that even before the scandal, Brandt's enemies inside his cabinet were no less fierce than those we sent from East Berlin. The strongest of these was no doubt Wehner.

A sour-faced, sharp-tongued man, Wehner was one of the few remaining links to the byzantine world of the prewar German Left, bitterly divided between Social Democrats and Communists before the war. As a young Communist he had undertaken secret work for the Party in Czechoslovakia and the Soviet Union. During the 1930s he had held a position in the Comintern leadership where, it would later emerge, he had betrayed some of his comrades to the NKVD. During the war, in Sweden, he was arrested and gave all his knowledge about the Communist Party and its members working in Germany to the Swedish police. Because of this betrayal he was expelled from the Party in 1942. As a postwar Social Democrat he was the only senior West German politician who knew members of the East German leadership from the prewar days, including Erich Honecker. They were separated

by many years, many secrets, and much bitterness and mutual recrim-
ination over Germany's fate, but they shared the special bond of a
common social and ideological past, which helped them bridge the
divide of the Cold War.

Despite his rather terrifying demeanor (it was said only partly in jest
that house pets ran under the sofa whenever his face appeared on television), Wehner had great sympathy for the effects of Germany's division
on people's personal lives. He simplified the procedures for exchanging
prisoners through a face-to-face meeting with Honecker in May 1973.
Pathologically afraid of the Soviet Union after his wartime experiences
there, he once confessed that he shook with fear before his first trip to
Moscow. But he and Honecker found that their youth in the Communist movement helped create a relationship very close to friendship. I
would go so far as to say that Wehner's journey from communism to
social democracy brought him closer to the East toward the end of his
life—even though he remained ideologically at odds with it—because he
felt closer to the GDR under Honecker than to his own Party.

From the start Brandt suspected Wehner's contacts with us, convinced that his colleague was negotiating with us behind his back. I
suppose the leadership of the Social Democratic Party had known
since the 1950s about the confidential contacts, but on what scale and
in how much detail Brandt was informed I do not know. Brandt suspected Wehner's closest colleague in the Bundestag, Karl Wienand, of
working for the KGB or my service. This was not an idle suspicion;
after unification, Wienand, who had been the SPD's secretary in the
West German parliament, was accused of serving as one of my agents.
All of the leading SPD politicians testified at his trial, which concluded
in mid-1996, and each confirmed that he had known that Wehner had
used Wienand to maintain contact with us. None of them, however,
knew the details of such contacts.*

In truth, Wehner and Honecker were not secretly plotting, and
there was no conspiratorial contact between Wehner and the Soviet
Union. Nevertheless, Brandt felt betrayed and his suspicions verged
on the paranoid. However, as the old saying goes, even paranoid people have enemies and there is no doubt in my mind that for political

---

*Wienand was sentenced to two and a half years in prison and was ordered to pay a fine of 1 mil-
lion DM. His appeal has not yet been decided.

reasons Wehner used his knowledge about the unusual—and unconstitutional—monitoring of Brandt's private affairs by the West German
criminal police for political reasons during the Guillaume affair. After
Guillaume was unmasked, Horst Herold, the head of the Federal
Criminal (Police) Office (Bundeskriminalamt), issued a report based
on an interrogation of Brandt's security team about the chancellor's
private life, a catalogue of his affairs with journalists, casual acquaintances, and prostitutes. The report stressed the allegation that Guillaume had been responsible for procuring women for Brandt.

Guillaume had of course been telling us about this kind of behavior
all along, which regularly raised the possibility of our blackmailing
Brandt over his private life. We never attempted to do so. First, we
knew that in the inbred, carefully protected political world in Bonn,
the press would not touch the information. In any case, it would not do
us much good, since we had no interest in destroying him, especially
since we had learned to deal with him, knew plenty about him, and followed the maxim of all intelligence services of working with the devil
we knew rather than getting accustomed to a new one.

It was the puritan Wehner who first realized the implications of
Brandt's behavior and exploited them. He approached Brandt with dire
warnings of the potential scandal that would result if Guillaume revealed
the piquant details of the chancellor's sex life in court. Wehner also
warned Brandt that he had become prone to blackmail from East Berlin,
though I do not think that Wehner really believed this was likely. It
would have brought us little gain, and Wehner of all people knew
Honecker well enough to realize blackmail of this sort did not suit the
East German leader's cautious style. Helmut Schmidt, already ambitious
to succeed Brandt as chancellor, maintained more discretion but did not
offer much help, either. Thus, Brandt, who enjoyed the highest regard
in the international community, was left alone by his own party colleagues to bear the realization not only that he had been spied upon by a
hostile foreign service since coming to power, but that his own country's
police and security services had been monitoring his weaknesses, and
their files could be used against him by his rivals at any time. He was
trapped, and in his estimation the only option was to resign.

Anticipating adverse political reaction in the East bloc and Moscow
to the discovery that we had spied on Brandt, I wrote a study, "On the

Development of the Coalition Crisis and Brandt's Resignation," which I gave to Honecker. I mention this because Brezhnev and later Honecker claimed that they had expressed displeasure at Guillaume's unmasking and claimed to have no knowledge of his existence, let alone his espionage. That may be true, but one month after Brandt's resignation I was informed by Mielke that Moscow agreed with my view that the genesis of the scandal was in West German domestic politics. In East Germany, where Brandt's strong following among ordinary people was grounded in the fact that *Ostpolitik* meant they could see family members in the West again, his political fall was unpopular. In Neustrelitz, unseen hands painted WILLY BRANDT STREET on a sign, and in Erfurt, where Brandt had first set foot in the East in 1970, anonymous posters appeared denouncing his betrayal. The post office in the northern town of Güstrow intercepted a sympathy telegram that three young women had tried to send to Brandt that read, "We hope that your successor will have the courage to take to a conclusion the process you began." Even then, I could hardly ignore that his fall from office was considered a disaster in both East and West and that my service was being blamed.

Conversely, the view persists that Guillaume's infiltration into the Chancellery was my greatest success. Willy Brandt's admirers—and there are many in the old East Germany—cannot forgive me for my role in his downfall. For that reason and for the record I must emphasize that I view the Guillaume case as the greatest defeat we suffered up to that time. Our role in bringing down Brandt was equivalent to kicking a football into our own goal. We never desired, planned, nor welcomed his political demise. But once the chain of events had been set in motion, they had their own momentum. Where was I supposed to have yelled stop?

The relationship between politics and intelligence work is often an uneasy one. From the time Andropov came to power in Moscow, and also under Gorbachev, the basic doctrine was that spying should not interfere with détente. At the same time, pressure was increasing to discover NATO's secrets. We were, as the old Russian proverb has it, supposed to wash the bear without getting its fur wet. The best way to guard against criticism in such a situation is to do absolutely nothing. Some of my colleagues achieved this feat, had no great successes, and enjoyed a peaceful life. Success has both its rewards and punishments.

Two weeks after Brandt's resignation, I tried to pull my feelings together and wrote in my diary:

> B. left his personal mark on our times and their course. He accomplished a great deal. Much of what made him so subjectively appealing was weakness in the real political world. So, suddenly, we have played the role of Nemesis without wanting to.

One can justifiably ask now whether the stakes were not too high, the risks too great to keep Guillaume in Brandt's office. One always has to reckon with the possibility that things might go awry and calculate the price of failure from the beginning. But is this really possible? Where does one stop? The logical consequence would be to shut down all foreign intelligence services. I do not see that happening anywhere, at least not yet.

Much later, in different times, I was personally to experience Willy Brandt's greatness of heart when, just before his death in 1993, he spoke out against my criminal prosecution on the occasion of the press conference announcing the publication of the French edition of his memoirs in 1991. I would have welcomed the opportunity to offer him my apology in person, but he had no wish to see me or Guillaume; he wrote that "it would cause me too much pain."

In mid-1995 Guillaume died after a long illness. I attended his funeral in the soulless new cemetery in Berlin-Marzahn, a vast high-rise housing project that stands as a concrete tribute to Honecker's grand, doomed vision of a worker's republic. At the last moment before the short secular service began, the doors of the building were thrown open and a wind-blown figure hurried in. I turned round, hoping to see Christel or Pierre, the boy who had grown up too fast, learned too late that his father had two lives, and had known only the fictional one. In the catalogue of victims of spying, children should be mentioned more often and the effect on their lives watched more closely.

But neither Pierre nor Christel came. They both stayed away, the wounds of the past too deep to heal before his death. The late arrival was his second wife, Elke, the woman we had chosen to care for him and who became the love of his late life. She sat silently, her eyes looking past the curious guests, remembering someone she had known and loved not as the famous or infamous agent Guillaume but as a retired man trying to make sense of his life while the system he knew and served so courageously crumbled around him. We walked out together into the scrubland of an untended graveyard, and the coffin was borne to earth. In keeping with Communist tradition, I cast a single red rose after it.

10

The Poison of Betrayal

Treachery is by no means as rare as we like to think. In ordinary lives friends or loved ones let us down, and at work close colleagues turn on us or plot our downfall to advance themselves. It is an unlovely but predictable part of our existence. Betraying one's country, however, is considered a grave breach of citizenship by most people, whatever their political convictions about the system in which they live. I have known all sorts of traitors whose acts were motivated by reasons both noble and base, and that includes men and women I have already written about who were prepared to divulge secrets to a foreign power out of ideological, financial, political, or plain personal motives.

But there is one class of treason that appalls and enthralls in a particularly intense way and is worth special examination: the traitor inside one secret service who delivers himself and his secret knowledge into the hands of another. Some people assume that a willingness to betray colleagues might make those who work in the intelligence world immune to disillusion when betrayal occurs among their own ranks. That is wrong. Betrayal is poison for every intelligence service against which the vaccines at our disposal have only limited effect.

The psychological culture of an espionage service resembles that of a clan or tribe, in which individuals are united by some greater goal and a shared sense of identity, ideological or otherwise. When this is ripped open, a poison of distrust enters the system. Agents in the field, even if their work is unconnected to the area where the betrayal has occurred, suffer a cold chill of vulnerability when they next approach a dead-letter drop (a place where one can secretly receive or send a letter, message, microfilm, and so on) or tune in to coded instructions from headquarters. It is also notoriously difficult to recruit new agents after a big defection.

For the masters as well there can be unsettling consequences. An intelligence service suddenly becomes the subject of the politicians' unwelcome interest after it emerges that something has gone wrong. Consider, for example, the earthquake that virtually paralyzed the CIA after the discovery of Aldrich Ames's treason. A traitor within an intelligence service betrays much more than the men or women whose names he gives away. He betrays the whole integrity of his service.

There are, of course, ways to minimize such risks. One is to create a strong collegial feeling, a team spirit in which each person cares about the others' safety and welfare on a personal and a professional level. Another is to build on existing patterns of loyalty—ideological, political, geographical—that date from childhood, ensuring that any officer who thinks of turning traitor is made to feel that so doing would make him a traitor to himself. The predominance of WASP, East Coast Americans in the CIA, the Oxford and Cambridge networks within the British secret services, and the family dynasties within Soviet intelligence are all protective mechanisms against betrayal.

The consequences of defection are so far-reaching that even the slightest suspicion must be taken seriously. I never labored under the illusion that my own officers were exempt from temptation, although I know from other Eastern bloc services how unwilling intelligence chiefs can be to accept that they may harbor an agent of destruction in their midst.

Of all the relations between Eastern intelligence services, those between the GDR and the Poles were the most fraught. However loyal the Polish Communists may have been to Moscow and its allies, European history ensured that the resentments of the might of both Germany and Russia had left scars. Our joint operations demanded great skills in diplomacy as well as espionage.

I once received information from a mole within West German intelligence to the effect that a senior employee of the Polish Interior Ministry had offered to spy for West Germany by offering his services to an official of the decoding department of Bonn's Warsaw embassy. I decided to travel incognito to Poland to warn my colleagues and took up a long-standing invitation from the Polish deputy minister of state security, Franciszek Szlachcic, for a weekend hunting trip at the ministry's exclusive reserve in Upper Silesia. As we stalked wild boar through the dark tangle of trees, I told him about the approach that was made. We agreed that the best course of action would be to meet privately with his counterintelligence chief and plan a sting. The plan was to catch the suspect red-handed by summoning him to a fake assignation at which some of my officers would masquerade as West Germans.

At the private meeting with the head of counterintelligence I discovered that Szlachcic, intent on showing me how seriously he took the matter, had invited a number of senior officers to help plan the details. Too many cooks very definitely spoiled the broth. We set up our trap and waited in vain for the man to turn up at the appointed meeting in a flower shop. A fall-back appointment did not work either. It was clear to me that there had been a leak from within the Polish Ministry of State Security itself from one of the many people who had heard the story. The last thing I heard, the Polish traitor-in-waiting had approached the British instead. I had no desire to go through the whole thing again and left the Poles to their own devices.

I never assumed that my own service was without weak links. The painful early lesson of our defections protected me against a belief in the moral superiority of all our men, although I like to think that the ideological bond that held us together was a very strong one. The challenge for both of the German intelligence services after the war was to build up a sense of identity and belonging strong enough to minimize the risk of betrayal from within. We did this more effectively than the West Germans, who have always viewed their intelligence operations as an adjunct of the civil service instead of trying to instill as we did a military sense of comradeship befitting the dangers inherent in an espionage service.

•

Each defection has its own history and teaches its own lessons. The one that hit me hardest came in 1979, at the height of revived Cold War tension in Europe, and involved an officer in one of my most secretive and efficient departments, Department B, a part of the Scientific and Technological Sector, known by its German initials SWT (Sektor Wissenschaft und Technik).

On January 19, 1979, my birthday, I was sitting in a meeting with intelligence chiefs in the region of Karl-Marx-Stadt. The session had hardly begun when I was called to the telephone. One of my deputies was on the other end and the tension in his voice was palpable. He came straight to the point. "It's SWT," he said. "Someone's gone." My immediate reaction, shared, I imagine, by intelligence chiefs the world over, was to engage in a bout of robust cursing. "But there's worse to come, Chief," said the voice at the other end. "The safe is open, some papers have gone and, damn it, so is the identity pass for the border." This was a pass—each department had just one—that could be used by a department member with business at the main Berlin border crossing, Friedrichstrasse station. The East German border guards would allow the person access to the Western side of the station.

Two days before at a meeting of my top cadres at a Party gathering, I had delivered my traditional New Year's address. "Never forget, comrades, the worst thing that can happen to us is for the enemy to manage to penetrate our ranks," I had said. It had been a cautionary tale, but now it had happened, and I was stunned. Especially painful for me was the realization that this defection came from SWT, a department to which I had devoted special attention because of my belief that the best espionage in the world would be useless if we failed to keep pace with the West's scientific and technological advances.

Inquiries to the border guards revealed that the pass had been used at 9:30 P.M. the previous night, so the defector had been gone twelve hours by the time anyone noticed. He had chosen his timing carefully, during the winter holiday season. In HVA's East Berlin headquarters, the vast, heavily guarded block in the Normannenstrasse, they were home, trying to figure out which of the department's officers was on leave enjoying a well-earned winter break and which was the traitor.

They drew up a list of suspects. By the time I reached East Berlin three hours later, it was clear that the man in question was Senior Lieutenant Werner Stiller, an officer of Subdepartment 1, which dealt with nuclear physics, chemistry, and bacteriology. One of the brightest officers in his department, he had an affable, confident manner and had just been chosen as the Party's first secretary in his department, a post usually given to someone considered particularly solid and reliable. Stiller was certainly the worst defection we had had in decades. (In 1959 Major Max Heim, who was a central figure in our work against the Christian Democrats, defected, leading to the arrest of a dozen of our agents. In 1961 Walter Glasse, an officer responsible for our work against American organizations in Germany, defected, compromising a number of our operations. Both men lived in West Germany and cooperated with West German intelligence when called upon.)

All emergency procedures were running. Warning messages were sent to the agents and informants Stiller ran in the West, instructing them to stay home and dispose of any incriminating documents, while our analysts pored over the lists of files, trying to work out what material Stiller had taken. The race was on for us to warn vulnerable people before the West Germans learned from Stiller's material where they should pounce.

We established that Stiller had taken with him the files with the list of informants. They contained the so-called companion-information lists of the entire Scientific and Technological Department, brief summaries of the reports recently delivered by agents and sources, and the code names of those who had compiled them. They could not alone betray the identity and whereabouts of our agents and sources, but counterintelligence in Cologne could use them to reinforce any suspicions it may have had. I had to admit that Stiller had shown some nerve and prepared his escape well. Taking the files of informants with him meant that he had something concrete to offer the other side when he turned up in West Berlin. He was clearly so serious about defecting that he was prepared to risk the death penalty by being caught with such materials. This meant that he either was already in the pay of the enemy, or intended to become so.

Just when I thought it could not get any worse, it did. Mielke's ter-ror-stricken voice on the other end of my emergency line informed me that one other set of items was missing from the safe: boxes filled with his own speeches and orders. Given the often meandering and repeti-tious character of Mielke's proclamations, this struck me as mainly embarrassing and hardly the worst of our problems that day. The min-ister did not, however, see it that way. I could not get him off the hot line. "What have those bastards got on me?" he roared over and over again. "What a f——g shambles! We might as well just invite the enemy to attend our meetings and have done with it! You all make me sick."

I bit my lip to control my anger, although I would have loved to yell back. But I had often experienced his childish tantrums and allowed him to let off steam. Then I made copies of his documents from another archive and sent them with a formal note that read, "Enclosed are copies of the papers bearing your signature which are now in enemy hands." That gave him time to absorb the shock before the first of these documents would be fed to the media by our gleeful foes in West German intelligence and thereupon published for all to read.

To comprehend how heavy a blow Stiller's defection was, it is neces-sary to understand the status of scientific and technological espionage at that time in the socialist countries. SWT was organized in the 1950s as a tiny department responsible mainly for helping us keep pace with Western developments in nuclear weapons technology. Several high-level Western physicists and biologists, perturbed by the prospect of West Germany's rearming itself, began to report to us that the building of nuclear power stations in West Germany was being organized in such a way that processing plants for combustion elements and isotope isolation could be converted quickly for military use.

This was already an area of a relentless propaganda war. The public responded fearfully to any suggestion that rearmament could be extended to the production of nuclear weapons. There was more than enough covert West German activity to keep us busy; technological advances in plutonium extraction were rapid, and a new generation of postwar entrepreneurs stepped up their involvement in Third World countries with nuclear ambitions, such as Brazil, Argentina, Libya, Pakistan, and South Africa.

But nuclear questions were also sensitive in East Germany. Our country had no development program separate from the Soviets'. Having taken control of East Germany's uranium-mining operations after the end of the war, Moscow continued to control them tightly until the collapse of East Germany and German unification in 1990. Wismut AG, with its headquarters in the south of the GDR, was ostensibly run as a German-Soviet joint venture but in fact was a state within a state run by the Russian military using German managers, engineers, and scientists.* This continued Russian control long after all other such ventures had been handed over to us, together with the undeniable fact that the Soviets were carting off valuable resources from East Germany for their own military needs, made the uranium project the most politically sensitive project in the country.

The precarious energy situation and balance-of-payments problems in our country led to intermittent calls for us to set up our own nuclear energy program. This was supported by people like the nuclear scientist Klaus Fuchs, who had settled in Dresden after his release from a British prison for passing secrets of the West's atomic bomb to Moscow. Fuchs also believed that the Soviet Union was cheating the GDR by paying too low a price for the uranium. I suspected that he was right, and my service found itself in the middle. On the one hand, we were passing to the Soviets most of the scientific and technological information we obtained. On the other, scientists in our own country argued that we could become competitive with the West only by forging ahead with our own technological development. The leadership became more and more interested in the evaluations of different types of reactors, and the pressure grew on my Scientific and

---

* My brother, Koni, made one of his best films about Wismut, *Sonnensucher* (*Sun Seekers*), which depicted the world of uranium mining as it really was in its early years—a sort of Wild East, peopled by desperadoes, cirminals, and returning soldiers anxious to make quick money under the watchful eyes of informers and the military command. The film was intended by Koni to be the first halfway honest cinematic reckoning with the problem of the Soviet presence in East Germany and the trauma that accompanied two nationalities that had been bitter enemies trying to come to terms with each other. Posters for the film had gone up all over East Berlin in 1956, and we were all set for the premiere when Walter Ulbricht panicked after being told that the Soviet ambassador, Pyotr Abrassimov, disapproved of any discussion of the uranium projects. Members of the Felix Dzerzhinsky regiment of guards, the Ministry of State Security's own soldiers, were sent out in the dead of night to tear down the posters, and the film was shelved for another ten years.

Technical Sector to provide this information without letting the Soviets know that we were even thinking about doing so.

I went to see Heinrich Weiberg, the wise old head of the SWT, for advice on what lines of intelligence we should be pursuing. He was a thorough academic and something of a misfit among the hardened veterans of the prewar Communist underground, who held most of the senior jobs in the State Security apparat. In fact, his sole political experience was in the Red Sports Movement, where he had been a passionate cyclist. He also had never acquired the hierarchical thinking that dominated our office culture, scorned the perks of his position, and insisted on turning up for work on an old bicycle. This made him a laughingstock among the middle and senior employees, who enjoyed showing off in their imported VW Golfs, or Citroëns and Fords for those higher up the ladder.

Weiberg insisted on enlightening me about every known detail of the reactors, whether or not I understood what he was talking about. I was accustomed to departmental heads giving me sharp, short answers, but he knew no form of communication other than the hour-long lecture, so I settled politely for a graduate-level class in applied physics. Weiberg was a believer in the fast-breeder reactor already under construction in West Germany. We were stuck with Soviet models whose risks were apparent to Weiberg. "We have to move on, Comrade Wolf," he said. "Can't you tell them [the politburo] that this is where the future lies?"

Fortunately for us the decision to start our own nuclear program was never made, mainly because of the cost but also because the leadership feared a falling-out with Moscow. A few years after this episode, the West Germans abandoned the fast-breeder technology because they were unable to solve the problem of cooling sodium. The only benefit my crash course in nuclear science brought me was the undeserved reputation in Moscow of being some sort of Renaissance man who could turn his hand to science as well as my other areas of expertise. I had taken in enough of Weiberg's thesis to be able to ask the right questions when I visited the nuclear research center near Lenin's birthplace of Ulyanovsk on the Volga. They sent a report back to my Moscow colleagues praising my astounding grasp of the subject.

●

By the mid-sixties, it had become clear to me that East Germany was lagging behind in the wider race for technological innovation. Millions were being pumped into research and development in West Germany, whereas our leadership, barring occasional outbursts of enthusiasm for some random project that had caught its fancy, starved scientists and engineers of resources and diverted spare cash instead to trying to satisfy consumer demand and thus prevent popular unrest.

It was after a conversation with frustrated scientist acquaintances that a way out of this misery suddenly dawned on me. If our agents were in a position to penetrate the political elite in Bonn and NATO headquarters in Europe, then why could they not gain access to industrial secrets? Although my main abilities and interests lay in political intelligence, I became increasingly obsessed by the potential of SWT. My family joked that it was late compensation for my unfulfilled boyhood dream of studying aeronautical engineering in Moscow; I still kept up my subscriptions to all the aviation magazines I could get my hands on, from the East or West.

But I could see that in chemical engineering, micromechanics, mechanical engineering, and optics, we had brilliant scientists who, because of the Western embargo on exporting technology to the Eastern bloc and the limited travel opportunities allowed them by East Germany, were busily engaged in the high-tech equivalent of reinventing the wheel. A little unofficial access to state-of-the-art Western research could go a long way, I reasoned, and besides, the leadership's appreciation of the intelligence services would rise if we could help them balance industry's books.

We would of course need far more specialists than we had. I discussed the idea with some of my senior officers and we agreed that the starting point would be a recruiting drive among science students. One of the first recruits was Werner Stiller.

An able physics student at Karl Marx University in Leipzig, Stiller was approached by one of our local talent spotters. When the local authorities were sure that he was a reliable prospect, he was sent to us in East Berlin, where he signed the document pledging himself "conscientiously and with all my strength" to the service of the German Democratic Republic through the Ministry of State Security. In an echo of the Communist adventure novels of his youth, he chose the cover name Stahlmann—"man of steel"—the same name assumed by my old boss. No sooner had he signed up than he and his two controlling officers downed a cognac.

Stiller was a handsome, thickset young man with a steady, intelligent gaze. He was too small a fish for me to have encountered personally, although he later liked to boast that he had met me. By his character, I would place him in the category of calculating, robust men rather than the fiercely ideological types we also had. Stiller was sent to Subsection 1 of the department, whose official purpose was to keep up with West German atomic research and monitor the deployment of all new weapons systems there.

By the time he defected, Stiller was in charge of a dozen unofficial sources inside the GDR and seven Western agents we had recruited, including Rolf Dobbertin, a Paris-based atomic physicist*; Reiner Fülle, a senior researcher at the Nuclear Research Center in Karlsruhe; one entrepreneur with the Siemens company; and another in the nuclear industry in Hanover. Stiller took with him information that also helped the West Germans discover that Professor Karl Hauffe, head of the atomic research program at Göttingen University, had been recruited by the KGB, although we controlled him from Berlin.

Besides focusing on nuclear developments, the department also expanded its industrial espionage, sounding out the West's burgeoning computer industry and searching for business contacts prepared to bypass the Western embargo. One of our best agents in this sphere was Gerhard Arnold, alias Storm, who as a young man had been sent to the West by us as a "sleeper spy." Since then he had risen through the ranks at IBM Deutschland and passed on its internal papers on the development of new systems and software. Arnold was a strange case in that he had long distanced himself from us politically and refused to accept our money but continued to pass us information because he felt a vestigial attachment to the East.

Computer research was particularly valuable to East Germany, which boasted the top microelectronics company, Robotron. But our research lagged far behind America's and Japan's. The only way Robotron could

*After serving five years in a French prison, in a retrial Dobbertin was acquitted of espionage. Dobbertin never denied passing along information, but called it "scientific developmental aid for my GDR colleagues."

even hope to keep pace was by acquiring Western knowledge and soft-ware forbidden to us under the embargo. Closely modeled on IBM, Robotron became so heavily dependent on surreptitiously acquiring IBM's technological advances that it was, in effect, a sort of illegal sub-sidiary of that company.

Capitalizing on his success, Stiller soon reached the rank of senior lieutenant. He was on his way up when he decided to defect for rea-sons that, as far as I know, were entirely based on his desire for a better life in the West. His marriage was on the rocks, and he had a lover, an East German waitress named Helga who had a brother in the West. Through this brother, Stiller had made contact with West German intelligence, probably in the mid-seventies. He worked out a deal to inform West Germany about the operations of his department in return for large sums of money and eventually a ticket to a secure life in the West. This is a fairly common pattern for prospective defectors. The problem, however, is that after the enemy service has hooked a person, it is more interested in keeping a new acquisition where he is—feeding valuable information from the heart of the enemy camp—than in welcoming him onto their territory. Of course the traitor sees it differently, particularly as months and years pass and his danger of exposure increases. The result is usually a battle of wills in which each side in the deal tries to pressure the other.

Stiller's luck was running out fast. In 1978, our counterintelligence service, whose job was to prevent espionage inside the GDR, picked up a coded letter sent by him to an address in the West that was known to us as a cover for West German foreign intelligence (BND). The head of our counterintelligence was unable to decipher the code or find the sender, but he ordered all mail sent to the West from the same postal district as the original intercepted letter to be screened. Sure enough, a postal telegram was picked up some months later. This time our counterintelligence did crack the code. It read: "I am unable to ful-fill your wish." Graphologists pronounced that the handwriting on the telegraph forms belonged to a woman; it was Helga passing on Stiller's message to his Western handlers that he had been unable to deliver a batch of microfilm.

There would have been no clear reason to suspect Stiller except that counterintelligence had by chance come across a meeting he had with an unknown contact at a time and place that did not fit with his own accounts of meetings with his known sources. No sweeping conclusions were drawn, but in 1976, when I ordered a clampdown on all but the most essential operations in the West because of a swoop on our agents in West Germany, we began to curtail his visits to West Berlin. He was, however, given permission to travel to Zagreb in Yugoslavia to meet one of his West German sources, where he also slipped to the BND information warning them how we had combined computer analysis with direct observation to arrest a number of their agents who had infiltrated Eastern military forces.

By the end of 1978, Stiller's nerve was cracking because he feared he was close to being discovered—rightly, as I found out too late. He forced the BND's hand, and they promised to look after him in the West and agreed to his defection. Whether deliberately or out of carelessness (for which the West German service was notorious, both in our circles and among their CIA colleagues), they gave him false identity papers that were so crude as to be unusable. Stiller decided to make his own way out of East Germany anyway using a departmental border pass.

Each department's single pass was kept under lock and key by the head of the department and had to be signed for whenever it was used by anyone with business at the Friedrichstrasse station. The main Berlin crossing point between East and West was a hive of espionage activity, with its rows of lockers (perfect for dead-letter drops) in mazelike corridors. The station was, technically speaking, in the East, but it was effectively divided into an Eastern and a Western half, with the border control in between. Any Easterner boarding the train on the Western side could still be arrested by Eastern authorities and hauled back.

Employees in the Scientific and Technical Department had complained that signing for the pass whenever they went to the station was an insulting sign of mistrust. Too bad, I thought, it still has to be done that way. But to simplify his life, the head of the department made his secretary the guardian of the magic pass. She kept a record of the comings and goings, which were monitored daily, but if an officer she knew and trusted came to ask for the pass, she cheerily handed it to him as if it were the key to the washroom.

In any event, Stiller's craftiness and highly developed sense of self-preservation got him out. Instead of risking the use of badly prepared papers, he broke into the department's safe to get the pass and a selection of the department's most valuable files as bounty for the West. He falsified a departmental assignment sheet so that it instructed him to cross to the Western part of the Friedrichstrasse station and deposit a case in one of the lockers there. To the travel controller on duty that night at the station, this would have looked entirely familiar. It was the same journey Stiller had made dozens of times before in the course of his work.

The files of that fateful night show that the two men exchanged banter about the awful weather, and Stiller, determined to distract the other officer from looking too closely at his papers, joked, "Maybe I'll request a transfer to your department. You get to sit in that warm cubbyhole all day. I could get used to that." The guard leafed through the documents: an instruction sheet bearing the "top secret" stamp, workplace pass, special border pass, and passport. Seeing that Stiller had obligingly laid the full complement of papers together for him, the guard looked no further. Our renegade walked through the double set of metal doors to the West. They clanged shut eight seconds apart, long enough for the officer to press a locking device if he were suddenly to have second thoughts and decide that he had better check that all the stamps in the documents matched exactly. No such thought occurred to him.

Up on the platform, Stiller walked quietly through the metal doors that brought him officially and irretrievably into the Western section of the station. Aware that East German counterintelligence officers were constantly on duty here, too, he meandered toward the lockers. Then, as he heard the roar of an incoming train, he sprinted the final yards and leapt through the doors as the red light flashed and the automated voice said, "Everybody in! The doors are closing." The final ten-minute journey, with the train still clanking through Eastern territory and him within the reach of any pursuers, must have racked Stiller's nerves. As soon as the train drew up in the rundown Lehrter station, the first stop on the Western side, he knew he was free.

Stiller actually got off farther along the line, changed trains, and headed to the nearest police station, which happened to be in the dull, lower-middle-class suburb of Reinickendorf. The officer on late shift, who was prepared for the usual procession of drunk drivers, brawlers, and would-be car thieves, must have done a double take when the smartly dressed young man entered, bid him a polite "Good evening," and added, "I am an officer of the Ministry of State Security of the German Democratic Republic and have just defected from East Berlin. Please inform [West German intelligence at] Pullach."

He was on his way to Pullach that very night. I would have loved to be a fly on the wall when he opened his attaché case jammed full of files stolen from the departmental safe. The only comfort to me was that Stiller, despite his undoubted abilities, was only a middle-ranking officer. Because of the careful security system I had built up, I could be certain that he did not know the identity of agents other than the seven he ran himself. But the papers he took from the safe carried hints that could lead Cologne counterintelligence to twenty or twenty-five more, and we had to write them off.

Our immediate task was to warn his contacts and agents. The nuclear reactor specialist Johannes Koppe and his wife fled by displaying great presence of mind. When the police knocked at his door in Hamburg and asked if he was Herr Koppe, he said no, that gentleman lived two floors up. Koppe and his wife then walked right out of their apartment with only the clothes on their backs, went directly to Bonn, and sought the protection of the Soviet embassy, which smuggled them out of the country. The counterintelligence then was confronted with a frustrating task: Koppe was an obsessive railroad enthusiast with a huge collection of timetables from dozens of countries and, worse, a set of model trains that snaked through his apartment. West German agents painstakingly inspected and dismantled the whole collection seeking espionage clues but found none. Eventually, as a reward for our blown agent, I arranged for the trains to be bought when they were auctioned off in West Germany (much to the initial dismay of Mielke, who saw no need for such demonstrations of loyalty) and shipped them to Koppe, who set them up again in his much smaller East Berlin apartment, where he lived a more crowded but happy life.

Another of Stiller's informants, Reiner Fülle of the Nuclear Research Center in Karlsruhe, had an even closer escape. He received the telephone warning when the arresting officers were already in his apartment. On his way from the car to the police station, one of the men slipped on the icy pavement and banged his head. Fülle bolted, lost the pursuing officers, and made his way undetected to the Soviet military mission in Wiesbaden, whence he was delivered to us in East Berlin.* Fülle could not adapt to life in the East and managed, two years later, to make contact with West German counterintelligence officers, who helped him to escape back to the West. Usually in such cases, we were aware of the withdrawn agent's problems and suspected that he might try to jump the border westward. In Fülle's case, we decided to let him go, reasoning that there was not much of value he could tell the authorities after his short time under our protection and surveillance. But there were no guarantees of leniency in such cases. Another of Stiller's agent's, Arnulf Raufeisen, who worked as a geophysicist in a Hanover nuclear research center, fled to East Berlin after our warning and also tried to defect back again in 1981. He was caught at the Hungarian border as he tried to cross into Austria. This time, the order from on high was to make an example of him; although a former East German spy, he was convicted in East Germany of espionage and sentenced to life in prison.

I had a bad conscience about Raufeisen. He had worked twenty years for my service, and I wanted to secure a swap or a pardon for him. I was unsuccessful, and he died in prison in 1987, a victim of both Stiller's betrayal and the random justice of the GDR. At the time of Stiller's defection, our desire for revenge burned very deep; I suppose Raufeisen got the sentence we would have liked to see Stiller suffer.

•

Stiller brought my enemies in Western intelligence something intangible but extremely important to them when he defected, and that was confirmation of my physical appearance. Although I had been head of East German foreign intelligence for two decades when he escaped, no one in the West had ever succeeded in securing a photograph of me, which earned me the complimentary description of "the man without a face." In fact, the Federal Intelligence Service did possess a picture of me, although they did not know it. I was captured on film without my knowledge during a trip to Sweden to meet with Dr. Friedrich Cremer, a promising contact in the West German Social Democratic Party. I

* Many years later, during my own committal procedure in Karlsruhe, I was guarded by the very same official who had let Fülle get away that January night. "Don't you go trying anything like that on us, Herr Wolf," he joked. At my age, I would not have given much for my chances anyway.

traveled there in the summer of 1978 to meet with him on neutral territory; we often used Sweden, Finland, and Austria for this purpose. Though this trip was partially an excuse to get out of the office, take a trip abroad with my wife, and—as long as I was in Sweden—meet with Cremer, there was another reason for my presence. The real reason for the trip was to meet with an important NATO source.

Perhaps because we were so careful about the security surrounding this important assignation, we let our guard down when that mission was accomplished and when it came to my meeting with Cremer— with unfortunate consequences for him. These ostensibly neutral Scandinavian nations had a suitably calm and unhurried atmosphere and their counterintelligence services did not seem overzealous, although I knew their loyalties were with the West. I met with our agents in the vicinity of the magnificent Gripsholm Castle, west of Stockholm, where we hoped to go unnoticed among the sightseers. Later, I remember noticing an elderly couple sitting in their car in the parking lot. The vehicle had West German plates, but there was no other reason to be suspicious, and I carried on with my meeting in the castle grounds. My colleagues informed me that they had arranged for me to meet with Cremer in Stockholm.

Later that day, as I wandered in the center of Stockholm, killing time before my appointment with Cremer, an agitated foreign couple, possibly Hungarian, rushed up to me and made it clear that I was being surreptitiously photographed. That was perturbing, but I could see no logical connection with the couple in the car. I carried on with my day as planned, meeting Cremer in the apartment that was used by the GDR embassy for traveling officials.

Our real mistake was to choose the northernmost port of Kappelskar as our place of entry, arriving from Finland according to the careful practice used by spies of avoiding travel direct from their home country to the territory on which they plan to meet a contact. As is normal in passage from Finland to Sweden, we went through border control without being asked to present our passports, so our presence was not registered. But at the harbor, the intelligence officer resident in our Swedish embassy picked me up. Swedish counterintelligence must have been working hard after all. They fed the number of our rented car into their computer and proceeded to monitor us as we drove to Stockholm.

The unusual preparations for special guests at the apartment must have attracted the attention of the Swedes to the mysterious arrival from East Germany, and they passed on their observations to their colleagues in West German foreign intelligence, with the result that I was under a tight net of double surveillance from the moment I set foot on Swedish territory. The West Germans returned home with my picture, snapped in Stockholm, but no one could work out who the mysterious East German was.

The photograph landed in a sealed box, along with blurred snapshots taken by West German counterintelligence of suspicious but otherwise unidentifiable figures. When Stiller arrived in the West, all these photos were spread out before him as a matter of routine. He immediately identified me, and from that day on, the right picture of me accompanied news reports in the West.

Knowing what the head of an espionage service looks like is not much of a gain in concrete terms for the enemy, but in my case, it was useful to the West in that it punctured some of the mystique that had grown up around my service and around me. I was no longer the spy without a face, but an ordinary mortal. Given Cremer's arrest and my own identification, we regretfully discontinued contact with the NATO source that had been the true reason for the Swedish trip. This break was, in the end, the most painful loss caused by Stiller.

After his escape, Stiller's Western masters turned him over to the CIA in America for a couple of years. He was given a false identity and was hidden, to the best of my knowledge, in Chicago, where he lost no time before learning English and picking up a banking certification. This was not a man who was going to end up poor under any system. When he returned to Germany and started working for a Frankfurt bank under an assumed name, we did in fact get to hear of it on the intelligence grapevine. One of our agents even brought us his address and asked for a big reward if he would bring Stiller to the border. Mielke promptly called me into his office and said in his characteristically rough manner: "That pig Stiller, can't we get him back?" I knew exactly what he meant: He was recalling the cross-border kidnappings of agents in the fifties. But this was the eighties. *Ostpolitik* and détente made such cloak-and-dagger operations politically untenable. To the minister's chagrin, Stiller remained free and prosperous, running his own company in Frankfurt. I consider him the only outright winner in one of the sorrier sagas of my career.

●

Thankfully it is not only bad news that comes out of the blue. One morning in the early summer of 1981, a large envelope appeared in the mailbox of the East German embassy in Bonn. In it was a letter addressed to the chief of Department 9 of the HVA, the foreign intelligence service. Department 9, responsible for penetrating the West German intelligence institutions, was the second largest in the service after the Scientific and Technological Sector and was one of the busiest. It was the department to which I felt most closely attached. Unlike most walkins—the term used for people who offer themselves to hostile services—this unknown letter writer used a precise form of address that showed he knew his way around the structure of East German intelligence.

In the envelope was a twenty-deutschmark note whose serial number was evidently intended to serve as a code in any future correspondence. The sender introduced himself as a specialist with a high degree of inside intelligence, which he was prepared to deliver in return for a one-time payment of 150,000 deutschmarks and a monthly fee of twice his present government salary for West German intelligence. His letter was written in large, capital letters. To whet our appetites, he gave us a tip-off about a planned West German attempt to recruit Christian Streubel, Stiller's superior in our SWT.

We had no idea of the sender's real identity. The security camera outside the East German embassy in Bonn had recorded only the photograph of a muffled figure depositing the letter. Despite the summer weather he had his hat pulled down and a scarf across his face. The confident, square block capital letters were all we had to go on.

It was a stroke of pure luck that we were able to figure out whose script it was. For some time, my service and the West Germans had been involved in a particularly long and complex game centering on one of my agents in the West code-named Wieland. His real name was Joachim Moitzheim.

A former student of the Jesuits, Moitzheim had been in Soviet captivity during the war, had worked for us since 1979 in the Cologne area, and had tried to recruit a source in the counterintelligence service (BfV), which was based there. This man, named Carolus, ran the counterintelligence computer (named Nadis), which contained centralized lists of those cleared for security, those who hadn't been cleared, and their files. Moitzheim offered Carolus one thousand marks if he would check on a name for the Americans. Carolus smelled a rat because he knew the CIA had access to Nadis themselves, and he reported the attempt to his superiors.

The attempt became known to two other men in West German counterintelligence, a brilliant senior officer named Klaus Kuron and Hansjoachim Tiedge, the head of the BfV's Security Clearance. Their job was to protect their service against Eastern infiltration. Tiedge and Kuron invited Moitzheim to a hotel, where they cornered him with their knowledge of his offer to Carolus. Threatening a lengthy prison sentence, they blackmailed Moitzheim into working for them as a double agent against the GDR. Worried that we would quickly figure out the ruse, the West Germans did not want Moitzheim to initially deliver disinformation to us. Instead, they supplied him with a lode of secret information on over eight hundred West Germans, including names of likely recruitment candidates for West German counterintelligence and those working on several classified defense projects. It was a major blunder, and one from which we greatly benefited.

While Moitzheim enjoyed the 2,000-deutschmark-per-month salary the West Germans paid him, he still felt at least a vague ideological inclination toward the East. He reported back to us that Kuron and Tiedge had tried to turn him, and he agreed to become a triple agent, working for us. It was in this capacity that Moitzheim identified the capital letters on the envelope as the handwriting of Klaus Kuron, the man who was supposedly his case officer in his role as a double agent.

When subterfuge reaches these proportions, the utmost care is required. Double agents (let alone triple ones) are always treated with special caution by spymasters. When someone has been turned once, the assumption is that they can be turned again. This particular game worked well for a while, with Wieland/Moitzheim informing his Cologne handlers about fictitious meetings with members of my staff in East Berlin—and then informing us that he had informed them. At the same time we asked our triple agent to provide genuine information from the heart of West German counterintelligence. We asked him to check out people in business whom we suspected of being linked with the security services and West Germans whom they suspected of working for us. Since we were not supposed to know that West German counterintelligence in Cologne was aware of Moitzheim's true relationship with us as a triple agent, they had to send back some genuine information to preserve his credibility. Otherwise they might fear that we would begin to suspect his second turning as a double agent. But we could not always be entirely certain how much of the information they sent from the Cologne computer was true, how much of it false. A Jesuit education was not bad preparation for this world of mirrors.

For its part, Cologne was anxious to gauge the extent of our real knowledge from the questions we asked Moitzheim. To keep Moitzheim's credibility with us and through it his cover intact, they obliged with wads of information, some of which we knew already. But there were some valuable undiscovered pearls along the way. Now we were faced with the fourth twist in this complex dance of the secret services. Kuron, the very Western officer who had run agent Moitzheim, wanted to work for the East too! This was exceptional, even for the entanglements of the spy business.

Kuron was a big fish with a faultless reputation who occupied a position at the very heart of counterintelligence, whose penetration is what secret services dream about. If we could secure his services, we would be able to gauge the level of Western knowledge about our operations and could adjust our defenses accordingly. It was like damaging the immune system at the heart of Western counterintelligence, the highest of prizes. But in a world of double and triple agents, we had to be sure that Kuron's approach was not itself a trap.

Exactly at the planned time, he made contact via the coded telephone number. We arranged a meeting with him, which we secretly filmed from a rooftop in order to have proof that he had approached us if this turned out to be an artful deception by the West Germans. But Kuron, who called himself Kluge (German for "clever one") when dealing with Moitzheim, lived up to his name.

He messaged again, saying that he wanted to take things slowly, so for a while nothing happened. It was 1982 by the time we persuaded him to attend a meeting in Vienna. All contact was made using variations on the code of the initial banknote he had sent us. Because of his seniority in Western intelligence, we kept the risks of association to a minimum. Every time he wanted to speak with us, he used one of several telephone numbers. He worked these out by listening to coded strings of numbers on his shortwave radio and subtracting from it the number of the banknote. It would be virtually impossible for anyone else to decipher our communications.

Still, I had a nail-biting weekend awaiting news from Vienna. Until the very final steps toward collaboration were taken by Kuron, we could not rule out the possibility that his offer might be a trap. Karl-Christoph Grossmann, deputy head of Department 9 (the department's work included analyzing the activities of West German counterintelligence), traveled to Austria with a young colleague. Günter Neels, second in command at the department, was also sent to Vienna separately to observe the deal, along with a junior officer to act as contact man. The elaborate preparations made that Viennese classic of intrigue, *The Third Man*, seem straightforward in comparison.

The meeting place for the most significant acquisition my service had ever made from the enemy's espionage organization was the entrance of Schönbrunn Park, a traditional setting for intrigue and romance during the Hapsburg era. The officers arrived separately, each checking that they were free from surveillance. Grossmann took up his position in the café at the opposite end of the park.

Exactly at the appointed time, the strong, upright figure of Kuron strolled into view. At the same moment, Neels approached the gate. For the benefit of anyone watching, the two men, strangers and from hostile institutions, greeted each other as if they were old acquaintances. Then they set off through the palace gardens. On seeing his quarry arrive safely at the other end, Grossmann climbed into a taxi, where he was joined by Kuron and the contact man, and the trio headed off to a quiet restaurant. Settled there comfortably, Kuron relaxed.

He was unembarrassed about his treachery, describing the frustrations to his career. His was a paradigm of unfulfilled ambitions of a type that fester throughout any civil service. Born into a simple home, he had worked his way up the intelligence ladder, although he had no university degree. His achievements were recognized by all his colleagues, but his lack of a formal qualification meant that he was being passed over for promotion. His salary of 48,000 marks (then about $25,000 dollars) was adequate for a comfortable if not luxurious life, but he knew that there was no possibility that it would ever increase.

"It has been a struggle," he said. "Everyone knows how good I am, but I'll never get any further." His voice was bitter and quiet as he added, "In the West, they say that there is freedom and an equal chance for everyone to achieve their potential. I don't see it like that. I can work till I drop and still end up being treated as a drone. Then they bring along some half-wit bureaucrat whose daddy has paid his way through school and he has a glittering path ahead, whatever he does. I can't bear it any longer."

Kuron's main concern was that his own four sons should have the means to get through university, since he could not afford to supplement their government grants. When his case became known after German unification, the Western press demonized Kuron as a particularly cold-blooded and greedy spy. But I see his motivation differently. I consider his decision to work for us as the act of a man who had internalized the pulsing message of the capitalist society to the exclusion of everything else and acted on it without scruple. Seeing that the successful and highly regarded people around him had bought their way to affluence and success, he sold his expertise in the only market he knew.

Some traitors, at least in their own minds, preserve for themselves the illusion that they are serving two masters when they enter the pay of their enemy while still working for their own country. But by the time Kuron made contact with us, he had lost any sense of identification with his own service. There was nothing left but hatred for it, he would later tell the court when he was called as a witness in my case. That sort of wholehearted transference of loyalty on the part of a mole who agrees to remain as an agent in place is an intelligence chief's dream come true. It does not happen often, but when it does, it is worth the high financial commitment demanded. Most people who approach the enemy and offer to work as a mole hope to do so for a short time and then, like Stiller, buy themselves a passage to the other country as a defector.

The only parallel for Kuron I can think of is Aldrich Ames, who provided the same sort of unstinting service for the KGB. In one important area Ames had a similar psychological profile. Like Kuron, he considered himself undervalued and unrewarded by the CIA, convinced that he was worth more money and attention than they paid him. Both liked money and lavish living. Neither felt that their honest work had been sufficiently rewarded. Both had deep knowledge of their service and knew that, if they set up their deals carefully, they would enjoy strong protection from the enemy service they embraced.

With Kuron we gained a supermole. Here was a man whose job it was to recruit East German and Soviet agents and turn them to work for the West. Now he was prepared to give us this information. True, his price was high and he wanted it paid into a numbered bank account in a third country, but the potential was enormous. As a highly professional spy himself, he also demanded a number of "exclusion clauses," like a Hollywood star negotiating a film deal, but again, we were willing to take the chance. He also wanted guarantees that the double agents whose identity he would disclose to us would not be arrested. This was not a sign of any particularly virtuous streak. What Kuron knew was that a series of arrests would in due course turn suspicion on the counterintelligence service in Cologne. I agreed.

So delighted were we with our new catch that we gave him the new code name Star. His identity was regarded as our top secret and his real name was never, ever spoken, not even in the privacy of my inner sanctum, which was deemed free of bugs. Further meetings followed in Austria, Spain, Italy, and Tunisia at which Kuron disclosed the names of East German agents whom his service had recruited.

Both he and I were extremely cautious about the location of our encounters, and we chose places that would sound like plausible holiday destinations.

•

The settlement of his demands was still outstanding. Kuron insisted on personal confirmation of the agreement by me. Before I asked Mielke's consent to pay out more than any other single source in the West had ever cost me, I wanted to take a look at Kuron in person. Issued a GDR diplomatic passport, he was brought from Vienna via Bratislava in a special plane to Dresden, where my son-in-law, Bernd, picked him up and brought him to a secret country house. Kuron was one of those people who were soon at ease in any surroundings, even a safe house in enemy country. We negotiated a precise financial deal in a very German way. There would even be a pension on his retirement from treachery. His salary was equivalent to that of an East German intelligence colonel. That day he revealed to me that two of our employees, Horst Garau and his wife, Gerlinde, go-betweens who worked for my service part time ferrying messages to and from our agents in the West, were also in the pay of West Germany.

Garau told West German counterintelligence the identity of the agents he knew. No arrests followed, again on the theory that such a move would blow Garau's cover as a double agent. But such information allowed the West Germans to monitor what the agents were doing and whom they met. As far as the participants were concerned, they were safe. But through Kuron, we now would know every move they made.

With business out of the way, we proceeded to drinks and dinner, served by the State Security Ministry's specially vetted staff. Kuron told jokes and I showed him some holiday films of East Germany, where I said I hoped we would be seeing a lot of him. He also lodged in my mind the name of his superior, Hansjoachim Tiedge. "Good brain once," mused Kuron. "Spends every hundred marks three times over and has one hell of a drinking problem." I filed that away for future use, never guessing that the high-living Mr. Tiedge might also present himself to me one day without the slightest effort on our part.

What happens to the agents or moles betrayed by someone like Kuron? To the best of my knowledge, neither the East nor the West German service ever arranged for anyone to be killed, either for revenge or to prevent the spread of their information. But neither service could deny that both used extortion and corruption. For instance, to turn Moitzheim, the West Germans offered him the brutal choice between a lengthy jail sentence and cooperation. We would probably have done the same.

Agents, as opposed to officers in the intelligence service, were not sentenced to death in East Germany after the 1950s. It was more valuable for us to imprison significant Western spies so that they could be exchanged for our own at some opportune time. The harshest sentences were reserved for staff officers who betrayed their country, like

Werner Teske, an officer in the Scientific and Technological Department who was caught in 1981 with files from the department hidden in his washing machine at home. He had been planning to defect to the West and take the material with him as a gift to West German intelligence in exchange for a good life on the other side.

Teske became a tragic footnote to history in 1981 as the last person executed in East Germany. The reasons for the decision to execute Teske remain something of a mystery to me. I am often blamed, in my capacity as head of the foreign intelligence service, for having permitted his death or at least for having failed to prevent it. Do I feel responsible for his fate? To answer honestly, I must distinguish between different types of responsibility.

As soon as Teske's treachery was discovered he was arrested by the Counterespionage Department, together with the Main Department for Interrogation, both under Mielke's control, and then handed over, like all espionage cases in the East, to a closed military tribunal, which by its nature put his defense at a serious disadvantage. At that point the case was out of our hands. By the early eighties, however, it was usual to commute to life imprisonment the statutory death sentence for severe instances of treason. While I knew that Teske's future was grim, I had no reason to believe that he would die. Odder still, the death sentence was carried out in June 1981 in a Leipzig jail, with no publicity, on the Soviet model of an unexpected pistol shot in the back of the neck. So this harsh sentence could hardly have been set for its exemplary effect, since not even my own officers knew about it. This indicates to me the muddled thinking to which the state had succumbed in its declining phase.

The year before, in 1980, Winifried Zarkrzovski, alias Manfred Baumann, a naval captain in the military intelligence network, had disclosed to the West Germans the names of several Eastern agents operating in West Germany. Mielke was furious. At a meeting I attended with other senior officers in 1982 he called for a clampdown on traitors. "Such mistakes should not occur in the thirty-second year [of East Germany's existence as a state]. . . . We are one heart and soul in this matter. We are not immune to having the odd bastard in our midst. If I knew who it was, I would have done with it once and for all."

This outburst showed that Mielke was dissatisfied with the judiciary's leniency toward treason. Although the courts were nominally independent in such matters, pressure could be exerted through the leadership in particular cases. Teske's fate may have been the result of such pressure. One aspect of it still puzzles me. Under East German law, he could only have been executed upon proof that treason had actually occurred. There was even a precedent in the case of an officer named Walter Thräne who had been preparing to defect when he was caught. The court refused the prosecution's demand for a death sentence or even life imprisonment, on the grounds that although the intention to commit treason was clear, the crime had never been completed. So even in the terms of our own strict laws, Teske's execution was illegal.

I cannot concur with my critics who say that I am directly responsible for Teske's death. But I must concede that I failed to criticize loudly and early enough the workings of a judicial system that was too closely allied to the state and could be manipulated in its interests. Each intelligence officer in the East knew that the death sentence was a distinct possibility for traitors. They said it themselves as they took up their first post: "If I ever break this, my solemn oath, I may be punished severely under the laws of the Republic and the contempt of the working people." The death sentence remained in force in East Germany until 1987.

But the death penalty is not justified for peacetime espionage. Looking back on the cases of treachery I have known on both sides, I risk the assertion that death would not have amounted to much of a deterrent. The motives governing the decision to work for the other side are complex and usually combined with a degree of self-confidence or arrogance implying that the traitor considers himself impervious to danger.

As for the infamous "wet jobs," or illegal unauthorized killings in espionage, they did and still do occur. It would be foolhardy for me to list suspicious disappearances at the hands of the CIA, for it would only open me up to the charge of suppressing the many breaches of law that were committed by the Soviet services. In the fifties, the Bulgarians and Poles had the reputation of being the most deadly services. East German counterintelligence is not blameless, although I again stress that the well-known and often rehearsed stories about traitors being kidnapped and killed were more likely the result of the amateurish use of powerful sleeping drugs in the course of kidnapping than of intended murder.

In fact, killing traitors is really a sign of weakness, not strength, and I would have considered it below my professional as well as my moral standards to become involved in such business. A wet job in the dramatic manner of spy fiction is a primitive and unproductive solution compared to the way we exploited resources like Moitzheim as a double agent and then triple agent to obtain the best possible deal. Such guilt that we bear lies in the exploitation of individuals, their weaknesses and greed. And those activities were not limited to the espionage services of the East.

●

Kuron took a professional pride in his work for us, often helping with projects that fell outside his agreed contract. I considered him so useful that I arranged for him to have day and night access to a special telephone number over which urgent messages could be passed back to the East. As a trusted member of West German counterintelligence in Cologne, he had access to most high-grade recruitment operations. Usually, he would let them run their course and then inform us, as it was in neither his nor our interest to awaken suspicions by spoiling West German recruiting attempts.

There was one exception, however. For decades we had had in Bonn an agent in the Christian Democratic Union, the party of Helmut Kohl. He was an old friend of Kohl's from the chancellor's early days in politics in the Rheinland and had also carried out some work for the giant Flick concern, representing the company's interests to the ruling Christian Democrats from 1981 onward. He knew all about the darker side of the deals between politics and industry in West Germany and was a valuable source of inside information on West German domestic politics for us.

One night, Kuron, on duty in his official role as a counterintelligence officer in Cologne, received information from a colleague that a suspected East German agent had been followed to a meeting with our Bonn political mole. The two had gone to an apartment and were under West German surveillance. Agents were about to swoop in for the kill. Kuron realized immediately that when the two men were found together, I would lose a valuable political informant in the West. So he quickly messaged to his emergency telephone number in code,

"Your men under surveillance in the Andernachstrasse." We took the extremely risky step of telephoning direct to the apartment and issuing a coded warning for our agent to flee, in the form of a message in a particular dialect about a wrong number.

We figured out that, as the surveillance had already worked one shift, they would be replaced overnight. If there was to be an arrest, it would take place in the early hours. So the two men put out the lights as if to go to bed, and shortly after midnight our agent slipped out through the underground car park and set off immediately for East Berlin via Switzerland. Next day, when the remaining man, our mole, left the flat, the West German agents must have rushed into the building only to find the mystery guest gone along with any shred of evidence of an espionage assignation with him.

The Western mole was later discovered, tried, and given a short suspended sentence. Given the sterner treatment of other moles, I cannot help thinking that somewhere in his network of contacts inside the body politic of Bonn, he had someone pleading for clemency on his behalf.

For six years, Kuron did sterling work for us. With the innocent help of his teenage son, who thought he was just doing his dad a favor for work, he had managed to figure out a method of recording computer signals onto a telephone answering-machine tape at an extremely high speed. This was a great improvement on our old system, under which the telltale bleeps and whirs of the coded letters could easily be detected by a counterintelligence bug. Under Kuron's system the sounds were speeded up, so that all the human ear could pick up was a slight distortion or short bleep that could just as well have been a fault on the line. At the other end, the message was played via a computer program onto a tape and could be deciphered as the tape was played back at a fraction of the sending speed. Kuron had gone one better by working out how the message could be transferred automatically onto a computer disc. The analyst then had only to slot in the discs for the high-grade security clearance and read the material off the screen. That shortened the decoding process by valuable minutes.

Our successes right up to 1989 indicate that technological superiority is of limited usefulness if the basics of the service are mishandled. That kind of expertise can be bought, but good organization, tight discipline, and the right instincts are not commercially available. For instance, it should have been obvious to Kuron's colleagues that he was living beyond his means, more and more so as the years went by. Unlike Aldrich Ames, Kuron was very circumspect as to spending money and inventing cover stories. He was highly professional in the way he maintained contact with us and lived a disciplined life. Furthermore, the man in charge of security clearance within the BfV in Cologne, Hansjoachim Tiedge, an alcoholic with a mountain of family problems and gambling debts, was hardly in a position to notice.

●

My suitcases were packed for a holiday in Hungary in the summer of 1985 when my hot line rang. It was a call from the Magdeburg region on the border with West Germany. A man identifying himself as Mr. Tabbert had arrived unexpectedly and demanded to speak with a representative of the foreign intelligence department. Through Kuron we knew that Tabbert was Tiedge's code name, so I ordered him to be brought to Berlin as quickly as possible, without further questioning. Remembering that the border guards tended not to give visitors to East Germany the most promising welcome, I added that he should be given a beer and some food. Karl-Christoph Grossmann, who had successfully handled Kuron's first approaches and whose Department 9 penetrated West German counterintelligence, was dispatched to pick him up on the Autobahn junction leading to Berlin in order to ensure that security was tight as he was driven through the capital.

From the start I knew that this was a big catch and that the West Germans would be extremely keen to get back this key security official, who had probably defected on a mere whim. He was installed in a safe house in Prenden, in the countryside outside East Berlin. My own country residence was there, and only a few hundred yards away was the underground bunker that the politburo had built to preserve itself from immolation if ever the Americans really did drop the atomic bomb. The area was therefore very heavily guarded. There was scant danger of our new friend's being snatched back by the other side.

Tiedge wanted to meet me directly, but I declined. I was already planning to retire and, knowing that this was a big case with many ramifications, thought it best to leave it to my successor, Werner

Grossmann. I reasoned that Tiedge would have the most trust in the first people he met in the East; this way we would avoid changing his handlers halfway through.

The man was in a dreadful state when he was brought in for a gentle interrogation. His unkempt appearance and bloodshot eyes did not suggest a highly placed member of a Western security service. Just to make sure, he was asked to produce his security pass, identifying him as an employee of the Office for the Protection of the Constitution (BfV) in Cologne. He identified himself as Hansjoachim Tiedge and explained in his high, dull voice, "I've come to stay. You're my last chance." I telephoned Mielke with the good news. Even with a prize defection in front of him, he was, as usual, more concerned with his own status and complained bitterly that the head of security in Magdeburg had not contacted him at once with the news. In the future, he snapped in his rough Berlin accent, "all lost and found items are to be handed in to me first!"

Tiedge confirmed what we knew from Kuron about his sorry personal circumstances. He was a heavy gambler and drinker. His wife had died in an accident at home after the two had been involved in a drunken fight. He had even been investigated on a possible manslaughter charge, but the final verdict was accidental death. He had unruly children who had never forgiven him for their mother's death and difficulties at work, where his tumultuous private life had led to disciplinary proceedings. Now he knew that the only reason he was being kept on in counterintelligence was to keep his inside knowledge safe where his superiors could keep an eye on him. His entire dignity, he said, was undermined. "If a case like mine had been presented to me for analysis," he reflected with admirable honesty, "I would have recommended that I be fired without delay."

I could not help reflecting, when I read the report later, that the head of security clearance in a Western intelligence service, a post that demands a squeaky-clean life, seemed to have an existence more suited to a character in a soap opera. Here was a man who had descended into such a psychological hell that he could see only two possible escapes, suicide or defection. "And I didn't have the courage for suicide," he told his interrogators.

A question that puzzled many people was whether Tiedge had been our agent before his defection. For the first time I can categorically deny that he was. The arrival of Tiedge in the East was as much a surprise to me as to everyone else. I had some inkling that he might wash up on our shore if things got much worse for him in Cologne, but we did not seek contact with him. He found us by hopping on a train one night and arriving in the East. He was an unusually frank defector. In fact, he was the only one I have ever encountered who candidly described himself as a traitor. He did not seek to prettify his decision with stories of ideological conversion. "Things are better for me in the second Germany than in the first!" he would say.

How true. We spent a lot of time, money, and effort virtually rebuilding this man from the alcoholic wreck that he had become when he stumbled across the border. Bloated and pale with dark-rimmed eyes, he resembled a giant panda when he was brought to the safe house. We engaged a nurse, a doctor, and a fitness instructor for him. They helped him stop drinking and lose almost thirty pounds in a month. Deprived of alcohol and subjected to a strict fat-free diet, Tiedge needed solace of some kind, and it emerged that he had a lively sexual appetite. We had available some women, members of the Party with links to the security services in the Potsdam area, who could be called on to befriend a defector and begin a liaison, as often happened in such cases. Under the emotional stress during interrogation, most men are ripe for female comfort. We ensured that the women we employed were prepared to indulge in sexual relations with these men.

They were not prostitutes, but down-to-earth women, Party members and loyal to their country, who were prepared to do this in return for some expression of what we used to call the gratitude of the state, which turned out to be a preferential flat or an advance up the waiting list for a car. All the same, our first candidate simply could not bring herself to go through with it with Tiedge. Another, a teacher, was found, and she managed to fulfill her brief, to our great relief. Tiedge was a particularly unattractive specimen of manhood, and I recall thinking that she must have been an extremely patriotic soul. But even the most sordid stories can turn out to have more pleasant results than expected. The two later married and as of this writing are still together.

Tiedge had a memory like a computer for names and connections and filled in a lot of the blanks for us, though not as many as he thought, since he was unaware that his colleague Kuron was in our pay.

The revelations in the press of Tiedge's unfitness for office that followed his defection reflected badly on the image of West German counterintelligence. In addition, the recently named head of the Federal Intelligence Service, Heribert Hellenbroich, an old friend of Tiedge's and his former boss at counterintelligence, was forced to resign amid accusations of incompetence within that agency. We rubbed our hands in glee at the turmoil, although I have later come to believe that Hellenbroich was one of the more honest and respectable heads of the West German intelligence service. I feel a twinge of sympathy for his predicament in having not one but two of my moles digging the ground of his career away from under him.

Tiedge's presence in the East also gave us an excuse to move against Horst and Gerlinde Garau, about whose treachery Kuron had informed us but whom we had resisted arresting because to do so would have exposed that we had a mole at work. As far as West German counterintelligence would know, they had been betrayed by Tiedge. Horst and Gerlinde Garau were arrested and he was sentenced to life imprisonment in December 1986. Gerlinde Garau was released after four months and warned not to speak of her experiences. Her husband was found dead in mid-1988 in Bautzen Prison. Gerlinde insisted that he had been murdered on my orders.

This was not so. Horst Garau was a sensitive and proud man who coped particularly badly with the harsh conditions of the prison. I am sure that he committed suicide in jail after it became clear to him that he was not on the West Germans' list of spy-swap candidates. Despite the pathos that has since attached itself to his case—he was betrayed twice by the men he trusted in West German intelligence—he was in my eyes a destructive spy. He did not deserve to die, but he did deserve prison.

On October 5, 1990, two days after the unification of the two Germanys, Kuron traveled to East Berlin to discuss his future with one of my senior officers. Treachery abounded as people rushed to save their skins. One of my elite officers had already succumbed to an offer to help the West Germans track down our agents. He was Colonel Karl-Christoph Grossmann, the same officer who had helped recruit Kuron and receive Tiedge. The rondo of deception had come full circle. The same man who had been entrusted with guarding our two top acquisitions from Western counterintelligence had turned traitor himself. I watched events unfold with a bitter sense of irony.

Grossmann's treachery meant that it was all over for Kuron and many more of our top agents. Kuron knew it too. Wordlessly, he took his final payment of ten thousand marks from the senior officer and agreed to the only offer East German foreign intelligence could still make to protect its threatened agents, an introduction to the KGB and a possible chance to escape to Moscow with the help of Soviet intelligence.

Obsessed with improving their relations with the West Germans, the Soviet Union provided us minimal help. After lengthy pleading and arm twisting by Werner Grossmann, who had succeeded me as head of foreign intelligence, the KGB had agreed to give asylum to any of our prime agents who wished it. Kuron initially agreed but soon changed his mind, fearful that he would never be able to get out of the Soviet Union once he had gone in.

With the excuse of returning once more to Cologne to discuss the offer with his wife, Kuron called the security clearance section of West German counterintelligence and explained that he had to discuss what he delicately called a problem. He was about to try one final game. He told his boss that he had been approached by the KGB and that he wanted to offer his services as a double agent to the West Germans. He offered to tell West German counterintelligence what the Soviets were trying to find out—the same activity he had practiced in the opposite direction for so long. Under the sort of pressure Kuron was subjected to, a defector, having made the huge psychological leap to the other side, is often capable of making it back again. It was a cunning gamble under pressure, but Kuron's luck had run out.

Upon arrival at the office block in Cologne where he had made his career, he was immediately detained and interrogated. That night, the most cunning of East-West spies threw in the towel and admitted, as he would later put it in court, that he had really only served one side, the East German Hauptverwaltung Aufklärung. Even with the help of Karl-Christoph Grossmann's evidence from inside our apparat, it took a year and a half for the West Germans to amass all the evidence against Kuron, so extensive was his espionage activity. In 1992 he was finally sentenced to twelve years in Rauschied prison. To the end he was unbowed. His comment on his fate was: "Compared with the pitiful lives that some people suffer, staring at the same gray filing cabinet all day, I have lived five lives."

Tiedge fled to the Soviet Union shortly before unification and lived there in modest comfort, sponsored first by the KGB and since then by its variously named but fundamentally similar successor organizations. It is said that he continues to work for them against the West, but I doubt this. After the twists and turns of the last few years of espionage history in Germany, I know from conversations with friends in the old and new services in Moscow that Russian intelligence had a jaundiced view of both German services. By the end of the Cold War, they came to the conclusion, which they still hold, that it was impossible to know with certainty for which side any German agent was working.

11

Intelligence and Counterintelligence

Now that the Cold War is history, it is easy to conclude that the Soviet Union was a mangy, ill-coordinated creature, inferior in many regards to its archrival, the United States, and doomed to failure from its inception. But during the four decades that the superpower conflict dominated world affairs, it did not seem that way at all. On the contrary, the West's fears that Moscow would fulfill Nikita Khrushchev's promise to catch up and overtake the capitalist countries was the motor that drove espionage and propaganda with a historically unprecedented intensity. Furthermore, the West's political imagination was profoundly influenced by the apparent success of Soviet espionage. East bloc espionage and counterintelligence was driven by fear of the declared Western policy of rollback and by Reagan's star wars threats. Each feared it would be overtaken by the other strategically.

As the ex-chief of what was recognized as the most effective and efficient Communist espionage service, I am well placed to assess our espionage successes and failures.

In intelligence circles East and West I had the reputation of being Moscow's man in the Eastern bloc. Yes and no. If people meant that I

Left: Else and Friedrich Wolf with my brother Konrad *(left)* and me in front of our house, Höllsteig, 1926

Below: Me, Stuttgart, 1929

Drummer group of the Karl Liebknecht School, of which Konrad and I were members, Moscow, 1935

Left: Me and Konrad, Moscow, 1939.

Above: Me (*second from right*) hosting "Treffpunkt Berlin" ("Meeting Point Berlin"), Berlin Radio, 1947

INTERNATIONAL MILITARY TRIBUNAL

3657

Pass No.

Date Issued

WOLF MARK F.

Name

MARK F. WOLF

SOVIET PRESS Rm 110

Other Date

is authorized to enter the Area of the

PALACE OF JUSTICE

SECURITY OFFICER

signature of bearer

Left: My identity card for the Nuremberg war-crimes trials

Below: After the accreditation of the GDR diplomatic mission in Moscow, November 3, 1949: president of the Supreme Soviet Shvernik *(fourth from left),* Ambassador Rudolf Apelt *(fifth from the left),* and me *(third from right)*

Bottom: (from left to right) Richard Stahlmann (Arthur Illner); A. G. Graur, liason officer and Soviet intelligence service advisor to the GDR in 1951; and A.M. Korotkov, head of KGB representation in Berlin (also liaison officer with the Red Orchestra in Berlin, 1939–1941, under the alias "Erdman")

Above: Friedrich and Else Wolf, Lehnitz, 1949

Above: State visit of Nikita Khrushchev and Anastas Mikoyan, East Berlin, 1957 (I am second from right)

Center: Congratulaions ceremony for the seventy-first birthday of Walter Ulbricht, chairman of the GDR State Council, East Berlin, 1964. I am fourth from left and Erich Mielke is second from right

Above: Ceremony for the fiftieth anniversary of the Soviet intelligence service, Moscow, 1971. I am on the far left, and A. M. Sakharovski is on the far right

Right: Me and Konrad at the Tenth Party Congress of the SED, 1981

Above: Y.V. Andropov presenting me with the Soviet Red-Banner Order, December 6, 1973

Right: Vladimir Kryuchkov and me at the First Main Directorate of the KGB in Yasenovo, near Moscow. Epigraph on memorial column reads, IN HONOR OF THE CHEKISTS OF THE INTELLIGENCE SERVICE WHO GAVE THEIR LIVES FOR THE SAKE OF COMMUNISM

Top: The Ministry of
State Security,
Normannenstraße,
East Berlin, 1977

Above: Promotion to the
colonel general by Erich
Honecker, chairman of the
GDR State Council, East
Berlin, February 1, 1982

Right: At my desk after the
promotion ceremony,
February 1, 1982

Top: Wreath-laying ceremony at Andropov's tomb, Moscow, Februrary 9, 1983

Above: My office at the Ministry of State Security

Left: Kryuchkov and me, East Berlin, 1984

Top: Zanzibar, 1964: Seif Bakari, member of the revolutionary council; Thabit Kombo, deputy head of the security branch; Dieter Hoffman; Rolf Markert; me; commissioner of Pemba; Ibrahim Makungu, head of the security branch

Bottom: Me with the Sudanese interior minister, Faruq Othman Hamadallah, May 1, 1970, East Berlin

Above: Me (in dark glasses) outside of Managua, Nicaragua, July 1985 (minister Tomas Borge is sitting on table)

Left: Me and Raoul Castro, Cuba, July 1985

Spies at work: a secret photo of West German vice-chancellor Fritz Schäffer *(center)* leaving the Marx-Engels-Platz railway station in East Berlin. The man on his left (in the light coat) is agent "Markgraf," and in front of them both is Captain Hermann Nebelung. Hidden is Colonel Willi Hüttner

Above: Shäffer being welcomed by Colonel Semyon Semyonovich Logachov and Hüttner, at the HVA safe house "Lieschen," East Berlin

Left: Günter Guillaume, at the Eleventh Party Congress of the SED, 1986

Below: Christel Guillaume after her release (*from left,* me, Christel Guillaume, her son Pierre Guillaume, and Christel's mother)

Above: Secret meeting with
Gaby Gast, Dresden, 1981

Left: Helga Rödiger, Eleventh Party
Congress of the SED, 1986

Right: Johanna Olbrich and me,
Eleventh Party Congress
of the SED, 1986

Top: Kim Philby and
me during a lecture
for HVA staff,
August 14, 1981,
East Berlin

Above: India Ink drawing by
Abel, given to me as a present

Right: Rudolf Abel, me,
and Soviet liaison officer
V. V. Kuchin, October 1967,
East Berlin

Above: Me with
George Blake,
August 1980,
Berlin (Blake
autographed
the photo)

Left: William
Borm ("Olaf")
and me, 1982,
East Berlin

Top: Klaus and
Margarethe Fuchs
congratulate me
on my sixtieth
birthday,
January 19, 1983

Right: Cover of
Die Troika, 1989
(*from left*,
George Fischer,
Lothar Wloch,
Konrad Wolf)

Left: Addressing a
protest rally,
Alexanderplatz,
Berlin,
November 4, 1989

Above: Andrea and me
with Yitzhak Shamir,
Tel Aviv, March 1996

Left: With Hannsheinz
Porst in front of the
Düsseldorf court of
appeals during my first
trial, September 7, 1993

Right: Me and Mielke

Below: Me with John Robbins, who served in the CIA's Operation Directorate. Robbins spent nearly eight years in Berlin, and was there during some of my most successful operations

COURTESY COLONEL JIM ATWOOD

Bottom: Me and former intelligence officers *(from left)* Hayden B. Peake (USA), and Dan Mulvenna (Canada) after a discussion on the role of espionage in the Cold War.

COURTESY COLONEL JIM ATWOOD

called the Kremlin or the KGB on Monday mornings for a chat about the week's work, they were wrong. But if they meant that I enjoyed a relationship of confidence and mutual regard with some of the most influential figures inside the Soviet state from the earliest post-Stalin days to the collapse of the Eastern bloc, they are right. By virtue of my fluency in Russian and the roots I had established there before and during World War II, I was in a unique position to cast both an insider's and an outsider's eye over the Soviet Union's thinking and the activities of its secret services throughout the Cold War.

The Soviet intelligence services had their greatest successes in America and Europe before and during World War II, when they were able to rely on the Communist Party and the intelligentsia of many countries, particularly in Germany and England but also in the United States. The Soviet Union was a beacon that attracted followers to its intelligence services out of deep conviction. The agents recruited at that time were the best, giving the Soviet Union the chance to catch up in the nuclear race, and many have remained undiscovered, even after the McCarthy period and the defection to Canada in 1945 of Igor Gousenko.

From our very beginnings, we in East Germany presented intelligence as an honorable profession. We were able to build on the experience and the legends instilled by great spies who had worked against the Nazis—Richard Sorge and his famous assistants, Ruth Werner, alias Sonya, who spied in China, Danzig, Switzerland, and Britain for the Soviets during the war, and Max Christiansen-Klausen, Sorge's radio operator; Ilse Stöbe, who spied from the heart of Hitler's foreign ministry; and Harro Schulze-Boysen, an officer in Goering's air force and head of the Rote Kapelle, which included Arvid and Mildred Harnack and Adam and Margarethe Kuckhoff. Our own apparat featured many veterans of the Communist movement during the Third Reich, like my first bosses, Wilhelm Zaisser, Richard Stahlmann, Robert Korb, and Ernst Wollweber. I was personally enthralled by their stories and saw the value of presenting them to our recruits as models for the role of spycraft in underpinning socialism. We even had a rather grand name for all of this: *Traditionspflege*, or the preservation of tradition. Part of the difference between the Eastern and the Western approach to running an intelligence service is, I think, seen clearly in the language we used to describe ourselves. The Central Intelligence

Agency and its West German equivalent, the BND, allocated each of its employees a rank based on civil service practice, while we followed the Soviet tradition of basing our service grades on the military's; the minister of state security had the rank of four-star general and down from there. We even had battle songs and a ministry choir avowing our eternal loyalty to the Cause. I translated one song from a Russian original dedicated to agents operating on foreign territory. It began:

> Our service is enlightenment
> Names remain secret,
> Discreet our achievements,
> Always within the enemy's sights.

There was a rousing chorus about the fighters on the invisible front, a stirring phrase that originated with the Chekists, Lenin's first secret police. We never called ourselves spies but *Kundschafter*, a good, strong Lutheran-German word meaning purveyor of information. The word "agent" was never used of our own side but was reserved for describing our foes. This is all very basic linguistic psychology, but it succeeded in creating a climate in which Eastern officers naturally thought of themselves as honorable and their foes as perfidious.

I must stress that the military aspects were decidedly secondary to the ideological, but in the West they did not go in for such mythmaking at all. As far as I can tell, what the CIA, Britain's MI6, and most other Western European services had in common was a rather dreary approach to their jobs and themselves. I do not mean that they were unprofessional—far from it—but that they were encouraged to see themselves not as glamorous or special in any way but rather as worker bees, gathering information for other far grander souls to process. We probably went too far in the other direction by introducing a military structure and great strictness about personal habits and morality into our services. But it did provide a strong sense of belonging, which underpinned the loyalty without which no secret service can function.

My firm belief is that hardly anyone becomes a traitor for money alone. The CIA was always inclined to use money as a recruiting device, and the KGB was not shy of doing the same. In the United States, in particular, the KGB eventually could no longer recruit enough agents out of conviction and had to focus on money. In the final years its greatest successes, culminating with Aldrich Ames, were walk-ins looking for cash and not agents recruited with a plan of infiltrating an institution, a process our service often began during a potential agent's student days.

To agents like Klaus Kuron in West German counterintelligence we paid plenty, of course, but that was the exception rather than the rule. The wiser Soviet recruiters realized that in fishing for potential moles in the West, they had to bear in mind that other factors are always at work. One of these is what I liked to call the erotic appeal of the East. By this I do not mean the prostitutes and pornographic videos occasionally supplied to help visitors pass their time, but the prickling excitement they seemed to feel at being received and feted on the other side of the Iron Curtain. We occasionally arranged wholly unnecessary visits to the GDR or even the Soviet Union for people we were targeting, because the usually unfamiliar sights (carefully chosen, of course) tended to move the heart of a suggestible Westerner.

I once used this method in recruiting a senior West German Social Democrat whom we code-named Julius. He was a regional newspaper editor and a man in a relatively high position with good contacts, including Willy Brandt and other leading figures of his party. I happened to be on vacation on a fishing trip on the Volga River at the same time he had been invited to tour a Soviet power station and inspect Stalingrad, which is on the Volga. Sensing he had an adventurous streak, I took Julius aboard a riverboat, and we disembarked and visited the small house of a worker and ate fish soup. There was a fine atmosphere of friendship and hospitality. I served as the interpreter while Julius asked about life, family, the battle of Stalingrad—the man had been a Stalingrad defender—and the current political and economic situation. The worker criticized Moscow, and we discussed failures of the socialist system. This frankness impressed Julius. The next day we visited a villa that had been prepared for a visit by President Eisenhower that had never taken place. I signed my full name in the guest book, Lt. Gen. Markus Wolf, which made Julius uncomfortable because his own name was nearby.

But the miniholiday deep inside enemy territory helped him shed his fears about being involved in helping the Soviet Union to secure world peace, as we phrased the appeal. It also gave him a prickle of forbidden excitement. He became a political source for us in his party, for which we paid to help support his private office, a type of political slush fund not unknown in many Western democracies.

I often said to my Russian colleagues: "You don't use your best weapon. You show them power stations, not the people. These people may live in poor houses, but they are more impressive to foreigners than anything else."

Soviet intelligence had been our model and in the early days our teacher in foreign espionage. Starting in the mid-fifties we traveled to Moscow for meetings with the Soviet foreign intelligence chiefs in the First Main Directorate and for a more general briefing from the KGB chief. Back then we were left in no doubt that our hosts regarded us as mere minions from an outpost of the proud empire.

Our accommodations were in the guest apartment in Kolpachny Pereulok that had belonged to Viktor Abakumov, the brutal head of the SMERSH terror network responsible for the liquidation of real and imagined enemies of Stalin during World War II. Abakumov was shot after Lavrenti Beria's death in 1953.

Built in grand pre-Revolutionary style, the three-story mansion had several apartments, an elevator, fireplaces, and a vast marble bathroom with a huge old bathtub. The sideboard in the dining room was filled with fine china and glassware, and there was a beautiful oval dining table hung with a low lamp, around which we would sit discussing the state of the world with our hosts. The windows were curtained with heavy drapes. The house had a fine library of Russian classics (rarely used), its own billiard room, and a cinema and was considered a marvel even among the senior ranks of the KGB, who loved this mixture of the old bourgeois taste and vulgar nouveau-riche luxury. Abakumov was reported to have tortured prisoners himself and followed Beria's practice of snatching attractive girls off the street, taking them home, and raping them. Who knows what horrors had taken place in the rooms where we were lavishly entertained? After the collapse of the Soviet Union, the press office of the Russian Intelligence Service was located there.

Mielke loved being entertained by the Soviets in grand style while I preferred our trips out of town to the cozy dachas deep in the forests, which reminded me of my childhood. Mielke never entirely escaped the insecurities of his working-class origins. He insisted on sharing a room with me because he was lonely—or maybe, given the surroundings, a little afraid. At night my companion would snore violently, which was scarcely a recipe for a relaxing week.

After 1953, the relationship with the KGB was constrained by the turbulence inside the Soviet leadership following Stalin's death and the execution of his henchman, Lavrenti Beria. Sergei Kruglov, who succeeded Beria, was replaced by Ivan Serov, who had been in charge of installing Soviet structures in East Germany: the big KGB office in Berlin, the placing of KGB representatives in all districts of the GDR, and the establishment of a huge Department of Military Intelligence in Potsdam. Serov was for letting the GDR run its own independent intelligence and counterintelligence operations. I first encountered him at a March 1955 meeting of East bloc security representatives. He was always in uniform, both in dress and in mind, and his speech focused on the need for all of us to combine our efforts against the common enemy, the United States. My Soviet guardian angel was Alexander Panyushkin, former ambassador to Washington and later the man responsible for foreign cadres in the Central Committee.

Once I took a coach trip through the forest of the hunting preserve of the security ministry in Wolletz, forty miles from Berlin, with Serov and the KGB resident in Berlin, Aleksandr Korotkov. Korotkov had served before the war as "Erdmann," the Berlin handler of the Rote Kapelle. They spent their time reminiscing as comrades in arms about putting down the Hungarian revolt. From them I got the impression that many of the KGB's leading generals had taken part in the repression.

Serov was replaced by Aleksandr Shelepin, who lasted only three harsh years (during which he approved the murder in Munich of Stepan Bandera, the Ukrainian nationalist leader, and personally decorated the agent who did it). Arrogant and ambitious, Shelepin was ousted for backing an unsuccessful putsch against Khrushchev in 1961 and was replaced by Vladimir Semichastny. He was as kind and friendly as might be expected from a former leader of the Komsomol, the party's youth wing.

Though affable, Semichastny was a sharp-minded, ideologically severe man who had climbed fast through the ranks of the KGB by making sure he was on the right side when Khrushchev was finally pushed out in 1964 in favor of Leonid Brezhnev. Semichastny's personal obsession was the pollution of the system from within by Soviet artists and writers; it was he who masterminded the vilification of Boris Pasternak and his novel *Dr. Zhivago*. He had little interest in foreign intelligence, which he left to Aleksandr Sakharovsky, who was highly respected by many members of his staff as well as by me. Sakharovsky treated me like a son, in accordance with our respective ages.

I tried to distance the HVA from the "operational excesses" of other espionage services in the East that also looked to the KGB for guidance. The clichés established by espionage movies and novels notwithstanding, physical violence was the exception, not the rule. I do not believe that either side set out to murder opponents, and most of those who died did so accidentally after being given too powerful a dose of knockout drops, often during a snatch. Such deaths were used against the Eastern bloc by the West to great propaganda effect in the stark, black-and-white newsreels of the fifties; indeed, we usually found out about such deaths through Western publications, since these were not the sorts of events that were bragged about internally.

This is not to say that we were not at times harsh in our methods. The HVA, as a result of its integration into the Ministry of State Security in the mid-fifties and in accordance with the Soviet espionage model, was linked to counterintelligence by many threads. For example, if Department 20 of state security, responsible for culture, was concerned with a certain "hostile-negative person"—to use the jargon of counterintelligence—and we found that a neighbor of this person was in HVA files, he or she was used to inform and provide information on the person, as long as other security conditions permitted. This spongy term, "hostile-negative," could be used against anyone who opposed, disagreed with, or only partly disagreed with the policy of the leadership. It was one of the worst instruments of Stasi persecution. If the HVA had information on the activities and contacts of East German writers who were living abroad, that information was given to counterintelligence. For our part, we benefited from counterintelligence knowledge of connections that GDR citizens had with the West.

Such exchanges of information were standard procedure throughout the Eastern bloc, and in the West as well. Some have claimed that the foreign intelligence service's collaboration with the counterintelli-

gence departments of the Ministry of State Security make me a collaborator in the ministry's surveillance and repression of East German
citizens. I am not going to claim that we had nothing to do with such
repression, but the relatively strict departmentalization of the ministry
meant that my service was explicitly not supposed to engage in internal
counterintelligence activities. The HVA was always a foreign intelligence service, and while we engaged in the standard bureaucratic
cooperation with counterintelligence, we had no domestic cases of our
own that involved arrests or convictions. Nevertheless, we were well
aware of what was going on and of counterintelligence's often harsh
methods. During the latter years of cooperation between the HVA and
the Ministry of State Security's counterintelligence departments, the
use of force was the exception rather than the rule, and it was neither
ordered nor approved by senior officers. Measures were, however,
taken to undermine and intimidate opposition groups, and its psychological effects were probably more damaging, ultimately, than any
physical torture would have been.

Such methods, almost inconceivable in scope and of infamous
sophistication, were used against the scientist Robert Havemann. A
convinced Communist who had been condemned to death under
Hitler and liberated by the Soviet army from the same prison as Erich
Honecker, Havemann, starting in the late sixties, publicly criticized
the political leadership of the GDR and demanded democratic reforms
of our stagnating system. His small residence in Grünheide, near
Berlin, was cordoned off and put under siege as if it were some enemy
stronghold. Every member of his family, every visitor, was kept under
observation by informers who literally encircled their everyday movements, and slanders were spread about their spouses, including stories
of actual or invented extramarital affairs. A former agent of my department named Knut Wollenberger was infiltrated into Havemann's
group of democratic reformers in order to pressure and subvert it.

Similar treatment was also applied systematically to the poet and
singer Wolf Biermann, a friend of Havemann's and a member of his
circle. After a tour of West Germany he was denied reentry into the
GDR and was illegally deprived of his citizenship.

Karl Winkler, a young poet and singer and an admirer of Havemann
and Biermann, was arrested on trumped-up charges of "public dispar-

agement" in 1979 and was deported to the West after a trial in which he was found guilty. He published a book describing the psychological torture of his imprisonment; we became acquainted—perhaps friends—after 1989, when I appeared at the rally in the Alexanderplatz seeking reforms. He came as my supporter during the court session in the summer of 1993. The following year, Winkler drowned in the Mediterranean under as yet unexplained circumstances.

All prisons undermine human dignity, but a great deal depends on those conducting the initial investigations and the nature of the jailers after the case is concluded. I have been told by my own agents of the psychological torture of solitary confinement by those who had been subjected to it in Western prisons. I never saw the prisons in East Germany, but the situation there must often have been particularly bad. Winkler's accounts of his own thirteen-month interrogation and incarceration before his deportation were an oppressive demonstration of the total disregard of prisoners' dignity, an experience shared by thousands. He later organized visits and programs about the Ministry of State Security and its prisons, and he and I came to understand and appreciate each other's concerns.

On learning of Winkler's experiences I was once again overcome by shame at the dark side of the ministry where I had held a senior position for so long. I felt no different when I met Walter Janka, an old Communist and companion of my father's, who told me of his prosecution and imprisonment after the upheavals of 1956, when he was sent to the notorious Bautzen penal institution. In December 1989, Janka and I presided at the Party Congress and tried to turn the Socialist Unity Party into a party of democratic socialists. I helped prepare a report on the crimes of Stalinism and of our own past, offering an apology to the people of the GDR. In the years that followed, I and my successor, Werner Grossmann, repeatedly said that our service could not escape responsibility for the internal repression, and we sought forgiveness.

Using the powerful instrument of the state security service against citizens holding different opinions, or those who sought to leave their own, unloved country, was tantamount to trampling on the ideals of communism's founders. Thus the chances of reform had been wasted, and our own responsibility and guilt by default remain a tormenting burden to this day.

I was adamantly against psychically violent or dangerous actions, but the same cannot be said of some of our "friendly" services. One day I received a call from the Bulgarian station chief in Berlin requesting a doctor who could be trusted to keep secrets to help them in "a difficult matter." When pressed he would say only, "We are transporting some goods that are in danger of going off."

It did not take me long to work out that the Bulgarians must have drugged a person they had "snatched" and failed to monitor the effect of the medication. A suitable medic was found with ties to the secret service, which meant that he was not easily shocked. An hour or so after arriving at the Bulgarian embassy, he telephoned me. "Too late," he said. "Those fools gave him a dose strong enough to kill a horse. They trussed up the poor fellow in the trunk of a car. No air and a knockout drug. A combination with predictable results."

Back on the line came the Bulgarian secret service man, now with a tremor in his voice. Having accidentally killed a defector, presumably after snatching him in his West German refuge for interrogation in Sofia, the Bulgarian's own head was now on the block.

"Would it be all right if we left the goods with you?" he pleaded.

"Certainly not," I replied.

We argued this back and forth for a while and finally referred the question to Mielke, who decreed that the corpse was the Bulgarians' problem. We waved the sad cargo on its way before rigor mortis could set in.

It seems impossible for me to persuade people that I did not use such methods. The explanation of our methodology in cases cited in this book should, however, make it clear to all but those who do not want to believe, or prefer to believe that James Bond is a real person, that it was not necessary to engage in the unseemly business of "wet jobs" and sleeping potions to run a highly effective intelligence service.

I knew, however, that even after Stalin's death, the Soviets still had a department that developed bizarre ways of killing enemies. Even within the KGB the existence of this department was a closely guarded secret. In addition to murdering Bandera with a poisoned bullet, the KGB assassinated the defector Truchnovich, the head of the Russian emigrant organization the National Workers Union, in Berlin, while attempting to kidnap him. One KGB man was dispatched to buyers throughout the Eastern bloc bearing wares such as untraceable nerve toxins and skin contact poisons to smear on doorknobs. The only thing I ever accepted from him was a sachet of "truth drugs," which he touted as "unbeatable" with the enthusiasm of a door-to-door sales-man. For years they lay in my personal safe. One day, in a fit of curios-ity, I asked our carefully vetted doctor to have them analyzed for me. He came back shaking his head in horror. "Use these without constant medical supervision and there is every chance that the fellow from whom you want the truth will be dead as a dodo in seconds," he said. We never did use the "truth drugs."

But death was always a risk, no matter what side you were on. The price for being discovered as a traitor early in the Cold War was very often execution after trial by one's own side. The first victim I heard of was a woman called Elli Barczatis, secretary to the East German prime minister Otto Grotewohl. Grotewohl had been a Social Democrat before the merger of the SPD and the Communists in the East in 1948, and his old SPD colleagues in the West had never given up hope that he might turn away from the Soviets and split the ruling East German party. He was very closely targeted by the West, but he being a satur-nine man, they went after his secretary. Barczatis was seduced by a Western agent and, it was later discovered during her interrogation, given the code name "Daisy." To my knowledge this was the first post-war use of a Romeo strategy by the intelligence services of either side to lure a person close to a political figure into cooperating with the enemy.

Barczatis's grim misfortune was that her case became public just after the execution of Julius and Ethel Rosenberg as atomic spies in the United States. The name of the game in espionage, as in other aspects of the Cold War, was parity. She was sentenced to death by guillotine in Frankfurt-an-der-Oder on the Polish border.

In this political climate, I could not fail to be fully aware from the very beginning of how rough the game had become. I do not claim ignorance of the brutalities of life within our own country; the random arrests and fear that penetrated the Communist apparatus in the fifties made me aware that no one was safe from allegations of treachery.

Things changed radically and for the better with the arrival of Yuri Andropov as KGB chief in 1967. Here at last was a figure I admired, unbound by protocol and aloof from the petty intrigues that had marked

the tenure of his predecessors. He was also exempt
Soviet arrogance, which automatically assumed that
was invulnerable. More keenly than anyone else in M
that the military intervention in Hungary in 1956, a
slovakia in 1968, was a sign of Soviet weakness rather than
was anxious for such events not to be repeated. Andropov distinguished
himself from all his KGB predecessors and successors by his political
and human qualities. The horizon of his interests stretched further than
any of them. He was able to understand major aspects of domestic and
foreign policy, ideological and theoretical problems, the necessity of
basic changes and reforms, but also their risks and implications.

My first in-depth meeting with Yuri Andropov came in 1968,
shortly after Russian troops had crushed the Prague spring. He had
been due to visit East Germany that summer, but the visit had to be
postponed because of the developments in Prague. It was autumn by
the time he came to us and we were all still rather dazed by what had
happened and wondered what the appropriate thing was to say. Among
the many virtually identical state banquets I attended, this one stands
out in my mind. We ate in one of our ministry's guest houses in the
northern Pankow district of East Berlin. (In the early days, the East
German leadership had all lived there in a neat estate, cheek by jowl
with each other, before security considerations persuaded them to
move outside the city to the Wandlitz compound in the fifties.)

The guest house in Pankow was a well-appointed villa that had been
chosen with a diplomatic eye to be elegant enough to show due honor
to our guests but not more grandiose than the settings of the dinners
the Soviets gave for us. The guests on the German side were Erich
Mielke, eleven top officers of the Ministry of State Security, and I. The
atmosphere that night was relaxed, a tribute to the changes Andropov
had wrought in the organization. The hard nub of fear—which had
been present during the fifties, a decade that despite Khrushchev's thaw
was scarred by the legacy of Stalin—had melted. Andropov held himself with dignity and, unlike many of his countrymen, could remain civilized after a few drinks. You could see everyone of even the most
modest intellectual pretensions heaving a sigh of relief. It was an
entirely male gathering. Even the servers were men, selected from the
ministry's special list of waiters regarded as trustworthy.

The conversation turned to Czechoslovakia, as I knew it would. Mielke had a lifetime obsession with the German Social Democrats, whom he blamed for "ideological diversion" in the socialist movement. He saw this dinner as an ideal opportunity to let off steam and impress our guest with his party solidarity for the Soviet Union's determination to crush the reform movement in Prague. He rose and spoke of the need to prevent "weakening" through social democratic influence, which dominated the reformist circles in Prague.

A wave of nods spread round the company. Then Andropov spoke. "That is not the whole story," he said, amiably but firmly. "We had two choices: military intervention, which would blacken our reputation, or letting Czechoslovakia go, with all the consequences that would entail for Eastern Europe. It was not an enviable choice."

Andropov took a sip from his water glass and the table fell silent, all eyes fixed on him.

"One has to look at the situation within each country and examine where the stresses and strains lie. The new [Communist] government is going to have a tough time of it in Czechoslovakia. And as for the Social Democrats, well, I think we will have to look carefully at our relations with them and what they represent everywhere."

The number of sacred cows that had just been slaughtered was breathtaking. For a start, he was brushing aside the strict ideological analysis of the intervention in favor of examining the internal problems of the country itself. Andropov's comments also implied that the Communists in Czechoslovakia had been slow to realize the extent of dissent and the work required to improve matters. Andropov's concern for the fate of the new leadership went directly against the official line, which maintained that the mass of law-abiding citizens were delighted to have order restored and the Communists firmly back in command. And the postscript, favoring contacts with all Social Democrats, was a veiled criticism of the visceral hatreds between the East German leadership and the main party of the left in West Germany. It was also prescient, given that in the following year the West German Social Democrats would launch their *Ostpolitik* campaign seeking a better understanding with the East. I was impressed by how intent Andropov was on overcoming the role he knew we expected him to play and by his honest talk in a forum where flattery and rhetoric were otherwise the order of the day. Emboldened by his attitude, we at the table re-filled our glasses.

This occasion was not the end of Mielke's outrageous statements. Until the 1970s he insisted on toasting Stalin and demanding "three cheers for our model and inspiration" to an increasingly mortified hall. He would hint heavily that it had been a great mistake for the Soviet Union to distance itself from Stalin's legacy. But that was in home company, of course. When the Soviets were present, it was different.

Unlike his predecessors, Andropov's main interest was foreign policy and foreign intelligence. He also introduced managerial structures into the KGB and installed a system of greater accountability. In foreign operations, he was quick to realize that the traditional practice of stuffing embassies and trade and other official Soviet representations with agents was not the best way to operate, since these institutions were very well monitored by foreign counterintelligence. I knew from my own, mainly abortive attempts to run agents from our Washington embassy that they could hardly move out of the building without having an FBI man on their tail, although years later I met Ivan Gromakov, who had served as KGB resident in Washington, and he maintained that FBI surveillance was easy to detect and had never proved an obstacle for him in dealing with his sources. The other disadvantage of operating under diplomatic cover was the risk of retaliatory diplomatic expulsions, which meant that any agent established in an embassy or similar post had a high probability of being thrown out of the country in one of the perennial expulsions. The Soviet Union's embassies were so overstuffed that in one year the British expelled a grand total of 105 suspected agents from the USSR's London's embassy. Andropov's shift toward the emphasis on illegals (infiltrating the agent into a hostile territory with a false identity, false papers, and an apparent justification for being there), while certainly better espionage practice, was deeply unpopular within the cadres, who preferred to have institutional support.

This shift to illegals was a reality we had already been forced by necessity to deal with. Because the GDR was not diplomatically recognized in the West until the Basic Treaty was signed with West Germany, we did not in any case have the luxury of using embassies as espionage bases and were far more reliant on the "illegal line" (we even used this old Bolshevik phrase). Andropov examined our methods closely and came to the conclusion that fewer agents should enjoy the comforts of institutional life and more should be sent out as illegals to make their own way. He studied the development of East German intelligence in depth and asked me to provide detailed examples of my approach to running agents. I was flattered to be asked and pleased to do so.

We never shared the names of agents. The first rule of our espionage tradition reached back to the revolutionary Communist Party's policy, and it was that one had access only to what one needed to know. This sensible restriction prevented outbreaks of mutual recriminations when treachery took place, preventing one service from trying to blame another.

Andropov's openness to information from outside the KGB also deepened his sense of the real relations between diplomats and intelligence officers within embassies as opposed to the officially reported ones. The KGB's occasionally arrogant approach to this relationship meant that in many embassies dealings between the ambassador and the official KGB resident were strained. This was exacerbated by the KGB's superior resources; it always was well funded, and its employees could afford their own cars, whereas only top-ranking Soviet diplomats had their own cars; other diplomats were forced to depend on the embassy's motor pool. KGB members could also claim higher meal expenses than bona fide diplomats. Not only were these discrepancies a source of resentment, they also helped foreign counterintelligence organizations to spot the KGB agents operating under diplomatic cover.

As for Andropov's wider political impact, I know that he was the source of many of the reformist ideas that Gorbachev would later claim as his own. He recognized that one of the reasons the Soviet economy had fallen so far behind the West's was centralized control and the total separation of the military and civilian sectors. Huge government investments in the military-industrial complex in the United States and other developed capitalist countries could be spun off by private companies into profitable civilian advances in high technology such as jet aviation and computers. But in the Soviet Union, the fetish for secrecy created an insuperable drag, as ministers from the GDR could testify from their own experience with Soviet military ministries. When I raised such issues with Andropov, he told me he was trying to put this line of thinking into practice in committees that he had staffed with civilian and military experts, who were supposed to learn from such comparisons between the two competing economic systems. Andropov regarded intelligence as an important instrument for learning from the other side to improve the socialist system, and his intellectual readiness to examine other ways contrasted with the stagnation all around him. He mused about the possibility of a social democratic "third way" led by Hungary and certain factions in the GDR, and even during the repression of Soviet dissidents, for which he was responsible, he was privately discussing Hungary's experiments in political pluralism as well as economic liberalism.

I often wondered what Andropov would have done if he had been granted a decade in power instead of just a few, ailing years. Surely he would not have done what Gorbachev did. He had expressed hopes of somehow subjecting socialized property to the free market as well as political liberalization, and surely the steps toward reform would have been more carefully thought out.

In dealing with other socialist countries, Andropov was never patronizing in the manner of Brezhnev, his predecessor, or Chernenko, his successor. Vyacheslav Kochemassov recalls that when he was appointed Soviet ambassador in Berlin, Andropov told him, "We need a new ambassador in the GDR, not a colonial governor." Whether the end of the old Russian imperial style would have led to a successful reform of socialism remains an open question.

Perhaps these recollections will help resolve the paradox that Andropov presented to the West. He was advertised as a closet liberal—even an admirer of jazz—but Western analysts found this difficult to square with his toughness toward dissidents. This missed the point. I can testify that he certainly favored reform, but it would not have come in a Western democratic manner, which he would have regarded as anarchic. Andropov's reforms would have been imposed from the top down, with all the limitations that would entail. But I believe such reforms would have taken a more measured and perhaps more successful path.

The fact that I admired Andropov doesn't mean I always got my way with him, especially when it came to my attempts to arrange a spy swap for Günter Guillaume in 1978. I figured that Bonn might offer

Guillaume only in return for someone really big from the Soviet side. This would enhance their reputation as big players in the game of global diplomacy, and a number of West German agents could be included to sweeten the deal for domestic consumption. As I doodled possible names on the back of an envelope, I saw that the key—and the problem—was Anatoly Sharansky. Or, more precisely, the Kremlin's obsession with him.

Like the moralist and Gulag chronicler Aleksandr Solzhenitsyn and the scientist and dissident Andrei Sakharov, the builder of the Soviet atomic bomb who had turned to the cause of human rights, Sharansky had in the five years of his concentrated campaigning for Jewish rights achieved cult status in the dissident world. This was a matter of charisma as well as luck in meeting the right sympathetic journalists— there were hundreds of other equally committed but thoroughly ignored dissidents in the Soviet Union. This shy academic by his suc- cess had become the target of a highly personalized degree of wrath in both the KGB and the Party. I knew from my experience of Moscow's dealings with internal enemies that this often worked its way out in a decision simply to get rid of the offending individual; Solzhenitsyn had been put on a plane to Germany; Sakharov had been sent (by Andropov himself) to internal exile in Gorky. So why not be rid of Sharansky too? But Andropov did not see it that way.

"Comrade Wolf," he said. "Don't you know what will happen if we give this signal? The man is a spy [Andropov thought Sharansky was involved with the CIA], but more important, he is a Jew, and it is the Jews he speaks for. Too many groups have suffered under the repres- sion in our country. If we give this sort of ground to the Jews, who will be next? The Volga Germans? The Crimean Tartars? Or maybe the Kalmucks or the Chechens?"

He was referring to the ethnic groups deported by Stalin from their homelands in a campaign literally to pull up potential sources of oppo- sition from their geographic roots. The KGB had a bureaucratic word for these groups that I had never heard before: *kontingentirovannye*. *Kontingent* referred to "quotas," or categories, of unreliable people. These "contingents" were regarded as disaffected potential enemies, and Andropov put their number at the astounding total of eight and a half million.

"We cannot carelessly try to solve all of these problems in these difficult times," he continued. "If we open up all the valves at once, and people start to express their grievances, there will be an avalanche and we will have no means of stopping it."

This was the frank Andropov I knew of old, cutting through the ponderous and mendacious official versions to reveal the bare-bones reason behind the Soviet Union's intransigence on human rights: fear—fear of the potential for conflict arising in Stalin's legacy of potential enemies within the country itself. Sharansky could become a figurehead not just for Soviet Jews, but for many, many more *kontingentirovannye*.

There now seems to be no evidence that Sharansky was involved with the CIA, but Andropov was absolutely convinced that he was. He would have had no reason to lie about this to me, of all people. But above and beyond any espionage connections, Andropov's main considerations lay elsewhere, and I was stunned by how openly he referred to potential ethnic problems. Andropov continued: "He will carry a flag for all the Jews. Stalin's anti-Semitic excesses have left these people with a big grievance against the Soviet state and they have powerful friends abroad. We cannot allow that at the moment." He was equally frank about the Soviet Union's decline, the start of which, referring to our meeting fourteen years before, he pinpointed as the 1968 invasion of Czechoslovakia.

I made several efforts to persuade Andropov to agree to swap Sharansky but failed every time. Andropov was allergic to his very name, and he usually became heated and shouted, "He is a spy and that's that." And that would end the conversation.

In the end, it was Guillaume's ill health (like Andropov, he suffered from kidney disease) that speeded up his release. The West Germans were forced to calculate that, however unwilling they were to show clemency, they would not get much of a swap for a corpse. Besides, Erich Honecker, after he succeeded Ulbricht, began to take the matter seriously and hint to Helmut Schmidt that unless something was done he might restrict prisoner exchanges and the reunification of families split by the border.

I met Andropov again in 1980 when I flew to Moscow with Mielke to present medals to some leading KGB officers on the occasion of the thirtieth anniversary of the founding of our ministry. These ceremonies were taken very seriously by both sides, the KGB and the East bloc intelligence services, and had reached a state of predictable reciprocity: They awarded us medals on their anniversaries, we replied in kind on ours. This was repeated throughout the Eastern bloc, and everyone lost count of the number of such awards received by the top ranks of the KGB. A special dresser was employed at KGB headquarters to ensure their officers wore the correct ones for each occasion. On this occasion Andropov was to receive a gold medal marking three decades of fraternal cooperation with our ministry. He was in the hospital but received the medal there.*

Nineteen eighty had been an uneasy year in Soviet-American relations. Arguing that the Soviet deployment of SS–20 mobile missiles in western Russia and East Germany demanded countermeasures, NATO had decided late in 1979 to deploy nuclear missiles in four European countries, including West Germany, if the removal of our missiles could not be negotiated within two years, by December 1981. This would bring missiles capable of striking most of Europe's major cities close to both sides of the Cold War frontier. Now the deadline had passed, and the mood in East and West Germany was somber. Some commentators likened the situation to the eve of World War I in 1914, when war threatened and one false step could unleash hostilities. This was dismissed by conservatives as left-wing scare mongering, but I knew that Helmut Schmidt had drawn this same historical analogy in talks with an envoy from Honecker.

---

*My final meeting with Andropov, in 1982, was more sobering. I had flown to Moscow to participate in a meeting of heads of East bloc foreign intelligence services. When I got there, however, I was informed that acute illness prevented Andropov from taking part in the meeting. It was the first I learned of the true extent of the poor state of his health. I was taken instead to meet him in the exclusive Kremlin Clinic in Kunzevo, a heavily guarded part of the city where Stalin had once had his summer residence. The clinic's protected location screened it from public gaze. Inside, Andropov had a whole apartment to himself, with his bedroom and treatment rooms separated by a brightly lit corridor humming with security cameras. Opposite were his study and a room for receiving visitors. He looked pale and flaccid. I waited outside with Andropov's deputy, Vladimir Kryuchkov, while Andropov himself spoke privately with Mielke. No one had mentioned the nature of his illnes, nor how severe it was. Any intimation of the general secretary's all-too-apparent mortality was taboo. After some minutes ticked by in silence, Kryuchkov asked me whether I could recommend a competent East German urologist, hastily adding that the nature of the leader's ailment was, of course, a matter of the highest secrecy.

Fears of a nuclear confrontation ran very deep indeed. In private conversation with Günter Mittag, Honecker's economics adviser and a frequent go-between on inter-German affairs, Schmidt complained of the increasing pressure on West Germany from Washington and added, "Everything is getting out of hand. We must keep in frequent contact." Panic could escalate very fast, he said, but Honecker should know that the Federal Republic was reliable. "Nothing crazy will happen on West Germany's side," he concluded. In other words, while the superpowers played their war game, we Germans should deal with each other and keep our heads down.

Andropov believed that the Americans were making a concerted effort to wrest nuclear superiority from the Soviets. "This is not the time for weakness on our part," he said, citing statements by President Carter, his adviser, Zbigniew Brzezinski, and the Pentagon that some circumstances could justify the use of nuclear weapons in a first strike against the Soviet Union. Andropov was also perturbed by rising Soviet losses against the Muslim fundamentalist rebels in Afghanistan, and I tentatively asked for his thoughts about the future of the operation. "There is no going back for us now," was all he would say.

His deepest vituperation was reserved for Chancellor Schmidt, who had agreed to NATO's two-track strategy of negotiating while planning the deployment of mobile nuclear missiles in West Germany. "The man has two faces," he complained. "But really, he is on the Americans' side. There should be no top-level contacts with such a man." I guessed that this was a reference to his previous private conversation with Mielke on the subject of Erich Honecker's contacts with Schmidt, many of which were hidden from the Soviets, a perennial source of irritation to them. Moscow fundamentally distrusted the openings between East and West Germany that *Ostpolitik* had brought about and wanted to keep control of any rapprochement. Andropov and Foreign Minister Andrei Gromyko were particularly keen to prevent a visit by Honecker to Bonn. The more threatening the international situation became, the more intensely Honecker and Schmidt worked at improving their personal relations. They kept contact on a special telephone line, while West Germany purchased the freedom of a steady stream of East German prisoners, the most accurate mirror of the state of relations.

From our intelligence sources in Bonn, we knew how sorely tested West Germany's loyalty to NATO was at that time. Schmidt had put himself into the difficult position because he had initially raised the question of Europe's defense after Moscow and Washington made their own deal on limiting intercontinental missile forces over the heads of the Europeans. Now the call by Carter to join an American boycott of the Moscow Olympic Games was the last straw. It split Schmidt's already fractious government, and we were informed by a source in the SPD that he could win by threatening to resign if the boycott was not approved. From our sources in key offices in the West German capital, we gathered how much he chafed under American pressure. The hardening of the U.S. line toward Moscow forced him to cancel a planned visit to East Berlin. Even then, his thoughts were focused on maintaining the German relationship rather than playing the superpower game. He insisted on straightforwardly canceling his visit to East Berlin himself, rather than trying to maneuver Honecker into a situation where the East would have to withdraw the invitation.

My service was responsible for passing to Moscow the proposed location and technical specifications of American Pershing II and Cruise missiles that were to be positioned in 1982 if negotiations failed. In fact, I knew a whole lot more about American nuclear strategy than about the Soviet deployment in Eastern Europe, thanks mainly to my chief NATO source, Rainer Rupp. The locations of the Soviets' mobile SS-20s were a carefully guarded secret even from us, although we were Moscow's prime ally—and the most forwardly placed missiles were, after all, on our own territory. Soviet arrogance in this irritated and alienated many otherwise loyal East Germans. Members of my service were called only to join in special exercises in preparation for an extreme-case scenario of a theoretical NATO first strike.

With the U.S. rearmament program and the advent of the aggressive Reagan administration, our Soviet partners had become obsessed with the danger of a nuclear missile attack, which they referred to by an acronym, RYAN, formed from the Russian phrase *Raketno yadenoye napadeniye*. The HVA was ordered to uncover any Western plans for such a surprise attack, and we formed a special staff and situation center, as well as emergency command centers, to do this. The personnel had to undergo military training and participate in alarm drills. Like most intelligence people, I found these war games a burdensome waste of time, but these orders were no more open to discussion than other orders from above. I no longer believed in the possibility of nuclear war in Europe, although I did believe that the confrontation between the two opposing global systems would intensify on political, economic, and other levels. At the same time, my doubts also increased that leading politicians on either side would understand and act on the changes taking place in the world. I began to think about how I could end my intelligence career and turn to a life of writing, but the rising pressures of my job in the atmosphere of more intense confrontation made me keep putting off the decision.

●

Despite Moscow's robust propaganda, I always knew the Soviet Union was far more vulnerable to a tough American line than it pretended. The SALT II disarmament negotiations between Brezhnev and Nixon made that clear to me. Jimmy Carter's election as president, however, left us unprepared; our initial files on him contained little information beyond a description of him as a low-profile peanut farmer. It was comforting that our intelligence sources in Bonn reported that the West Germans were similarly unimpressed by the new commander-in-chief. But when Carter announced a record defense budget of $157 billion to pay for MX and Trident missiles, Cruise missiles, more atomic submarines, and a reserve force of eleven thousand, the reaction in Moscow was one of barely controlled panic. "We cannot fight them with funds," a leading Soviet nuclear strategist confided to me. "Thank God we are good at other things."

By this time, some of the gaps in policy between East and West Germany had closed independent of our respective masters in Moscow and Washington. Herbert Wehner, still parliamentary floor manager and power broker in the ruling Social Democrats in Bonn, was so disconcerted by U.S. nuclear policy that he made substantial efforts to keep contacts open between Bonn and East Germany. Through Wehner's assistant, Karl Wienand, we acquired a confidential paper written by Wehner indicating the extent of his distrust of Washington's intentions. Wehner was unsparing in his criticism: "The CIA has distributed the bacillus of possible war between the two Germanys. That is not an invention. The neutron bombs are being tailor-made for the Ruhr and for Berlin. I share Schmidt's skepticism about Carter. Not because he has dark intentions, but because he is apt to try every possible variant. That approach can go wrong very easily."

As mentioned earlier, I believe Wehner knew of his assistant's links to East Berlin. His disillusionment with communism would have prevented him from ever becoming a direct source for us, but he was happy to let it be known that, regardless of the political risk to himself, he would signal to the East even the slightest nuclear danger in order to safeguard German interests. Wehner further developed contacts with the GDR through the spy-trading lawyer Wolfgang Vogel. In the end, I believe that Wehner trusted Honecker more than the leaders of his own party. We were even told by our contacts in the West that Wehner had left instructions for his personal papers to be deposited in the East after his death.

At the same time as we were perturbed by incomprehensible shifts in American policy, the changeable nature of Soviet foreign policy throughout this period caused us any number of problems. No sooner had Honecker adapted himself to the new *Ostpolitik* and steered toward a more generous interpretation of Western social democracy, than Moscow would send out signals to stop.

The questions put to me by my own personal Soviet contact officer, Vladimir Budakhin, indicated how, despite all the toasts and warm rhetoric, the relationship between Moscow and East Berlin was doomed to misunderstanding. Whether it was the building of a motorway between Hamburg and Berlin through our territory, the opening of an East-West shipping canal, or business negotiations with the West German industrial giants Krupp or Hoechst, the Soviets were always there with suspicious questions and objections. Usually this resulted in the postponement yet again of the long-desired meeting between Honecker and Schmidt.

Honecker suffered from the illusion, reinforced by the Kremlin-model mini-personality cult he permitted, that he could solve such problems single-handedly. When he received via Wehner information about confidential contacts between the Soviets and Bonn about which East Berlin had not been informed, he merely commented,

"They can decide nothing without us." History shows this was his great mistake.

I also made a cardinal error in underestimating the consequences of our total dependence on the Soviet Union. My lifelong bonds with Moscow and the amicable relationship I enjoyed with Soviet intelligence allowed me to believe—mistakenly—that the KGB was dealing with the HVA as an equal. I knew that we sent Moscow a waterfall of information: political and military intelligence about their frontline foes, technical manuals about the U.S. National Security Agency's electronic espionage, identities and methods of CIA agents, and such quantities of scientific and technological information that the Russian liaison officer had to add an assistant to handle it. Only a trickle came the other way. But this was something my senior intelligence partners in Moscow admitted and sought to redress on a personal level, and the slow nature of changes in Moscow lulled me into thinking that we would always be near the top of the Kremlin's foreign priorities. That had certainly been the case under Stalin, Khrushchev, Andropov, and Chernenko. Gorbachev's inexplicable decision to leave our fate in the hands of NATO in 1989 thus would come as a brutal shock.

That said, we had grown accustomed to the Soviets' behaving, in military terms at least, like an occupying power who expended scant concern for our sensibilities. Honecker had often expressed to Moscow his concern at the concentration of arms, soldiers, and now nuclear hardware in East Germany. I was uncomfortably aware of the gap between his real influence and what he perceived as his influence. It was wide indeed, but such self-deception was part and parcel of the way we lived our life in this frontline outpost of the Soviet empire. As the missile row between Moscow and Washington intensified in 1979 and Moscow threatened to deploy even more weaponry in East Germany, Mielke said to me one day, "There is no way we are going to spend billions on behalf of others and chop down trees to clear more space for tanks and missile launchers. Nothing will happen, you'll see. Just more negotiations."

Needless to say, when the huge Soviet SS-20s rolled in during the dead of night disguised as log deliveries, the woods were chopped down without further discussion.

•

Perhaps I am in danger of lionizing Andropov. He certainly deserves criticism, even from an admirer, and it is true that his treatment of dissidents was harsh. His decisions (and they were his, to all intents and purposes) to strip Solzhenitsyn of his citizenship and exile Sakharov to Gorky are all part of the same mind-set that resisted the release of Sharansky. He pursued the stability of the Soviet Union above all other considerations. His interest in the permissible forms of political pluralism was confined to watching the experiment of Hungary's "goulash" communism (as it was half mockingly, half disparagingly called by the rest of us) while practicing a far stricter form of the doctrine at home. But he was more careful than Gorbachev in his changes in the Central Committee and initiated the struggle against corruption to a much greater extent than did his successors.

Andropov's decision to elevate Vladimir Kryuchkov to the position of chief of the First Main Directorate of the KGB was logical but not especially wise. Kryuchkov had been Andropov's close aide ever since Budapest in 1956. He knew Kryuchkov understood foreign policy and presumably thought that entrusting foreign intelligence to someone he had formed in his own image would prevent a relapse to the old internal schisms and narrow vision.

Kryuchkov's stature within the KGB had grown with its involvement in Afghanistan, where he was credited with organizing special operations after the invasion. But he lacked Andropov's breadth of understanding and was not by disposition a leader. Without his master to guide him, this competent and intelligent number two was lost. I caught a glimpse of the extent of Kryuchkov's hero worship for Andropov when I visited him in 1982 to congratulate him on becoming head of the KGB. Afterward, over dinner, he recited to me some of Andropov's poems. It was the first I knew about these and they were surprisingly good, rather melancholy and romantic offerings, imitative of Pushkin and Lermontov with their emphasis on lost love and the regrets of old age. That increased my regard for Andropov, but I did think it a touch comical that his successor at the head of the KGB busied himself learning by heart the love poetry of the new general secretary of the Communist Party of the Soviet Union.

When I arrived in Moscow, Kryuchkov always took me to a private room behind his front office, poured me a large Scotch, and said, "Tell me what's going on." When Mielke was around, things were much less direct, with a lot of beating of the political drum on both sides, never-ending toasts about the glory of the Revolution and the success of communism, which was rather strange given that of all people, these two heads of the security services were the ones who knew that things were not going well in their countries.

No visit to Kryuchkov was complete without a visit to the theater. He went often and prided himself on having seen all of the major productions in Moscow and collected the programs, which he hoarded in his office. This earned him a reputation as a cultivated man. In fact, his attachment to the theater grew as much out of his like of collecting things as anything else. I discovered this during one of his visits to East Germany in the mid-eighties. *Faust* was being staged in the Weimar National Theater. Kryuchkov's German was poor, but he nevertheless insisted on going, doubtless knowing that this was one of the central dramas in the canon of world literature. Eight hours of *Faust* demands more concentration than even I could readily muster in my native language, but I was happy to go through with it for the sake of German-Soviet friendship. An hour or so into the play, I shot a sideways look at my guest and caught his eyes closing. Clearly, Goethe was rather heavy fare for him, too. At the end of the first part, it was clear to me that he had no idea what was going on. "I think I've got the hang of it," he said. "Let's skip the rest." He left clutching his program proudly as the latest addition to his collection.

Even if I did not respect him as much as Andropov, I had good relations with him. It came as an immense shock to me much later when, in August 1991, during my stay in Moscow, he attempted his amateurish putsch against Gorbachev. Key groups in the security and party apparatus were deeply unhappy about the amount of self-determination Gorbachev wanted to cede to the Soviet republics, so I was less shocked at the attempt itself than at the operetta manner in which it was conducted. Old KGB colleagues complained bitterly to me that they had not even been informed of what was happening. As they saw the disorganized nature of the putsch and the helplessness of those involved, it was no surprise that they refused to back it openly.

●

The special sense of being part of a family attached to the KGB and its allied services was one source of the Soviet KGB's superiority. But the KGB also had weaknesses, the principal ones being a top-heavy Party bureaucracy and the bedrock of distrust within the organization itself. The latter reflected its inability, despite the best efforts of Andropov and Kryuchkov, to rid itself of the shadow of Stalin and Beria.

Furthermore, for a long time, alongside the carefully nurtured feeling of belonging to a nobility in the KGB went an appalling lack of gratitude toward agents who had risked their lives for the organization—often they were disowned or neglected by it when they were of no more use. East Germany, deemed the most reliable in intelligence terms within the bloc, was used as a dumping ground for a number of exploded spies Moscow wanted hidden away. This was a financial as well as an organizational strain on East Germany, since the internal accounting within the Eastern bloc always worked in the Soviet Union's favor. When a retired agent was presented to us, he came with paltry financial resources inadequate to the task of settling him in a comfortable apartment and finding him a suitable job.

Both the KGB and the GRU (Chief Intelligence Directorate of the Soviet General Staff, a.k.a. Soviet military intelligence) recruited East Germans. Despite the close ties between our two countries and our two espionage services, they liked to have their own people, and we were not told who they were. We would only discover that they had been using an East German to spy, usually in West Germany or NATO, after his capture. After such a spy had served his time or was swapped for an imprisoned Western agent, the Soviets expected us to look after him personally and financially. This was tricky. Once an agent is known in the West he cannot be used there again. Neither was I keen to have such people working in any part of the Ministry of State Security, where they would have access to secrets or could overhear sensitive information.

Worst of all, they often suffered from depression or other psychological trauma, since the Soviets gave them little support or reward for their work and their sacrifices. This cold rejection made many feel that their Soviet masters blamed them for getting caught, even though for most the reason for failure lay elsewhere, usually in the careless planning or execution of their meetings with Soviet instructors ("couriers" in the West) or in treachery by someone back in Moscow. I was disappointed that the Soviets made so little effort to reward these burned-out agents, often not even awarding them a medal for their pains.

One such Soviet agent for whom I had the greatest respect was the atomic-secrets spy Klaus Fuchs. He had played a crucial role in the Soviet nuclear program by giving Beria, who personally oversaw nuclear strategy, American and British details of work on the plutonium bomb and on uranium-235. He thus made the greatest single contribution to Moscow's ability to build an atom bomb. Having moved to Britain before the war to escape the Nazis, he was working on nuclear programs at the Harwell Research Station in Britain. Fuchs was cut from the same human cloth as Sorge and Philby, and like them, this brilliant man voluntarily put his knowledge at the service of the Soviet Union. They all truly believed that only with the help of the USSR could Hitler be defeated. The discovery that scientists in Nazi Germany were working on the bomb prompted Fuchs to pass his secrets to Moscow.

Fuchs's Communist convictions were deepened by his experience in Nazi Germany. He was present at the explosion of the first atom bomb by the Americans at Alamogordo, New Mexico, on July 16, 1945, and signaled the news so quickly to Moscow that Stalin was notably unsurprised when President Truman hinted to him about a powerful new weapon only eight days later at the conference of the wartime victors at Potsdam.

On the orders of Soviet military intelligence, Fuchs remained silent for over thirty years after his arrest in Britain in 1950, neither publishing his memoirs nor giving interviews, even to Soviet or East German publications. After being released by the British in 1959, he lived in Dresden, but for a long time we were not even allowed to approach him. In the 1970s, it was finally agreed that my Scientific and Technological Sector should be able to use him to provide occasional advice on energy policy. It was made clear to me that we were not to discuss Fuchs's espionage achievements.

The thought that the man who had made the greatest contribution to nuclear espionage was living in my country, answering periodic questions about the merits of various cooling systems and the trickier points of nuclear physics for my colleagues but unable to talk about his great intelligence coup, left me no rest. I had put great effort into building up a sense of tradition and belonging within my service by having the lives and deeds of great spies on our side memorialized in films and books. I knew that Klaus Fuchs would make an ideal subject for such a study. Of course, it was unthinkable that I should approach him without political clearance. It took several attempts to persuade Erich Honecker to back me in trying to persuade Fuchs to tell me his story. After some delay I was finally given approval to visit him together with a senior colleague who understood nuclear physics. We were the only non-KGB or -GRU men ever to be allowed to interview him about his past after his resettlement in East Germany. Our meeting with him in 1983 was conducted on our agreement that its contents should be exclusively for internal use in my service. We were able to persuade Fuchs to be videotaped, and this tape is the only footage of him in the GDR.

I met him in a guest house in Berlin where he stayed during meetings of the Party, of which he was a member of the Central Committee. I found someone physically incongruous in the role of superspy. He was a cartoonist's notion of the brilliant scientist, with a high forehead and rimless glasses out of which watchful eyes stared thoughtfully as I plied him with questions. This stare had impressed everyone who met him, including Professor Max Born, Fuchs's mentor and former partner in nuclear research in Edinburgh, who remembered him from his student days as a very nice boy with big sad eyes. These eyes came to life when Fuchs began to talk about theoretical physics. He still had a boyish enthusiasm for the subject and could expound for hours on end on quantum theory and his own outstanding research contribution to the creation of the bomb: the discovery of the calculus of variations during the implosion inside the plutonium bomb. He remained a researcher heart and soul.

"I never considered myself a spy," Fuchs told me. "I could not see why it was in the West's interest not to share the bomb with Moscow.

Something with this unimaginable destructive potential simply had to be held in common by the great powers. It was abhorrent to me that one side should be able to threaten the other with such great force. That would be like a giant treading on Lilliputians. I never thought that I was doing something culpable by passing the secrets to Moscow. It would have seemed an evil negligence for me not to have done it."

In 1941 Fuchs contacted Soviet military intelligence (the GRU) through his friend the economist Jürgen Kuczynski. The GRU assigned him a series of constantly changing couriers. His favorite was Kuczynski's sister, Ursula Beurton, alias Ruth Werner, whose code name was Sonya. The resourceful Werner lived, to all outward appearances, as a quiet mother of two small children in Oxford. In fact, she was one of the Soviet Union's top spies in Britain and would eventually be awarded the rare honorary title of colonel in the Red Army—the only woman to receive it. Werner would bicycle with Fuchs to the woods near the Churchill family seat at Blenheim. He then would pass over secrets, which she stuffed under her bicycle seat. Fuchs had no intelligence training and refused to learn radio codes or to take microfilm pictures. He simply made copies of the information he wanted or researched it, then wrote it out later from his prodigious photographic memory. The delivery system was breathtakingly simple, even naïve from an intelligence point of view. There was no dead-letter drop. The secrets were passed hand to hand, which would have been a gift for counterintelligence if it had been watching. Fortunately, there were no British suspicions of Fuchs at this time. He was less impressed with the Russian couriers. "Unlike Ruth, they were visibly afraid in my presence," he said. "There was one in particular who used to look round all the time to see if he was being followed. I am no professional in these matters, but that seemed to attract more attention to us than simply getting on with it."

Ruth Werner, who, amazingly, managed to flee Britain after Fuchs's arrest, became a close friend of mine back in East Berlin. She once admitted to me that she had taken a peek at the secrets but could not understand a word of them—"They were just strings of hieroglyphics and formulae written in such tiny writing that they just looked like squiggles."

Those squiggles changed the world's balance of power by breaking America's nuclear monopoly earlier than otherwise. Fuchs was reserved with us about his personal role in the development of the Soviet atomic bomb, and in fact Moscow never confirmed to him until two years before his death what the value of his information had been. This was an attempt to confuse the West into thinking that the Soviets might have had other undiscovered nuclear spies. This pretense ended only when the Kremlin cleared for publication the memoirs of Professor Igor Kurchatov. Kurchatov confirmed that Fuchs's information had saved him several years of research by enabling him to model his approach on what he learned was the successful American approach for the first Los Alamos bomb.

When I gingerly approached the subject of his arrest in 1950, it was immediately clear to me that I was prodding a thirty-year-old wound that had not healed. Fuchs was determined not to break down in front of us, but the effort in controlling himself showed in his strained face and involuntary twitches. He told us the story of his great mistake with such deep regret and emotion that it sounded like a second confession.

I am sure that he suffered most from the fact that, since his release from jail in 1959, he had not been given the opportunity to speak directly of his discovery with his Soviet handlers. I could not understand why, in over twenty years, Moscow had never taken the initiative to make it happen. There had been no gratitude, no acknowledgment of his service, not even questions about what had gone wrong. This silence from the country he had served purely out of conscience and at great cost to his liberty and scientific career weighed on him like a daily burden.

Fuchs did not give his opinion on these omissions. But I suspect that the reason for his masters' cruel silence lay in the Soviets' suspicion that he had betrayed the names of couriers or other agents during his interrogation by MI5, the counterintelligence department of the British Secret Service. I, however, believe that no proof of Fuchs's guilt existed.

Fuchs told me that when he realized the British suspected him, he had been confident that he could deflect suspicion. He was questioned after the arrest of the British scientist Allan Nunn May in 1946 on charges of espionage, but he had the impression that British counterintelligence was quizzing all scientists who had met Nunn May and felt that he had acquitted himself well. "The pressure built up in 1950, when I was called several times to see the authorities in Harwell, British intelligence officers among them," he recalled. "I was still confident. But they were obviously working on me, because they knew that my father had gone to live in East Germany and I was questioned about that too. Finally, they started to refer to information from New York, and it was clear that the CIA had passed on information about me."

This uncomfortable situation continued for some time. It is difficult to see why the Soviets did not attempt to get Fuchs out of Britain, given the degree of interest in him by the authorities at Harwell. One can surmise that they neglected to do so for the simple reason that they wanted to continue mining as much material as possible out of Harwell, and Fuchs's safety came second to that. That would also explain Fuchs's distress so many years after his arrest.

In the end, it was a simple psychological trick rather than any hard evidence that trapped Fuchs. The deputy director of Harwell, a close friend of Fuchs's, openly discussed with him the suspicions that he was a spy. He simply asked Fuchs whether it was true or not. If Fuchs said no, his friend emphasized, the whole of Harwell would rally round him and stand by him to a man.

This was, I imagine, a move cleverly planned by British counterintelligence, using their extremely good psychological profiling system. They had found Fuchs good at withstanding questioning; he would not break simply under more of the same, so they would try something completely different. Watching him work at Harwell, they concluded that Fuchs took his friendships very seriously. They would have put the words into the deputy director's mouth, knowing that for Fuchs, the thought of lying directly to his friend would be painful. The British were right.

Fuchs, unable to bring himself to lie, stuttered and then was silent in response to his friend's question. "From that moment on," Fuchs told me, "I was in a trance. I cauterized my fear by working hard and pushed it out of my mind. There were encouraging signs, too. None of the security officials at Harwell wanted to believe that I was a traitor, and they refused to carry out any more interrogations. When they came to arrest me, I just thought, quite blankly, 'So this is the end.'"

It amazed me that Fuchs was so naïve about espionage that it had never occurred to him to find out what sentence he might receive. "I climbed the steps to the defendant's box in the courthouse as if in a dream," he said. "They said to me, 'Do you know what sentence awaits you if you are found guilty?' And I said, 'The death penalty, I suppose,' because I had read somewhere that that is what happens to spies. They said, 'No, fourteen years,' and I was so relieved. It was only then that I thought I would live and that there was a future."

Nine years later he was released from prison and brought to East Germany on Soviet orders. He must have expected them at least to meet him there. But from the moment he set foot outside the prison, he was passed over to East German diplomats like a parcel. Only after I made contact with him in 1983 were his old handlers in Moscow, Vladimir Barkovsky and Alexander Feklisov, allowed to contact him again and bestow the Soviet Union's belated acknowledgment of his services.

Fuchs was a sensitive and vulnerable man. He did not have the constitution for espionage and his inability to lie to his friend, while it showed his human quality, was a weakness in an agent. True to the dictum of the British writer E. M. Forster, he would sooner betray his country than his friend.

12

" A c t i v e   M e a s u r e s "

In his sobering play about the practice of communism, *The Measure Taken*, Bertolt Brecht rationalizes the more extreme activities undertaken to strengthen the Revolution thus:

What baseness would you not commit,
To stamp out baseness?
If you could change the world
What would you be too good for?
Sink in the mire
Embrace the butcher but
Change the world.
It needs it.

Although none of my staff would likely have known this fragment, we had all internalized such rationalizations in pursuit of a better, socialist world. Almost anything was permitted, we felt, as long as it served the Cause.

In my case, this meant presiding over a small but effective working group that went by the name Active Measures (Aktive Massnahmen). Our political purpose was to weaken Bonn's international position,

weaken the Hallstein Doctrine, which mandated the diplomatic isolation of East Germany, and stop West German rearmament. The central focus of our task was not "lying" or "deliberately misleading," but
a method of disseminating uncomfortable and embarrassing facts. Call
it psychological warfare. We did play our share of dirty tricks, but that
was not our prime function. We combined true and false information
and disseminated it so as to strengthen our policies, weaken Western
policies and organizations, and compromise individuals. Disinformation was not necessary as long as former Nazis moved into high positions in West Germany, the government of the Federal Republic
pressed its program of rearmament so soon after the nation's cata-
strophic defeat in Hitler's military adventures, and the West German
media themselves were eager to print political scandal.

The small group engaged in "active measures" grew into the HVA's
Department 10, which was formally set up in 1956 with the express
purpose of influencing the Western media and confusing and misleading our opponents in Western Europe and America as they formulated
policy toward the Soviet bloc. The spiritual father of this enterprise
was one Ivan Ivanovich Agayanz, a highly cultivated intelligence specialist whose successors at the KGB were hardly worthy of tying his
shoelaces.

Germany during the Cold War was an ideal locus for such measures. We of course shared a common language and history. The Eastern Bureau of the Social Democratic Party floated balloons and sent
leaflets over our territory at the behest of the U.S. secret services, so of
course we were not alone in this practice from the very beginning.
Bonn's defense ministry also set up a "Psychological Defense" section,
which had nothing to do with defense and mainly conducted psychological warfare. This we learned from a former destroyer captain, Wilhelm Reichenburg, who worked for the section under our code name
Admiral and provided us with secret intelligence documents. After his
retirement in 1978 he became chairman of the defense policy working
group of the Bavarian Christian Social Union Party in Munich, until
his arrest in 1984, when he was accused of spying for us for money for
fourteen years. Prior to his arrest, we had tried to warn Reichenburg
and his contacts at a meeting in Amsterdam's Rijksmuseum under
Rembrandt's *Night Watch*, but that rendezvous fell through. In any

case, testimony at Reichenburg's trial compromised a leading figure in West German counterintelligence who had been closely linked to him, from our point of view a not undesirable side effect in discrediting the West German service, despite the discovery of our own man.

The CIA also ran an elaborate psychological warfare program in the 1950s and 1960s. The links between the CIA and organizations like Radio Free Europe and RIAS (Radio in the American Sector) are well known; of all the various means used to influence people against the East during the Cold War, I would count these institutions as the most effective. They provided excellent counterpropaganda, using information from dissident groups and from citizens who had fled the satellite countries because they were at odds ideologically with the regime. Moreover, they were fast on their feet when any sign of instability arose in the Eastern bloc, providing timely and detailed accounts of action that were invaluable to our opponents in planning a quick response to events that were hushed up or glossed over by the Communist media.

I was fairly knowledgeable about this business, and my experience at German People's Radio (Deutsche Volkssender) in Moscow in the 1940s proved a useful foundation. The model for the station, which called on its German listeners to rise up against Hitler, was the Soldiers' Station Calais (Soldatensender Calais), broadcast from England and run with great flair and expertise by Sefton Delmer. Delmer's intention was to provide reports that came as close to the truth as possible, reporting real events mixed with invented stories about the degree of antifascist resistance in the German army, the Nazi Party, and the SA militia. The stories were delivered in the same sort of language—right down to Nazi jargon and jokes—used by ordinary people rather than the stilted, ultradignified tones of Soviet propaganda on the main state radio. From prisoners of war and intercepted soldiers' letters, we learned how effective this was in influencing opinion against the Nazi leadership and the war.

We decided to overhaul German People's Radio along the same lines as Delmer's station and created the fiction that it was being broadcast from inside Germany, not Moscow. A complex mythology of contacts with the underground resistance was built up, and we followed Delmer's rule of mixing fiction with fact, experimenting with the proportions until we achieved, I like to think, a station that rivaled the American and the British wartime efforts.

In Department 10 we took a similar approach, seeking out contacts with suitable Western journalists. We tended to avoid the correspondents accredited in East Berlin, who we assumed to be subject to vetting by West German counterintelligence. We concentrated instead on freelance investigative types who were less fussy about the contacts they made and the company they kept and were quite happy to receive a document from anyone as long as they got a story out of it.

We were even in communication with Gerd Heidemann, the eccentric journalist for *Stern* magazine who marketed the forged Hitler diaries in the eighties, though we had no knowledge of the undertaking at the time. As far as we knew when we established contact with him he was interested in searching for the treasure said to have been aboard one of the last German planes to leave Germany as the Allies moved in on Berlin. Heidemann was convinced that the cache had been buried by Nazi sympathizers somewhere near the East German border with Czechoslovakia, and in a complicated deal made under top secret conditions with the Ministry of State Security he was allowed to excavate in the region. Alas, no treasure was forthcoming, but his reputation as someone who had secretive links to the East later gave him the perfect excuse for suddenly producing the supposedly long-lost diaries with a claim that they had come from Moscow. This invention eventually was unmasked as a forgery, but not before it tarnished the reputation of a number of distinguished Western publications that had been taken in and historians who had vouched for its authenticity.

Although the HVA was not involved in that hoax, forgeries were a creative part of Department 10's work. Whether we were targeting the West German government, big business, a publication, or a political party, the intention was always to undermine the public credibility in the new and largely untested institutions of the nation and thus sow doubts about the Western political order. Department chiefs were led into the temptation of following the advice of the founder of German Protestantism, Martin Luther: "Each lie must have seven lies if it is to resemble the truth and adopt truth's aura."

Nevertheless, my principle was to stick as close to the truth as possible, especially when there was so much of it that could easily further the department's aims. We disseminated genuine information about the Nazi connections of numerous leading West German politicians and judges, not least President Heinrich Lübke; Chancellor Kurt-Georg Kiesinger, a former member of Goebbels's propaganda staff; and Hans Filbinger, prime minister of Baden-Württemberg, who as a Nazi prosecutor had been responsible for death sentences for soldiers and many others.

The work of discrediting the West was highly specialized. The officers evaluated the content of bugged telephone conversations between ministers of state or bank chiefs, looking out for information withheld from the public on touchy subjects like arms exports or political intrigue. Having spotted weaknesses and cover-ups, they would collate the information into a fat file and, using our undercover agents in the Federal Republic and West Berlin, allow it to come into the hands of journalists whom we knew would follow up on the stories. Transcripts were generally sent unchanged, and we tried to divert suspicion to the West as the source of the telephone taps, which were known to be conducted on a huge scale by the U.S. National Security Agency. Embarrassed by the publication of genuine but suppressed information, the targets were badly placed to defend themselves against the other, more damaging accusations that had been invented.

Unfortunately, this highly professional specialty developed its own momentum, and the officers who did this work prided themselves on being able to provide convincing imitations of the modes of speaking or expression typical of hundreds of different West German institutions. Its practitioners were tempted to use their skills in foolish ways, which I regret to say I allowed so as not to inhibit the initiative and inventiveness of these imaginative people. They exceeded the limits of what even an intelligence service should tolerate, such as the creation of the fictitious transcripts of what the kidnapped German industrialist Hanns-Martin Schleyer told the Red Army faction before they murdered him in 1977. Somewhat ironically, Herbert Bremer, the man in Department 10 who meticulously produced this false document from a mountain of genuine information, was one of the first to sell his story to the media after the collapse of the GDR.

Unlike some of my more energetic and imaginative colleagues, I did not in my heart of hearts believe that this sort of undertaking would bring the capitalist order crashing to its knees. More prosaically, I saw its main usefulness to lie in knocking out of the propaganda game some particularly persistent and inventive opponents of the East who had a high degree of influence on policy and public opinion. The newspaper magnate Axel Springer was our chief enemy in this battle. Springer, whose empire included the mass-circulation *Bild-Zeitung* as well as *Die Welt*, the most respected paper in West German government and administrative circles, was violently opposed to any diplomatic recognition of East Germany. Until the mid–1980s his papers printed the GDR's German initials, DDR (Deutsche Demokratische Republik), in quotation marks. Springer used his newspapers to undermine the treaties acknowledging the division of Germany and normalizing business between the two estranged parts. Our leadership, anxious for world recognition and for the trade and diplomatic opportunities that would follow such agreements, gave instructions to the intelligence services to take all measures possible to counter opposing Western voices.

Like Springer's tabloids, West Germany's mass-circulation magazine *Quick* was a populist platform for such voices. This was a great stroke of luck for us: Its editor, Hans Losecaat van Nouhuys, the one source who resulted from our early attempt at setting up a phony brothel, had remained an informant for my service through the 1950s under the code name Nante, delivering valuable material from his inside knowledge of Bonn politics. By the mid-1960s, his work for us had petered out, but he was foolhardy enough to imagine that it would never come back to haunt him. (It amazes me that otherwise intelligent Westerners who got involved with enemy secret services believed they remained masters of their own destiny. No cooperation with an intelligence service is ever forgotten. It can be unearthed and used against you until your dying day.)

We decided to break our own rule of never betraying the identity of an agent and let it be known that the editor of a magazine virulently opposing the treaties with the East had himself been in the pay of East Berlin for many years. We combined this leak with another operation, namely an investigation into the death of a West German businessman named Heinz Bosse, who had good connections in Bonn and had died in an automobile accident in East Germany. Bosse did in fact have some contacts in East German intelligence and had been paying a courtesy call on them when his car skidded off a wet road as he drove back to the West. Rumors immediately started to circulate about the mysterious death of a man who had several mysterious connections with both East and West, including contacts with Karl Wienand, an SPD parliamentary staff member. His crash was simply a tragic accident and we were anxious to prove it, not least because any suspicions about his death would be a powerful deterrent for any of our other Western sources and agents to make occasional trips East for consultations or to hand over material. We took the rare step of inviting a *Stern* magazine investigator to research the accident and allowed him access to the autopsy and all the other relevant reports.

We then used the *Stern* reporter's trip to the East as an opportunity to interest him discreetly in the tale of van Nouhuys. That did not take much doing, since *Stern*—which in general took a liberal line—was *Quick*'s keenest rival. The story duly appeared in *Stern* as we wanted it. Van Nouhuys was fired, but *Quick* embarked on a long court battle against *Stern* about whether the story was true. It took years for the courts to decide in favor of *Stern*, a sign of how difficult it is to resolve through the methods of the law disputes originating in the complex world of intelligence.

Personal histories in Germany are prone to the oddest twists. Soon after the fall of East Germany and the opening of the Stasi files, in which the details of van Nouhuys's treachery were stored, together with hundreds of thousands of other fateful, reprehensible, and tragic life stories, I opened a tabloid newspaper to see Hans van Nouhuys's byline staring at me. Ever adept at changing his tune to suit the times, he had transformed himself into an expert on the Ministry of State Security and the foreign intelligence service of East Germany.

●

The trouble with "disinformation" departments, as every spy chief in the world knows, is that they have an unfortunate tendency to take on a life of their own. The specialists who work there want to try their hand at more and more daring tales. One of the episodes about which I still have the most qualms came from the department responsible for churches and dissidents; it was not under my control, and in this case the perpetrators were egged on by Moscow. During the early 1980s, concerned that neo-Nazi activities in West Germany were spreading to dis-affected youth in the East, this department literally manufactured its own provocative neo-Nazi propaganda in imitation of the crude and hysterical Western style and mailed the leaflets to West Germany. As hoped, the leaflets were taken as authentic, caused an outrage in the West, and awakened the fears we had hoped to provoke, leading to a debate in the Bundestag. I found this grisly comedy dangerous; some of the Soviet sponsors of the idea would have been happy to see us actually promoting neo-Nazi rallies for the sake of embarrassing West Germany.

A fundamental weakness in Soviet bloc intelligence was the con-stant political pressure to produce evidence of Western evils for use in propaganda broadsides against the enemy. The propaganda battles of the Cold War were conducted in a moral vocabulary that hid the real technological and military substance of the conflict. But for public consumption on either side of the Iron Curtain, it was vital for their respective governments to demonize the enemy and thus to be able to claim that they were acting legitimately and ethically while the other side was breaking the rules of civilized behavior.

The most poisonous fruit of this was occasional sheer invention on the part of intelligence officers determined to prove to headquarters that they were effectively countering the enemy when they were doing no such thing. It was known that Moscow's intelligence officers sta-tioned in embassies abroad occasionally sent back accounts of meet-ings with agents and sources who simply did not exist, so as to appear hardworking to their bosses back home.

That sort of behavior could not have gone undetected for long in the foreign intelligence service, because all information gathered by agents and sources was carefully analyzed by officers without delay, so that manipulation and fantasy were likely to be detected as raw infor-mation was cross-referenced. The risks of such behavior were far greater in the counterintelligence service, however. There, Mielke created a hothouse atmosphere by placing unrealistic demands on his officers in order to prove to the Soviets and our own leaders that his men alone were saving the GDR from Western spies. In 1979 this cul-minated in the sorry tale of the ASAs.

Occasionally deserters from our Volksarmee fled to the West and, finding life less glamorous and easy there than it looked on their television screens, opted to return to East Germany. The position of such deserters was always precarious. They were allowed back because their return made good propaganda and produced a highly effective deterrent against further desertions. At the same time, the returned deserters were distrusted by the state. In order to secure decent housing or jobs, they had to prove in intense and not always polite questioning that this time they would remain loyal to the socialist state. It does not take Freud to conclude that at that point they were psychologically very malleable.

One aim of the questioning was the discovery of any returnees who had been exposed to Western intelligence recruiters, and if so, what methods had been used. Alas, the ministry's Department 9 office in the Suhl region (Department 9 was responsible for interrogation) was yielding scant results in this field. Hardly any of the people questioned by its officers had been confronted by Western espionage recruiters, or if they had, it was on a level that the departmental chief did not consider high enough to impress headquarters back in East Berlin.

One day, two middle-ranking officers reported that they had just finished interrogating a returned army deserter who confessed to being in the pay of the Americans. This was a far better find than someone merely working for the West Germans. The officers reported that the man had been trained in subversive, violent techniques by U.S. officers in the resettlement bases for escaped Easterners. Years of our own propaganda about the West's plans to mount a hidden war inside the East were bearing fruit. The man claimed that the Americans had called each trained Easterner an "agent with special structural tasks," or ASA, the acronym for the German term *Agent mit spezieller Auftragsstruktur.*

This should have set alarm bells ringing. For a start, this was a very German-sounding and not American-sounding name—more specifically, East German in its linguistically low-brow and portentous quality. The outbreak of ASAs soon gathered momentum. A mixture of suggestion by the interrogators and the perception by the returned deserters that the more colorful their tale, the more favorably they would be received by the authorities ensured that one after another admitted to being an ASA. Berlin headquarters of Department 9 joined in the game, with other districts following; Rostock on the

Baltic even contributed a story, provided by an ASA, about a mysterious submarine.

Mielke rejoiced at the news, which confirmed all of his most alarmist prognostications about Western infiltration of the East and the need for heavy surveillance of the population. In a meeting with Andropov at which I was present, he boasted he had significant information about the dangers of hidden war. He passed to Andropov a top secret document detailing the whereabouts of an alleged U.S. mini-submarine and, shooting a sharp glance at me, emphasized that this was the result of his counterintelligence work rather than of the HVA foreign intelligence service under my leadership.

What the Soviets made of these documents no one ever dared ask, for shortly afterward, a colleague in the military intelligence of the Ministry of Defense warned me of a scandal brewing. Their marine and strategy experts had declared, on analyzing the claims, that it would have been physically impossible for the Americans or anyone else to have placed a submarine in waters where the purported agent with special structural tasks claimed to have seen it. One after another, the claims of the ASAs started to collapse. The discovery that it was all fantasy came not from investigations within the service but from the famous lawyer Wolfgang Vogel, who had been called in to defend the hapless ASAs (while confessing to involvement with the supposed ASA effort helped their case, such deserters still faced prosecution for desertion). Wisely, Vogel thoroughly investigated their stories and discovered that most had been planted by the Department 9 interrogators themselves. Worse still, it appeared that senior figures in our investigation department hardly believed the ASA stories at all, but when faced with an avalanche of exciting claims and an eager appetite for them in counterintelligence in East Berlin, they could not or would not stop the whole business from developing its own internal dynamic.

Mielke reacted quickly and forcibly, removing the head of the main Department 9 and holding an investigation. He issued a stern lecture on the need for security services to respect the law. He called for more careful controls over interrogators and a constant regard for the rights of citizens. "A confession does not replace the need to establish the truth independently," he thundered. "The motto that it is better to arrest one too many than one too few is not acceptable." Was this a new Mielke, we wondered? It was quite a relief when he finished this homily with a rousing order of the day, "Comrades, the enemy must be treated as the enemy—no quarter!" At least we knew that he was back to normal.

Whether he ever admitted to himself that the ASA farce was the result of the hothouse atmosphere he had created, I do not know. The entire senior staff at Department 9 in Suhl was quietly changed, although none of those responsible were punished. Discretion, the minister clearly thought, was the wiser approach.

●

One of the greatest pressures on governments East and West throughout the 1970s and 1980s came from the burgeoning peace movement. Fear of nuclear conflict roused strong opinions and protest among citizens otherwise indifferent to protest. Three hundred thousand people flocked to a peace demonstration in Bonn protesting NATO's decision to place missiles in Europe. Such antinuclear protests in the West broadly suited our purposes, since they provided political complications for NATO policy makers. The political pressures were often so annoying that we were accused by Western leaders of fomenting the huge demonstrations and controlling the peace movement.

In fact, the protests did receive financial support from the East; meanwhile, we faced our own problems. We were in the awkward position of trying to support the peace movement in Western Europe as a propaganda weapon against Washington while our secret police in the East spared no effort to repress "ideological diversion" among the burgeoning peace groups at home. Mass protests like those in Bonn and at Greenham Common in England had no chance of being allowed in the Eastern bloc countries, but we were aware that the peace movement had taken root in our own societies and that it represented a potential challenge to Soviet influence. In East Germany, the theme was particularly disturbing to a leadership accustomed to using peace as an essentially Communist ideal. But the Soviet deployment of SS-20 missiles in East Germany in 1980 discomfited local populations. Although long separated, East and West Germans started to identify strongly with each other through their mutual abhorrence of the bomb. The issue also provided a powerful focus for larger dissatisfactions in our society. The Protestant church produced many peace activists from within its clergy, and they used the shelter of the church to channel protests that were thinly veiled criticisms of nuclear policy.

Moreover, the peace movement brought into the public eye a group of prominent intellectuals who were active supporters of Soviet and Eastern bloc dissidents, including Solzhenitsyn, who was exiled to the United States; Wolf Biermann, a popular East German singer and poet who shared Solzhenitsyn's fate of being stripped of his citizenship; and Heinrich Böll, the West German writer and Nobel Prize winner. In Moscow and the Eastern European politburos, fear arose that those attracted to the appeals by these respected figures would coalesce into protest against the Communist regimes on other issues. We also had to fear the leading West German peace activists, since after the Helsinki Agreement on Human Rights was signed by the Soviet Union in 1975, it became increasingly difficult to justify banning such people from entering the Eastern bloc.

My role as head of foreign intelligence, with a good knowledge of the political climate in Western Europe, was to concentrate on the effect of the disarmament campaign on the foreign policies of the NATO countries and to work out how the East could profit from divisions within the Western alliance on this emotional issue.

In Germany, the German Union for Peace (Deutsche Friedensunion—DFU) had been formed following the 1968 student protests, by people who were close to if not directly involved with the German Communist Party. This was not, in its first stages at least, the result of artful planning by our side. Moscow and East Berlin were quite happy to let far-left activists set up such groups and then see what happened. Even I was amazed by how quickly their ideas took root in society at large. In a 1979 memo to my staff I wrote:

Among young people from well-situated families a fundamental shift in values is under way. Personal advancement and material well-being are declining in importance for this section of society. Engagement in the wider questions of mankind, solidarity and a "we-feeling," or being locked into a group sharing interests and ideals running contrary to those of the capitalist state are considered the truly worthwhile undertakings.

This shift offered us a new recruiting ground for intelligence sources. But we had to proceed carefully and decided not to recruit directly within the peace movement. Accidents happen all the time in espionage, and if it had been discovered that we were manipulating the leading figures in the antinuclear protests they would have lost credibility and been seen by their followers and the population at large as mere Soviet stooges. In a number of cases we did, however, approach likely targets; if they agreed to work with us we recommended that they quit active involvement in the disarmament campaigns. That was a doubly sensible precaution, since such pro-disarmament citizens were watched carefully by their own country's counterintelligence organizations for any suspicious contacts.

In the battle between supporters and opponents of the nuclear deterrent, the public's view of Moscow's and Washington's intentions was all-important. We placed great emphasis on counteracting American propaganda about the Soviet threat. In this undertaking, the work of one organization was paramount. It was a small section of the peace movement with a name that sounded like a contradiction in terms, but its influence over the disarmament debate was huge in comparison to its size. Its name was Generals for Peace (Generale für den Frieden).

Formed in 1981, the group consisted of former generals and admirals who had all given up their commissions because they disagreed with NATO's nuclear doctrines. There was retired General Count Wolf Wilhelm von Baudissin of the Bundeswehr (the West German army), the son of an aristocratic family and a man of great social as well as military influence in Bonn; General Michael Harbottle of Britain; Admiral John Marshall Lee in the United States; Admiral Antoine Sanguinetti in France; General D. M. H. von Meyenfeldt in the Netherlands; General Nino Pasti in Italy; and General Francisco da Costa Gomes in Portugal. Soon they were joined by newly retired General Gert Bastian, formerly commander of the Bundeswehr's elite 12th Panzer Division. A highly respected soldier who had been wounded on the Russian front and was an adviser in the Ministry of

Defense, he had achieved the ranks of colonel, brigadier general, and major general before finally landing the plum job as head of the 12th Panzer Division. Frightened by what he saw as regressive tendencies in the West German military and a creeping return to Nazi nostalgia among his fellow senior officers, he hotly opposed the deployment of U.S. nuclear weapons in Germany, and in 1980 he laid down his commission and devoted himself to the peace movement. His private life was divided thereafter between his long-suffering wife, Charlotte, and his new lover, the charismatic, elegant Petra Kelly, a woman whose charms could make the most aggressive of hawks listen to her calls for gentler policies.

The brains and motivation behind Generals for Peace were provided by a man called Gerhard Kade, a former officer in the German marines who had become a historian at Hamburg University and a prolific writer on peace issues. As a thorough researcher on the links between the senior military and the armaments industry in Germany and America, he was already a thorn in the side of the defense establishment.

The message of Generals for Peace was the same as that of the various European disarmament campaigns, but peace protesters always are fascinated by the military, and the nine generals soon found that they had cult status in the movement. All had direct experience of the Second World War, and many bore wounds from its battles. This gave them an authority that the mainly young leaders of the peace protestors lacked. At the top of their profession in their respective countries, they had the additional authority of having been involved in strategic planning involving the nuclear deterrent. No one could say that they did not know what they were talking about.

Kade and von Meyenfeldt did the bulk of the work in setting up Generals for Peace. But what Kade's friends and colleagues in and out of Generals for Peace did not know and would have been horrified if they had found out was that a good deal of Kade's ideas came from Moscow and a substantial amount of money and other help came from East German foreign intelligence.

I did not give orders to my men to penetrate Generals for Peace. That was not necessary. The top officers in Active Measures, Department 10, knew that their job was to find indirect ways to support any groups in the West whose activities might be useful to us, and Generals for Peace, with its anti-NATO stance, public support, and touch of media glamour, was a logical target.

At the end of 1980, one of my officers came to me with the fruits of his department's labors. They had conferred with Gerhard Kade through a source in Hamburg. Kade had suggested a meeting and we dispatched two officers from my service, armed with the thin pretext that they were representatives of the Institute for Policy and Economy, a name we occasionally used as a handy cover. The useful thing about this story was that a Westerner, if he had any knowledge of East Germany or even much common sense, could gather that he was talking to the foreign intelligence service without the need for the embarrassment or fright that would have been engendered by a formal introduction. We used both shadow and light to conceal ourselves, unlike the Americans, who always struck me as too ready to admit openly that they came from the CIA or FBI.

After a few meetings, Kade was registered under the cover name Super by my officers. This did not mean that they definitely considered him to be an agent—we regularly gave people cover names when we were secretly investigating them. But in Kade's case I would judge that the award of a flattering cover name implied that they considered they had struck a deal with him. He certainly raised the subject of Generals for Peace and told them that the organization needed funding if it was to publish its views widely enough to influence public opinion. The officers negotiated an annual grant, which I approved.

The money was paid directly to Kade. It was not a huge amount, but the relatively small number of the members of the organization meant that the money would contribute handsomely to travel expenses and publishing costs. At the same time, Kade also had contacts with the foreign intelligence department of the Ministry of State Security in Moscow and prepared discussion papers, based partially on consultations with KGB sources, that formed the basis of Generals for Peace campaigns.

It would be wrong to conclude that anyone in Generals for Peace knew of Kade's contacts with foreign intelligence, or that all documents issued or statements made by Generals for Peace had been inspired by Moscow or Berlin. The generals were acting out of conviction. They did, however, often use lines of reasoning introduced by

Kade. Listen, for instance, to Gert Bastian in a radio interview in East Berlin in 1987:

> INTERVIEWER: Do you think that the speech of the Soviet foreign minister [Gromyko] could serve to strengthen peace-stabilizing momentum?
> BASTIAN: Yes, I think so. I believe that the suggestions coming from Moscow recently have been very constructive and I hope that they find a positive echo in the West. That is already the case in a small way, but not with enough clarity and definition, as I see it. I hope that that improves and that during the present President's time in office, we make a concrete step in the right direction: namely the removal of nuclear weapons in Europe.*

I have no evidence that Bastian knew where the funding for Generals for Peace came from. Von Meyenfeldt, who was close to Kade and present at the very inception of the organization, had more reason to be immediately suspicious if not cognizant of KGB and Ministry of State Security involvement.

Since the tragic deaths in 1992 of Gert Bastian and Petra Kelly, probably in a suicide pact, I have been deluged by researchers, friends, and journalists asking whether the opening of the ministry files might have led Bastian to take his own life and Kelly's. As far as I know, the files have yielded little beyond records of routine surveillance during their visits to the East. To some of their erstwhile allies in the Green movement who have voiced the suspicion that the relevant files have been destroyed I would say this: A number of highly sensitive intelligence files were destroyed between November 1989 and January 1990. But as far as I know they covered only live agents and sources who were ranked by us as being of top importance. I do not think that the files on Kelly and Bastian came into this category. Gerhard Kade, who died in Berlin in December 1995, never admitted to his contacts with Eastern bloc security services and was remembered as he would have wished, as a researcher and campaigner for peace.

It was of course vitally important that we should not be identifiable as a sponsor of this organization, whose credibility rested on the fact

*Berliner Rundfunk, a broadcast on the visit of a delegation from Generals for Peace to East Berlin, August, 10, 1987.

that it was not hostage to the NATO and Warsaw Pact camps. Kade eventually persuaded the Soviets to provide a general to take part to give a better impression of balance. Unlike the real Generals for Peace, who had distanced themselves from the state and the military to found the organization, the Soviet general was simply delegated from his usual job to the task of being the peace general and was far from pleased with this task.

When the generals' campaign became a great success, various East German departments rushed to claim the credit for the fact. Most annoyingly for us, Erich Honecker's brother-in-law, Manfred Feist, an incompetent functionary who had got his job as chief of foreign propaganda in the Central Committee through his family connections, told the East German leader that it had all been his idea.

●

Generals were not the only figures we attempted to influence. William Borm was a very old man who was usually seen in the front ranks of the antimissile demonstrations. Under the Nazis Borm had been a factory director in Berlin; he was later arrested by the GDR for reasons that were not clear—he maintained close contact with the British Secret Intelligence Service—and was sentenced to ten years in prison. After nine years, at the end of the 1950s, he was released. We in the foreign intelligence service received lists of those who had been released, and I decided to make contact with Borm, who had now resettled in West Berlin. He and I became friends, and it became clear to me that Borm was an old-fashioned economic liberal, conservative and aristocratic, whose Freemasonry, with its ideals of justice and equality, had helped him survive the rigors of his imprisonment. There he had studied Marxist literature and found ideals similar to his own. He respected me and others as Marxists, although he never became one.

When in 1965 he was elected to the Bundestag as a Free Democrat from West Berlin, he collaborated closely with Brandt, who was then the leader of the Social Democrats and had played a major role in fighting the Cold War. We paid for Borm's parliamentary office, and he gave us information about his party and Brandt's *Ostpolitik* treaties with Poland and the USSR—information not too different from what a diplomat might receive in a foreign capital, but we had no diplomatic representation in Bonn at the time. He made impassioned speeches in favor of Brandt's openings to the East, including one supporting the 1972 Basic Treaty recognizing the two Germanys. When Hans-Dietrich Genscher abandoned the Social Democrats and swung his Center Party's support to Helmut Kohl, Borm refused to follow, even though we urged him to do so in order to maintain him as an asset inside the Free Democrats. But Borm stuck to his principles and organized a splinter Liberal Democratic Party, even though it had little chance of success and indeed soon broke up. When Borm started appearing at the head of protest marches, he lost his intelligence value; we knew West German counterintelligence would henceforth keep too close an eye on him. Nevertheless, it was our funding that had helped Borm reach a position of influence, and we believed that he would continue to steer things in an agreeable direction. Unfortunately, his death on September 2, 1987, at age 92 put an end to his honorable activities.

●

If I were asked now whether I regretted this manipulation of the many genuine people who supported Generals for Peace and drew inspiration from it in their fight against the nuclear threat, I would have to answer that I do not. In this case I do not have the same belated scruples as in some others. We did not start Generals for Peace. What we did was to give institutional and financial support to an organization that had grown up out of justified fears among members of the military that the arms race was dangerously out of control. That reflected a view widely held by the public at large. It was an entirely respectable position to take in tense times and I still applaud those who braved the anger of their military colleagues and rejection by their friends and families to do so. And, of course, none of us could have seen in those fearful days at the beginning of the 1980s that the arms race would end not with a nuclear bang, but with the whimper of the Soviet Union's collapse.

13

Terrorism

and the GDR

On September 13, 1993, Yassir Arafat, chairman of the Palestine Liberation Organization, and Yitzhak Rabin, the prime minister of Israel, sealed with a handshake on the White House lawn the accord that represented a historic step toward peace in the Middle East. One year later in Oslo both the Israelis and the Palestinians were awarded the Nobel Prize for Peace. In the years before these inspiring events, contact with Arafat or his organization had been enough to stigmatize one as a sympathizer or even a sponsor of international terrorism. Almost two years later, on November 4, 1995, it was Rabin who paid with his life at the hands of an Israeli terrorist. Such are the ironies of history.

It is widely said that future historians will count the GDR among the most active supporters of terrorism. I and my work have been swept up in these accusations, the harshest of which come from the Americans. They seem to forget their own long history of supporting brutal dictators and attacking legitimate governments, overtly and covertly—from overthrowing Mossadegh in Iran, Arbenz Guzman in Guatemala, and Allende in Chile to supporting the Somoza family dictatorship in Nicaragua and too many others like them in many parts of the globe.

Many of these unholy alliances were, on both sides, the tragic product of the Cold War. There is no question that the release of Ministry of State Security files has shown that the ministry of which my foreign intelligence department, the HVA, was a part cooperated with several organizations such as the PLO, and that the GDR supported some of these groups involved in politically motivated terrorism.

Because I was the chief of the foreign intelligence branch of the ministry, it is not surprising that I am assumed to have known everything about my government's relationship with terrorists. I was in fact aware of many ties East Germany maintained with organizations deemed in the West to be terrorist. But, as I will explain, I was excluded from important operational details. My primary responsibility was intelligence: the gathering of information, preferably secret. That is spying, not terrorism. I was never personally involved in the planning or execution of terrorist acts.

To understand this paradox of a spymaster ignorant of foreign entanglements, it is necessary to write about two things: first, how the national liberation struggles of the Third World became entangled in the Cold War; and second, how the Ministry of State Security's rigid separation into fiefdoms made for an absolute fetish of conspiracy and secrecy.

These explanations are not meant to excuse what happened, and I want to make it clear that my purpose is not to exonerate myself. The fact is that the GDR and its intelligence services supplied technical and financial support for organizations we considered legitimate, and some of these organizations engaged in terrorism against civilians as a part of their strategy. It also protected terrorists who had escaped from the Federal Republic. I was not engaged in this, others were. They did their work, I did mine. Perhaps it also was fortunate that Mielke, the minister of state security, preferred that I did not know, because this freed me to focus on my mission of obtaining secrets abroad.

There is more than enough responsibility to be shared and regret to be expressed. I must stress that whatever we did that was wrong cannot be excused by what the West did under its own banner in the battle against communism, which left Vietnam and some countries in Central America and Africa in ruins after the geopolitical battle was over. That was the way the war was fought on some fronts; while I did not abet terrorists as such, we certainly did train people in methods that were later abused.

This may sound cynical, coming from someone whose country was routinely criticized in Amnesty International's reports for its treatment of people imprisoned for crimes against the state. I would not claim that our domestic interrogation and remand procedures were beyond reproach, nor that I spoke out sufficiently against their harshness at the time. But I still make a distinction between regimes in which human dignity and liberty are curtailed as the result of an overzealous policy of state security—which was the result of East Germany's internal repression—and the systematic use of torture to punish political opponents. The line between overzealous behavior and barbarity was frequently crossed in the Third World, and, however inadvertently, we and our Western opponents helped people cross it. Did we know full well that what we were offering might be used in ways with which we disagreed? Of course, but I do not believe that Honecker or even Mielke ever knowingly sanctioned terrorist or violent acts against civilians. As the head of the foreign intelligence service, I do accept responsibility for these abuses—not guilt. This is a moral distinction that I hope readers will accept in the interest of coming to terms with the excesses of the time.

The debate over the different definitions of "guilt" and "responsibility" has become more and more intense in recent years. To put these terms in their historical context, only a small minority of Germans were actually guilty of the terrible crimes that were committed under the Nazis, but all Germans who lived willingly under the Nazis bear a responsibility for them. This is not just an academic distinction. Crimes are a matter of law, responsibility a matter of conscience. As far as the law is concerned, suffice it to say that with all archives open to a zealous staff of prosecutors in the Federal Republic, they have been unable to produce any evidence, let alone proof, of my complicity in acts of violence. I have also filed three libel suits against newspapers that reported that I knew that the GDR was sheltering West German terrorists when the Ministry of State Security was doing so; I did not. Furthermore, I have been refused a visitor's visa by the U.S. State

Department on the grounds that I had dealings with terrorists. I have seen no evidence to support these charges. (It is worth noting that the CIA had no compunction whatsoever about inviting me to the United States in 1990, although perhaps the State Department was quite unaware of this invitation when it barred me six years later.)

As my story will make clear, different departments in the same government, even those as closely connected as the departments handling foreign policy and foreign intelligence, do not necessarily know what the other is doing—whether the department is located in Langley, Virginia, that section of greater Washington, D.C., known as Foggy Bottom, or in East Berlin when it was the capital of the GDR. I will relate here what I know and let the reader consider my guilt, which I reject, as opposed to my moral responsibility, which I accept.

●

It was through our dealings with the Third World that we became involved with national liberation movements, and this helped prepare and condition us for tolerating liberation organizations that employed terrorism. In retrospect this process has a certain inevitability, but it did not seem inevitable at the time. It all began in Africa about halfway through East Germany's short history. On January 18, 1964, the tiny Republic of Zanzibar, consisting of two islands off the East African coast, declared its independence. That was scarcely a world-shattering event. One African colony after another was declaring its independence around that time, and apart from the collectors of exotic stamps, no one paid much attention to Zanzibar.

The new country forced itself on our attention by suddenly offering diplomatic recognition to East Germany, making it the first nonsocialist country to defy Bonn's Hallstein Doctrine, under which West Germany imposed on every country except the Soviet Union a choice between one Germany or another. (Moscow was made an exception to emphasize Bonn's view that we were merely Moscow's puppet; they alone had the right to maintain relations with both Germanys.) Zanzibar chose us; we did not choose them. Quite possibly the president, Sheikh Obeid Karume, was unaware of the diplomatic implication of his choice when, encouraged by some members of his youth organization who had once visited a summer school in East Germany, he formally embraced our country.

Aside from the broader diplomatic implications, this recognition by an African state meant new opportunities for the intelligence services. Or perhaps President Karume was sharper than we thought, for alongside the notice of formal recognition came a stream of demands for financial help and security advice, particularly in the sphere of internal intelligence gathering and border protection. Our reputation in those fields had evidently spread far, which was a compliment of sorts.

Flattered by the attention, Mielke looked around for a candidate to serve as adviser to Zanzibar's nascent security services. We agreed on General Rolf Markert, a former inmate of Buchenwald concentration camp who had become a senior policeman after the war and now worked as the head of a regional branch of the Ministry of State Security. As we had virtually no diplomatic presence in Africa at the time, it was agreed that someone with knowledge of foreign affairs should accompany Markert. On a whim, I suggested that I go myself.

It was a daring idea then for the head of foreign intelligence to travel to a place whose real allegiance was still unclear, crossing territories with strong NATO affiliations to get there. Mielke hesitated for a while before finally agreeing. I had to listen to a long lecture on the need for absolute secrecy and was warned not to mention the mission even to my deputy. Mielke took personal charge of my security arrangements and even supervised an emergency rescue plan for me if it should turn out that I had walked into a trap. Markert and I were given an array of false East and West German passports in different names. Our ages were altered in the documents, and, much to our amusement, we were packed off to a disguise artist for masks to be made. Mielke insisted we wear them during the journey. Our disguises of course matched photographs in the false identity documents, which described us as experts on adult education.

We departed in February 1964, and the first stop of our flight was to be Cairo. Markert and the head of the real diplomatic delegation flew first class, but in order to draw less attention to myself, I registered as a lowly first secretary and flew in tourist class. The first excitement was a sandstorm that forced us to land in Athens, justifying Mielke's fears about my being apprehended on NATO territory. Markert and I were separated from each other and taken to different hotels for the night. This caused some anxiety, since we all knew that an East German passport offered no protection in a NATO country. The next morning, I struggled for a full half hour to glue my false beard back into a position that would even approximately match my passport photo.

There were additional long stopovers in Cairo, Addis Ababa, and Mogadishu. At last we reached Nairobi, where our passports were taken away and we were refused a connecting flight. We surmised that our route had been followed since Cairo, where we had had to register with British officials to obtain a visa for the East African Union (Zanzibar, Tanganyika, Kenya, Uganda). After a nerve-racking wait, we were saved from further inspection by the intervention of the Kenyan foreign minister, Oginga Odinga, who later became vice president. His son was studying in East Germany, and seeing the familiar name of Deputy Foreign Minister Wolfgang Kiesewetter on a list of our traveling party that was presented to him, he ordered that we all be allowed to continue our journey. Our arrival in Zanzibar was greeted by the entire government, a guard of honor still clad in uniforms of the old imperial British style and a police orchestra playing Viennese waltzes. They had requested that we bring along the music for the East German anthem, but until they learned the tune we had to make do with Strauss. Our deputy foreign minister had the greatest of difficulty inspecting the guard of honor to the lilting strains of the Blue Danube.

Being an East German in postcolonial Zanzibar was a pleasure indeed. On national holidays like May First, which had been introduced in our honor, we were quickly recognized and taken to the heart of the crowd. The people had enthusiastically absorbed the government's expectations of us. The singers who led the crowd in their chants made up rhymes praising the beauty and richness of the German Democratic Republic, which had clearly achieved the status of a fairytale land of plenty in the public imagination.

As wonderful as such celebrations were, not all went well. Our attempts to impose firm work plans and routines during our stay were hopeless. All too often, we would turn up for meetings only to find that people had been ousted from their jobs and someone else, who had no idea of the state of negotiations or plans, was there. At first, such things seemed minor inconveniences when compared to the long tropical evenings spent strolling among the elegant villas where we lived, the now disused golf course, the Indian cemetery, and the mud huts on the edge of town. There the men sat talking and smoking at dusk while the women continued to work in the fields.

Our dealings with Ibrahim Makungu, later appointed chief of security, were initially difficult. We needed to know his honest assessment of the country's priorities, but Makungu had been ordered by the president to reveal nothing and find out everything he could from us. In fact, he took secrecy so far that he even refused to tell us his real name. I found it out only when he left one of his frequent mysterious notes in Swahili in which he canceled a planned meeting, ending with the words "Our work is difficult and secretive. Simba." I asked the cook who Simba was and learned not only his full name but some of his history. In the old days, the cook said, Makungu had worked for the Special Branch of the British colonial police.

Coming from a country where everyone in the ruling party was united in support of its established goals, we were unfamiliar with a government of individuals who were divided by contradictory goals and interests. Some of our partners regarded themselves as Socialists, while the strict Moslems regarded them and us with evident mistrust. But none was shy in presenting demands and then criticizing us when we failed to deliver the goods. They would mournfully show us crumbling boats, old radios, and fraying telephone cables left behind by the British, hoping that we could restore the infrastructure of their entire country.

The leadership of Zanzibar was split between President Obeid Karume, who as a former sailors union leader spoke like an English trade unionist, and his vice presidents, Abdullah Kossim Hanga and Abdulrahman Mohammed Nbabu. They supported with equal and opposite fervor the Soviet and Chinese models of communism, by now bitterly opposed to each other. Hanga had studied in the Soviet Union, while Nbabu insisted on demonstrating his attachment to Mao Tse-tung by playing a scratched copy of the "Internationale" loudly at state receptions. This grab bag of ideologies probably explains why Zanzibar had picked East Germany as its prime partner. I soon had no doubt that our presence here was based on a simple political calculation: Because the East African Union countries depended economically on traditional trade and financial ties with Britain, an outright link with one of the two Communist superpowers would have been unwise. We were economically advanced enough to be a useful supplier of advice and basic security infrastructure (it would take years before Zanzibar advanced as far as requiring technology), but small enough not to annoy any other sources of income.

A few months after our arrival, the island was alive with rumors of a possible union between Zanzibar and Tanganyika. This concerned us too, since Tanganyika was ruled by Julius Nyerere, who maintained close links with London. If a union did come to pass, we suspected that the British government would put pressure on Zanzibar to end its association with us. Worse still, we were in the unwelcome situation of being intelligence advisers in a country where none of our partners within the country had the slightest intention of telling us what was going on.

On April 24, 1964, we received news that the union was to take place and that the new country would be called Tanzania. The day before, I had been assured that no such move was planned and had flown to the smaller island of Pemba to inspect the new security office. I got the news while sitting among the new recruits at dusk answering questions about the relationship between Marxism and religion. I broke off the visit in some irritation and flew back to the main island. An East German cargo ship had delayed its departure to take me home, but after three months of frustrating work I could not bear to leave without seeing for myself whether Zanzibar would remain loyal to us. We also now had personal and financial stakes in Zanzibar, having built up a small flotilla of ships for the border guards and trained sailors and engineers in East Germany. Contrary to our fears, Zanzibar did keep a high degree of autonomy. Nyerere's picture always hung only slightly below Karume's in public buildings.

Our efforts were untainted by the cynicism that later permeated our dealings with the Third World. We were convinced that, by helping Zanzibar, we were contributing to the freedom of the African people and helping them toward a better life. But I would be lying if I said we did not take pleasure as representatives of East German intelligence in conducting an operation in a part of the world where the British and West Germans had been kings of the espionage jungle. I remember in particular a trek that brought us to a U.S. satellite tracking station in

Zanzibar. Outside stood a very dark-skinned soldier with a very big gun, and when we came he pointed the gun at us as we tried to explain. Finally we persuaded him to let us enter. There I was, on my first voyage into the capitalist world, standing in an American satellite station, no less.

In many ways we were naïve about the effects of our intervention in Third World countries. Our intelligence-gathering skills, honed by the experience of the Second World War and the Cold War, were transferred through our well-trained liaison officers and specialists. Prompted by their diligence, the security service in Zanzibar reached ridiculous dimensions. Relative to the size of the population, it was soon far bigger than our own, and it rapidly acquired a dynamic of its own over which we had no more influence. Karume was much more adept than we had suspected at playing off external powers against each other, and our status was eroded by the arrival of the Chinese en masse in 1965. We were particularly embittered when, having managed to secure the delivery of trawlers, which the government had begged us to provide, our bounty was eclipsed by the simultaneous arrival of a Chinese delegation bearing agricultural equipment. The embarrassment was exacerbated by the realization that the trawlers were not suited to the waters in which they would have to operate.

The Chinese were extremely smart at establishing themselves. Within a few weeks, Ulbricht's picture had either been removed from public display or was outflanked by bigger and more prominently hung pictures of Mao. Moscow took this symbolism very seriously and demanded reports of how many pictures of the Chinese leader had appeared and where. We then conducted a senseless exercise in counting them.

Before I left Zanzibar, I made a brief acquaintance that stayed in my mind. All foreigners on the island were invited to harvest cassava, the most important food of the region. We were greeted by musical bands and dancing troops and then set to work slashing and gathering the crop until our backs ached. Next to me worked a small, energetic man with alert features, the U.S. consul in Zanzibar. Together we were taken aside and told in the nicest possible way that we had mistaken the tiny, tender bunches of cassava for weeds, uprooted them, and thrown them into the waste pile. I wonder whether this American, whose name was Frank Carlucci and who was not only a valued American diplomat but eventually deputy director of the CIA, ever knew who I was.

Despite our experience in Zanzibar, the basic motivation for the spread of our operations into the Third World did not disappear: We continued to seek diplomatic recognition for the German Democratic Republic. By 1969 we were flooded with visits and requests for help. Syria and Egypt broke the Hallstein Doctrine and sought us out, followed by Sudan, both North and South Yemen, Congo/Brazzaville, Kampuchea, and the Rhodesian liberation movement, ZAPU. One reception for Egypt's interior minister meant that all our windows had to be cleaned twice on Mielke's orders, and the ministry's courtyard was flooded with honor guards and youth choirs. I began to feel that these links were becoming an unwelcome and unnecessary burden, however adventurous it may have been to visit exotic locales. They distracted both Mielke and me from our primary task of keeping the upper hand in the foreign intelligence war in Europe. I always concentrated our efforts in West Germany, but now middle-ranking officers were being siphoned off to Third World assignments for long periods, bogging us down in a variety of countries led by tenuous governments and shadowy people. However frustrating I found it, though, these assignments were out of my control. The initiative for such cooperation came from the political leadership, and the intelligence services were expected to follow orders.

For some time, our relations with Egypt were deemed to be particularly valuable. After the Six Day War in 1967, President Gamal Abdel Nasser had let it be known through his interior minister, General Sharawi Gomaa, that he wanted to exchange intelligence information with us. My deputy traveled to Cairo and was received with full protocol honors. It emerged that Nasser wanted our help in investigating the Israeli penetration of Egypt's government and military—which Nasser believed was why Egypt had lost the war.

Nasser was bitterly disappointed when we told him that we had no agents in Israel, but it was true. In fact, during the thirty-three years I headed the foreign intelligence service we never managed to penetrate Israeli intelligence. There was pressure from Moscow to do so, and some efforts were made in the early years to recruit Jewish emigrants to Israel, but this never succeeded. On the whole, I came to accept that we got the information we needed about the Middle East from sources in the United States, West Germany, and, eventually, the security services of the PLO.

I was anxious lest we become entangled in the Middle East, but the Soviets were fixated on Israel as an enemy. I would never have wasted time and money on intelligence gathering simply to get even with the state of Israel on behalf of the Arab world. I viewed Israel like any other target country. Once it was clear to me that the ratio of effort to result was unsatisfactory in terms of penetration, I simply canceled our attempts to gain agents in Israel.

In any case there were also signs that the Egyptians were playing a double game in proposing to exchange information. We asked for intelligence about the activities of the NATO nations' espionage in the Middle East and were introduced to the head of Egyptian intelligence, the Muhabarat. He was cagey and used a pseudonym during the first meeting. We knew that he also dealt this way with the CIA and we were unwilling to risk having our questions handed to the Americans. To increase our confidence in them, our partners in Cairo took my representative to visit a secret rocket-production plant, which had been built by an Austrian firm with the help of Pilz, a former colleague of the German rocket scientist Wernher von Braun. The Egyptians thought that the plant was being sabotaged and wanted us to track down the offenders. Wary of having my service seen as a sort of intelligence consultancy that could be hired out at random to solve the domestic problems of other countries, I refused the request.

I believed that we had to keep a sense of commitment and political solidarity in our foreign operations rather than make ad hoc deals with states whose ultimate loyalties were not with the Soviet Union and Eastern Europe. Within a short time, it was evident that the exchange with Egypt would not produce results, and we ended it, although we maintained personal contact with Gomaa and his Interior Ministry. After Nasser's death in 1970, his successor, Anwar Sadat, accused Gomaa of treason. Our contacts with Cairo were reduced to a single liaison officer in the GDR embassy, whose main concern was its security and that of the staff. We relied on our legal residents—members of the branches of a secret service posing as diplomats in all foreign embassies—for information about West German, American, and other NATO intelligence activities in Egypt. Our residents in Cairo would send their information home to HVA Section 3, covering the Middle East, which would pass it up to the chief of Department III, covering the Third World, who would then pass it to my deputy, General Horst Jänicke. He would pass to me only information that he deemed of sufficient importance. The same applied to our residents in Washington and at our United Nations mission in New York. They filed to Department 11, covering the United States, which would then pass it up to the chief of Department XI, and from there it would be filtered to Jänicke.

A few months before Nasser's death, in May 1969, a group of progressive officers had seized power in Sudan under the leadership of Gaafar Mohammad Numeiry, the chief of the Sudanese military academy. Ignoring the vicissitudes of our efforts in Zanzibar, we deemed Sudan a promising territory and a possible gateway to the Middle East. The Revolutionary Command that had seized power was intent on creating its own version of Arabic socialism and had asked for the usual security and economic help from East Germany to do so.

My knowledge of Sudan was vague indeed. I knew only that the north of the country had a long tradition of struggle against British colonial rule. The Sudanese distrusted Egypt because it had long served as Britain's proxy in the region. Internal strife between the Muslim north and the Christian-animist south created chaos. Streams of refugees from Congo, Zaire, and Ethiopia deepened the country's poverty. Its strategic position meant it was swarming with secret services and mercenaries, operating unchecked and very often at cross-purposes even with their own side.

During my first visit shortly after the revolution, it was clear to me that the young officers I met had only a nebulous idea of the socialism they were now supposed to defend. They were motivated by other factors: the desire for national independence, military comradeship, and a desire to reinforce Islamic beliefs under another name. One proudly told me that he was a socialist because he fed the poor every Friday. My conversations with Numeiry were impersonal and to the point. I once accompanied him to a public meeting and watched him spring from his jeep; deliver a short speech punctuated by whistles from the men, cries from the women, and organized choruses of approval; leap back into the jeep, and roar away, all within a few minutes. My more intimate contacts were with Faruq Othman Hamadallah, head of the Interior and State Security Ministries. Most of the police and security men had learned their trade under the British or the Egyptians and they still seemed very British in their manner. When they entered or left a room, they would clamp a short stick smartly between fist and elbow and wheel around in a marching step.

I first met Hamadallah in his garden. He was a tall, athletic man whose black skin glistened with health. He continued stroking his sheepdog with one hand as he beckoned me in with the other. He told me soberly of the difficulties in building up a security service strong-willed and objective enough to cope with the complexities of his huge country. Beside us at the table sat another, smaller khaki-clad man who was introduced to me only briefly and had an Arabic name. I would meet him again later when East Germany began dealing with South Yemen—he was Mohammed Saleh Muteea, the security chief, who later became foreign minister of Yemen; his life was ended when he was poisoned in prison as a result of disagreements within the Yemen ruling party.

Hamadallah was one of the few African politicians with whom I developed a close personal as well as professional friendship. He visited me several times in East Berlin and spoke with great insight and feeling of his country's problems and the complexities of the relationship between the Arab world and black Africa. Although he had never before visited a socialist country, he had surprisingly mature ideas about a possible African road to socialism. He told me of his fears that Numeiry would dissolve the revolutionary council and activate Western contacts. "You can't help us with this," he said glumly. "We have to solve this problem ourselves."

His prediction soon came to pass. In 1970 Numeiry changed course and banished Hamadallah and other leftists from the revolutionary council. The following year, in the wake of an attempted leftist putsch, Numeiry purged all socialists from his government. Hamadallah was in London at the time and, against our advice, decided to fly back to the country to regroup his forces against Numeiry. The British charter plane carrying him was forced to land in Libya by its ruler, Colonel Muammar Qaddafi, who promptly extradited Hamadallah and a colleague to Sudan and Numeiry. He was sentenced to death in Sudan.

Later, I saw pictures of him on television, before the sentence was carried out, talking quietly with his guards and smoking a cigarette. An hour after the filming was finished, he was executed. I felt real pain and loss at the news. Yet another friend had lost a good and worthwhile fight. Even now, I believe that with Hamadallah, Sudan lost one of its very best men, who was years ahead of his time and his country. In this violent and changeable political climate, it was impossible for us to continue our work as intelligence advisers to Sudan. We left in 1971 and never returned.

Shortly before we pulled out of Sudan, I became involved with one of the most notorious mercenaries of this century, Julius Steiner (not to be confused with the Julius Steiner who was a member of the West German Bundestag and whom we had bribed). Born in Munich in 1933, Steiner was an exemplary mercenary. He began the relevant part of his career in the French Foreign Legion as a member of its aptly named Special Missions Unit, which fought the forces of Ho Chi Minh in the Vietnamese war of independence against France. After the defeat of the French in 1954 he turned his abilities to prodigious warmongering in Algeria during the war that ended in that country's independence from France in 1962. His first great independent venture was in the Nigerian civil war, which broke out in 1967 over conflicting oil interests. In the region of the country with the most oil, which had declared its autonomy under the name Biafra, he trained Biafran commandos, and so began his connections with a number of secret services in Europe, the Middle East, and Africa. Steiner helped turn Biafra into the most militarized territory in Africa, supplied through West German and other arms dealers with $20 million worth of weaponry, including the then state-of-the-art Cobra and Roland rockets. His private army of several thousand men marched under the banner of a skull and crossbones.

When this venture collapsed, Steiner was hired by the southern Sudanese rebels. This move was of interest to British intelligence. Steiner was supplied with maps and radio equipment by Beverley Barnard, the former British military attaché in Sudan and owner of the Southern Airmotive company, and a colleague, Anthony Duvall, a representative of the British secret service who acquired his knowledge from working under the cover of West German humanitarian aid groups.

Our information showed that through this channel, Steiner made contact with the CIA, who saw in him a way through which they might overthrow Numeiry's government. Through a post office box in Kampala, Uganda, Steiner was able to pass lists of requests for weapons to the Americans through a Mr. Preston from the U.S. embassy in Kampala. Describing himself as a representative of the African Society for the Promotion of Humanitarian Aid in Southern Sudan, Steiner was able to organize the training and arming of a ruthless guerrilla force that shed much civilian blood in the south as well as attacking the Sudanese police and military. Steiner had established his headquarters and airstrip in the remote territory of Tafeng, near Juba. Juba was the principal city in southern Sudan and the entrepôt for personnel and armaments from Uganda, whose government was supported by Israeli military advisers. This was the nearest I came to the sort of bewildering and exhilarating African world described by Joseph Conrad in *Heart of Darkness*. During festivities held there in our honor, we watched the tribal dancing, mesmerized by the drumbeat and the motion of the dancers. Suddenly, an old man, his naked body smeared with ashes, ran toward us brandishing a short spear and a fish. My guards leapt in front of me, one protecting my torso while the other two apprehended the man. Afterward, they told me that I had escaped an assassination attempt orchestrated by the rebels.

In secret talks held in Khartoum with the Sudanese and Libyan leadership, we agreed to help capture Steiner. This was achieved partly through our intelligence efforts to establish his exact whereabouts on a particular day and was partly due to withdrawal of Uganda's support under pressure from the Organization of African States.

Once he was under arrest and facing execution we acceded to the Sudanese government's request for help with his interrogation. My main task was teaching the Sudanese that interrogations (Steiner's and others') should serve to extract useful information from the prisoner about treasonable activities still in progress or being planned, not to exact revenge by means of intimidation and torture. But our influence repeatedly proved to be minimal and we stood powerless as our advice was misused, whether in Zanzibar or the other states with which we maintained close contact over the years, such as South Yemen, Ethiopia, and Mozambique. Our techniques depended on isolation and warnings, not gross physical punishment or sheer fright, but rarely did we hear that much restraint was exercised.

Our advisory role dealt with interrogation methods only as a secondary matter, and in Zanzibar we had no specialists in interrogation methods. What we did try to impart was a principle known to every member of the GDR security service: that a confession without further evidence was of no legal value, and a confession extorted by violence was of no value at all. Interrogators in the GDR had received special legal education, and the main investigation department, Department IX, reported directly to the minister of state security. I do not know the details of their legal training but I am sure the principles of obtaining legal evidence were taught. Of course interrogation tactics also were taught, but I doubt that the methods they used to make a prisoner talk differed greatly from those used in the West. Torture and physical coercion were forbidden, and if someone used such methods, it happened against orders. I am certain extralegal interrogation has occurred in the West. Sheikh Bakari, the member of the revolutionary council responsible for security, once came to me in Zanzibar proudly claiming that he had obtained a confession from an enemy of the president by ordering him to dig his own grave and then having his captors fire twice into the air. The cruelest example was Ethiopia, where the extent of murder and torture was so horrific that it was difficult to accept the reports we heard. Like our Western opponents, we sadly discovered that police and security forces in Africa were regarded by those who held power as mere tools to be wielded at will in multifarious tribal, ethnic, and personal rivalries, and not as methods of eliciting information.

In Steiner's case, I managed to convince the Sudanese that a man of his stamina and tough psychological makeup would reveal useful material only if he had the expectation of being treated fairly. Two GDR interrogators were allowed to visit him. Despite his robust resistance to previous questioning, he was visibly relieved to see Germans arrive in his cell to talk with him, even if they were representatives of the other Germany, against whose ideology he had fought in various parts of the globe. I decided that our best tactic was to use a personal touch in dealing with him. We managed to secure from his Algerian wife their wedding photo album and to arrange for some of his relatives to send letters. This gesture softened the mercenary and prompted him to start talking more freely about his involvement in Sudan's tangled conflict. In the end, we were able to secure from him a comprehensive picture of a web of different interest groups, front organizations, and secret services.

But while we were pulling one set of strings in the region, West German foreign intelligence and its allies were busily pulling others. In a complicated series of events that finally resulted in Numeiry's shift toward the West, Steiner was finally released to live in West Germany.

The stories of Sudan and Steiner illustrate the scope and limitations of the influence of intelligence work in the Third World. Although we examined strategic, economic, and military factors before becoming involved in a developing country, we, like the West, saw our activities primarily as part of a greater struggle for influence and an attempt to color the globe our shade of red. But over time we realized that diplomatic recognition in return for intelligence and military help had led us into a costly spiral. Long before I left office, my staff and colleagues in the Central Committee with whom we worked had come to the conclusion that our attempts to export wholesale our economic system to developing countries was neither efficient nor desirable. These efforts devoured energy and resources but did not bring sufficient return either to us or the host countries to make them worthwhile. We had spent more than we had gotten, and the consolation prize of being recognized diplomatically by a scattering of relatively insignificant countries was not enough.

Still, there was a time in the late 1960s and early 1970s when our alliances with the Third World and our activities there made us feel as though we were winning the Cold War. We saw ourselves as contributors to a spread of socialist influence that would tip the balance of global power in our favor. Leonid Brezhnev, firm in his belief that the correlation of forces was moving in the Soviet Union's favor, sought to implement a sweeping policy of support for radical left-wing governments in the Arab Middle East and down through the Horn of Africa.

This fit well with the mind-set of Erich Honecker. Triumphant at having secured the Basic Treaty with Bonn in 1972 that accorded the GDR the diplomatic recognition that came with full sovereignty, he was free to explore parts of the globe hitherto closed to us and was discovering them with childlike enthusiasm. He thus conceived an ambition to become an international statesman. Psychologically, it is easy to understand Honecker's drive to involve his country in the affairs of the wider world. He was a man of limited vision but great pride. His aim was to be remembered as one who had made life better for ordinary working people in East Germany (to the end of his days, he could reel off how many new houses and inside toilets had been built under his rule). But he knew that in the history of the Communist movement in Germany he would always rank below his predecessor, Walter Ulbricht, the first leader of East Germany. With diplomatic recognition, Honecker set out to trump Ulbricht's achievement.

In our heart of hearts, we knew that his stream of contacts with Third World leaders and his hopes of being received in Washington, Tokyo, and Bonn were the triumph of ambition over common sense, but our small country bolstered itself with this false sense of importance. The mentality, combining *folie de grandeur* and small-mindedness, is best captured in the mock slogan that did the rounds as a joke among more daring souls on the diplomatic circuit: "Our GDR is the greatest GDR there is."

In addition to Honecker's drive to extend our contacts throughout the Arab nations came our proud desire to be regarded by the Soviets as the most efficient and daring intelligence partners in the bloc. Moscow's esteem was gained through the kinds of foreign operations that Mielke had initially been unwilling to embrace. Trained as a tough counterintelligence man, his pride and joy was the unmasking of enemy agents, real or imagined, inside East Germany. At meetings with his opposite numbers in the KGB he would boast about the number of arrests made by our counterintelligence teams. The Soviet response was indifferent; it was no more than they expected. Instead, our prestige with them was measured in terms of the information we obtained through our foreign intelligence about the NATO countries and the successes we chalked up in Africa and later the Middle East.

Thus there was a steady progression from our involvement in Africa to dealings in the Middle East and with organizations that used terror as one of their methods of securing international attention. The bridge between the African and the Arabic worlds increasingly became South Yemen. After a revolutionary regime seized power there in 1969, we established a large corps of advisers in Aden. Our links with South Yemen were more extensive than elsewhere, including economic aid, technical and educational assistance, and the provision of military advisers and specialists in external and internal intelligence gathering. The whole country was our playground, and a stint there—"learning to ride camels," we joked—was part of the training of a whole generation of our officers.

Unlike the situation with our other operations in the Middle East, we were welcomed with open arms in Aden. The country was fighting an espionage war of tremendous intensity with its neighbor North Yemen, which was supported by Saudi Arabia. The fact that we came from a divided country and were engaged in our own intelligence war against our estranged West German brethren convinced the leadership in Aden that we were the partners most able to understand and help them. The Soviets, keen to have reliable reports from this unstable region and to shore up their allies in Aden, encouraged us to commit ourselves heavily there.

There were also Mozambique and Ethiopia. We entered Mozambique, along with the Soviet Union and Cuba, after the collapse of the Portuguese dictatorship brought the Marxist Frelimo government to power in 1975. The new government remained under constant siege from the Renamo rebels backed by the white regimes in Rhodesia and South Africa. We had high hopes of making a substantial difference; large training programs for intelligence officers, the military, and police were carried out in East Germany. For six years our ministry played host to over a thousand Mozambican trainees, whom we schooled mostly in counterespionage, the establishment of effective border controls, and the prevention of smuggling. In Mozambique, training was under the command of our station chief; I went to Mozambique only once but was generally informed as to what was going on. The civil war in Mozambique, an expensive and time-consuming enterprise for us, was the first in which we were forced to face up to the fact that by supporting Frelimo we had become targets ourselves. Eight East German agricultural experts were killed in 1983, mowed down by Renamo forces. Even by the time of my visit the year before, the situation was no longer remotely tenable for us.

Internal power struggles in the government were exacerbated by debates between the Soviet military and the KGB over the proper way to handle a conflict that was careening out of control. I realized that even our best suggestions for increasing the efficiency of our joint efforts were not reaching the right ears in Moscow and we began to scale down our work, although we continued to provide weaponry and technical support until 1987.

In Angola, we offered some intelligence and military support to one of the three factions, the MPLA, the Marxist group founded in 1961 to oppose Portuguese colonialism, but we readily let the Cubans oversee military strategy in that politically complex war. Initially, at least, the Cubans were enthusiastic and proud to have been dispatched by Fidel Castro to fight on the other side of the world. They fought well, thanks to their ingenuity and their experienced intuition about guerrilla warfare, but the Angolan wars turned out to be inconclusive and a huge waste of human life and prosperity, and it is very likely that the involvement of the CIA on one side and Soviet-backed Cubans on the other protracted Angola's agony.

As for Ethiopia, the Soviet and Cuban intelligence services there considered us to be little more than a potential source of weapons. Moscow's position was to oblige them. This business was handed over to KoKo (Kommerzielle Koordination), the GDR's secret trading arm. In a number of countries we advised the military commands we backed as to which Western technology or electronic weapons were best suited to Africa's extreme climate, and in a few urgent cases we secured arms directly for our client countries through KoKo.

While we escaped the disaster in Angola, things went badly wrong for us in Ethiopia, where we were drawn in along with the Soviets and Cubans. Our goals were unclear and the savagery of the twin wars with neighboring Somalia, which switched from being a Soviet to an American client in 1977, and the territory of Eritrea, which had been seeking to secede from Ethiopia, ran far deeper than anything we could hope to influence, let alone control. One tragic incident symbolized the helplessness we felt as we became ever more entangled in the bloody affairs of the Horn of Africa.

In 1973, it was decided in East Berlin that Werner Lamberz, a young politburo member, and Paul Markowski, head of the foreign affairs department of the Central Committee, should try to negotiate a truce between the warring factions in Ethiopia by bringing the Eritreans first to the negotiating table as a sign of goodwill. Moscow backed the move and the two men set off together with my deputy, Horst Jänicke.

Lamberz and Markowski were to fly from Tripoli, Libya, by helicopter to visit Colonel Muammar Qaddafi in his tent in the desert and attempt to persuade him to use his influence with the Eritrean leadership. On their way back, the helicopter crashed and both were killed. The news hit me hard. I knew both men well and they were among the very few who, even at this pre-Gorbachev time, could be said to harbor reformist tendencies. Lamberz in particular was the favored candidate of the intelligentsia and many young Party members to succeed Honecker in the distant future.

The mysterious setting of Lamberz's death fed rumors that it might not have been accidental. I too was concerned that it might have been the work of saboteurs and it fell to me to review the reports on the accident. It emerged that the Libyan helicopter pilot was not qualified for night flying but that Lamberz had insisted he fly them back. This seems to have been the correct explanation for the fatal accident.

This tragedy further discouraged direct intelligence links with Libya, though later when Tripoli requested our help in securing military technology it was arranged on a financial basis. Libya was one of the few countries in the region able and prepared to pay handsomely for the skills or special equipment Colonel Qaddafi required. Only one other significant contract was drawn up: Qaddafi's personal guard was trained at a secret camp outside East Berlin by the department of the Ministry of State Security that provided bodyguards.

After the funerals of Lamberz and Markowski in East Berlin, my deputy and another Party representative took their place in Addis Ababa to try to negotiate a peace settlement in honor of our dead colleagues. But they failed because of the strong opposition of Ethiopia's president, Haile Mengistu Mariam, an early sign that our work with Ethiopia was doomed. Although we had formally been invited there to train intelligence officials, we soon found ourselves devoid of influence and with only scant insights into the often senselessly brutal security apparatus. The Soviets also there had the same problems, despite being able to offer far more manpower and technical assistance.

The only representatives of the socialist camp who seemed to have access to the wheels turning within wheels turning in the Ethiopian state were the Cubans. As their confidence and professional competence grew, they became the best intelligence operators in Africa. They had an understanding of the continent's mentality and a sense of events that we lacked.

From the beginning, Moscow made the same mistake in Ethiopia that it made over and over again in its involvement in foreign conflicts: It tried to use military solutions in countries where the infrastructure and terrain rendered this approach hopeless. We and the Cubans thought that in case of the failure of political solutions, partisan movements would be a more effective method of fighting. Another source of disagreement was the scope of our involvement. I believed that by concentrating on, for example, Ethiopia we would make more headway than by spreading our resources. In the end it didn't matter. All of us were slow to realize that African statesmen, of whatever ideological hue, in the end followed their own vision of their countries' development. Whatever our intentions or methods, there was very little we could do about that. By the end of the 1970s we had scaled back our presence, leaving with some regret over the high costs we had incurred financially and in terms of personnel for so little result.

The United States made the same mistake of becoming bogged down in too many unwinnable and morally dubious campaigns, and as a result its government was frequently perceived by its own public opinion as being on the wrong side. We had one small advantage over the West in our operations in the Third World: our ability to keep our activities secret, or at least opaque to our people, because of powerless parliaments and official control of the media.

Soon after the 1979 Soviet invasion of Afghanistan, Vladimir Kryuchkov, the head of KGB operations there, asked the GDR to provide officers to contribute to intelligence-gathering in that distant, tribal snakepit. This time I put my foot down, telling Mielke that we were already overextended in our foreign operations and that there was no conceivable benefit to us in joining in the conflict in Afghanistan. A flat no was a highly unusual response to any request from Moscow, but we prevailed, and events would prove how wise we were to avoid that quagmire. Our contribution was limited to assistance for a hospital and providing a venue for meetings in Berlin between the leaders of the mujahideen and Moscow's favorite in Kabul, Najibullah.

•

All of us, as Communists, bore in mind the words Lenin uttered after his brother Alexander was executed for plotting to assassinate the Tsar:

"We will go another way." The class-based, revolutionary theories in which we believed left no place for random terror. Random terrorism was, in our eyes, the equivalent of throwing a brick through a bank's window: satisfying perhaps at the time, but it does not stop the bank from opening up as usual the next day. By the late 1970s, the ministry and my department were involved in a number of alliances with forces that used terror as a tactic: the Palestine Liberation Organization; the freelance Venezuelan terrorist and assassin Ilyich Ramirez Sanchez (ironically named after none other than Lenin), who was known as Carlos the Jackal; and the West German terrorist group that called itself the Red Army Faction (RAF) but was also known as the Baader-Meinhof gang after its leaders, Andreas Baader and Ulrike Meinhof. Our enthusiasm for such partnerships varied from case to case, far more than I would ever have been able to admit publicly at the time.

In 1969 the Cairo resident of our intelligence service had begun clandestine contacts with Yassir Arafat of the Palestine Liberation Organization and George Habash, head of the more radical Popular Front for the Liberation of Palestine. The initiation of contact grew directly out of our sympathies for national liberation movements. In our view, the Palestinians were the only group among the countries decolonized since World War II that had not obtained their legitimate national rights. They had been denied their land not only by Israel but by Egypt and Jordan. Intellectually isolated as we were in the GDR, we knew little of the complexities of the Arab-Israeli struggle, and although we all knew of Hitler's extermination of the Jews, even I as a Jew knew little of Israel's fight to establish itself.

At the end of 1972, East Germany formally opened political contacts with the Palestine Liberation Organization, and Honecker received Arafat in East Berlin. Immediately after the meeting, our service was ordered to establish intelligence links with the PLO. Moscow backed the move with great alacrity, since the PLO was in the process of being accorded observer status at the United Nations, and the Soviet Union was keen to develop a variety of contacts with the PLO's leadership.

But there was also a darker side to the Soviets' and our enthusiasm for the PLO. At the August 1972 Olympic Games in Munich, Palestinian terrorists from the Black September group had stormed the living quarters of the Israeli athletes, killing two who resisted and taking nine captive (an attack that was as much of a surprise to us as it was to the rest of the world). The rescue operation mounted by Hans-Dietrich Genscher, then interior minister, was an amateurish affair that ended in the deaths of all the remaining hostages as well as their captors, and it was strongly criticized afterward in West Germany and Israel. For us in East Berlin, such an event on German soil (even if it was in the other Germany) was a sobering reminder of how easy it was for terrorists to export their grievances. A working group whose membership included some of my staff was ordered to draw up a policy paper considering the goals of the Palestinian movement from the standpoint of its ideology and our security. Offering Yassir Arafat's Fatah wing of the PLO semi-diplomatic status in East Berlin seemed to be a useful precaution against being the target of an attack. We were particularly concerned about protecting the upcoming World Youth Congress in East Berlin.

Further talks were held in Moscow between Arafat and the head of my department responsible for Arab countries. We agreed to help the PLO on the condition that it end terrorist attacks in Europe. Arafat agreed and named Abu Ayad (whose real name was Salah Chalaf) as the man who would deal with us in the future. Soon, Palestinian fighters were invited to Ministry of State Security camps hidden in the East German countryside for training in intelligence and counterintelligence and the use of guns, explosives, and guerrilla tactics. This was routine training for national liberation groups and was overseen by my department and also by two ministry departments, Department HA-II (counterespionage) and AGM (Arbeits gruppe des Ministers, the Minister's Working Group), responsible for military tasks and training.

In return for our aid and training, we hoped to gain access to PLO information on American security, global strategy, and weaponry. We had great respect for Palestinian political intelligence gathering and believed Abu Ayad when he boasted of his contacts at the heart of the U.S. government, NATO, and the arms trade. Impressed by the Palestinians' supposed worldwide network of contacts through its diaspora of highly educated professionals in many countries and not just the Middle East, we hoped they would bring us details of summit meetings and open channels of information where the Soviets shielded their knowledge from us. On the whole, we were disappointed. In fact, about the only particularly valuable intelligence we got from the PLO during the entire time we worked with them were accounts of the preparations for and substance of the Camp David agreement between Israel and Egypt.

The Palestinians did provide insights into the shifting politics, alliances, and enmities of the Middle East, which raised our general level of expertise in the region. Our formal contacts with the PLO also facilitated the operations of our intelligence officers in Damascus and Aden. Through them we learned of the extent of covert CIA and West German involvement in the affairs of the region and the identities of the officers stationed there, always useful information when they were transferred and turned up at other stations under diplomatic cover. The Palestinians also identified these agents' sources, which also helped us figure out who was on whose side.

Our service had little information to give the PLO in exchange. They certainly received no special intelligence from us about Israel, for we had none. Our target remained West Germany as the frontline state in the Cold War, and this was not a priority for the PLO. We did, however, give instruction. My senior officers were called in to give lectures on intelligence gathering and encoding and decoding, and to pass on our experience of counterespionage techniques to Palestinian visitors. We of course guessed that this information might pass to terrorist commandos against Israel or their trainers.

During the savage Israeli intervention in Lebanon in 1982, our modest presence there took on inordinate significance. With Beirut in ruins, there was an interval during which Moscow lost contact with its embassy and its KGB officers in the Lebanese capital. Our officers were the only ones able to maintain radio and personal contact with the leadership of the PLO and, acting as Moscow's proxy, our men were instructed to pass on the PLO's reaction to events. They ventured forth, risking their lives among the shooting and bombings to meet their Palestinian partners. The vicious, criminal brutality of the Israeli assault on the refugee camps of Sabra and Shatila and the numerous civilian deaths that resulted shocked even these officers, who were no strangers to the harsh enmities of the Middle East, and they were deeply affected by it.

Our sympathies were already influenced by Moscow's pro-Arab line, and the Israeli intervention pulled such officers even further toward the Arab world. Of course, a closer examination of the long history of Israeli-Palestinian hostilities was discouraged. Knowledge of the Bible (traditionally important in Lutheran Germany) was of little importance in our socialist schools. My Jewish roots gave me a certain sensitivity in this matter that others lacked, and I also knew of the Arab links to Hitler's Germany. It never failed to shock and unsettle me during my visits to the Middle East when camel drivers or street vendors, hearing German spoken, would run after us shouting, "Heil Hitler!"

●

Mielke essentially mistrusted me as a member of the intelligentsia and perhaps for other reasons (although I never heard him make any anti-Semitic remark beyond an occasional anti-Jewish joke); furthermore, our ministry was pervaded by a culture of secrecy that threw up institutional barriers to communication. I lasted because Mielke knew I had the patronage at the highest levels of the KGB, which could of course be useful to him as well as dangerous to challenge. To Mielke I was essentially a good collector and analyst of information but was unsuited for the hard class struggle that had formed him on the streets of Berlin, and when he could keep me out of the loop, he did. From the beginning of the HVA, he had put the Department for Special Tasks—behind-the-lines sabotage, destruction of pipelines and atomic stations—under his control, even though in Moscow these functions were under the First Main Directorate, that is, foreign intelligence, corresponding to the HVA. After I retired, this department was returned to my successor at foreign intelligence.

Thus it came about that contacts with terrorist groups were organized not by the HVA but by a ministry group called Department XXII. It reported to General Gerhard Neiber, one of Mielke's four deputy ministers of state security, whose main task was to command the border control.* Department XXII was essentially a parallel counterintelligence department and did not come under my jurisdiction.

*At that time and until 1985 Mielke's deputies were Rudi Mittig, Neiber, Wolfgang Schwanitz, and I. Schwanitz, sharp and ambitious, was the youngest; he was in charge of technological espionage systems and communications. Mittig was in charge of internal surveillance of the economy, transport, the government bureaucracy, dissidents, the church, and the cultural establishment. It was one of the most hated functions of the regime. Until 1982, Mielke actually had a first deputy minister, Bruno Beater, a tough intriguer who had been with the service since its beginnings under Soviet tutelage. After Beater retired, no one was formally named first deputy minister so that Mielke could withhold his public preference from any candidate successor. It fell to Rudi Mittig to deputize for Mielke when the minister was away. When Mielke was finally removed in 1989, Schwanitz became the head of the Office for National Security (Amt für Nationale Sicherheit—ACNS), the successor to the Ministry of State Security, but his tenure was short-lived.

Neiber gradually became responsible for counterintelligence in the army and police and eventually was also in charge of the ministry's counterterrorism activities. Neiber was a very friendly person who had a large number of well-appointed guest houses under his control. He served as a good host for the delegations from foreign intelligence services. He was not the kind of person to sign death warrants, not a brutal man, but was certainly a man who followed orders. Thus, after unification, he was accused of participating in the execution of a man named Gartenschläger, who broke through the border fence four or five times and destroyed parts of it.

Neiber was directly responsible to Mielke, and his Department XXII was technically an antiterrorist unit. Until 1979 it had been relatively small, but the decision to widen our dealings with "forces involved in armed struggle," as we put it, meant that it had to grow fast. Within a few years, it had more than eight hundred employees, although I believe only about twenty of them knew about the direct contacts with terrorist groups. It is now known that these contacts included the Irish Republican Army, the Basque separatist movement, ETA, and Carlos the Jackal. I did not know of these connections at the time and indeed I never met Carlos or other international terrorist stars. I left the contacts with the Palestinians to my Middle East specialist, whose code name was Roscher (I will not use his real name here). Roscher maintained limited personal contacts with PLO functionaries, PLO security people, and George Habash of the Palestine Liberation Front. He did not, however, have contacts with Abu Nidal or Carlos, and his information about their activities came indirectly through his PLO associates. Roscher's avoidance of Abu Nidal and Carlos was the result of my orders to our people to avoid terrorists and terrorism, and as far as I am aware he consistently followed his orders. Roscher was only selectively informed about Department XXII's contacts and was certainly not informed about "hot" contacts. "Hot" contacts were those that involved Carlos or other especially violent terrorists and terrorist groups. These contacts were known only to a small number of officers in Department XXII. No one from my department knew about such contacts.

Roscher reported to me about his contacts when he thought the information would be relevant to our intelligence mission. Usually this involved a request for training, support, and so on. I reported such requests to Mielke, and he decided on them. After this there was not much for me to do, since the training programs generally were run without any direct involvement on my part or my personal support.

The majority of Arab terrorists who were hidden in the GDR entered at the border under Arab diplomatic cover, which was not my responsibility. In addition to opposing Department XXII on political grounds—I was worried that it could backfire on my service—I opposed it on grounds that any bureaucrat the world over would understand: Department XXII was poaching on my own turf, invading our foreign intelligence functions by setting up a parallel service. I knew that no good would come of it for me and for the country as a whole, and I was right.

As the years went by, it became clear that the PLO saw us as just another cog in their wheel, and that our hopes of controlling their activities were in vain. We were also concerned that our identification with Arafat's wing of the PLO would expose us to revenge by others, so we were gradually drawn into offering hospitality and training to a spread of Palestinian fighters. These eventually included Abu Nidal. On the recommendation of Roscher, who learned about the brutality of Abu Nidal's organization from his regular contacts with Arafat's secret service, I signed a memo opposing any contact with him, but to no avail, and East German military instructors trained Abu Nidal in Soviet rocket-launching techniques.

When we wanted to make friendly gestures without committing ourselves too deeply, we would offer holiday facilities or educational opportunities. George Habash kept an apartment in Dresden to visit his daughter, a student at the technical university there.

In 1979 Mielke ordered a secret study of all this by the ministry's analysts. Entitled, "On Activities of Representatives of the Palestinian Liberation Movement and Other International Terrorists and Their Attempts to Involve the GDR in the Preparations for Acts of Violence in the Countries of Western Europe," it listed many of the terrorist activities of the groups we were aiding and indicated that we had information that the PLO and their allies were planning to use their access to East Germany as a forward position from which to mount terror attacks. The proximity and ease of access to West Berlin were extremely useful to them. The report's contents were later published by Dr. Richard Meier, formerly my opposite number in West Germany, in a book accusing me of abetting terrorism. He deftly omitted the most significant part of the report, its summary paragraph, which warned: "Those activities from the territory of the GDR will result in political risks and jeopardize our national security interests."

Far from being an endorsement, the report Mielke had commissioned turned out to be a warning.

But there was no discussion of this in the ministry's collegium, nor indeed was there any formal discussion of the activities of Department XXII, or the morality or otherwise of our involvement with terrorist organizations. I heard occasional comments or expressions of reluctance, which made it clear to me that opinions within the ministry were divided about our work with potential terrorists. Some simply took their orders and did not consider too closely the consequences of what they were teaching our Palestinian or South Yemeni partners. Some voiced a practical objection—the fear of being caught. Mielke was terrified that our Palestinian connection would become public. He was especially nervous that news of our training and support for the PLO would emerge before sensitive summit meetings with other world leaders. As a result, the program was often suspended at short notice while we begged Abu Ayad to forgo violence. That worked for short periods, but over the long run it was a forlorn hope.

●

Our principal aim—preventing our own territory from serving as a base for terrorism—became impossible to ensure once the ministry had made the acquaintance of Carlos the Jackal. Our most problematic customer, he arrived for the first time in East Germany in 1979 through South Yemeni connections. He was hardly a person of great importance, but his flamboyant behavior made him a star of the Western media, although my service neither controlled nor even to the best of my knowledge met him. His story, as I have pieced it together, is worth telling in order to illustrate what we had gotten ourselves into. It was like having a tiger by the tail.

It was immediately clear that Carlos liked East Berlin, probably because it offered more comfort and a better nightlife than most of the other places he was able to hole up in. He took a suite in East Berlin's

Palast Hotel, much to the distress of our security people since the Palast was favored by Westerners. Carlos traveled on a Syrian diplomatic passport and was in the habit of announcing his arrival with only a day or two's warning. In fact, our ministry managed to limit him to only several stays.

I and my officers were no admirers of Carlos. From staff reports, he emerged as a loudmouth, a spoiled bourgeois-turned-terrorist who disregarded all the basic rules of discretion, thereby endangering those who worked with him. During his visits to East Berlin, counterintelligence constantly monitored his movements. He ignored their pleas to spend his time quietly in his room; instead he settled down late in the bar with his pistol stuck in his belt, drank copiously, and flirted with the women. The prostitutes all reported to State Security, but it was still risky for him to be seen and worrying for us that he might be spotted.

Our main concern was getting him out of the country as soon as possible, no simple task. One of the most difficult aspects of liaison with terrorists like Carlos was that the power relationship between us and them had an unfortunate tendency to reverse itself. Originally, Carlos was grateful for assistance in organizing his clandestine life. But once he sensed that we were less keen on his presence, his mood turned nasty. He began to make the same threats toward us that he carried out against enemy governments, warning those who tried to dissuade him from a visit that he would seek out East German targets abroad. When Carlos's West German wife, Magdalena, was arrested in France in 1982, he asked us to help spring her from jail. When we refused, he threatened to storm our Paris embassy. We ended up in the bizarre position of having to increase security at our embassy to protect it.

Why did we tolerate people involved with terrorist activities? Mielke, who personally ran our dealings with them, held the view that they might be used in "the most serious case"—his euphemism for all-out war with the NATO nations. I never heard him state it directly, but his theory seemed to be that the terrorists we befriended or, as in the case of the Red Army Faction, sheltered could be used as behind-the-lines guerrilla forces for sabotage against the West. Had I been asked about this harebrained idea, I certainly would have opposed it. We could hardly control someone like Carlos inside East Germany in peacetime, so how would he prove dependable or even useful in the chaos of war? It seemed like the most wishful thinking to me, and I believe Mielke was really driven by a sense of inferiority toward both the West and the Soviet Union on the one hand, and on the other by an advanced case of hubris. He wanted to become internationally significant—even if it meant becoming entangled with organizations like the PLO or the Red Army Faction.

Despite the promises we had exacted from the PLO and others, two terrorist attacks were nevertheless launched from East German territory. The bombings in Berlin of the French consulate in 1983 and the La Belle discotheque in 1986 were in many ways the logical culmination of the decision to allow terrorists to use East Berlin as an occasional base. Mielke never expected this to happen, but dealings with the terrorists simply swung out of his control.

One way in which our ministry could slightly limit the activities of these groups was by controlling what they brought in and out of the country in their luggage. Like anyone else entering the country, these groups passed through screening at the airport and were usually found to be carrying or transporting weapons. It was decided by border control that they should be allowed to carry the guns, since going armed was clearly second nature to them.

On April 5, 1986, an explosion in the La Belle discotheque in West Berlin, a frequent haunt of U.S. servicemen, killed two soldiers and a woman, and one hundred and fifty people were injured. The Americans claimed that the attack was orchestrated from within the Libyan embassy in West Berlin and responded by bombing military bases and suspected terrorist centers in Libya. The White House also claimed that the East German government knew in advance of at least the intent to mount the attack, if not the details.

In fact, the La Belle attack was also the result of a serious sin of omission and culpable cowardice by the Ministry of State Security. A report came from Neiber's border control officers that Libyan diplomats had entered the country with explosives in their luggage. Their identity and terrorist connections were well known. Counterintelligence sources in the Middle East had reported plans for a Libyan attack somewhere in West Berlin, so there was every reason to suspect that the explosives were intended for this purpose.

After unification, it was confirmed that my foreign intelligence service was not aware of the acts that led to either the bombing of La Belle or the 1983 bombing of the French consulate in West Berlin. Yet another mystery remains: What did the Americans know, and could they have prevented the bombing? It took less than one day for President Reagan to announce that the United States had definite proof of Libyan involvement. Even if the so-called proof that this was true was merely the result of a Russian tip-off, there were other curiosities. The main organizer of the bombing, a man named Chreidi, had easily traveled back and forth between East and West Berlin during a period of heightened security measures at Checkpoint Charlie. More ominously, PLO sources, quoted in documents kept at the ministry, implied that Chreidi was no mere Libyan terrorist, but in fact in the secret employ of the United States.

Ten days after his announcement, President Reagan authorized a massive assault on Libya. A total of 160 aircraft dropped more than sixty tons of explosives, missing their ostensible target—Qaddafi himself—but leaving dozens of innocent civilians dead and injuring hundreds. As terrible as many of us found the La Belle bombing, it was hard to decide whether the murder of the soldiers and the woman in West Berlin or the murder of many more Libyan civilians was the greater act of terrorism.

●

In addition to protecting foreign terrorists in East Germany, Department XXII also looked after members of the Red Army Faction who had been given sanctuary in the East. The RAF sprang from the radicalism of the 1960s and the violence of Germany's political traditions. It conducted a campaign of terror and assassination of West Germany's political and especially economic leaders to destroy capitalism by methods we Communists in the East had long since forsworn. Though its leaders, Andreas Baader and Ulrike Meinhof, committed suicide in prison in West Germany, their supporters to this day believe they were murdered by the authorities. In the years after unification, my name would be linked to these Red Army Faction members, but, as was the case with Arab terrorists, I and my service were kept ignorant of the Red Army Faction's presence within the GDR.

Some of these hidden Red Army Faction members were given new identities and new lives by the Ministry of State Security, including Susanna Albrecht, accused of leading an assassination squad to the home of a friend of her father, Jürgen Ponto, chief executive of the Dresdner Bank; and Christian Klar and Silke Maier-Witt, involved in the kidnapping and murder of Hans-Martin Schleyer, the president of the Association of German Industrialists. Three RAF members—Inge Viett, Regina Nicolai, and Ingrid Siepmann—escaped from West Germany to Czechoslovakia, where the authorities there asked them if they wanted to contact East Germany. They agreed and were eventually brought to Berlin on Mielke's orders.

The Red Army Faction was already in decline within a year or so after many of its left-wing sympathizers published statements in the West disavowing them. The leadership of the group feared mass arrests and decided that any activists who wished to retire could do so without fear of reprisal or betrayal. The technicalities of resettlement were carried out by an inner group of Department XXII officers. These officers' identities were kept secret, even from me, and foreign intelligence was in no way involved with resettling the Red Army Faction members. Mielke was always anxious to have control over things only he knew about. There was no operational reason for him not to share this knowledge with me, but given that Department XXII reported directly to him, there was also no reason why he should. In any case, my policy from the beginning was to keep as far away from the Red Army Faction members as possible because some could well have been turned by Western intelligence and planted with us.

If there had ever been any danger of Red Army Faction terrorists mounting attacks on targets in West Germany from the East, I am sure that I would have learned of it from counterintelligence. I don't think this danger ever existed. They were encouraged to live as quietly as possible. Each terrorist was given a cover story. One might say that he had been in trouble with the police in the West because of radical pro-socialist protest activities, another that she wanted to be close to an aged parent in the East. They were ordered not to mention their terrorist past, although being human beings possessing a fatal desire to tell the truth, some revealed their RAF atrocities to new husbands or wives in the East. The main way in which they stood out among their new colleagues in the factories and offices in the East was by their obstreperous devotion to socialism. For example, after the collapse of East Germany in 1989, it emerged in the press that Inge Viett, who lived in Magdeburg under the pseudonym Eva Maria Schnell, took her comrades in the factory branch of the Party to task for embracing monetary union with West Germany far too eagerly! Sigrid Sternbeck, settled with her lover in the far north of the country, reported that her new factory colleagues were unconvinced by her cover story, and it was whispered that she must be one of my spies who had been withdrawn from the West.

The reason behind the decision to take in the former RAF members lay perhaps in the same fear of becoming a potential target. But in the case of the Red Army Faction, Mielke's approach was laced with a desire to embarrass West Germany by keeping the ex-terrorists out of the grasp of the judicial process. Some of the RAF members received training in Syria and South Yemen in more advanced firearms and explosives techniques than they brought with them from West Germany, and a special annual session was held to train them in the use of Soviet RPG-7 antitank guns. Training sessions also took place in East Germany for retired RAF members still living in the West. The published records show that in 1981 and 1982, a group was instructed in firing weapons at the passenger seat of a Mercedes. A live sheepdog had been tied down as a target; the animal was killed, the car was blown up, and the trainee terrorists were shown how to dispose of the wreckage.

Mielke started out believing that the RAF would offer insights into the West, and at the same time having them among us would protect us from their violence, but this grisly example of the ministry's efforts to improve the skills of even officially retired terrorists supports my belief that Mielke continued to harbor the notion of using them in a possible war between East and West. He took this possibility very seriously.

West German intelligence certainly suspected that the men and women whose faces adorned post offices on the "most wanted" list were in East Germany. The existence of these alienated social outcasts from the West probably reminded Honecker and Mielke of their own youth in Germany as underground fighters against the Nazis. But any sense of common cause would have been dispelled, I expect, by longer exposure to these spoiled, hysterical children of mainly upper-middle-class backgrounds. Their style of combat rarely demanded that they show the bravery and ingenuity that enabled the Communist Party and its intelligence networks to keep operating in Germany under Hitler. I can put it no better than Helmut Pohl, an imprisoned Red Army Faction member who is thought to have been one of the main planners of this rump terrorist organization's activities. Speaking about his training in the East, he said in an interview, "We could not stand all the theory and formality and the grand words about world peace. For all the good it did, we might as well have read *Neues Deutschland* [the East German Communist Party newspaper]. There was a climate of constant irritation between us. By the end, we were probably as unbearable for them as they were for us."

•

The dividing line between freedom fighters and terrorists is usually determined by which side you are on. One struggle to which we made military and financial contributions that left me with no regrets was our help for the African National Congress, the liberation movement in South Africa. There were no strategic considerations in our support for the ANC. We regarded its battle against apartheid as a legitimate liberation struggle, although we did not regard it as a force that could take power, an assumption that made me smile years later at the irony when I saw Nelson Mandela enjoying the benefits and burdens of power in a South Africa without any legal color bar.

But there was nevertheless a political motive mixed in with our help. We wanted to strengthen the left wing of the ANC, and this had to be done very carefully, both by us and the Soviet Union. There would have been no net gain in exacerbating splits in the liberation movement between the liberals and the pro-Communists, thus allowing the traditionally anti-Communist white rulers to strengthen their hand. We and Moscow agreed that the most useful strategy for securing support for socialist policies in the ANC would simply be to help as promptly and generously as we could, so that we were seen as allies in the broader struggle.

From the mid-1970s onward, East Germany trained guerrilla fighters for the ANC. This belonged in the realm of military rather than intelligence cooperation and was handled through the AGM (Minister's Working Group) and General Alfred Scholz. Two groups of forty or fifty ANC fighters were trained at a Party school in the East German countryside. East German military intelligence, which operated separately from my foreign intelligence service, dealt with their travel plans, which were of course kept strictly secret. They traveled via Tanzania or Angola, were flown to London, and then changed planes to be flown aboard the East German state airline to East Berlin. This was considered the best route for shaking off South African intelligence. The subterfuge worked.

There were never any leaks about their military training in East Germany. I found out about it in the late 1970s, when Joe Slovo, the leader of the South African Communist Party, sent a request through the Central Committee of the East German Party for us to train small groups of ANC members in counterintelligence. He explained that the ANC was in danger of being penetrated by agents of the South African government and that they lacked the basic knowledge to build a counterespionage system to prevent it. This message from Slovo was passed to us from Honecker's office with a notation, "The general secretary has agreed."

We arranged for eight to ten ANC men to be trained in a special department of the Ministry's Legal College (Juristische Hochschule) in Potsdam, outside Berlin. This college, our invention, was an institution of many uses, all of them connected to the Ministry of State Security. Retired officers ran courses there ranging from basic foreign affairs for new recruits to lessons in countering spies. Under the close attention of a general borrowed from the top ranks of our counterintelligence department, the ANC learned how to spot potential moles, confuse them, and track them down without giving themselves away.

The courses began every three to five months, and the South Africans were fervent students, soaking up all the knowledge we felt we could safely give them on the known methods of their enemy service and the psychology of interrogation. Some basic instruction on the principles of Marxism-Leninism was also included, but our student guests politely made it plain that this was not what they had come for. By this stage, the basic rule of all such cooperation was that it was unwise to force our worldview on our partners. Out of this channel of communication with the ANC we hoped one day to establish methods of legalizing agents we wanted to send abroad by sending them first to South Africa, where they could establish false identities with the help of our new intelligence contacts there. This was only just starting to come to fruition about 1988, so we never had the chance to see how workable it was.

●

When thinking about the GDR's aid to terrorists, and especially the attacks on the French consulate and the La Belle disco, no one who had anything to do with it can avoid the question of personal responsibility, guilt, and complicity. The dead were not victims who fell in a fight for freedom; they supported neither our worldview nor even our overvalued security doctrine. These sorts of attacks, like the 1993 attempt by a small terrorist group on the World Trade Center, demonstrate the responsibility that everyone assumes when dealing with such forces for whatever motive. But these are perceptions in hindsight. Our cooperation with the PLO under Arafat and other such groups was part of a complex political maneuver for which I am personally responsible, and I know it. It was a collaboration in the service of our political leadership, and we were just as politically motivated in its implementation as in the past assignments in the Third World.

When judging our activities in the Third World and with groups many deemed terrorist, I hope that the positive desires of each side in this extreme, hard Cold War confrontation will leave behind a few traces. The blood of Patrice Lumumba, Che Guevara, Salvador Allende, Yitzhak Rabin, and the many victims whose names are remembered only by their families and friends should not haunt or obstruct the progress of events. The pictures of the election of Nelson Mandela to the presidency of the Republic of South Africa and of the handshake of Jews and Palestinians are what should inspire us.

14

E n e m y   T e r r i t o r y

The intelligence world, East and West, was a realm of moral shadows. Its practices were often unethical, its methods dirty. Given this fact, it seems to me that the CIA was at a peculiar disadvantage in having to take part in a sort of democratic pantomime to satisfy the requirements of the American Constitution, regardless of whether or not they were relevant to intelligence work. No secret service can ever be democratic nor, however much politicians may wish it, open to constant scrutiny and still perform its tasks properly. In the CIA, much of senior officers' time was taken up preparing documents and summaries of their work to present outside the agency, always with half an eye on the reaction of politicians and the press.

In the East, we erred too far in the opposite direction. Although we had to produce papers and reports for the political hierarchy, which meant that there was some formal scrutiny of our espionage services, there was no real oversight. Our political masters were so fundamentally insecure that they insisted on getting any information that could have a bearing on potential threats to their position and were none too fussy about how it was obtained. Erich Honecker specialized in telling West German politicians whose trust he sought that East German intelligence had been given orders to stay away from them. Once back home, he would devour intelligence reports about them assiduously and strongly imply that he wanted more information, not less.

The behavior of CIA counterintelligence, my personal experience of which is narrated at the start of this book, suggests to me that they were more concerned with quieting worries that a mole was active in the CIA than in actually finding him. Gus Hathaway told the Senate Intelligence Committee in 1985: "There has never been an agent of the Soviet in the center of the CIA itself. We may have failed to find such an agent, but I doubt it." This in spite of the fact that the defector Edward Lee Howard, dismissed by the CIA two years earlier for drug offenses and petty theft, had subsequently revealed secrets of the agency's Moscow operations to the Soviets; his treachery was not uncovered by the CIA itself but was unveiled only through the defection of a senior KGB official, Vitaly Yurchenko. Strictly speaking, Hathaway's statement was true, since Howard was out of the service by the time he passed over the secrets. But the blanket assurance it contained was not. Having met Hathaway and judged him to be a serious, conscientious intelligence officer, I ask myself why he should have been content to whitewash the agency's weaknesses in this way. My hunch is that he feared letting down the CIA in public at a time when its standing was declining.

The CIA's miscarried attempts to unseat Fidel Castro and its haphazard tactics in Central America had brought down its reputation among conservatives and liberals alike. Assessments made by our officers in the Washington and New York stations regarding American intelligence in the 1970s and 1980s showed it to be far less respected than in the 1950s and 1960s. This, as any management consultant could have said, had an effect on the morale of its officers. The organization came to be seen not only as secretive and underhanded—quite normal judgments of a powerful intelligence service—but seedy, a reputation no intelligence service can afford. Secret services are psychologically unstable places and their internal mind-set is quickly reflected in performance. Reports on the traitor Aldrich Ames revealed a high level of self-hatred within the CIA. Ames not only disliked his own agency, he despised it. I do not think that the same is true of a Soviet traitor like Oleg Gordievsky. Moscow's traitors changed sides for a mixture of ideological and personal reasons, but while they knew what was bad in the KGB, they didn't lose their awe of it until Gorbachev's reign.

Ames was not the first mediocrity to be rewarded within the CIA. In the 1970s, the Americans ran an agent code-named Thielemann whose task it was to make contact with East German diplomats, businessmen, and academics visiting West Germany and to try to recruit them. It was basically a good idea of the CIA's to home in on useful East Germans when they traveled outside their own country, and was far less risky than operating inside the East. But we learned of Thielemann's activities when, in 1973, we began to undertake an intensive analytical survey of CIA operations working out of Bonn. By simply monitoring casual approaches to our countrymen at cocktail parties, sports clubs, bars and cafés, and other public gathering places we were soon able to draw up a list of CIA workers.

By 1975, Thielemann had settled full time in Bonn. Unbeknownst to him or the CIA, we had worked out his real name, Jack Falcon. At first we simply tailed him, noting his targets and establishing what he was looking for. Gradually, we started feeding him targets—agents working for us who would allow themselves to be recruited by Falcon as a source and give him a mixture of unimportant secrets and disinformation. The idea was to throw the Americans onto false trails in their own inquiries and lead them to mistaken conclusions about our work. Poor Falcon thought that he was doing a splendid job recruiting so many willing and knowledgeable East Germans. To one particularly trusted source he boasted that the CIA had promoted him and given him a raise because of the success of his recruiting drive. This caused great mirth in our ministry's counterintelligence department. Its senior officers had concocted most of the worthless secrets themselves.

In fact, spotting CIA operatives in Bonn was ridiculously easy. Quite unlike my own insistence on careful preparation and slow, almost imperceptible approaches to a potential recruit, they always set off on a frantic round of making contacts. Targets we had planted often complained of the agents' poor level of knowledge of the economic problems of the East, which made it hard to know what line to spin them because their basic information about the East was so sketchy. For a time in the late 1970s and early 1980s the quality of the American agents was so poor and their work so haphazard that our masters began to ask fearfully whether Washington had stopped taking East Germany seriously.

Later, we learned that the United States was obtaining its key data on East Germany from electronic surveillance in West Berlin and West Germany. It was a bit odd that the CIA bothered to send men snooping around incompetently on the ground when most of the valuable information they wanted was in the ether. But in my experience, no technical method can substitute for good human intelligence and judgment, and—however incompetent their attempts—someone at the CIA must have agreed. You can intercept a phone call, but without a sense of the context it is easy to misinterpret; a satellite photo can tell you where missiles are at the moment, but a source in the military command can tell you where they are headed. The problem with technical intelligence is that it is essentially information without evaluation. Technical intelligence can only record what has happened so far—not what might happen in the future. Human sources can give information about plans, can analyze the political and military outlook, and can place documents and conversations in context. As any intelligence officer knows, far too much of the job is spent sifting through mountains of data in search of a valuable nugget; an overreliance on technical intelligence might double the number of nuggets but will certainly triple the size of the data mountain to be sifted through. Even though the role of technical intelligence will increase and will supplement what used to be done by human means at great expense and risk, it can never really substitute. It is the human factor that makes an espionage service successful, not its high-tech bells and whistles.

By the late 1980s, we were in the enviable position of knowing that not a single CIA agent had worked in East Germany without having been turned into a double agent or working for us from the start. On our orders they were all delivering carefully selected information and disinformation to the Americans. We knew this because Edward Lee Howard had worked on the East German desk. He met Falcon after Falcon was brought back to CIA headquarters at Langley and rewarded for his successes inside East Germany. From Falcon, Howard had been able to learn that there were only six or seven agents working for the CIA inside East Germany. We were able to account for all of them as our plants. This was later confirmed by the CIA itself, which revealed after the fall of East Germany that all its agents there had turned out to be manipulated by the Ministry of State Security.

In 1987–88, Howard, by now resident in Moscow and under the KGB's protection, visited East Berlin and told his minders from the foreign intelligence service in detail about the CIA's operations and its espionage priorities in military installations and research institutes. What was really news to us was Howard's disclosure that the CIA kept a target list of the economic elite and academics of East Germany. If any of them applied for a visa to visit America, his or her name was passed on through the consular department to the U.S. secret services and thence into a vast data bank. During that individual's visit to the United States, whenever his or her name was mentioned in a monitored telephone conversation, fax, or telex message, the U.S. authorities recorded it and passed it to the CIA for evaluation. East Germany may have had a justified reputation for snooping and bugging, but our technical limitations alone ensured that we could not match the Americans on this point.

One institutional weakness in American intelligence that the Ames case should have highlighted is its vulnerability to political gestures. In recent years, the post of director of Central Intelligence has been akin to that of a football coach who gets booted out after a bad season. The advantages of such a policy are purely cosmetic in giving the public the idea that a new broom has arrived, until, a few years down the line, he can be damned equally for incompetence. That is no way to increase the efficiency of any intelligence service. On the contrary, the period after a major defection or arrest of agents is the very time continuity and steadiness are demanded at the top. I never believed mass firings were an appropriate response.

When Werner Stiller disappeared, I recommended only a change of his immediate section head. There was no pressure on either me or the minister for state security to resign. What good would it have done? Much better for us all to keep our desks and work out how to stop it from happening again. Incidentally, I see little evidence that the CIA ever did sit down and figure out how to stop it from happening again. Certain sections of its operations—the Soviet section in particular springs to mind—seem to have gotten by on a wing and a prayer. If there had been a thorough investigation after Howard's defection, Ames might have been caught sooner.

Espionage services do themselves no favors by giving in to ignorant politicians' calls for heads to roll whenever an accident such as this becomes public. I always felt a sneaking sympathy for Heribert Hellenbroich, whose career as head of West German foreign intelligence foundered on Tiedge's defection. Hellenbroich, who had been head of the Office for Protection of the Constitution, was new to the BND job; he had some disagreements with the new chancellor's advisers (especially Klaus Kinkel) and became the scapegoat for failures that were really the fault of prior staff selections and the lack of total control endemic to a secret service.

My meeting with Gus Hathaway was, of course, a bizarre ending to my Cold War relations with America. For the three and a half decades during which I was chief of East Germany's foreign intelligence, the United States was a distant and hostile country. Following our Soviet counterparts, we used the German word *Hauptgegner,* "principal adversary" (*glavni protivnik* in Russian) to describe the United States. In Moscow's eyes, and by extension in ours, America was the source from which all imperialist evils flowed. I did not, however, harbor any personal animosity toward the United States. Of course, I knew about and abhorred the obsessive anti-Communist activities of Senator Joseph McCarthy and the infringements of justice committed with the support of the CIA in Latin America. But my internationalist upbringing prevented me from falling into the stupid anti-Americanism that afflicted many socialists. My knowledge of America was grounded in what I had learned in the Soviet Union from American friends, from my personal experience as a radio reporter in Berlin and in Nuremberg covering the trials, and from the Western newspapers and magazines I read daily. Of course I applied a strong ideological filter to what I read, since it was my job to debate the assumptions and conclusions about politics and ideology contained in the reports and to justify the opposing Soviet position as best I could. Inevitably, this drove a wedge between me and American friends like George Fischer. As a captain on Eisenhower's staff, he often came to Berlin in the immediate postwar period. We were delighted to see each other again, but it was hard to ignore the prickle of distrust that had entered the relationship.

Much of the knowledge of U.S. political thinking, intentions, and fears that I was able to gather came from the two men who were my first American agents. They were never discovered, so even though they are both dead, I do not intend to name them here other than by the cover names we used for them: Maler ("Painter") and Klavier ("Piano"). Both were born in Germany, had been close to the Communist movement in their youth, and were Jewish. Both had to flee their homeland under the Nazi threat, found asylum in the United States, and concluded their studies there, one as an economist, the other as a lawyer. By dint of their German birth and their professional knowledge, both were recruited into the Office of Strategic Services (OSS), the forerunner of the CIA. During Senator McCarthy's witch-hunt in the early fifties, the OSS was denounced as a nest of left-wing intellectuals. Paradoxically, Stalin used the OSS connections of Noel Field* as a pretext for a bloody orgy of persecution against Communists in several countries in 1951–53, including Czechoslovakia, Hungary, and East Germany. What I heard about Field made me certain he never was a spy but a naïve idealist who tried to help antifascists and therefore maintained contact with the OSS. But his case was an example of the terrible machinations by Stalin and Beria to justify the purges in Eastern Europe.

In that climate, many of our intelligence officers were wary of recruiting any American, lest they open themselves to charges of having fallen into an American trap. But I knew that we badly needed information about American thinking. We had made contact with the economist, Maler, via a friend from his early student days during the Third Reich. The two had been members of a Jewish resistance group that attempted to blow up a Nazi exhibition. Most of the group's members were arrested and thirty-five of them killed. Maler managed to emigrate; his friend survived the concentration camps. The friend was a senior figure in the financial world in East Germany, and through him we managed to make contact with Maler, originally in the hopes of reactivating his OSS contacts.

But it turned out that Maler's wider contacts in the United States were equally interesting. He was a deep and original thinker who still regarded himself as a Communist. He had many influential friends in Washington and was able, at our behest, to introduce himself to the American ambassador in Bonn and the head of mission in Berlin with a

---

*During World War II, Noel worked with a humanitarian organization, the Unitarian Universalist Service Committee, that among other things helped Communist emigrants. Field consequently had contacts with Allen Dulles of the OSS.

letter of recommendation from John Foster Dulles. Most usefully for us, he informed us of the various intelligence contacts that Ernst Lemmer, then West Germany's minister for inter-German questions (i.e., dealings with the East), had had during the war (when he was a Berlin correspondent for foreign newspapers), ranging from networks in France and Switzerland to contacts with the Russians. I never used this material about Lemmer, but in my safe lay a copy of a signed commitment by him to work with the KGB. Maler was a rich man and took from us reimbursements only for expenses, never payment from us for his work, which he described as bringing light to the shadowy areas of the West.

While Maler concentrated his efforts on Europe, Klavier, although resident in Germany, was more often an operational insider in the United States. Klavier was a German trained in the law who emigrated to the United States, where he worked as a lawyer and later joined the OSS. Dissatisfied with the handling of war criminals in West Germany, he offered his inside knowledge to GDR historians. He worked with us only on condition that his wife must never know—she was a West German and, as he put it grimly, a mortal enemy of the East. However, he did take money from us, which he used to build a retirement home in Switzerland. Klavier had been a member of the prosecuting staff at the Nuremberg trials, where he specialized in preparing the case against the German steel magnate Friedrich Krupp, whose financial support was central to Hitler's political rise and whose industrial support was essential to the Nazi military machine. Klavier's motive for working with us was a fear of creeping re-Nazification in West Germany. He could not accept the easy rehabilitation of old Nazis, who were then restored to their old jobs in the judiciary, industry, and finance.

Klavier's Jewishness was the strongest influence on his political thinking and he amassed a large archive, which he left to me, of the proceedings of the Krupp trial and of Adolf Eichmann's trial in Jerusalem. It was through him that I first became aware that my father's journey from humanitarian to Communist was strongly influenced by his social awareness as a German of Jewish ancestry. Klavier was also a friend of the influential journalist Walter Lippmann, who was close to the Kennedys. Before President Kennedy's summit with Khrushchev, Klavier was able to tell us from his conversations with

Lippmann that Kennedy was going to drive a hard line. We passed this information on to Moscow, but I do not know if it influenced the summit. As it turned out, Khrushchev rattled Kennedy by driving an even harder line than his American counterpart.

I valued information from foreign correspondents and columnists highly because they often seemed to me to be better informed and less hidebound than Western diplomats. Over the decades, we tried to recruit a number of U.S. and British journalists as sources, but we failed. Our only journalistic sources were German, and mainly on minor newspapers. (Among our own journalists we did not consider it proper to recruit directly, although bureau chiefs of the East German news agency and our newspapers who were stationed abroad were expected to confer with members of the foreign intelligence residency in our embassies.) Unlike the head of the counterintelligence department, I did not resent foreign correspondents' freedom to roam our country. The early policy of harassing them and making their stay unpleasant seemed counterproductive to me. I assumed that any one of them might well be an intelligence agent and that we should direct clever disinformation at them, giving them scoops and insights that somehow benefited us rather than driving them away full of resentment.

The international recognition of East Germany in the early 1970s made it easier to acquire knowledge about America directly. The Department of American Studies at Humboldt University in Berlin and the American section of the Foreign Affairs Institute were set up with our backing and had senior staff loyal to us. But we were in awe of the reputation of the American and British counterintelligence services (the FBI and MI5, respectively) and proceeded very carefully before launching operations in those countries.

We graded Britain as only a Category 2 country, as far as our intelligence interest was concerned. It was handled by the department that handled France and Sweden. We did manage to infiltrate several people through the West German consular department in Edinburgh, where the vetting procedure was more lax than in London, but very few of these illegals remained in Britain because our government preferred to maintain good relations with London, especially given the effects of superpower politics on our dealings with America. One of our targets was Amnesty International. Mielke deemed it a subversive organization and would have dearly loved to infiltrate it to discover the source of its information from the Soviet Union and Eastern Europe. We never succeeded. Another reason why we did not bother to spy much on Britain (apart from the usual intelligence gathering by the foreign intelligence resident inside East Germany's London embassy) was that we had another source—in Bonn. For about a decade starting in the middle of the 1970s, a political counselor in the West German Foreign Ministry, Dr. Hagen Blau, gave us access to all the intelligence the West Germans had on Britain and was one of our best sources in the West German Foreign Service. He had a Japanese wife and also sent us valuable information when he was posted in Tokyo.

●

Until the early 1970s, the Hallstein Doctrine governed West German foreign policy; Bonn refused to recognize any country that recognized East Germany, so our formal contacts with America were scant. Our main espionage efforts on American territory were devoted to expanding our knowledge of its science and technology. It was a slow process. The FBI was efficient, if heavy-handed, in its approach to suspicious aliens, and our lack of an embassy or any other representation meant that any East German seeking to settle in the States automatically attracted the attention of the FBI. I considered that any operation of ours on U.S. territory had to be particularly well conceived and executed to offset the risk of adding vulnerable agents to the stockpile of potential tit-for-tat expulsions that were a regular feature of East-West relations during the Cold War.

We did manage to settle a handful of illegals. They were given identities as doppelgängers, which meant their biographies were modeled on those of real people, some of them dead, whose names they were given. This lessened the danger of their falling victim to random checks showing that they did not officially exist. Under our method, they existed all right—as two people sharing one identity. They had to be legalized in a third country where vetting procedures were not so strict. We often used Australia, South Africa, or Latin America for this purpose. They had to live in the interim country for a couple of years before moving to America so as not to arouse suspicion, and we told them not to recruit any sources for some time after that. We sometimes joked among ourselves that by the time such illegals became fully operational, we had forgotten who they were or why we had sent them.

The big disadvantage of this system was that it was vulnerable to the same detection method successfully used by West German counterintelligence in the second half of the 1970s. Many of our illegals in the U.S. were exposed by a vetting process based on identifying a number of attributes—for example, single man, middle-aged, changing job in different countries, and so on—that when clustered could be used to narrow the pool of suspects among the population at large. This was the fate of one of our most promising agents, Eberhard Lüttich, codenamed Brest. After his arrest in 1979, Lüttich gave all his knowledge of our operations to the Americans in a plea bargain for a lighter sentence. This was a particularly heavy blow for us, since before being settled abroad he had worked in the intelligence apparat in East Berlin, where he was highly graded as an officer with special tasks (Offizier in besonderem Einsatz). We had placed implicit faith in him, settling him first in Hamburg, where he was hired by an international moving company, and then engineering a transfer to New York. Lüttich's assignment was overseeing the running of intelligence sources in the States in particularly difficult cases and when discovery seemed imminent. He also used his profession to inform us about the transport routes used by the U.S. military for its equipment and recruited sources who informed us about armament and troop movements.

Lüttich was arrested in 1979 in a joint operation by the American and West German authorities. He betrayed the identity of the West German man and address we used to pass instructions from East Berlin. Worse still, he told the West Germans and through them the Americans that East Berlin could relay one-way radio messages to its agents in America using a recently erected transmitter in Cuba. It had taken decades of work to create a transmitter sensitive enough to do this and it had provided a great boost to our global communications.

Another disadvantage of the infiltration method was that it was rare to be able to send out a married couple, since arranging two false identities in tandem is a very difficult task indeed. We tended to send single men in the hope that they would enhance their immigration status by marrying American women. But the Romeo strategy that had served us so well in Germany didn't work in America. The head of my American operations explained that by the 1980s American women were too emancipated to be easily wooed into marriage. They also seemed to have had an inconvenient habit of bringing out the best in the men—or, from an intelligence point of view, the worst. In some cases, our men revealed to their wives or girlfriends their real profession without our permission. We only allowed this step after the relationship was cemented by time and therefore had reason to believe that the spouse would accept her husband's double life. But America is a confessional society, and the desire to tell all afflicted more of the agents we planted there. In such cases, we had to end our work with them. Most remained in America under their false identities and carried on with the civilian lives we had arranged for them as cover for espionage activities that now did not take place.

In the wake of Lüttich's discovery, I decided to withdraw all of our U.S. agents. That meant ripping up and starting again with all the intelligence work that was not conducted from our embassy in Washington and representation at the United Nations. With a heavy heart, I ordered the recall of promising spies, among them a married couple who had been in the States for five years and established themselves at the University of Missouri as assistants to several professors engaged in scientific research and teaching jobs, and an unmarried officer who had been placed in a situation similar to Lüttich's.

As for our official representatives, their intelligence work was unproductive despite its huge costs because in our experience, Eastern European diplomats were so thoroughly monitored by the FBI that it was extremely difficult for them to hook recruits or develop unsuspecting sources. Although our intelligence presence was comparatively very small, the Americans considered us a high risk and devoted considerable resources to monitoring the activities of our embassies. In all my time as spy chief, we were never able to run intelligence sources through this channel. Residents in our Washington and U.N. missions concentrated instead on protecting the diplomats from compromising advances, on checking the buildings for bugging by the Americans, and on perfecting security conditions for confidential conversations. Our diplomats fed information to the ministry's counterintelligence department, but this included no earth-shattering revelations about what made America tick.

Very occasionally, the embassy intelligence officers in Washington would pass on some fortuitously overhead remark by Presidents Reagan or Bush, a juicy piece of senatorial gossip, or the insights of a top industrialist. More likely than not, it would also appear a few days later in the newspapers.

I do not think that we ever got the hang of successfully operating in America. The Soviets, who conducted in-depth surveys of common American psychological profiles, were far better prepared for this society. Nevertheless, the Soviets believed that my country's forward geographical position in Europe and our immediate proximity to the American sectors of Berlin and Germany gave us certain advantages in penetrating the United States. From the 1950s onward, we were asked by the KGB to contribute information on our "principal adversary" as well as to monitor U.S. relations with and activities in West Germany. Complicated and unsatisfactory though our operations were in America itself, we were able to make up for that in Germany with a veritable smorgasbord of sources just outside our own front door. The social factors most helpful to us in recruiting Americans in Europe were the antiwar and antiestablishment atmosphere of the sixties, plus the popularity among young intellectuals of the writings of the political philosopher Herbert Marcuse, such as *One-Dimensional Man.* The large number of American citizens working with the U.S. military in Germany and America's large diplomatic corps gave us a large pool of potential recruits. Moreover, under the Allied agreement on the status of Berlin, many of these people had free access to East Berlin, so they aroused no suspicions by visiting our side.

One of our principal targets was the headquarters of the U.S. military in Heidelberg. There, too, we found it easy to make contacts with potential sources. Unlike the English and French, who tended to keep to themselves during their postings, the Americans were usually happy to make friends and had fewer reservations about following up an invitation from a relative stranger for a drink, a meal, and a chat about life as an American in Europe. We also found that the Americans had a more pronounced inclination to make a quick dollar in unconventional ways. The Soviets, far more experienced than we, maintained that material interest, as they put it, was very often the reason Americans agreed to help a foreign power, even if they had plenty of money to start with. We noticed that when American officers tried to tempt East Germans into cooperating with the CIA, one of their first steps was to offer large sums of money, whereas in our recruiting we continued to play on ideology or, sometimes, motives of revenge. Only when that failed, or if it was clear from the start that the would-be recruit was out for money, did we offer it.

Several offers of what we called "the commercial variant" were conducted successfully through a Turkish middleman called Hussein Yildrim, who worked as a motor mechanic at the U.S. army base in Berlin. Yildrim's work in the garage offered an ideal opportunity to fall into casual conversation with technical experts. He had a shrewd idea of what people earned and could guess from conversations about dream cars which of the employees was especially dissatisfied with his income and might be prepared to boost it by selling secrets. He introduced us to several potential sources in the U.S. military.

None of these contacts of Yildrim's was as important or productive as Specialist James Hall, an American working in electronic espionage for the National Security Agency. This communications agency is so secret that American officials are instructed to declare ignorance of its very existence, and its employees joke that its initials stand for "no such agency." Penetrating it would be a great coup. Yildrim picked out Hall as someone who reacted with particular frustration to the effect of the declining dollar on his lifestyle and recommended we approach him.

Hall was stationed in Teufelsberg, known to us as America's Big Ear. Built on a hill of wartime ruins in West Berlin—hence its name, which means "devil's mountain"—in a physical environment deemed by experts to be particularly favorable for receiving electromagnetic signals, the neutrally named Field Station Berlin was America's central electronic surveillance installation in Europe, a vast, intricate network of sophisticated bugging devices with branches strung along the East German–West German border. It employed thirteen hundred highly skilled technicians who intercepted radio and telephone messages, then analyzed and graded them, and passed on to U.S. and NATO authorities any valuable information they contained. The operation far exceeded anything run by the Warsaw Pact, so the best way for the Soviet Union to fight this surveillance was simply to know as much as possible about it and find ways of eluding it.

Before Hall came along we had little idea of how much sound the station could pick up, or from where. We had learned something of the basic structure from some sources in Teufelsberg, whose personnel included sections of the American 6912th Electronic Security Group and the 26th Signal Unit of the British army. We knew that Teufelsberg was the center from which interceptions were made of GDR Party telephone communications, the radio and telephone traffic of the East German air force, and communications by the Ministry of State Security. Too late, we also found out that the Americans had managed to crack the radio codes in which the daily situation report of internal and external politics was delivered to the Central Committee.

Günter Mittag, who was responsible for economic policy in the GDR, used these monitored channels to communicate with our central economic and financial offices, thus dropping a fresh daily picture of our economy right into the Americans' laps. The West Germans repeatedly requested access to this information but were always refused because the Americans did not trust them to keep such high-quality intelligence secret from us. It was, I think, the right decision—although if the West Germans had had direct access to Mittag's reports and had combined them with their own knowledge of inter-German trade, I suspect they would have come much earlier to the conclusion that East Germany was economically on its knees.

But with Hall in place, we were receiving a steady flow of secret and top secret documentation of the functioning of Teufelsberg. Both Hall and Yildrim had hefty financial appetites. Klaus Eichner, deputy head of HVA's Department 9, was responsible for evaluating the information Hall provided. At times Eichner reported directly to me and I had a high opinion of his instincts and methodical thinking. "We've struck a gold mine here," he told me. "As long as this source is careful, this could go on and on." During the five years Hall spied for us, we paid him well over twice what he was earning with the army—a total of $100,000 and, during one particularly productive phase, $30,000 in a single year. These were large sums by our standards, but very little when compared to the value of his information to our government and Moscow. During this time Hall was promoted to supervisor in the analytical section of electronic intelligence, and the quality of his information rose accordingly. After returning to the United States for further

training in 1985, Hall was assigned to the military intelligence battalion of the 5th Army Corps in Frankfurt, eventually being promoted to
head of electronic warfare and signal intelligence operations.

In Frankfurt, Hall would meet Yildrim at the PX and while shopping hand over a plastic bag of stolen documents. Yildrim would then
drive alone to a small apartment Hall had rented in the city and copy
them. This sometimes took until late into the night. The Turk would
then drive back to Berlin and Hall would return the original documents. To earn more money Hall began to provide more information,
so much, in fact, that our analysts complained that they could not keep
up with it. For this reason, I suggested that the material be passed on
to the Soviets, since in addition to the concrete details that were of
interest to East Germany, there was much information of general
strategic importance that could be better used in Moscow—although
we never revealed our source to them or the nature of our operation.

We also had the documents analyzed by the chief of the ministry's
department of radio intelligence and counterintelligence, since the
technical details were above the heads of our regular analysts. His subsequent report contained one salient piece of hitherto unknown intelligence that was of vital importance for military planning. It found that
the ELOKA electronic warfare system was now giving the United
States and its NATO allies pinpoint knowledge of the whereabouts of
Warsaw Pact commando centers and troop movements from East
Germany across the Soviet Union. In other words, despite the efforts
of the Warsaw Pact generals to disguise troop and weapons movement,
every important shift was instantly picked up by the Americans at
Teufelsberg and relayed to Washington or Brussels.

Among the most important documents we received from Hall was
the National Sigint Requirements List, a four-thousand-page document describing how to use signals intelligence ("sigint") to close the
gaps in military and political intelligence. From this we obtained very
useful information about where the CIA and the State Department felt
they were lacking knowledge. This was extremely valuable since we
could infer where those organizations would increase their activities
and then take relevant countermeasures. Another outstanding success
was obtaining a report code-named Canopy Wing, which listed the
types of electronic warfare that would be used to neutralize the Soviet

Union and Warsaw Pact's command centers in case of all-out war. It detailed the precise method of depriving the Soviet High Command of its high-frequency communications used to give orders to its armed forces. Once we had passed this on to the Soviets, they were able to install scrambling devices and other countermeasures.

Hall's deliveries were so vast that we suggested he slow down so as not to expose himself to suspicion. One package from him contained thirteen complete documents, directives, and work plans of the NSA and the Intelligence and Security Command and included detailed plans of the development of radio intelligence planned by the United States for the next decade. He also provided classified information on Ronald Reagan's pet star wars program of antimissile defenses. U.S. military counterintelligence, which we considered so impressive inside the United States, was clearly not doing much of a job at Teufelsberg. When Hall moved back to the States, he kept up his contact with us. Unfortunately, his greed pushed him into the trap of trying to double his illicit earnings by offering the same material to the Soviets, a move that brought him to the attention of the FBI. He was arrested in December 1988 together with Yildrim after they attended a meeting in a hotel in Savannah, Georgia, with an FBI agent posing as a Soviet intelligence officer. The report on Hall's activities read in court confirmed that the documents stolen by him helped our service cripple American electronic surveillance of Eastern Europe for six years. Hall pleaded guilty to ten charges of espionage and received a forty-year sentence. Yildrim, his Mephistopheles, was also prosecuted for espionage.

Also of key importance was the information we gained on U.S. electronic espionage from James Carney, code-named Kid. Carney was an air force sergeant who, as a linguist and communications specialist, served at Tempelhof airport in West Berlin, used as an air base by the U.S. Air Force. From the NSA headquarters at Fort Meade in Maryland, there was a direct link to its European branch in Frankfurt and on to Berlin-Teufelsberg. Carney's information showed us in detail how this communications system was able to pinpoint dozens of vulnerable Warsaw Pact targets within minutes of the outbreak of war. Some of its capabilities sounded so fantastic to me that I had to call in experts to evaluate and explain them in plain language. For example, there was a team in West Berlin monitoring the Soviet air base at

Eberswalde, about twenty-eight miles northeast of East Berlin. Carney's documents showed that the Americans had managed to penetrate the base's ground-air communications and were working on a method of blocking orders before they reached the Russian pilots and substituting their own from West Berlin. Had this succeeded, the MiG pilots would have received commands from their American enemy. It sounded like science fiction, but, our experts concluded, it was in no way improbable that they could have pulled off such a trick, given the enormous spending and technical power of U.S. military air research.

Carney's weakness as a spy was his psychological state, which was far from robust. He was a homosexual and suffered from acute paranoia that his personal life might be used to discredit him in the army, where homosexuality was forbidden. In 1984, after returning to America, he asked for sanctuary in East Germany, claiming that his lover, who worked in the same field of communications, had been found dead in the bathtub with a plastic bag over his head and that this was the work of an unspecified spy service out to get him. We were worried that he was on the verge of confessing everything, and although we did not know whether to believe the bathtub story, we feared he might be under surveillance and was likely to be arrested if he tried to leave the States. How to extricate him from this vulnerable position? We decided to resort to a daring tactic that we used only in extremis but always with success: Carney was given false Cuban papers, which got him out of the United States to Havana. From there we flew him via Moscow to East Berlin.

Once he was with us, our main challenge was to make him as comfortable as possible. This was not easy, given the sleepy pace of life in the East and the relative dearth of consumer goods and excitement. But we were extremely anxious to prevent him from plunging into a depression and wandering into the U.S. embassy to tell his story. Carney was given a job monitoring English-language radio messages from the British and U.S. embassies and institutes in West Berlin and writing down details that might interest us. It was not high-grade intelligence work—I did not feel that he was stable or trustworthy enough for that—but at least it kept him in touch with his home country.

In 1989, with the end of East Germany approaching, his case officer and the head of the American section had to think fast about what to do with him. He was offered resettlement in South Africa at the Ministry of State Security's expense but turned this down. Neither did he like the idea of being packed off to Moscow. We could do little but offer him a flat and a subsistence package in Suhl, in the south of East Germany, where he would be less exposed. Early in 1990, Carney disappeared from Suhl. Some of our officers believed he had been kidnapped by the CIA. More likely they found him alone and depressed and managed to persuade him to come home. If his hunters promised leniency, they did not deliver it. Carney was sentenced later that year to thirty-eight years in prison by an American court.

In the cases of both Hall and Carney, there was no doubt that they had betrayed their country to the East. Another case that was not so clear-cut, however, was that of Jeffrey Schevitz, the last American to be tried for spying for East Germany. But it was never clear whom he was spying for—or, more precisely, whom he was spying for more. Schevitz arrived in West Berlin as a peace activist in 1976 and passed us information from the John F. Kennedy Free University Institute for American Studies, from his post as guest researcher at the Foreign Policy Society in Bonn and, later, from a nuclear research center in Karlsruhe where he worked from 1980 to 1994. Schevitz passed on information concerning West German efforts to weaken U.S. nonproliferation policy and on the COCOM (Coordinating Committee for East-West Trade Policy) regulations covering the export of high technology. Schevitz himself claimed that he had obtained the information through contacts with a former head of intelligence in Helmut Kohl's Chancellery. But Schevitz also claimed that his U.S. case officer was Shephard Stone, the director of the Aspen Institute in Berlin, a meeting place for eminent politicians, intellectuals, and journalists from East and West, and that he was working as a double agent for the United States from the beginning. Schevitz maintained that Stone had promised him the CIA would own up to his connections if he were ever arrested, but Stone died in 1990 without leaving any record about Schevitz. The court rejected his explanation but mysteriously gave him only a suspended sentence of eighteen months.

I do not know the full truth of the matter. My service knew that Shephard Stone was involved with the CIA, but not in the way that Schevitz implied. We were convinced that the conversations held at Aspen were frequently recorded and passed on to the CIA. But as for

Stone's relationship with Schevitz, we had no proof one way or the other.

Parallel and complementary to our Cold War espionage against America ran our interest in NATO's strategic planning. I have already recorded the work of Margarete, our female source at SHAPE (Supreme Headquarters, Allied Powers Europe) during the 1960s. We were also lucky enough to recruit and keep, for seventeen years, a much more valuable agent, a German NATO official named Rainer Rupp, who was aided by his British wife, Anne-Christine, in passing some of NATO's most sensitive secrets to the East.

Rupp was a true child of the 1960s. Thousands of young West Germans had marched in anger at the 1967 decision by Chancellor Kurt-Georg Kiesinger and Vice Chancellor Willy Brandt to receive and honor the Shah of Iran, whose antidemocratic regime was reinforced by the terror of his secret police. The demonstrations against the Shah's visit turned violent, and in the melee, Benno Ohnesorg, a student who belonged to the Evangelical Students Congregation, was shot dead. Sixty people were arrested and the student movement was born. Rupp, studying economics in Düsseldorf, joined the nationwide protests that followed. During one of these he marched next to an older man who invited him afterward for a beer and a bowl of goulash and some political debate. The man, who called himself Kurt, shared Rupp's concern that right-wing radicalism was on the rise. The two demonstrators ordered more beer and talked about the hypocrisy of the democratic West in receiving murderers like the Shah with pomp and honors, all because of Iran's oil.

Suddenly Kurt steered the conversation away from street protests. "Sometimes," he said to Rupp, "a single man can be worth a whole army." It was a bold, swift attempt to recruit Rupp, and it worked.

Rupp soon realized that his drinking partner was from East Germany—although whether he was aware that Kurt was an operational agent working in the Bonn area at the time, I am not sure. The twenty-two-year-old student, hostile to the order of the world around him, agreed immediately to meet Kurt in East Berlin. Two additional officers met Rupp and were delighted with the potential offered by his talents. He spoke English and French and had a sky-high IQ and a good grasp of political economy. One of our officers suggested a job at

NATO, now headquartered in Brussels. Rupp had no firm career plans in mind when he finished his studies, and he agreed. He left Düsseldorf University and enrolled for his final semester in Brussels, to make it easier to apply for a job there. He had brilliant grades, and after his graduation he was given a place as a researcher at the Institute for Applied Economics. From there it was easy for him to move to a job with NATO, writing analyses of the effect of the arms industry on national economies. Rupp passed all this material and his other observations of work and attitudes within NATO HQ via courier to us in East Berlin. We gave him the code name Topaz. His wife, whom he married while working at NATO, was a naïve, good-natured woman who did not seem to take on board the significance of the fact that they spent their honeymoon in East Berlin.

After the marriage Rainer moved up in the NATO hierarchy and was soon providing us with detailed information on the defense capabilities of all NATO member states. Until 1977, Anne-Christine, by now aware of the nature of her husband's mysterious trips to Amsterdam to meet his handler and his photographing of documents in the cellar, was actively helping him. She had moved to a job in NICSMA, the NATO Integrated Systems Management Agency, where she also smuggled out material. She stopped spying after the birth of her children. Rainer Rupp carried on until 1989, unwavering in his commitment and providing NATO gems such as the *Crisis Handbook*, the three-hundred-page *Armed Forces Plan*, the *Final Document on Preventive Measures*, and, in the early 1980s, details of the alliance's first-strike intentions. But Rupp's main value to us lay in the analytical awareness he brought to the reports and in his ability to summarize and put into accessible language what we called NATO Chinese—the blur of acronyms in which the organization works. Vladimir Kryuchkov, the KGB chief, was fascinated by Rupp's material and even asked to see the original English drafts so that he could claim to have read exactly what the NATO generals read.

I had hoped that this book would be written without including Rupp's story—that his work for us would never be revealed. But what were once our best-kept secrets are now laid open to scrutiny on the mortuary slab of a vanquished system. I believe, however, no further big agent will be revealed as a result of exposing the operations of East

German foreign intelligence. When the GDR fell, I saw no reason for Rupp to be exposed. His place within NATO in Brussels made him safer, so I thought, than our agents inside Germany. I was also confident that even if there was suspicion of a NATO source, no one would guess his real identity. As it turned out, his code name was betrayed by Dr. Heinz Busch, a military intelligence analyst in my service who started passing information to the BND in 1990. Busch knew the code name, although not Rupp's real identity. In 1994 Rupp was sentenced to twelve years in prison and fined 300,000 deutschmarks for betraying secrets that, the court maintained, would have had disastrous consequences in case of war. I disagree. I believe that his decision to share NATO's secrets with us contributed to the climate of détente. Without him, we would have known less about NATO and feared it more.

Like many others, I regard Rupp's conviction as patently illegal. A principle of both international law and the German constitution guarantees equality of citizens vis-à-vis the law. How can it be that after the peaceful unification of two states recognized under international law, the spies of one state go unpunished, are even given indemnifications if they were imprisoned, whereas those who worked for the other state are sentenced to long prison terms and hefty fines? For some spies the Cold War is finally over, for others it continues.

15

Cuba

I certainly would never voluntarily have risked going to America, but chance had it that my first contact with that continent took place in New York, a city I knew only from the poetry of Brecht, the music of Kurt Weill, and gangster films starring Peter Lorre. The year was 1965. Four years had passed since the fall of the Cuban dictator Batista, and at the Cubans' request I was flying to Havana to advise Fidel Castro's government on setting up an effective intelligence service. Later, Cuba would join Czechoslovakia in the first league of socialist countries skilled in the practice of espionage, but back then it was merely a beginner. I was told to advise on everything from the first principles of covert work to the creation of secure decoding and filing systems. Cuba's recent liberation inspired me and I set off in high spirits for this tiny socialist island adrift in a sea of capitalism. The usual route to Havana from East Berlin was via Prague with stopovers in Scotland or Canada. In my case, however, Mielke was adamant that I should not even land in a NATO country. "Who knows what they know about you and what would happen if something went wrong," he said darkly. Instead, I was to fly to Moscow and connect there with the Russians' regular nonstop flight to Havana.

With two officers I landed in Moscow on January 6, 1965, in the depths of a particularly harsh winter. The temperature had fallen well below zero Fahrenheit, and we shivered as we were hustled through Sheremyetevo airport and into cars waiting to take us for talks with the then KGB chief, Vladimir V. Semichastny, and his head of foreign intelligence, Aleksandr Sakharovsky. They briefed us on their links with the Cuban Interior Ministry and gave us information about the numbers and activities of the KGB liaison officers already stationed there.

That evening we set off again in a massive turboprop AN-124, the most powerful carrier in the Soviet Aeroflot fleet. The stewardess, Maria, without doubt a KGB employee, lavished attention on our small delegation. Most of the other passengers were Soviet naval officers or military experts traveling with their families to new posts in the outlying reaches of the Communist world. There was a sense of pioneering work. The only two other foreigners were Chinese, evidently diplomatic couriers. They sat directly in front of us with the handles of their leather bags wound tightly around their wrists. They watched the bags at their feet almost continuously, as if they feared that we were about to spring up and steal the diplomatic baggage of the People's Republic of China. The back of the plane was completely empty. The seats had been removed in order to lighten the plane and ensure, as we were comfortingly informed, that its fuel lasted as far as our destination, about eight thousand miles away.

We flew throughout the night and, as the sun rose, glimpsed the Canadian coast from our window. Several more hours passed, enough by my calculations for us to be approaching Cuba. The plane had already started descending. I was already shaving in preparation for our reception in Havana when I noticed that the sun was not where it was supposed to be. I returned to my seat as air turbulence caused the aircraft to shudder alarmingly, before suddenly plummeting downward. It was unnerving that there was no announcement that anything was out of the ordinary, and I could see the sea hurtling toward us. I had only seconds to wonder whether this is what it feels like when a plane crashes, but the next thing I knew we jolted onto a runway, and the brakes were screaming. I pressed my hot head to the window and saw a sign. It read, WELCOME TO JOHN F. KENNEDY AIRPORT.

We all sat in stunned silence, mentally running through the same obvious questions. What had happened? Had we run out of fuel? Had there been a near accident? Had the Soviet pilot suddenly decided that his future lay in the Free World? I especially wondered what the hell were we, emissaries of an Eastern bloc secret service bound for our lone ally on the other side of a tense world, supposed to do now that we had been catapulted into America, the very heart of enemy territory.

As the engines whirred to a halt, a convoy of police cars raced to surround the plane. Sirens screamed. "Shit," breathed my neighbor. We braced ourselves for the storming of the plane. But nothing happened. For several hours we sat in the plane on the tarmac, bewildered and feverishly running through the possible scenarios. None of them afforded much comfort. The three of us in our delegation had GDR diplomatic passports but East Germany was not yet recognized by the United States or the United Nations, so we did not even have a representative to turn to in the States. I carried a small document case whose contents indicated our real professions. I quietly shoved it under the mattress of a child's pram that, thanks to Aeroflot's casual luggage restrictions, stood in the aisle near me.

By now the aircraft was surrounded by photographers and journalists. I noticed that one actually had his press pass sticking in the band of his fedora like a reporter in *The Front Page.* They were arguing with the U.S. security men to let them aboard the plane. I prayed that the guards would turn them down, dreading the reaction back in East Berlin when my photograph—my face was still unknown in the West—turned up for all to see, and on the front page of the *New York Times,* no less. This was, I would later discover, the first time since the Cuba crisis in 1962 that a Soviet plane or ship had landed in America. The unheralded arrival of our airliner was nothing short of a sensation. Through the window I could see the photographers urging us to wave. I pulled down the shade. The arrival of the press restored our sense of humor, the best companion in such a situation. We started to mime Mielke's imagined responses when he discovered that his foreign intelligence chief and two other senior intelligence officers, armed with information and technical help for America's enemy ninety miles offshore, were stranded on the tarmac of JFK Airport. We imagined what he would say to Moscow: "Comrades, I sent them with you to ensure the absolute security of their mission. Now I hear that they have not only been exposed to the enemy, they have been flown directly into his hands."

Behind the hangars I could see the highway throbbing with the morning traffic. My mind wandered down hitherto unexplored avenues of speculation. What would it be like to arrive here as a normal passenger? Could I simply just stroll through Arrivals, show my diplomatic passport, and call up, say, George Fischer? Or Leonhard Mins, another Communist exile who had been my parents' close friend during our days behind the Arbat? He had been the channel through which my father was able to communicate with us during his internment in France. My half brother Lukas, the product of my father's first marriage, must also live somewhere near New York, if I remembered correctly. I felt strangely free. It was a rare, fleeting moment of normality in a life that usually was lived in far more constrained circumstances owing to a mixture of history, personal fate, and my own convictions.

Reality intruded soon enough. I surveyed the potential intelligence implications of my unexpected presence on American soil. What could the Americans accuse me of if they were to identify me? Would it suffice to detain or even try me here? At that time we were in the process of training some of our most promising agents to be infiltrated into America as illegals with false identities. Fortunately, none had yet been posted to the States because the infiltration program had been interrupted by a defection from the HVA department that monitored the activities of American institutions in the Western sector of Berlin. One of those arrested in the wake of this defection was an interpreter from the U.S. military mission in Berlin who had supplied us with secret information about Washington's policy toward both parts of divided Germany. It came from transcripts taken during the visits of Eleanor Lansing Dulles, the sister of John Foster Dulles and a senior American State Department official with special responsibility for policy on Berlin. For passing to us exhaustive documentation of this talkative lady's views, our informant had been given a substantial sentence for treason. What if I were caught and identified as the official responsible for this operation?

This train of thought was interrupted by a nudge from my colleague. He pointed at the Chinese in front of us. The two diplomatic couriers had opened their hand baggage and were steadily devouring the bundles of paper within. We were touched by their devotion to duty. Chewing and swallowing were the only weapons they possessed against the class enemy. But the sheaves of documents were thick and they had no water to help digest this unappetizing fare. Should we, in the name of proletarian internationalism, offer to help? We briefly conferred and decided with some relief that that might constitute an unwarranted intervention in Chinese affairs with unforeseeable consequences for relations between our two countries.

By now the temperature in the cabin had dropped. The only ventilation came from fresh, cold air being drawn into the cabin from outside. The thermometer sank well below freezing. Dressed for the tropics of Cuba, the passengers shivered. More unpleasant hours passed before the Soviet consul finally appeared with flasks of hot tea. He could not tell us much. "Moscow is negotiating with Washington," he repeated. He explained that we were on the ground because the plane had run short of fuel. In the wake of the Cuban missile crisis in 1961, all landing and refueling agreements for Soviet-bloc aircraft flying to Cuba had been suspended as part of the program of sanctions against Fidel Castro. A total of eighteen hours passed before the pretty KGB stewardess whispered to me that Washington was going to let the plane refuel and leave, albeit with two Air Force officers on board as observers, doubtless with instructions to have a good look at the passengers.

I tried to pass on the good news to the Chinese but only succeeded in alarming them further. By now, their digestive capacity was exhausted and they had begun to take turns using the toilet for their orgy of destruction. Before the door closed, I could see one of them at the wash basin, frantically rubbing the hard Soviet soap across silk paper into which secret messages must have been encoded. Perhaps they were instructions for the Latin American guerrilla groups, many of whom took their orders directly from Chairman Mao. At any rate, these instructions would reach their destination only verbally. Every five minutes the toilet flushed noisily. We took off again near midnight. That was my first stay on the North American continent. I had not seen much of it except for a tempting piece of the New York skyline and the highway next to the airport.

It was still dark when we finally saw the more propitious sign welcoming us to José Martí Airport in Havana. The adventure was not yet over, however. The Cubans had not been informed of the presence of two American officers on board and there was another lengthy delay during which a decision was taken on whether any of us would be allowed to disembark or whether we should all be flown back to Moscow. Such were the delights of international air travel during the Cold War.

Eventually, Cuban security officers managed to extricate our delegation. The rest of the passengers had to wait. We raced through the night in a roomy Buick. I was enchanted by the old American cars, driven with wild abandon along the stony streets of the capital. We were brought by our driver, Enrico, to a spacious white villa and informed by Umberto, the security man who was to be our minder-clad untropically in dark suit, white shirt, and tie-that the home had belonged to a millionaire before the Revolution. "Before the Revolution" was a phrase we heard dozens of times a day and always contrasted with the advantages that had come with Castro's socialist leadership. Coming from a country that had had communism imposed on it by the Red Army in the wake of the Nazi defeat, I felt a swell of warmth and pride in these people who had taken their fate into their own hands and made their own revolution. Umberto introduced the driver, Enrico, as the best pistolero in all Cuba. We need have no fears, said Umberto earnestly, about our safety on the island.

Although we were drooping with fatigue, we could not resist taking a turn in the gardens. The night air had a sweet heaviness about it that was alien and yet beguiling to me. We marveled at the lush vegetation, the velvet darkness of the sky, and the loud chirping of the cicadas. "Imagine," said the youngest of our team, "socialism, real socialism-and in a place like this!" That was the nearest thing he could imagine to heaven on earth. I was not quite so impressionable, but nonetheless uplifted by the thought that this beautiful, once-oppressed island had managed to find its own way to liberation.

The day after our arrival, like all official visitors we were taken to see the statue of José Martí, the father of Cuban nationalism-and also to be shown the U.S. warships anchored off the coast, a powerful reminder that the country was under constant enemy surveillance. The uprising against the Batista regime was still the stuff of daily recollection, the bullet holes in the walls still fresh. Unlike the predictable receptions I had endured in Moscow and other socialist countries, the Cubans had a disarming way of encouraging foreigners to enter their realm of experience. We were instructed to put on fatigues and taken to Colorado Beach in Oriente province where Castro and his eighty-two followers landed in 1956, in the Granma after their passage from Mexico, to start the fight for Cuba's liberation. We visited the Bay of Pigs and were proudly shown the twisted remains of an American B–52 bomber.

I do not need to rehearse here the full incompetence of the CIA's operations in Cuba. Suffice it to say that we were amazed that an organization that had access to the West's top strategic analysts could make such a clumsy mess of an intervention as they did of the exiles' disastrous invasion of Cuba. Moral relativism is always unappealing, but when American journalists ask me in accusing tones about my service's involvement with terrorists in liberation struggles, I have difficulty suppressing the counterquestion as to whether American-backed campaigns of sabotage and arson in Cuba reflect a vision of civil society.

My intelligence partner in Cuba, Manuel Pineiro, came from the ranks of the barbudos, the bearded ones who survived Castro's march through the Sierra Maestra and the bitter battles in the mountains before Havana was taken. Raul Castro, Fidel's brother and second-in-command in the politburo, and Ramiro Valdez, then interior minister, were intent on building up a security service that would give them timely, accurate warnings of American intentions toward the island. Valdez, like many others in the Cuban leadership, struck me as less of a statesman than an adventurous operative always ready to have a go. On our journeys he would order the driver and bodyguard into the backseat of his Cadillac, beckon me into the front, and set off at a hundred miles an hour. I would feign terror and cry out "Patria o muerte"- the revolutionary slogan, "My country or death." He loved this pantomime and would drive even faster, until my fear was real. His passion was baseball and he insisted that we see his team play. When their performance failed to satisfy him, he stormed onto the field, sent off the player he most disapproved of, and took his place on the team for the rest of the afternoon.

Valdez's professional interest was in the gathering and analysis of political and military information. But, embarrassing for me, he also had excessive expectations of the technical help that we could offer. On his desk lay piles of purloined Western catalogues showing the latest designs in bugging and remote-control devices, supersensitive micro-phones that could pick up sound in the open air across great distances or record conversations through walls, miniature receivers and radio transmitters, miniweaponry and old but impracticable favorites like poison-spitting pens and knives hidden in the heels of shoes. It was a boyish view of intelligence work, an armory out of his imagination and that had precious little value in determining the actions of a powerful enemy whose technological capacity would always be immeasurably greater than anything Cuba could produce. I tried to explain that a small country must find other ways to win the intelligence war and that in any case, the Soviet Union and not the GDR was responsible for supplying Havana with technical expertise. As our conversation turned in circles, his disappointment in me as a traveling salesman of espi-onage equipment grew increasingly obvious.

The role of Soviet advisers was kept entirely secret in Cuba in the early years. Valdez never mentioned them and seemed discomfited by my suggestion that he approach them for material help. Unlike the East Germans, who routinely invited Soviet intelligence men to social events and stressed cooperation, the Cubans kept their helpers out of sight, perhaps to strengthen popular support for Castro by implying that he ran everything. So seriously did the Cubans take this secrecy that when I wanted to meet with a KGB man whose name had been given to me in Moscow, the Cubans tried hard to prevent me. In the end I had to shake off a persistent Cuban tail by diverting his attention and suddenly drop-ping from his sight to make my own way to the Soviet embassy. Later on relations became less strained. A further reason for the Cuban distance toward the Soviets was the distrust sown by the Cuban missile crisis. Valdez spoke bitterly about Khrushchev's decision to withdraw nuclear missiles from Cuba as part of the deal to resolve the crisis. "When it comes down to it," he said, "the superpowers will look after their own interests. We small ones should stick together."

The Cuban Communist Party was still in its infancy in those days, so residual political divisions could not be hidden. Traveling around the island, I became aware of the many kinds of resentments that still lingered toward Castro and his bearded ones among the ranks of the original Communist Party and the workers' movements. Older Com-munists tended to distrust Castro's personality cult and felt that he needed more support and a wider social base than his ministerial team could provide. When I returned to Havana and met up with Ramiro Valdez or Raul Castro, it was immediately clear to me that the substance of my conversations in the provinces had been reported back. This was an amusing feeling for a spymaster who spends most of his working life collating and analyzing just such reports about others. But the Cubans were so direct and unashamed about this practice that it would have seemed churlish to complain. At one point Valdez referred outright to a question I had posed in the countryside about the internal stability and coherence of Castro's government, which he then proceeded to answer in glowing detail.

We could not resist using the ever-open ears of our companions to play a small trick on our hosts. One evening I returned late to our villa to find my colleagues waiting with a bunch of flowers and a bottle of vodka that they had purloined during our stopover in Moscow. They had remembered my birthday, which I had forgotten in the excitement of the trip. Anyway, I had no desire to indulge in the full Cuban birthday protocol, which would doubtless consist of hour-long speeches about my health and happiness. So we had a few tots of vodka by ourselves and went to bed. The next day, Umberto had done his detective work and insistently asked about the cause of the nocturnal celebration. With suitable solemnity I told him that we had been marking the successful launch of the first East German *Sputnik*. Of course there was only one *Sputnik*, and that had been launched by the Soviets a few years earlier. But Umberto swallowed the story whole, fetched another bottle and glasses, and delivered a weighty speech about the East German space project and how it marked—exactly how was left unclear— a great advance in Cuban–East German relations.

But it was another question that really puzzled him: How had we managed to receive the momentous news without his knowing about it? Swearing him to absolute secrecy, I told him that the news of the *Sputnik* launch had reached us via a special minitransmitter, small enough to fit into a pocket and strong enough to receive signals from East Berlin. I named this fictitious device the "Gogofon" and told the gullible Umberto that its very existence was a state secret of the highest order, that I possessed the only one in the world, and that it was still in the test phase. Umberto swore on his life not to tell a soul.

He managed to keep his word for a full day. The next night, at a dinner given by the interior minister, we were pressed on all sides to give details on anything new at home in East Germany. I replied that we were quite cut off from home in Cuba. There was a short pregnant pause and then Commandante Pineiro burst out, "But what about the Gogofon?" I had to admit to the company that we had played a joke on our minder, after which poor Umberto was known simply as Gogofon.

My contacts with Pineiro deepened over the years. Despite its ama-teurish beginnings, Cuban foreign intelligence developed quickly and well. My early relationship with Castro's leadership meant that I was occasionally able to use the island when I needed to hide someone. In return I would sometimes procure for Pineiro the listening, decoding, and special photography devices he desired. After the murder of Sal-vador Allende in Chile in 1973 and the campaign of terror against the Left under the rule of General Augusto Pinochet, we were able to use Cuba as an escape route for Chilean refugees. Erich Honecker's daughter was married to a Chilean, so East Germany exerted itself in helping the opposition there. Honecker liked the idea of East Ger-many offering humanitarian aid to those in need. Aiding Chile and other Latin American countries where the Left was being purged by military and far-right governments also proved popular with young people in the East. It is not an exaggeration to say that these cam-paigns in the 1970s strengthened East Germany by giving the belea-guered country a patina of respectability.

Pineiro also told me of his last conversations with the Argentinian Che Guevara before that one-man guerrilla band withdrew from Cuba, bitterly disappointed by the Soviet decision to end the Cuban crisis by withdrawing its missiles. "Che thought he could repeat Cuba elsewhere and take the pressure off us," said Pineiro. "But Cuba was unique, and I think we all knew that even before he went." When Guevara was killed in Bolivia in 1967, a young German woman, Tamara Bunke, died with him. Her parents had emigrated from Germany to Argentina when she was a child. An interpreter who had accompanied an East German youth delegation to Havana, she had remained without permission, had fallen in love with Che, and had run off with him on his last rebellion. This combination of romance and revolution made her a popular idol for East German teenagers. After her death my deputy reminded me of a long-forgotten encounter on our first visit to Havana. He had stopped to exchange a few words with a good-looking young woman in uniform at the entrance to the Cuban Interior Ministry. It had been Tamara. Shortly afterward she disappeared with Che. I take it that at the time of my visit Pineiro was helping them prepare their expedition to Bolivia, but Che Guevara was never mentioned to me during my visit to Havana. The Cubans were already observing the first, most important, rule of successful intelligence work: No one must know anything he does not explicitly need to know.

In contrast to Pineiro and Valdez, I found Raul Castro to be a far more steady, well-educated, and statesmanlike figure. Unlike his more emotional colleagues, he took a cool strategic view of Cuba's situation. I never heard anything from him hinting at distance from or disappointment in the Soviet Union. He was the only one there who turned up for appointments on time, a trait highly unusual in Cubans. His friends teased him for his punctuality and called him The Prussian. He had busied himself with Marxist theories and military theory during his exile in Mexico and was keen to show visitors that despite Cuba's geographical distance from the Soviet Union and Eastern Europe, he was versed in the ideological debates of communism and in military techniques.

In 1985 I visited Managua, Nicaragua, coming from Cuba as a guest of Thomas Borge, the interior minister. We celebrated six years of the Sandinista Revolution and I was impressed by the way the Nicaraguans had managed to combine liberation theology, humanism, and Marxist theories into a coherent government program. I was always moved by the revolutionary energy of Cubans and Nicaraguans who had given so much to change their countries. There was—at that time at least—little of the complaints and blame of others for misfortunes that I so often heard at home. I envied those countries that had made their revolutions themselves, and in my heart of hearts I knew that the countries of Eastern Europe would always resent the Soviet postwar occupation, which forced them to adopt socialist governments.

Return visits by the Cubans to East Berlin were always fraught with anxiety from the point of view of security. Fidel Castro loved foreign travel, and as the burden of his responsibilities at home grew, he was at his most relaxed on visits to friendly countries far from home. Of course, relaxation for the high-spirited Cubans was rather different from the way we solid northern Europeans envisaged it. Staff of the personal-security department responsible for protecting Castro and his delegation during visits to us blanched at the memories of all-night singing and drinking sessions and the Cuban tendency to pick up complete strangers—usually pretty Cuban women studying in East Berlin—and invite them back to their residences to party. I heard that Fidel, frustrated by the attempts of his East German minders to get him to bed early, climbed out of his room and down a drainpipe to rejoin the festivities elsewhere. After that it was considered best to find some way of entertaining our visitors more satisfactorily. Someone hit on the idea of inviting the girls from the state television ballet company to flirt and dance with the Cubans into the night, which kept them out of trouble. But inconvenience aside, whenever I heard about the Cubans' lust for life and experience it made our existence seem drab, governed as it was by the dual German imperatives of duty and hard work.

●

We cooperated far less with Nicaragua than with Cuba. The Cubans would complain bitterly to us that Managua leaked like a sieve. In the early days after Nicaragua's revolution, having taken part in the armed struggle was considered proof enough of loyalty. Poor vetting in the security services was one reason the American-backed contras were able to make such headway. We tried to seek out partners there among the most stable ranks of the security services. Perhaps aware of their sloppy reputation, they were obsessively secretive in dealing with us and insisted on holding talks in the open air rather than the Interior Ministry headquarters.

Our main contribution to Nicaraguan security was the training of security guards for the president and ministers. This became quite a cottage industry for the East German Ministry of State Security. Our reputation for personal security was high, and country after country in Latin America and Africa requested our experts to train their guards. We generally obliged, relieved to find a way of helping needy allies without having to commit ourselves to major involvement in their internal security operations. We also supplied a small amount of technical backup such as specialized photo developing and enlarging equipment. In contrast to the material we supplied to African countries, these contributions were always beautifully cared for and proudly displayed on return visits.

It was for Chile that we exerted ourselves most. At the time of the September 1973 coup d'etat against Salvador Allende, our security services were not represented in Santiago at all. I had closed down our minimal presence of two operatives two years before, although we had not stayed completely out of intelligence. Earlier that year, my service had warned Allende and Luis Corvalan, the Communist Party leader, of an impending military coup, which they disregarded because they believed Chile's armed forces were too deeply rooted in the tradition of civilian control to meddle in politics. Our warning was based on information from West German intelligence, which was well represented in Chile and fully aware of the insurgents' intentions, and the CIA's.

At the height of the fighting in Santiago some of the leadership of the Unidad Popular sought asylum in the East German embassy. The most prominent among them was Carlos Altamirano, general secretary of the Socialist Party. East Berlin had broken off diplomatic relations with Santiago, which meant that formally we could do nothing to help. But Erich Honecker, anxious at this time to expand East Germany's bilateral ties and our influence, was determined to help the Socialists escape. His daughter was married to a fellow activist of Altamirano's, so the fate of the harried Socialists was of emotional as well as strategic importance to him.

We set in train one of the most complicated rescue missions we had ever conducted. A team of our best officers was dispatched at top speed from East Berlin to check out the permeability of border controls at Chilean airports, at the port at Valparaiso, and at the road crossings to Argentina. From Argentina, we improvised a remarkable operation. The prisoners were smuggled out of the country in cars with hiding places constructed in much the same way that escapees from the GDR were secreted in cars to get past the Wall. When the controls suddenly tightened and this became too risky, we diverted cargo ships to Valparaiso and smuggled some of the prisoners aboard in jute sacks with the cargos of fruit and canned fish. It took nearly two months to smuggle Altamirano out of Chile—through Argentina to Cuba and on to East Berlin.

Our hard work in Chile did not go unnoticed by American intelligence. Negotiating through the Americans, Wolfgang Vogel was able to exchange Corvalan for Vladimir Bukovsky, a dissident writer and intellectual held by the Soviets. For Cuba, the lesson of Allende's Chile was a bitter one. Raul Castro told me that the military coup there had so unnerved the leadership in Havana that the civil defense program was expanded and he and Fidel stopped traveling together or appearing on the same public podiums.

When I think about Cuba today, it is with a feeling of regret and sadness for the crumbling of the hopes it once embodied. It was already a sobering experience to revisit Cuba in 1985, twenty years after I had first set foot there. Constant shortages and economic failure left Cubans everywhere in a state of evident disillusionment. Already, a debilitating sense of being left alone and vulnerable had set in. "Who will help us now if the Americans invade?" asked one senior security official bitterly. It was true. Moscow had the heavy burden of Afghanistan. Mikhail Gorbachev's opening to the West meant that there could be little real assistance for Cuba. As my plane approached Havana—this time without an unscheduled stop in New York—I was haunted by a sense of discomfort and disappointment. The practice of communism seemed to be moving further and further away from the ideas I had embraced in my youth and with which I had returned to Germany in 1945. There was a yawning gap between the wishful thinking of the politicians—Castro included—and the reality experienced by the population, day in and day out. Gorbachev's rise to power did provide a glimmer of hope, and I mused that perhaps this change in Moscow would help Cuba and Nicaragua find new ways of dealing with their unenviable geopolitical situation vis-à-vis America.

What I failed to see was that Gorbachev's new course would completely isolate Cuba and in Nicaragua lead to the defeat of the Sandinistas. Socialist countries in Latin America were effectively cut adrift from Moscow in security terms, and for the first time the Kremlin made it clear it accepted and would respect America's sphere of influence. At the time of Gorbachev's ascent, I thought this would produce a liberalization and an increase in personal freedom that would benefit Cuban socialism. How wrong I was.

My last visit to Cuba was in the spring of 1989, by which time I was swamped by our own problems in Germany, many of which were shared by Cuba. Both our countries had rejected Gorbachev's political openness and economic reform—the twin policies of glasnost and perestroika. I was filled with foreboding by the sight of long lines in front of shops with little to sell and outside foreign embassies with even fewer visas to offer. I could not imagine how Castro's administration could survive this. It is one of history's more piquant ironies that my own state, deemed by analysts East and West to be far more stable than Cuba, collapsed a few months later. Erich Honecker, who had once offered East German help to the vanquished socialists of Chile, ended his life in exile in that country on May 26, 1994, having been denied long-term asylum by Moscow.

All around me I have seen the defeat of socialist idealism. Allende's democratic socialism was bloodily defeated in Chile. The pluralistic structures and innovative practices that had made Cuba in the years after the Revolution appear so refreshing to me have also crumbled, leaving an authoritarian regime. I watch with interest and some pain Castro's attempts to liberalize and remotivate Cuba from within, without even the symbolic help of the Soviet Union. He must feel like the loneliest man in the world. In this matter I am of the same opinion as Günter Grass, the most significant living German writer, who wrote, "I have always been an opponent of the doctrinaire system in Cuba. But when I see today that it is nearing its end without any alternative, at least no other than a Batista, then I am for Castro."

16

The End of
the Old Order

The establishment of the independent trade union Solidarity in Poland under the leadership of Lech Walesa in 1980 sent shock waves through the Eastern bloc. They were particularly keenly felt by Poland's immediate neighbor, the GDR; it was feared that the upheavals could spread across the border. The leading role of the unions in the Polish uprising was especially perturbing to the Communist leadership because the strikes fatally undermined the Party's claim to represent all working people.

The HVA had provided good intelligence in the late 1970s about the spread of dissatisfaction in Poland. We had our own sources of information in Walesa's circles and that of the leading intellectual, Adam Michnik. But the relations between the secret services in Warsaw and East Berlin had never been easy, and the Polish authorities would not take our warnings of unrest seriously.

With the future looking threatening, we formed special working groups on Poland inside our ministry in Berlin and in provincial headquarters near the GDR's border with Poland. For my foreign intelligence service, the top priority was discovering the intentions of Western governments, political parties, secret services, and private organizations such as foreign labor unions supporting Solidarity. Our Polish counterparts asked us to keep tabs on Polish émigré organizations, especially at Radio Free Europe in Munich and the magazine *Kultura* in Paris. During the most intense period of unrest we also gathered information inside Poland itself with the agreement of the Polish Interior Ministry. We worked out active measures to influence public opinion in Poland and also learned what the émigré section of West German intelligence in Poland was doing so we could counter it.

But neither our warnings nor Poland's own internal monitoring made a difference. Solidarity was a truly revolutionary organization that overturned the conventional wisdom of Eastern European dissidents that economic and social stability must be the basis for reform. By contrast, the striking workers sought confrontation with the Communist state on all fronts and demonstrated that the latter lacked the self-confidence to fight back. The imposition of martial law by General Wojciech Jaruzelski in December 1981 only slowed down a process that had its own dynamic.

By 1981, I was already starting to think about retirement. Not only had I achieved most things I had set out to do in my professional life, but the progress promised by the Basic Treaty of 1972 had ground to a halt, and Erich Honecker had become just another elderly leader clinging to power. There was some talk of my seeking election to the Central Committee and possibly moving up to the politburo, but political preferment in these conditions was not what I wanted. Anyway, Mielke was determined to block me. I said nothing but noted in my diary:

> Mielke does not understand that that is no longer what I want. For one, it would mean another tie and that would curb my personal choices. To choose this route would be a waste of my energies, since our elected powers have no real influence. Why bother?

I had started to read more widely than ever before, opening my mind to new ideas and critiques of our system, which we called "real existing socialism." One of the most influential books was Peter Weiss's *The Aesthetics of Resistance*, which combined a treatment of the causes and effects of Stalinism with personal recollections and an eloquent narrative. I also spent hours talking to my brother, Koni, about his idea for a film or book called *The Troika*. He had decided to tell the story of his boyhood friendship in Moscow with Lothar Wloch, the son of a prominent German Communist family, and Victor and George Fischer.* Thirty years after the war, the four met again in the United States. Koni had fought in the Red Army and had become a respected filmmaker and head of the Academy of Arts in East Germany. Lothar had returned to Germany after his father became a victim of one of Stalin's purges, and the collapse of the 1939 pact with Hitler opened the way for his service in the Luftwaffe against the Soviet Union. After the war he settled in West Berlin to become a successful entrepreneur in the building trades. George Fischer became a captain in the U.S. Army, and I suspected that he might have links to American intelligence. Despite their very different lives and beliefs, the troika found that the human spark of their early friendship had survived the Cold War.

By 1980, Koni was preparing to make the film, but he was already suffering from cancer. He died in March 1982, and it was left to me to complete my brother's work. Every day I carried his notes and outline to my office, scribbled my own comments, and planned research. It soon seemed clear to me that this work was of more lasting value than simply continuing to run an effective espionage service. The excitement that I used to feel when recruiting new agents and plotting operations now came only when I worked on the book.

Amazing, [I wrote in my diary], how alive Koni now seems to me again. . . . Many people seem to expect me quite naturally to take up where he left off. There are many hopes and human contacts to be kept alive. It seems so important to so many people who knew him. For the first time in my life, I am aware that the clock is ticking. It is time to get on with things.

Early in 1983, I received the most depressing insight yet into the state of the Warsaw Pact. Our chief mole in NATO, Rainer Rupp, had managed to secure for us a microfilmed copy of NATO's East-West

---

*My brother intended to combine Victor and George into one composite character, thus making for a threesome, the meaning of the title *The Troika*.

study of the balance of global power. It was a masterful analysis of the weaknesses of the Soviet system and its decline in military efficiency and economic power. Reading this document, I knew that the West's analysis of the East bloc's malaise was accurate and I also knew that there was no hope that the "concrete heads"—as our elderly leaders were mockingly called by their critics—would make any attempt to change things. We seemed to be locked into a precipitous spiral of decline. All of this sapped my professional morale and my energies, leaving me deflated and with increased misgivings.

I prepared myself to present Mielke with the document, accompanied by an analytical commentary from our side. From there, it would be handed on to Viktor Chebrikov, the head of the KGB in Moscow, and to General Secretary Konstantin Chernenko. The tone of our "commentary" would have to be just right, and I labored with my brightest young team to ensure that it would neither veil the bleak picture presented by the NATO study nor express any high-handed Schadenfreude about the miserable portrayal of the Soviet Union.

During our trip to Moscow in February 1983, I took the opportunity of telling Mielke that I was already thinking about the timing of my retirement. I had reached sixty, Mielke was seventy-five. It was time for both of us to start thinking about our successors. He waved his hand dismissively. I pressed the point, and after some hesitation, he agreed in principle to my retirement but loftily added that he would decide on the timing. He had heard about my plans to carry on Koni's work on *The Troika* and sneered, "Intelligence chiefs don't make films." But the subject had at least been broached.

The political and social dissatisfactions spreading throughout our country had permeated the thick walls of the Ministry of State Security. In our private sauna, where senior officers felt that they could speak more openly than elsewhere, two senior foreign office officials had told me of their frustration with the aging and unresponsive leadership in Moscow and East Berlin. My interlocutors in the sauna confided that all was not well between East Germany and Moscow. Chernenko distrusted Honecker's approaches to Helmut Kohl and feared that the West Germans were trying to foster a pan-Germanic national identity that would supersede socialist solidarity. In a meeting in Moscow in 1984 he warned Honecker that the GDR would end up "the ultimate victim of all this." "You ought to remember," he added, "that the development of relations between East and West Germany must always respect the security interests of the Soviet Union first and foremost."

This warning was evidently intended to squelch Honecker's ambition to make an official visit to Bonn. The meeting, my two sources in the sauna said, had broken up in a frosty atmosphere. Honecker, enraged at his humiliation, had indulged in a rare show of temper once he was alone again with his delegation and mocked Chernenko's schoolmasterly act. When he returned to East Berlin, Honecker poured out his frustrations to Mielke and declared that, whatever Moscow's objections, he was determined to find a way to visit Bonn. The Soviet press meanwhile began a campaign attacking Honecker.

Because of my fluency in Russian and my connections in Moscow, I was asked to intervene and called Chebrikov. He curtly rebuffed me with a reminder that such things were matters for the Party, not the secret service.

The impasse over Honecker's desire to visit Bonn dominated all other questions with Moscow. I had never known a period when things were so strained. It took months of delicate diplomacy even to arrange a direct telephone call between Honecker and Chernenko, since neither wanted to be seen to be ready to compromise. Through telephone surveillance, we picked up a fragment of conversation between Klaus Bölling, the press spokesman of the Bonn government, and another senior West German official discussing the tug-of-war between Moscow and East Berlin. "This is turning into a really big deal," Bölling observed, "It's more exciting than *Dallas* and *Dynasty* put together!"

An August 1984 summit between Honecker and Chernenko lasted only one day and ended in failure. Our general secretary found himself in the same position as millions of his citizens: prevented from visiting the West. He was obliged to execute an abrupt about-face vis-à-vis the West, which he promptly did by declaring that the "broader meteorological climate" was not conducive to an East-West German summit and the summit must be suspended. Through clenched teeth he quietly told his aides, " 'suspended' does not mean 'canceled.' "

Honecker felt he had been left in the lurch by the Soviet Union, economically as well as diplomatically, because Moscow was steadily reducing the amount of oil it exported to East Germany at below-market prices. "We will have to rely on ourselves," he would say, refusing to acknowledge that East Germany had neither the wealth nor the power to act alone. He became obsessed by annoying Moscow with such meaningless gestures as improving relations with China.

By this time, thinking people in the GDR and in Moscow, too, sensed changes on the way, for the country, for the East bloc, and personal changes, too. Around this time I met with Hans Modrow, the head of the Communist Party in the Dresden region, a soft-spoken, gray-haired man with thoughtful features and a pleasant manner. Quite unlike many other more bumptious and unreflective senior Communists, he lived simply in a three-room apartment, drove an ordinary car, and never made use of the grand privileges enjoyed by Party bosses. He was also noted for his plain speaking, an art rarely practiced in a party where the norm was to produce cosmetic versions of the truth. "I am not paid my salary to write doctored reports," he told me. It was clear that I had a soulmate in my frustrations.

We spoke about Manfred von Ardenne, an eminent physicist from an aristocratic family who had built up his own institute high on a hill outside Berlin. A rare example of someone who had managed to slip the leash and work independently, he got away with it because his results far outranked anything delivered by the state. Von Ardenne, already over eighty years old by this time, had strong views on the country and the whole Eastern bloc. He feared we had fallen irreversibly behind the West in the scientific and technological race and that this would finally destroy us.

Modrow was only a regional Party secretary and had no obvious prospect of entering the politburo. It was clear that outside of the Central Committee I could have no direct influence on the Party's course under Honecker, and von Ardenne was too old and too unenthusiastic about the GDR's internal political struggles to do more than fight in his corner on behalf of scientific research. So our hopes for necessary changes came to rest on Modrow.

Our meetings eventually led to outlandish reports that we, later called the reformers inside the Party, were plotting to make Modrow leader and impose Soviet-style reforms in East Germany. The truth is, alas, more modest. When Mikhail Gorbachev succeeded Chernenko in March 1985, Modrow and I both saw this as a remarkable and welcome change. I wrote in my diary:

> Now at last, after all the old and ill leaders in the Kremlin, a new general secretary and new hope. It looks like a breakthrough. Until now, we have done most harm to ourselves. No enemy could have achieved what we did in terms of incompetence, ignorance, self-aggrandizement, and the way we have torn our own roots out of the thoughts and feelings of ordinary people.

After that, Modrow and I met about twice a year for talks, but I made no attempt to push him to power. Had I done so, I would be proud to say so now. The bitter truth is that both he and I were too slow in making our desperation clear. The fact that neither of us disguised our dissatisfaction among friends and trusted colleagues does not excuse us from not having worked actively to reform the system. Like many other, less influential people, we waited in vain for a redeemer to emerge as a successor to Honecker from within the system and set a new course.

●

I had another, entirely personal reason for my desire to quit. My second marriage was in trouble. I had fallen in love with another woman. I had previously met Andrea briefly on a visit to Karl-Marx-Stadt, my second wife, Christa's, hometown, and then again when she and her husband visited our dacha in 1985. As a young woman, she had spent four months in jail for attempting to flee the country. Hearing her story years later was a grim reminder for me of the internal repression practiced in my country. I considered my own work in foreign intelligence to be a separate and more defensible sphere of activity, but I could not help but be ashamed at the brutal tactics against internal opposition and those whose only desire was to leave the country.

Early in 1986, I went to Mielke and told him what had happened. An old-fashioned puritan in sexual mores, he was incensed. When he calmed down, he tried to persuade me to remain married for the sake of appearances and said that we could arrange for Andrea to be installed in East Berlin so that I could see her whenever I chose. He was not a man with much insight in matters of the heart. His great concern was security. My wife had been employed by the Ministry of State Security in Karl-Marx-Stadt and she understood a lot about my work. He was terrified that, embittered, she would leak stories about me and my operations to the West.

I refused this offer and insisted on marrying Andrea. Mielke was furious. I learned from colleagues that he had ordered my telephones tapped. I was now experiencing the same discomfort as ordinary East Germans who were suspected in some way by the state. My ex-wife too was kept under constant surveillance, lest she make contact with our enemies. She managed nonetheless to slip the leash and, during a holiday in Bulgaria, struck up a relationship with a West German businessman whom Mielke was sure had been sent to lure her into a Romeo trap by the intelligence services. I faced the unpleasant irony of seeing my own Romeo tactic used against my ex-wife. For a while I braced myself for the shock of seeing her picture and the details of our life together in a West German tabloid. In the end, after some financial and job inducements from the Ministry of State Security (and perhaps suspecting, with some justification, that she was being lured into a honeytrap by the West German secret services), she opted to stay in the East.

Mielke finally agreed to my retirement in the spring of 1986, after the man I had groomed as my successor, Werner Grossmann, was ready to take over. My departure would represent a major change in our intelligence service after nearly thirty years, and we were anxious for it to occur as smoothly and as naturally as possible. I negotiated a separation package with Mielke, including a new Berlin apartment, where I reside to this day, overlooking the River Spree. For all the privileges the nomenklatura enjoyed under our system, I knew that in the last analysis they were linked to our jobs. The state gave and the state could take away. I asked for a driver, a secretary, and an office in the ministry while I wrote about my intelligence experiences, for use by the ministry, and worked on *The Troika*. In return, I would be available to advise my successor and Mielke.

My retirement ceremony in November 1986 was conducted with all formal honors. Mielke wanted to announce it briefly and in traditional Soviet style: "Owing to serious health problems . . ." But I was perfectly healthy and saw no reason to begin my new life outside the intelligence services with a lie. I insisted on a more truthful if cryptic announcement: "At his own wish, General Markus Wolf has retired from the Main Directorate (foreign intelligence)." The stiff official send-off was in sharp contrast to the small farewell party I threw after my official farewell. There, among my most trusted colleagues, I laced the words of genuine affection and appreciation I felt for my team with the occasional oblique reference to the fears, frustrations, and difficulties I knew they shared. "A good Communist," I told them, quoting Bertolt Brecht at his most wry, "has many dents in his helmet. And some of them are the work of the enemy."

I praised Gorbachev's reforms. The officers exchanged glances, knowing that the ideas of perestroika and glasnost were being roundly ignored by our leadership. I left them with a poem written by my father entitled "Apologies for Being Human" ("Verzeiht, Dass Ich ein Mensch in . . .") an accurate summary of his character and, I think, of my own. It translates roughly as follows:

> And if I hated too much
> And loved too wild, too free.
> Forgive me for being human
> Sainthood was not for me.

Andrea and I hid ourselves away in the country and I buried myself in Koni's notes about the three-way friendship that had survived the Cold War. I was, for the first time in many years, blissfully happy and at ease with myself. I knew that the book, with its implicit critique of Stalinism and praise for the durability of human ties despite the enmity of the two ideologies, could be a major event in our world. I was determined to broach a subject that had never been openly discussed in East Germany: Stalin's terror and the random nature of his mass arrests. The book was published simultaneously by two German publishing houses in the East (Aufbau) and West (Classen) within the framework of Gorbachev's glasnost, which had been rejected by Honecker as a model for our country.

With a director friend I also undertook a film about my father's life. When the film *Apologies for Being Human* was to be shown I was informed that a passage about Stalin's crimes was to be cut. I protested, but it was shortened while I was out of the country. This experience of the senseless attempt to suppress the past (and by implication the present) was the last straw. Unlike most East Germans, I was lucky in having access to the general secretary. I approached Honecker with anecdotes from others who had been forced to stand helpless while politically sensitive parts of their work were randomly amputated. As always, Honecker was extremely courteous and even agreed that it had been bad manners not to have told me or the others that changes had been made. Then he admitted that he had personally made the decision to cut the discussion of Stalin's atrocities from the film and made no concessions of substance. When I complained that it was impossible to portray the 1930s in the Soviet Union without reference to Stalin's crimes he replied, "But don't you see? These days history is being falsified over there day in, day out. Glasnost has a lot to answer for in that regard."

I plowed on.

"You can't tell people for decades that everything the Soviet Union does is right and then turn your back on it so abruptly. People place great hope in Gorbachev here. They don't accept that what he is doing is bad. They compare his openness to the policies on the media here, and they want more freedom of speech and publication. This is not something that will go away."

Honecker jutted out his obstinate jaw and said, "I will never allow here what is happening in the Soviet Union."

Desperate for a realistic response, I asked whether he was aware of the swelling numbers of protesters who were finding moral support under the auspices of the Protestant church in East Berlin and Leipzig—the people who would, within months, form the core of East Germany's peaceful revolution.

"They are fools and dreamers," he said. "We can deal with people like that."

In March 1989, my first book, *The Troika*, was published in an atmosphere of rising social tension. The East German authorities had just banned an issue of the Soviet magazine *Sputnik* that contained newly published research about Stalin's crimes. The conflict between the GDR and Moscow was now out in the open, with East Berlin effectively censoring the Soviet Union.

I decided to use the simultaneous publication of the book in East and West Germany to make a public stand for perestroika and against the moribund regime. I distanced myself from the ban on *Sputnik* and told one Western TV interviewer who asked how I felt about Gorbachev, "I am cheerful and happy that he is there."

Next day I heard that I was a subject of discussion at the weekly meeting of the politburo. Mielke phoned to tell me that my views were regarded as an attack on the Party leadership and informed me that the politburo had decided I should give no more interviews about the book at the forthcoming Leipzig book fair. To borrow a crude but effective saying from American politics, I was discovering what it was like to be outside the tent pissing in after a lifetime of being inside pissing out. I did not flout the politburo's order directly, but I continued my reading tour around the country. It coincided with the worsening of the domestic crisis. There was rising resentment over the sham electoral procedures that allowed the Socialist Unity Party to continue in power unopposed after the May election.

By summer, the exodus of East Germans to the West through Hungary's newly opened borders was in full spate. Like several of my more thoughtful colleagues who knew the Ministry of State Security from the inside, I was concerned about the possibility of violence. Resentments that had stewed for decades were very close to boiling over. I approached Egon Krenz, the solid, unimaginative functionary everyone expected to succeed Honecker. I told him that I feared bloodshed if nervous internal security forces were deployed against demonstrators without a clear idea of how to deal with a situation they knew only from their manuals. I gave him a written aide-mémoire about the necessary next steps, but he remained dejected. "I know, Mischa," he said, echoing comments I had heard years earlier from Andropov, "but you know how the politburo runs. If I say one word of this in there, I'll be out of my job the next day. Remember, Gorbachev only became general secretary after he had kept his mouth shut under three predecessors."

On October 18, Honecker finally fell from power in the time-honored manner of authoritarian rulers who have lost the respect of their inner circle and are asked to go. No one person took responsibility, but no leader of the GDR could have been unseated without Mielke's active agreement. Krenz was installed as general secretary and appeared on television making conciliatory noises. But he was ill-equipped for the extremely arduous task he faced.

I knew that the time for discreet words was over when Bertolt Brecht's energetic and principled granddaughter, Johanna Schall, invited me to join in a demonstration on November 4 in East Berlin's vast Alexander-platz, which was to be a plea for peaceful change. I joined the writers Christa Wolf, Stephan Heym, and Heiner Müller and the leaders of the New Forum opposition group Bärbel Bohley and Jens Reich. Gazing across a sea of homemade posters demanding an end to one-party rule, it became clear to me that my Socialist Unity Party's monopoly was at an end. For me, that meant shedding a lifetime of ideological commitment. I still believed that the GDR could be—at least for a substantial period of time—preserved separately from the West with a government incorpo-rating socialist beliefs but permitting far greater freedom of speech, assembly, and property. I tried to persuade the half million at the rally and the millions more watching on television not to resort to violence, but as I spoke, protesting the atmosphere of incrimination that made every member of the state security organizations scapegoats of the poli-cies of the former leadership, I was dimly aware that parts of the crowd were hissing me. They were in no mood to be lectured on reasonable behavior by a former general of the Ministry of State Security.

So I learned painfully in those moments that I could not escape my past. I would have to learn to bear responsibility for activities of my ministry and those aspects of the system I had served and perpetuated, even though they lay outside my own experience, knowledge, or con-sent. I cannot say that the crowd's reaction entirely surprised me, but my overwhelming feeling was one of relief and pride to be able to stand up at last and speak the truth. That night, I went home and slept soundly for the first time in weeks.

On November 28, West German Chancellor Helmut Kohl pub-lished a ten-point program for the unification of Germany. From that day on, especially on December 4, at the regular Monday demonstra-tion in Leipzig, isolated posters had already begun to appear demand-ing GERMANY, ONE FATHERLAND (DEUTSCHLAND, EINIG VATERLAND). But there were no such calls that day in East Berlin. Many different views were heard from the speakers and marchers about the future shape of their country, but there was an overwhelming sense of communal endeavor. Looking back, I suppose that was the last day of our socialist dream. Five days later, I was at a writers club in Potsdam discussing *The Troika* when a young man wrenched open the door and shouted, "The border is open." That is how quickly history is made. Within a single night, the old world, the world to which I had devoted my life's work, disappeared. That evening, television sets everywhere broadcast images of the Berlin Wall crumbling. The concrete barrier that had physically reinforced ideological division would in the days to come be reduced to souvenir chunks. From now on I would have to become accustomed to a new world, one that I knew only as an enemy and where I would be a stranger, a refugee from a fallen utopia.

●

On January 15, 1990, an angry crowd—including several well-prepared groups—stormed my old ministry and seized files, which were then handed over to Western secret services. Carefully selected parts were published, and since Mielke's and my names were the only ones familiar to the public, almost no day passed when I was not subjected to fierce attacks, above all in connection with the discovery that former terrorists of the Red Army Faction were being sheltered in the GDR. It made no difference that there was no evidence or proof of my own involvement with the RAF; that I had been working in a different part of the ministry involved was enough to incriminate me in the accusers' eyes.

By summer I was faced with a vengeful situation. A bill granting amnesty to GDR intelligence services had been blocked in the parliament in Bonn. I had no doubt that on Unity Day, October 3, 1990, I would be arrested. After consulting both lawyers and friends I decided to leave the country for a while. I was hoping to work from abroad to protect my former staff, the last of whom had left the ministry in April 1990. Before leaving I wrote letters to the federal president, Richard von Weizsäcker, Foreign Minister Hans-Dietrich Genscher, and Willy Brandt saying that another emigration from Germany would be impossible for me:

It is the country of my parents. Here they found a field of activities for themselves, after a long emigration. My parents and my brother are buried in Berlin. And to me, Germany is the place of my toil, my strength, my love, my activities in a positive view as well as in failed and wrong attempts.

And I wrote to the federal prosecutor, Alexander von Stahl:

For me, and for the members of the staff of the intelligence service who were engaged in the Cold War in the same way as members of other services, the war seems to continue. There are to be victors and vanquished, retaliations without mercy.

I wanted to leave no doubt that, while I might leave Germany for a time, I would return without hesitation once guaranteed fair proceedings. I also told the chief of the Berlin station of the KGB, Anatoly G. Novikov, that I intended to leave Germany for a while. He smiled and said that the KGB was aware of West Germany's attempts to offer immunity from prosecution in exchange for information. He did not tell me how he had learned this, but he said the KGB was pleased that I had not complied. A few days later, after he had reported our meeting to Moscow, I received a message from him to contact the KGB for help at any time I was in danger.

We agreed that my wife and I would, in extremis, make our own way out of Germany to avoid the Soviets' being seen to be responsible for my escape. If necessary, I would phone a secret number and they would come to my aid. It was the best of a bad bunch of offers. I still hoped that if we could hide out in Europe unnoticed for a few weeks, the witch-hunt in Germany would die down and I could return.

Andrea and I packed our bags discreetly on September 28, six days before unification, and set off for Austria. We used our real passports and our own car—I was determined not to be caught in any petty illegality and never traveled on false papers—and drove across the border like any other late-summer tourists heading for the mountains. The border guards cast a cursory glance at our documents and waved us on. When we were well out of their sight, we stopped and hugged each other like children playing hooky from a strict boarding school.

For two months, Andrea and I drove through the Austrian countryside, keeping to small hotels and boarding houses and sometimes receiving hospitality from good friends we knew in left-wing Austrian circles. We were not in disguise, and when the story broke after October 3 that I had fled Germany, my face began to appear regularly on the front page of newspapers, which naturally turned up in the hotel lobbies and reception desks. Amazingly, no one seemed to associate me with the "most wanted spy" who had disappeared. Once or twice, Andrea would see someone looking rather too closely at me, or hear a whispered exclamation, and we would move on without ceremony. It was an extraordinary time, at once terrifying and exhilarating. I felt strangely rejuvenated. But I knew that we could not go on forever like some German Bonnie and Clyde.

We tried to reactivate the Israeli option without success. Despite the original promise, there was no visa waiting in Vienna, and I did not want to draw attention to myself by hanging around the Austrian capital to pursue it. (I did not get to Israel until 1995, when the Israeli newspaper *Ma'ariv* invited me for a well-publicized visit with retired members of the Mossad and a meeting with the former prime minister Yitzhak Shamir.) One night, over dinner in an Austrian village, I looked at Andrea's pretty, careworn face and knew that no other option was open for us then but Russia. I retained a shred of hope that Gorbachev, as a friend of Helmut Kohl's, would plead for clemency on our behalf. From Austria I addressed a letter to him but received no answer. In November 1990, I took out the secret KGB contact number that had been given to me in Berlin before I left, uttered the code word to the Russian voice on the other end of the line, and told him that the time had come.

Two days later, Andrea and I were picked up by a Russian go-between at the Hungarian border and driven across the plains of Hungary. After a day's rest, we proceeded into Ukraine, and from there to Moscow, arriving exhausted but hugely relieved that our days on the run were over.

In Moscow Leonid Shebarshin welcomed us at foreign intelligence headquarters in Yasenevo and we raised several glasses to my escape. But the atmosphere was strained. My hosts were embarrassed that I had not received more support from Gorbachev. Although he knew me well, Kryuchkov sent greetings through Valentin Falin and the Central Committee rather than receiving me directly. The KGB chief advised me not to return to Germany. It was clear that the leadership was ambivalent about my presence. On the one hand, it felt bound by the past to offer me shelter in Moscow. On the other, it did not want to make a fuss about my being there, since relations with Bonn took priority.

For the first time in my life, places that had always said yes to me in Moscow started to say no. Or rather, in that ineffably Russian way, they gave no any answer at all. As part of research for this book, I tried to consult some old NATO documents that had been obtained by my agents and passed on to Moscow by me. They never appeared. Of course, I was never refused outright. I was just told that access to the secrets I myself had given Moscow was impossible for "technical reasons."

I spent my time trying to find political and legal support for my former staff members, agents, and myself, and also seeing old friends from my youth and pursuing my culinary interests, collecting Russian recipes for a cookbook I later published. My son Sascha, who was being looked after by Andrea's daughter by her first marriage, Claudia, visited now and then.

I lived comfortably in Moscow until August 1991. But I felt the necessity to be with my family and former colleagues in Germany. To remain in the Soviet Union meant to live quietly, actually as an émigré. In the summer, Andrea and I had been invited by the Central Committee to holiday in Yalta, on the Black Sea coast, in a dacha reserved for the political elite. At the same time, Mikhail Gorbachev was vacationing not far away—a holiday that was to be his last as leader of the Soviet Union. For it was there that he received an uninvited delegation of politburo colleagues from Moscow announcing a coup, masterminded by none other than Kryuchkov, the KGB chief.

Kryuchkov was not my favorite KGB boss, but I never thought that a man of his caliber would get himself involved in such a half-baked action. It hardly took an intelligence chief to see that it was a farce from the start.

The failed putsch was the last straw for us. My lawyers had visited me twice to discuss the timing of my return to Germany. Now the decision to leave was pressing. It was clear that Gorbachev's days were numbered and that Boris Yeltsin would soon bid for absolute power. I expected no favors from him.

So at the end of August, by which time a shaken Gorbachev was back in the Kremlin, I made an appointment to see Leonid Shebarshin. He had taken over as temporary chief of the KGB, now that Kryuchkov was disgraced and under arrest. He looked dazed and strained under the pressure of events. With the Soviet Union in disarray and the KGB split between supporters and rivals of the putsch, the last thing he needed was me and my problems. Still, perhaps he would try to hold me back, make a last gesture of solidarity toward a fellow intelligence officer.

He listened to me carefully as I explained my intention to return to Germany, then spread his hands palms upward in a Russian gesture of helplessness. "You see the way things are here, Mischa," he said. "You've been a good friend to us, but there is nothing more we can do for you here now. Who would have thought it would end like this! Go with God."

We decided to take a brief holiday in Austria on the way back, not only to recuperate from the stresses of the past weeks, but because it was a better base from which to communicate with my German lawyers and arrange for my return to take place as quietly as possible. This turned out to be a false hope. The Soviets, through carelessness rather than malice, had revealed in their formal statement on my departure that I had gone to Austria. The Austrian police and secret service were ordered to find and arrest me. Then they were to deliver me into the hands of their German colleagues.

Nevertheless, I saw no reason why we should oblige the publicity machine with an early return. We began our travels again. But commentators and cartoonists started laughing, then sneering at the incompetence of the Austrian authorities in being unable to find a retired spymaster in their small country. Daily reports appeared in the papers, and the whole thing became a farce, so we went to Vienna, where I turned myself in. The Austrian police could not have been more polite. They found us discreet accommodation away from the press, and, almost a year after I had left Germany, with the help of my lawyers we arranged for my homecoming.

The Germans ensured that it was a stylish affair. Crossing at Bayerisch Gmain, we found guards were waiting for us at the border. Politely, they bade me get out of the car and cursorily searched my luggage—for weapons, explained the embarrassed official. My eldest son, Michael, had traveled to meet me on the Austrian side, delighted to have a part in the drama. He took my car, while Andrea and I were ushered into a bulletproof Mercedes once we crossed the border. A second such car followed with the public prosecutor and my lawyer.

Just beyond the border the German authorities had arranged a stop in a hotel for refreshments. In the lounge, the public prosecutor somberly produced my arrest warrant and read it to me. Then we made our way to the office of the supreme court in Karlsruhe. Despite the unusually late hour the prosecutor succeeded in obtaining my immediate imprisonment. Shortly before midnight I was committed to the only double-barred cell of the Karlsruhe prison. After eleven days, I was released on my lawyer's application. Bail was set so high that I was only able to raise it with the support of friends and on conditions that were correctly called spiteful.

●

Legend has it that during my two long visits to Moscow, in the spring of 1990 and again from November 1990, I took along GDR intelligence files and handed them to the KGB. This entertaining thought is part of the lively speculation that surrounds the fate of these files, but it is sadly wrong, for reasons of simple intelligence practice. I had been out of office for three years when East Germany collapsed and had been succeeded by Werner Grossmann, my own choice. A diligent man, Grossmann was favored by the younger, technocratic members of the service. It had never been my intention to cramp my successor's style after retirement, and Grossmann also made it clear that he wanted to lead by himself. Very occasionally, he would consult me for advice on cases begun when I was in command, but he generally preferred to go his own way. One piece of advice that I did give him when I handed over the key to my office was never to put the agent files onto any kind of computer disc. I had spent the initial years of the computer boom resisting pressure from bright young things who insisted that our filing system was cumbersome and inefficient. The Ministry of State Security files, as everyone now knows, thanks to horrified media reports, took up several miles of space in the archives. While I do not contest that East German state security was afflicted by an obsessive desire to collect and file information on its citizens and those it perceived to be its enemies abroad, I would gently remind the headline writers that one reason for this was the primitive state of computerization in the East. I doubt the CIA is short of files, but I am sure it stores them more tidily on magnetic chips and tapes.

As I mentioned earlier, quite early in my career I had worked out a complex cross-referencing system, which meant that anyone trying to identify an agent from our files would need to obtain access to three to five (depending on the security rating) pieces of separate information and security clearance to read three sets of interconnected documents. The central registry contained both agents (organized by first name, last name, date of birth, and place of birth) and hundreds of thousands of other persons who were registered for completely varied reasons. Card registers were kept separately in each department, each one handling at most sixty to one hundred agents. For each agent there was a card with a code name, address, and territory—which could be his ministry, company, or other organization. The cards never carried the agents' real names, and the small card pack in each department was usually kept in the custody of a trusted senior officer. In crisis or wartime, his job would have been to remove them from the ministry to our temporary headquarters. Any unauthorized person would have had to trawl physically through a massive quantity of paper in search of a match. Such a conspicuous operation to match the code name of an agent with his real one would inevitably attract attention—quite the opposite of what would have happened if even these separate files were on computer discs. The ungainliness of the operation troubled me little because I and my senior officers kept the names of most important agents in our heads. Since I had first used the model of the spider's web to identify connections between existing spy networks in Germany after the war, I found it perfectly easy simply to slot in new names in my head. I rarely had to remind myself who an agent was or what his field of operation was.

On computer, security for such information would have been provided by levels of clearance and code words. Time and time again, experts tried to persuade me that a computerized system was fail-safe. It always sounded convincing until a few weeks or months later, when a newspaper report would appear about some twelve-year-old hacking into a military computer from his bedroom. I have never trusted computers.

What had to be protected at all costs was the central coded card index, which was the key to researching the identity and operation of an agent. I cannot say with certainty what happened to it. If I had still been in charge, it probably would have gone to Moscow when East Germany collapsed, but there was no formal drill for the files in the event of the breakdown of the state. We in the HVA assumed that in wartime the files would go to our central war headquarters in Gosen, on the eastern border of Berlin, but every department had its own emergency location. In 1989 the destination of the files was at the discretion of the head of GDR foreign intelligence.

How much the Russians would have made of the card files if they had gotten them is difficult to say. There has been much speculation that Moscow would activate these agents on its own behalf and continue spying on the West using their knowledge, which was indeed deep and specialized. This seems highly doubtful to me. If I had been the head of Russian foreign intelligence, I would have considered these agents far too dangerous to use. The sobering experience of the last turbulent years shows us that social upheaval can turn even seemingly loyal people into traitors. German unification was such a powerful jolt to all of us and such a challenge to our loyalties that it was no longer easy to predict how our agents, officers, and sources would react. By mid-1990 they knew that we had been left out in the cold by the Soviets. There was great bitterness among our officers toward the Soviets, and when senior officers visited me the conversation inevitably turned to Moscow's failure to help them after the many toasts we had drunk together.

Later that year I heard a rumor from within the KGB that discs containing highly classified material from the HVA had found their way to the CIA and were being decoded in a massive operation. It was the first I had heard about such material being placed on discs at all. Soon afterward, Rainer Rupp and even contacts like Karl Wienand were arrested. The raw material for these discoveries could have come only from a central card register containing details about our agents operating in the West.

Where had such material come from? Had it been transferred to discs? The war scare of the early 1980s had prompted elaborate measures for evacuation and even the construction of a special bunker in Gosen, from which I was supposed to continue running my agents—as if I would have been able to reach them by radio or any other means in case of an atomic holocaust. I thought the whole enterprise was slightly mad, and I visited the bunker only once, remarking that if atomic war broke out, we would never have time to reach it anyway. In the fever of these ridiculous preparations, I now believe that the agent registration cards were centralized and computerized, on whose orders I do not know. Once that happened, copying the disc with the list of agents would have been a relatively simple matter for a senior officer.

I therefore conclude that one of our agents sold the data to the CIA for a considerable sum of money and a promise of immunity from the German prosecutors. Remember, the head of my American department had turned down an offer of one million dollars for just such information. One reason I believe it went directly to the CIA, and not through the Russians, was the appearance of stories in the press claiming that GDR intelligence handed over its files to the Russians at their KGB base in Karlshorst, in Berlin. For various reasons I find this so unlikely that I believe the story was a piece of deliberate disinformation to conceal a direct deal between the CIA and one of our officers.

If I am right, that would have made it the greatest single intelligence haul in history. The Germans no longer hid the fact that much of the information on which they based the prosecution of dozens of our agents was passed on to them as a goodwill gesture from America. During my own and other investigations, it was obvious that the interrogators were working from lists of code names and trying to find out real names. For example, Heinz Busch, one of my former intelligence analysts, told the prosecutors under questioning in 1990 that we had an agent in NATO and revealed his code name. But Rainer Rupp was not unmasked by name until the late summer of 1993, after German newspapers reported that the CIA had permitted German intelligence to inspect some of the names—kept in a separate file.

This took place at CIA headquarters in Langley, Virginia, and not until two or three years after they got the names. Why would the CIA wait that long? From the CIA's point of view, the identification of East German agents was a mere by-product of an operation whose scale and intensity indicated that it was about something else altogether. Their quarry was closer to home, the mole gnawing away, year after year, at the very heart of U.S. security. They knew he was there. They knew the damage he was doing. But they did not know his name, which is what had led Gus Hathaway to me in the spring of 1990.

When Gaby Gast, our brilliant, highly placed agent within the Federal Intelligence Service (BND), went on trial in 1991, it was evident she had been sold out much earlier and for a much lower price. Her lover, Karlizcek, was intent on saving his own skin and deserted her, refusing to give mitigating evidence on her behalf and publicly announcing that they had no future together. As a citizen of the former GDR, he was given a suspended sentence for his espionage activities (this has been the outcome in every case except mine!). As a West German, however, she was considered a traitor to her own country and received a sentence of six and a half years. Karlizcek celebrated his freedom with a lavish lunch in an Italian restaurant opposite the courtroom, while his lover of over twenty years was taken to the Neudeck women's prison in Munich. It was clear that his loyalties were neither to her nor to us; for him it was just a job.

Gaby's arrest and conviction was the hardest blow for me during a period rich in personal disappointments and defeats. In a letter from prison, Gaby furiously expressed her bitterness at being betrayed by a leading officer of East German intelligence. I could not help but feel at fault, since I had promised her again and again that she would never be discovered and that we would always protect her. But a Judas had revealed her, and I was distraught by my inability to help her. The thought of Gaby in a prison cell, anxious about her child, plagued by self-recrimination and the sight of her motives and actions being subjected to the distorting prism of the highly unsympathetic German media, burnt in my brain.

Perhaps the only thing I could do was to help Gaby strengthen her resolve. She worried that my professions of solidarity were nothing more than a charade, that I had said only whatever it took to convince her to work for us and that now my declarations rung hollow. In response, I wrote a letter reminding her that "at no time were you a mere cog in the wheel, or simply one of the many whose fate is tied up with the events which have, to one extent or another, made victims of us all. It is hard to talk about these matters in a letter, and as much as I believe that I understand you, our experiences were always different—in the past few years, even more so. Still, we are bound together by circumstance. [My references to solidarity] were in no way part of a tired old verbal ritual. They reflected what I truly and deeply felt."

She and I have gone back to writing each other supportive letters. She phones me often and has declared that our continued acquaintance gives her strength to bear the torture of confronting the past. She has become active in a group campaigning for an end to the prosecution of other agents whose cases are slogging their way through the courts. Nowadays our communications do not have to be in code or go through secret channels, which is a tribute to the fact that in the direst adversity, two spies became two friends.

Though Gaby's lover was able to escape charges of treason on the basis of having been an East German citizen, no such logic applied to me. On May 4, 1993, I found myself making my way through crowds of insistent press and curious public into the provincial high court in Düsseldorf to face an inquisition into my life's work. Flanked by my two lawyers, Andrea and I edged our way forward. Raising my eyes to the tower that adorns the building, I glimpsed the eagle that was the heraldic symbol of the German Reich, its wings outstretched, a rare vestige in postwar Germany of the Kaiser's reign. A throng of reporters gathered around the door, intent on producing their required sensation of the day. They surged greedily toward us.

We made our way through the main hall of the building and into the cellar, where my trial was to take place. There we found ourselves confronted with yet another stampede of journalists at the back entrance. I grabbed Andrea's arm and we hurtled downstairs into the quiet of the courtroom.

Opposite me, on the other side of the U-shaped podium, sat the prosecutors, clad in purple. I had come to know their faces well since the day of my arrest on the Austrian border and a subsequent short hearing before the Federal Supreme Court in Karlsruhe. There was not an empty seat in the house.

My presence in this courtroom was laden with irony. Here was I, the former head of East German foreign intelligence, being tried by the united Germany's judiciary for spying against the Federal Republic. Odder still, this was the very same room in which Günter Guillaume and his wife, Christel, had been tried in 1975. The courtroom had been specially built into the cellar to make bugging impossible during that case, at which senior ministers and BND and BfV officials gave testimony that was kept secret.

This emotion-laden choice of venue was not accidental. The federal public prosecutor's office for Karlsruhe had made its application specially to the Düsseldorf court to open the case there. Even before the Guillaume trial, the Düsseldorf court had earned itself a reputation for unbending harshness in its sentencing. Its judges ranked as some of the strictest in the country. The list of charges ran 389 pages. Its content and the curt treatment with which the objections of my defense were met by the public prosecutor's office even before the trial opened left me in no doubt as to what lay ahead.

Five judges duly appeared and took their places. The formal part of my trial thus began. During the preliminaries, I examined the faces of the judges. There were four men and one woman. I had encountered them once before, the previous year, when I had appeared as a witness in the trial of Klaus Kuron.

Kuron's trial was an unpleasant taste of things to come, and the sight of him in the dock, slumped and aged by the stress of the trial, had given me a jolt. So this, I thought, was what unification looked like close up. Back then I had been able to give my evidence and leave, but now I was stuck here with these same judges, who, seated in their black robes under the giant eagle, looked somehow fantastic, like characters from the pictures of Hieronymus Bosch or the nightmare world of Goya. During the next long seven months, I would get to know their expressions and even their gestures very well.

The presiding judge, Klaus Wagner, had a wide face, lifeless gestures, and watchful eyes, features that gave him a startling resemblance to an elderly owl. He exuded a sense of modesty and calm but could at any time swoop aggressively down upon an unsuspecting witness. Between him and a thin-faced female judge (who seemed intent on scribbling down every word of the proceedings) sat a younger judge with albino features. He was anxious to portray himself as the next in line after Judge Wagner but was rarely allowed to get a word in and gloomily restricted himself to filling his superior's water glass.

The fourth judge seemed mainly responsible for making sure that the relevant documentary evidence for each point in my case was produced and promptly busied himself behind a vast mountain of files and papers. It was hard to place the fifth judge, who seemed to have little or no role in the proceedings and restricted his participation to an occasional inscrutable smile that would flit across his face, only to disappear as fast as it had come.

As I stared at these representatives of what for me could never be other than an enemy's judiciary, I could not help but reflect on the central irony of my life: My success had been my downfall. I was in the dock for running the most successful espionage service in Europe, East or West.

My defense began by demanding that the trial be adjourned until there was a decision from the Federal Constitutional Court in Karlsruhe, Germany's highest, as to whether it should proceed at all. My hopes had been raised by the fact that the Berlin court that was to try my successor, Werner Grossmann, had refused to proceed with the case until there was a ruling on whether there was a firm legal basis for trying spies from the East in a united German court. But the judge in the Constitutional Court dismissed my lawyer's objection out of hand.

Our second attempt was to demonstrate, though questioning witnesses and producing evidence from government files, that there had been no juridically relevant difference between the activities of the East and West German intelligence services. This would have rendered a central point in the prosecutor's case void, namely, that I was guilty of treason for passing on intelligence information to the KGB. We could also have parried that the Federal Intelligence Service (BND) was no less industrious in passing information to its American ally, the CIA.

Unfortunately for me, no such parallel could ever be drawn in court, since the judge overruled our objection on the ground that the activities of the BND were not a matter for his court. Thus, the central argument of the public prosecutor's case was the assertion that my intelligence service was the servant of an unjust regime. He therefore argued that our service was fundamentally aggressive, whereas the equivalent services on the other side in the Cold War were by contrast defensive and therefore acceptable. The legal foundation of his argument rested on West Germany's Basic Law (Grundgesetz), under which the Federal Republic claimed sovereignty over all former German territory.

As soon as the court in Düsseldorf turned down the petitions of my defense team, I felt that I could save the court's time by announcing a guilty verdict in advance. The prosecution alleged that I had been for many years head of the foreign intelligence service of the German Democratic Republic, the Main Intelligence Directorate; clearly, it required no evidence or witnesses to prove that. The chief public prosecutor further declared that he had incriminating evidence against me proving that I had met personally and given instructions to agents. I had no need to trouble the court with an examination of these meetings, since I had no intention of denying the allegations. I was proud to have been a hands-on boss and not someone who sat behind a desk ordering others into the dangers of espionage.

"I have submitted myself to this trial because I want to live in the country that is my homeland. I respect the laws of the Federal Republic of Germany, whether or not I agree with them," I said. "But I only became a citizen of the Federal Republic on October 3, 1990. Until that day, I was a citizen of a different country."

The German word for treason is *Landesverrat*, which quite literally means "betrayal of country." Common sense would dictate that the accusation against me was absurd: Which country was I supposed to have betrayed? I certainly did not betray my own country, nor the people who worked for me, and I saw no earthly reason why I should be in the dock for betraying someone else's.

During the seven months that followed, I was accused of running thirty important agents, some of whom appeared as witnesses. This gave me the chance to observe and once again meet many people who had been bound to me by work and political conviction. For that, at least, I owe a perverse debt of gratitude to the court. Like me, most of them had seen the irretrievable breakdown of the order of the world in which they believed. Yet their belief in themselves and their personal dignity remained intact and provided great consolation and encouragement.

It was a strange stream of individuals who appeared in the witness box. From a variety of backgrounds in East and West Germany, they had cooperated with my service for many different reasons. My most poignant encounter was with Gaby. When she entered the courtroom at my trial, she turned her face away from me. This was interpreted by the journalists covering the case as a gesture of rejection, but it was the result of a highly emotional moment. The model of a cool witness, she refused to bow to the prosecution's efforts to portray me as the Svengali who had hired and held female agents through blackmail and other pressures. She looked pale and drawn as she pulled her last mental resources together to answer the judge's questions, and I knew what a severe strain this must have been for her. Her conviction, like Kuron's, was another painful reminder to me that the honor I had believed to be invulnerable in my service had not stood the test of different times.

Another fascinating figure to take the stand was Hannsheinz Porst, the entrepreneur and multimillionaire who had wanted to use his ties with us—at a time when any such contact was a criminal offense in the eyes of the federal authorities—to promote the normalization of relations between the two Germanys. Unification had exposed him, too, and the man I had last encountered as a young and agile businessman appeared in the witness box as an elderly gentleman with a shock of white hair and a bushy beard. He still stood by the desire for national reconciliation that had led him to work with East Germany and described the charge of treason against me as absurd.

Also making an appearance was one of my "super-Romeos," Herbert Schröter, and the sight of him brought back all sorts of memories of madcap schemes and daring ruses. After Herbert's achievements were listed, the prosecutor remarked, "I suppose you think you're God's gift to women?" Gauche and expansive as ever, our former officer strode over to me in the dock, gave a half salute, and bawled, "It was a pleasure to work with you, Herr General." That was the last I saw of him.

The courtroom was bursting at the seams the day Günter Guillaume appeared as a witness. No one would have recognized him as the same character who was once Willy Brandt's right-hand man. The seven years he had spent in prison after his discovery, and a subsequent heart attack, had left their mark on him. He had only agreed to testify after the public prosecutor's office had made it clear that he risked a second trial if he did not oblige by giving evidence. But when asked about his personal feelings about deceiving Brandt over a long period, Guillaume coolly replied, "I have respected and served two people wholeheartedly in my life: Markus Wolf and Willy Brandt." There was a piquant moment when he repeated his claim that he had succeeded in passing on to us Brandt's Norway papers, and I could not stop myself from giving him a wry smile. But my defense and I had agreed that I would not say anything that could damage Guillaume or lead to fresh legal proceedings against him: The last thing either of us needed was a public spat between two old colleagues.

Klaus Kinkel, then the foreign minister of the united Germany, was asked by my defense to testify because he was in the Ministry of the Interior at the time of Brandt's downfall before later becoming head of West German intelligence. Kinkel was party to much of the sordid background to the case, which only now would receive a long-overdue airing through this trial. We both had been born in the small city of Hechingen under the castle of the Hohenzollern kings.

Here the former heads of foreign intelligence for East and West Germany faced each other in court. My activities had landed me there as a defendant, while Kinkel had progressed to a career as a senior statesman, welcomed in Washington, London, and Moscow without his intelligence background worrying anyone. Kinkel's staff had gone to extraordinary lengths to ensure that we would not meet on the way into the courtroom. I knew that he disliked me intensely and hated the thought that the outside world, seeing us on opposite sides of the court, might find even a shred of moral equivalence in what we had done in our opposing official positions. So Kinkel arrived at the very last moment and sat down in the witness box. After a couple of moments, even he seemed a little ashamed at not acknowledging me, and nodded curtly in my direction.

Kinkel answered only a few questions of no great value, but my encounter with him was in many ways symbolic of the trauma that East Germans were facing after unification. Their lives were on the slab, and the West held the scalpel for dissection. The teacher in the West could accuse the teacher in the East of being a bad educator, just because he had taught within the rival system, no matter how professional or well respected the Eastern teacher was. The Eastern diplomats lost their jobs because they were, in the new jargon, "system-immanent," while the Western diplomats with whom they had until recently held negotiations moved on up the career ladder. The spy on the Eastern side ended up in the dock, the spy on the Western side in the witness box.

In spite of the absurdness and frequently voiced legal doubts regarding my prosecution, the court indicted me on December 6, 1993. The charge of treason carried a six-year prison sentence, and the court found me guilty. My lawyer appealed this decision with the Supreme Court, which in turn asked the Constitutional Court for a decision. In June 1995 the Federal Constitutional Court judged that officers of the GDR intelligence service could not be prosecuted for treason and espionage. Thus, on October 18, 1995, the Federal Supreme Court had to accept the application of my counsel and overturn my conviction, sending it back to the court in Düsseldorf.

Watching former agents and moles pass in front of me in the courtroom, I was forced to ask myself whether it had all been worth it. It is a question with which I was confronted repeatedly as I looked back on my life to write this book. My intention then and now has been to examine the historical intersections that marked the second half of the twentieth century, and to look back at my contributions to them as head of an intelligence service whose high performance could not prevent the end of the system it served. The Cold War was not a time of blacks and whites, but of many shades of gray. We cannot look at what has happened without remembering this, and we cannot move forward without keeping it in mind. As I said to the court during my trial:

> No legal process can illuminate a period of history rich in contradictions, illusions, and guilt. . . . The system in which I lived and worked was the child of a utopia that, since the early nineteenth century, has been the goal of millions of people, including outstanding thinkers, who believed in the possibility of freeing humankind from repression, exploitation, and war. That system failed because it was no longer supported by the people who lived within it. And yet I insist that not everything in the forty-year history of the GDR was bad and worthy of erasure, and not everything in the West good and just. This period of historical upheaval cannot be dealt with adequately through the clichés of a "just state" on the one hand and an "unjust state" on the other.

Does this mean that there is no blame, no responsibility? Of course not. The Cold War was a brutal struggle, and terrible things were done by both sides in the name of winning it. But now that the Cold War and the GDR have slipped from the front pages of newspapers and into the history books, we should not forget that things were never as clear-cut as both sides' propaganda machines made them out to be. We should take the words of the great contemporary Japanese philosopher Daisaku Ikeda to heart: "One cannot, without reflection, make some into bearers of goodness and others into miscreants, judging them by relative positive or negative criteria. These, like everything else, change according to historical circumstances, the character of a society, the times and subjective points of view." Only by seeing things in such a light can we truly learn the lessons that the Cold War, and the lives of each of us who helped fight it, have to offer.

17

Epilogue

A lifetime spent in intelligence is a mixture of glory in our occasional successes, misery when our best work is ignored, and the daily banality of working within any bureaucracy whose principal task often is delivering unwelcome news to its political masters. I find it hard to imagine that the high professionals we faced in the Cold War feel very differently about the course of their lives, except of course that their side won. My life has been marked not only by my role in the secret battles of the Cold War but by watching the abuse of power practiced in the name of the socialist ideal in which I still believe.

I was always inspired, and tried to inspire my service, by tales of agents who came before us. These traditions motivated my officers and agents on either side of our borders, but there was always a nagging question. During the time that Hitler ruled Germany and threatened the world, heroes like Richard Sorge, Harro Schulze-Boysen, and Leopold Trepper delivered to the Soviets warnings about German military plans; lives could have been saved if these warnings had been heeded, yet Stalin ignored them. The great tragedy of these men's lives was that they served a system that did not tolerate critical minds and where one person could make all decisions and judgments. A system that does not allow dissent also ignores dissenting information. And so it was with the system that ultimately evolved in the GDR, one that also did not tolerate dissent and critical minds.

In later years I managed to contact some of the Rote Kappelle survivors. Details about this organization were more accessible for me in Western publications than in our own ministry's archives. Mielke kept files about the Nazi era under his personal control in a special section of the Investigations Department, and try as I might I could not gain access to them. I was interested in how these people of such varied backgrounds and political convictions dedicated themselves to resisting Hitler. How had they overcome their doubts, their fears? What was the source of their inner strength to swim against the tide and battle an omniscient and barbaric regime? Such issues of the moral and historical responsibilities of individuals were largely passed over in publications within the GDR.

We who fought in the Cold War operated on a less exalted level than those who resisted Nazism. If this account of my life has demonstrated anything, it is the limits of what intelligence can accomplish. We can look back on our work with satisfaction not because we overturned the other side with some bold and unexpected stroke, but for precisely the opposite reason. The intelligence services contributed to a half century of peace—the longest Europe has ever known—by giving statesmen some security that they would not be surprised by the other side.

The statesmen on both sides, our clients, did not always want to admit that to themselves. The courage and suffering involved in obtaining information really has nothing to do with its significance. In my experience, the efficiency of a service depends much more on the willingness of those who receive its information to pay attention to it when it contradicts their own opinions. The problem starts with the limited number of people who usually have access to reports and how they make decisions. Since they are swamped with information that they have little time to digest, the bureaucracy that moves the material to them plays a decisive role in the quality of decisions they finally make. There is usually a wall of secrecy between this bureaucracy and the intelligence services, and in my time there was little opportunity for consultation about what really mattered. Ultimately the results of the work of my overt and covert colleagues landed on a very limited number of desks, mainly chosen by Mielke's whim.

In an authoritarian society errors of judgment are practically inevitable. The deliberations of the SED politburo usually degenerated into a formal, time-wasting marathon. In the rare collegium meetings of the Ministry of State Security, Mielke's lengthy monologues were generally followed by discussion of commonplaces and superfluous peripheral matters.

The Western democracies also appear to have found no practical way of solving the same problem of evaluating the significance of intelligence. The Bay of Pigs disaster offers eloquent testimony to this: The decision to start this hopeless adventure was offered to President Kennedy by an incompetent foreign intelligence service following the wishful thinking of pigheaded politicians. In West Germany, the BND's reports to the chancellor's office were regarded by most people who received them in Bonn as wastepaper, as far as I could tell. Helmut Schmidt, who became chancellor as a result of the Guillaume spy case and was frequently aggravated by other, similar cases during his term in office, once made a typically tart comment to Michael Kohl, the GDR ambassador in Bonn. "You should stop with these damned espionage cases," Schmidt said. "You don't learn anything new from such garbage anyway. It's all stale crumbs. Neither side gets any military information it really needs to know. . . . The really big secrets are carefully protected, both by the United States and by the Soviet Union. Spending money on spying is unnecessary and just makes the intelligence services feel self-important enough to justify their budgets and maintain their staffing levels."

Nevertheless the BND remained directly under the chancellor's control, and he and his chief of staff remained frequent guests at BND headquarters in Pullach. In my diary, I remarked in 1977 that secret services are "really creatures unto themselves. Whether we get genuine and usable information or not, our reputation does have one certain effect: Everyone knows that no significant facts or operations can be kept secret for very long. This alone has a real effect in guaranteeing peace and making sure that international obligations are fulfilled."

This entry sounds rather self-serving and could easily create the impression that I overestimated the impact and the significance of the information my service provided. But I was often skeptical about the value of my own work, particularly in conjunction with anniversary celebrations in our country. Immediately after the GDR's anniversary in 1974, I wrote: "In the discussion of the usefulness of secret services, besides the question of *cui bono*, the issue of whether what they do is of any use at all comes up with increasing frequency. And who among us honest insiders would answer without first thinking hard? The question does not only concern the secret services—the armed forces wolf down many billions more in funds. Still, almost all the reams of paper produced by NATO and stamped with the codes 'cosmic' or 'top secret' are, when you get right down to it, not even worth using as toilet paper."

Other critics compared our activities to children's games—KGB agents watch CIA agents, who, together with the BND, the Mossad, or the British Secret Intelligence Service shadow the KGB. One such critic said: "For this, call-girls are laid before diplomats, umbrella tips are poisoned, and aging Western secretaries get roses from Eastern cavaliers. No country in the world thinks it can get by without a secret service. The main work of most of these bloated agencies consists in making life difficult for each other. The Germans, in their divided nation, have brought it to the point of being a true championship, one Pyrrhic victory after another."

To outsiders, the world of secret services must sometimes appear absurd, their activities at best a senseless game, at worst immoral. Now that the Cold War is over, their value is being measured against their huge cost more widely, openly, and urgently than before. The CIA in particular is under attack for spending billions without foreseeing the internal collapse of the USSR and being penetrated by a mole who destroyed the agency's entire spy network inside the Soviet Union.

I would reckon that the giant apparatus on both sides could be cut by at least half without any loss of efficiency. But while it is true that in the age of satellites and computer hackers, technological intelligence, which does not come cheap, has to be used, human agents cannot be completely replaced. Technology can only establish the situation of the moment; secret plans, options, and other considerations will remain concealed even from the most sophisticated satellite.

Moreover, the acquisition and development of high-quality human sources definitely does not depend on the size of the staff back at headquarters. On the contrary, I would also reckon that the number of any country's good spies is in inverse proportion to the size of its bureau-

cratic apparatus. I worked on that assumption in my service, in contrast to the prevailing policies in the rest of the Ministry of State Security. By the end its staff amounted to eighty thousand employees,
incomprehensible for a small country of seventeen million people, and
finally no help to its survival anyway. I fought constantly against
Parkinson's Law. When I left the foreign intelligence service in 1987,
the staff numbered more than three thousand, but another thousand
workers were added before it was dissolved some four years later—all
the time running about the same number of agents in the West. Such
agents numbered little more than one thousand in the Federal Republic during the last decades, and little more than one tenth of these were
important sources.

So even if intelligence services are indispensable, their size can be
considerably reduced if their tasks are precisely defined. They certainly can be used against international terrorism and the burgeoning
worldwide narcotics mafia, and cooperation is essential in limiting the
spread of nuclear weapons. But it seems doubtful that government
spies can be of much use in industrial espionage when the corporations
themselves have their own established services to seek out their com-
petitors' secrets.

What concerns me more is that if secret services—undemocratic as
they are by their very nature—are not reduced, the temptation will forever remain for governments even in democratic nations to spy on and
control their own people. It goes without saying that they will be used
to abuse civil rights in undemocratic nations like the GDR, but control
of secret services even by a democratic legislature is difficult if not
impossible. The very nature of secret agents severely limits and usually
prevents the type of disclosure essential to public accountability—
indeed, that may be the whole point. Even supervisory committees limited to a few, hand-picked members of parliament, as they exist in the
German Bundestag or the U.S. Congress, are unable to pierce the
essential secrecy. The endless history of scandals in all parliamentary
democracies is proof of that.

As long as there are political conflicts and armed forces ready supposedly to solve them, no nation will dispense with a service to reconnoiter
the intentions and capacities of a potential enemy. At best, democratic
parliaments and governments can try to ensure they stick to their allot-

ted tasks and nothing more. But the fight in the dark will continue. That fight, whatever its results, is not a game. It takes place in the real world and will exact years in prison, destroy careers, and can cost lives. This is a high price for information that cannot determine a nation's political course and can perhaps only influence it, if that. At the end of a life in intelligence, I have to ask myself whether that price is too high.

I closed my trial in Düsseldorf with the following statement: "At seventy years of age you can certainly ask yourself what the balance of a whole life looks like. The word 'treason' has been spoken many times [during this trial], and I have asked myself whether I did in fact betray any of the moral principles that have accompanied me throughout my life, principles that had been so dear to my family, my friends, and those I sought to emulate. I know now that we erred frequently, that we committed many grave mistakes, and far too often recognized errors and their causes when it was too late. But I still cling to the ideals and values that guided us as we tried to change the world."

In telling my story, I hope I have made it clear that I never knowingly betrayed my ideals, and therefore I cannot feel that my life was without purpose. I, as well as my many friends and contemporaries, have not lived in vain, however arguable our decisions sometimes have been, however painful the wounds—to ourselves and others—we inflicted.

When I think back to the days of my youth in the Soviet Union, what first comes to mind are not Stalin's crimes or the pact with Nazi Germany, but memories of a life during wartime. The Second World War was the crucial event in the lives of millions of people, and it was a war that thankfully ended the Third Reich. How could anyone who fought against Hitler's barbarians have considered himself a traitor to Germany? My own contribution, and that of my family, to the fight may have been small, but I am proud of it nonetheless.

I feel the same way about my attempts after the war to publicize and make the world aware of the causes of Nazi tyranny, its terrible crimes against humanity, and the existence of former Nazis in the West German power structure. Hitler's long shadow was one of the reasons I agreed to the idea of working for a secret service. This was not treason.

Even putting aside the Nazi legacy and our battle against and fear of it, I am also proud simply that I had my share in maintaining the status quo in Europe, a status quo that may have been tense and chilly, but which ultimately avoided the unthinkable—but not always improbable—endgame of nuclear war.

But this pride is tempered. As much as I feel the need to plead for a fair-minded assessment of the GDR, and as much as I would prefer to stress its anti-fascist origins, I would never allow myself to pass lightly over the dark side of its history. I know that there was a great deal wrong with the GDR, including a terrible amount of repression. I am perfectly aware of my own share in the responsibility for this. I was part of the system, and if people attack me (as they often do) as if I had been head of state, as if I had had total control over everything that happened in the GDR, then that is something that I will have to bear.

Since the momentous events of 1989, I have asked myself repeatedly why the GDR failed so miserably and spectacularly. I've wondered whether I waited too long before saying loudly what I really thought and felt. It was not lack of courage but the futility of protest throughout the history of the GDR that made me hold my peace. Too often I had seen how vehement protest only served to heighten oppression and further suppress freedom of thought. I believed that patient, quiet negotiation would, in the end, be more productive in a country where any open debate was doomed to be denounced by a leadership that was too hysterical and insecure to act sensibly. Was I wrong? Perhaps, but unfortunately there is no way to go back in time and act differently. I often think, especially when I am with one of my ten grandchildren, of a letter my father wrote my brother back in 1944. He advised him never to refrain from forming his own opinion. To this I now add that it is important to have the courage to fight for one's opinion if necessary, even if one has to face repression. I have learned that one must always respect another's way of thinking and never try to force another into conformity. But for much of my life, and most of my career, I chose to wait patiently for change.

I can clearly recall how nervously we all waited for a change of leadership to take place in Moscow, knowing that it would inevitably have a tremendous effect in East Berlin. When the long-expected reforms finally came with Mikhail Gorbachev's ascension to power, no one was more enthusiastic for our future than me. But we did not foresee that the change had come too late; glasnost was not going to really solve any of our problems. The time had run out on the utopian idea hatched in Russia back in 1917.

So what remains? Thinking back and remembering how confident we were in our belief that we could make Marx and Engels's theories work, that it would be possible to form a society where the great ideals of liberty, equality, and fraternity would finally exist, it is sometimes hard to comprehend how we could have failed. When we were young, it often seemed that the strength of our faith would be enough to transform the world. But now I must admit that we failed not because we were too socialist in belief, but because we were not socialist enough in practice. Stalin's crimes were not the logical outcome of Communist theory, but a violation of communism. Nevertheless, the sacrifice of personal liberty to party doctrine, the manipulation of people, and the falsification of history all came out of Stalin's Soviet Union and were quickly adopted by most of the countries on our side of the Iron Curtain. The sad reality of the GDR had more to do with these abuses of power than with democracy and socialism, and this is why East Germany finally suffocated. I freely admit that our system was incomparably inferior to most of the pluralist democracies of the West, even taking into account the advantages of our social security system. The great lesson that I learned from the decline and fall of East Germany is that freedom of thought and expression are as fundamental to a modern society as the advantages we had achieved and were so proud of.

For most of my compatriots, life in a reunified Germany has proven less glamorous than expected—work is often difficult to find, rents are excessive and hard to afford, and many feel the deep loss of everyday solidarity that was a hallmark of life in the GDR. It would be neither just nor sensible to judge life in a Western democracy like Germany by comparing it to an ideal socialist society, but I know that there are many of us who cannot accept the idea of being part of a society where the rich are getting richer by the hour while the poor continue to get poorer. I wonder how people in the United States, rightly proud of their country and its many achievements, can accept the fact that at least forty million Americans live in complete misery. I am very uneasy at the prospect of a society and civilization based solely on money. Money can be as powerful as any governmental system, but often its effects are less visible without being less brutal. In the Eastern bloc, the abuse of power began by manipulating ideals; in capitalist countries, the idea of personal freedom often merely serves as a disguise for business interests. Perhaps this is why, even in the nations that "won" the Cold War, so many citizens are unhappy and cynical about the role of political systems in solving problems.

Nevertheless, I remain both an idealist and an optimist. I am certain that many young people still dream of a better future for everyone, of a world more humane than our present one. I do not believe that utopian ideas are nonsense, but something deeply needed by mankind. Indeed, without some utopian faith we would run the risk of relapsing into utter barbarism, into the sort of brutality that could lead to the destruction of not just a nation, but of the planet. I am certain that the younger generation, and the generations yet to come, will find a way to realize the ideals I once held and still do hold dear.

Not far from my apartment in Berlin is a memorial to Marx and Engels. In the fall of 1989, as East Germany drew to an end, some young people spray painted the words NOT GUILTY across the memorial. They were right. I would like to think that they shared my belief in Marxism's potential. The Cold War is over, and my work may be done, but I have not lost my faith. I often take down from my shelves a book by the Swiss scientist Jean Ziegler. The title encapsulates well my feelings at the end of the century, as I draw toward the final act of a life that has been richer in good and bad than I could ever have imagined as a young child: *A demain, Karl. Until Tomorrow, Karl.*

Index

He meant that those of us who had served the East were now powerless in the new Germany. In my case, there was a more than realistic
chance that I would be sentenced for high treason and spend a few
years scrubbing out a cell.

I would be lying if I did not admit that the temptation to comply
was great. I wanted my freedom. But I knew very well that it would be
at the expense of the liberty of the men and women who had devoted
their lives to my service and, in the case of our agents who had worked
underground in the West, the risk of years in prison. What would they
think of me, the man they had called the Chief, if I sold them out now?
I thanked Diestel for the convivial evening but declined the offer.

"I'll leave others to do the betraying," I said.

"There will be no shortage of applicants," he said as he turned to
go. "If you change your mind, you'll always have a ride to Boeden's
office with me."

●

There was no shortage of other bidders. One offer had already
come from a place I would never in my wildest dreams have imagined
could serve as an escape route to freedom.

On May 28, 1990, two American gentlemen arrived at the gate of
my country house. They introduced themselves with disarming candor
as representatives of the CIA and presented a large bouquet of flowers
and a box of chocolates to my wife. I was not sure whether the flowers
were intended as congratulations or a wreath.

The elder man, thin-faced and graying, was dressed in a somber suit,
immaculately pressed shirt, and striped tie. He introduced himself as
Mr. Hathaway and described himself as a personal emissary of William
Webster, then the U.S. director of central intelligence, upon whose
authority he said he was acting. He spoke precise, formal German.

"A bureaucrat," my wife, Andrea, whispered to me as we retreated
to the kitchen, she in search of a vase for the flowers, I for my cigarettes and ashtray. Hathaway was one of those fanatical American anti-
smokers and tried to persuade me not to light up. I jokingly asked
whether this was a new CIA campaign and he laughed, dutifully but
without real warmth.

His companion, younger and stockier, introduced himself merely as Charles and said that he was head of the agency's Berlin station, although he seemed to me to have the build and manner of a body-guard. He spoke little and barely reacted to the conversation, although it later emerged that he also spoke German. Andrea was reminded of the Americans she knew from TV films about the Vietnam War.

They had been careful not to use the telephone to contact me, evidently wary of taps placed by the KGB or the West Germans. Instead, they had latched on to the fact that a collector of military uniforms in the United States had approached me, asking if I would be prepared to sell some East German dress uniforms. Inspired by this new channel of communication between East and West, they had decided to approach me.

Since the Wall had come down, I also had occasionally received friendly letters from an ex-CIA operative in Europe by fax. He never seemed to be trying to get anything out of me; his tone was that of one spy paying professional tribute to a worthy adversary. But now, I could not help wondering whether he was also part of this carefully planned approach.

Whatever the route, someone at CIA headquarters had managed to find out the name and address of my loyal personal assistant, Eberhard Meier, and had contacted him and asked whether I would be prepared to receive two American callers. They were highly professional, never used the telephone or mail that might be intercepted, and always found other ways of passing messages to me through my assistant, never directly. I told my aide to have them come to my villa, a more discreet meeting place than my apartment in Berlin. Still, I mused, it was unclear what they wanted. After four years out of office, it was a little late for a kidnapping, but what else could they be after?

With the resources of an espionage service no longer behind me, I had to go back to first principles and surreptitiously tape the meeting on a machine hidden in the sideboard. Anyone with even a passing acquaintance with espionage techniques knows that one never permits contact with a hostile power without a recording of the whole encounter to protect against blackmail.

Hathaway passed the time of day for a while, sympathizing with my plight in the impending unification and the inevitability of my arrest.